THE ARCHAEOLOGY OF CALIFORNIA

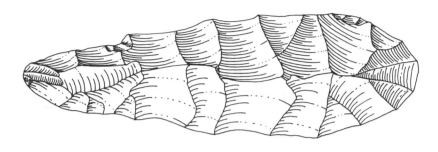

The Archaeology of California

JOSEPH L. CHARTKOFF AND
KERRY KONA CHARTKOFF

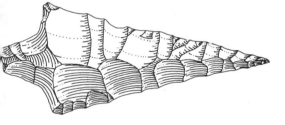

Stanford University Press, Stanford, California 1984

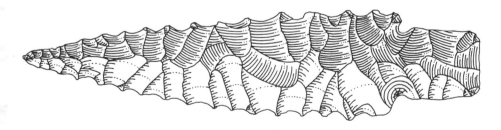

The preliminary report was supported by PSW Grant No. 35, Pacific Southwest Forest
and Range Experiment Station, Forest Service, U.S. Department of Agriculture, and is
in the public domain. The copyright claimed by the publisher covers the revisions
and new matter presented here, including the new illustrative matter.

To our parents, Daniel and Janice Kona
and Jean and Wilma Chartkoff, and
to our sons, Zachary and Eli Chartkoff

PREFACE

Beneath the urban sprawl and golden hills of California lies one of the nation's richest archaeological records. More people lived in California prehistorically than anywhere else in North America, and they left behind a correspondingly large and varied body of remains. Archaeologists have been studying these remains for more than a century, and more research may have been conducted on the prehistory of the Golden State than on that of any other part of the nation. Paradoxically, although most people are fascinated by archaeology, many Californians know much less about the archaeology of their own state than they do about that of Mexico, Egypt, and the American Southwest. Furthermore, and even more surprising, professional archaeologists in the rest of the country know very little about California's past and have a difficult time relating their own area's archaeological record to that of California. This book was written to help remedy these deficiencies.

The lack of popular and professional understanding about California's archaeology is not due to the peculiarity of the data or to the lack of published material. Little is found in California sites that cannot be found elsewhere, and there is a substantial literature describing the excavation of California sites. The reasons are more particular.

Archaeology has been conducted in California for a long time—at least since the 1870's—and this research has produced a considerable literature. But in the main, most of this literature consists of reports written by and intended for a small group of scholars. Very little has been written for the general public, which is one reason the public is ignorant about a subject it ordinarily would find interesting. Some summaries have been written about the archaeological remains found in the state (for example, Aikens 1978; Heizer 1964; Jennings 1974; Meighan 1965, 1978; Willey 1966), but they were written for academic audiences, not popular ones. For lay people, they are hard to find and harder to follow. Nor do they offer overall summaries and interpretations of the state's past as a whole; rather, they present the archaeology of the several regions of the state as separate (and unrelated) entities. Relatively little effort has been made to relate the archaeological records of various parts of the state to each other, and the non-professional exploring these summaries on his own tends to find it hard to achieve any sort of overview. At the same time, because the framework used by archaeologists in most parts of the continent to organize the archaeological record is not used by California specialists, it is hard even for scholars to see the relationship between California's past and the past elsewhere.

The writing of popular syntheses of California's archaeology has also been discouraged by the apparently changeless character of California. In other regions, the beginnings of farming, the introduction of widespread pottery manufacture, or the construction of great earthworks or pueblos provides easily understood benchmarks against which to measure the course of prehistory. The prehistory of California, generally lacking such obvious features, has been marked by smaller, subtler changes. This has led archaeologists to foster a greater sense of change by emphasizing the differences between sites more than their similarities. This emphasis has inhibited the development of syntheses, whether popular or professional.

A tendency to regionalism, too, has worked against synthesis. In many states there are only one or two major archaeological programs, operating throughout the state from universities or other central sponsoring institutions. Researchers working from one of these institutions generally acquire an overview of the state's archaeology. But in California, there are no truly statewide university research programs, and research is not concentrated at one or two institutions; there are, instead, unrelated research programs at more than two dozen colleges, universities, and museums. These programs tend to concentrate on the archaeology of their immediate areas, and the communication of research goals and results among institutions in different parts of the state is often limited. The state's great geographical extent and environmental diversity have exacerbated the tendency to regionalism. As a result, many archaeologists have assumed that a synthesis of California's archaeology was not even possible (for further comments, see Heizer 1978b: 13).

Further, California archaeologists have tended to specialize in particular time periods rather than address the entire archaeological record. Some workers concentrate on European-American sites of the Historical Period but not on the Native Californian sites of the same period, and vice versa. Others specialize in late prehistoric sites, others in the early postglacial period, and yet others in the archaeology of Pleistocene Paleo-Indians. California's rich archaeological record and large body of researchers have permitted such specialization. However, this concentration has worked against the development of a broad-gauged overview of the whole of the state's archaeology.

Even should such overviews be developed, the lack of popular interpretation would likely remain a problem, since many archaeologists reject the notion of writing for general audiences. There have been notable exceptions, of course, but they have been rare in California. The most successful popular interpretations are localized or specialized works written by people not trained as archaeologists. An example is Campbell Grant's *The Rock Paintings of the Chumash* (1965). Many university-based archaeologists receive little encouragement to write for nonacademic audiences. Professors who compete for tenure or promotion find that their success depends on their scholarly publications, not on works for a more general readership. What popular writings exist were more often than not written by dedicated amateurs rather than professional archaeologists who presumably have the most to say (see, for example, Smith & Turner 1975). And it is no secret that professionals, concerned more with accuracy than with style, often find it difficult to write for the general public.

Another factor inhibiting popular synthesis is the system of government contracts for environmental-impact studies that now fund most archaeological fieldwork in California. Though they serve other needs, these studies have produced few published scholarly reports and essentially no reports for the general public, let alone popular overviews of the state's archaeology. None of the funding agencies has underscored the importance of informing the public of the results of such research, nor has any heretofore specifically funded the preparation and publication of popular works. To the contrary, many project reports are withheld from the public to protect archaeological sites from the vandalism that invariably occurs when site locations are widely known.

Popular syntheses are nonetheless needed. Knowledge about the state's archaeological record represents, after all, an important part of the cultural heritage of all Californians. Knowledge of the past has the power to enlighten and enrich the lives of those who command it.

Public appreciation can also serve a more practical purpose. Vandalism is one of the most serious threats to California's archaeological resources, second only to expanding urbanism. By alerting the public to this fact, and by demonstrating what archaeology is about and why the destruction of archaeological resources represents such an irreparable loss, popular syntheses can perhaps reduce at least the casual vandalism that arises from simple ignorance.

By vandalism we mean the destruction of archaeological resources by individuals, usually without permission and in violation of the law, and in all cases without any compensating contribution to our knowledge about the past. Basically there are three kinds of vandalism. Malicious vandals are those who destroy sites for personal gratification. They deface rock-art sites, ride all-terrain vehicles through fragile desert sites, or disturb unguarded archaeological excavations. This sort of vandalism is difficult to understand or control, except by restricting access to sites and by imposing severe penalties on violators. In general, the weight of the law has not been laid against archaeological vandals, even when they are caught in the act, partly because many judges and prosecutors perceive little value in California's archaeological sites.

Another kind of vandalism is easier to understand: the "mining" of sites to recover objects for sale in the antiquities market. A substantial commerce exists throughout the nation in antiquities of all kinds, including prehistoric artifacts, usually without regard to the actual ownership or origin of these objects. A great many artifacts in this trade were originally looted from sites, despite the fact that such looting often destroys the site and renders it useless for study. The illegal antiquities trade has become a severe problem not just in North America, but anywhere in the world where archaeological remains are felt to have commercial value. Some private collectors are openly contemptuous of archaeology, and resent the practice of museums' preserving collections for scholarly study. Such collectors value artifacts only as isolated objects to be owned and enjoyed, and are not concerned with the fact that the removal of an artifact from its context or collection destroys most of the information that the artifact could provide. The combined motives of personal profit and desire to possess objects of antiquity make commercial vandalism extremely difficult to control. Given that most commercial mining is illegal but that violators are rarely punished, it has been a relatively safe activity for its devotees, even though it is pursued at the expense of the public's heritage.

A third kind of vandalism, in intent a form of recreation, is "relic collecting" or "pothunting." Sometimes it is mistakenly confused with amateur archaeology (see Appendix C). Relic collectors are usually well-meaning individuals who enjoy the out-of-doors, are fascinated with ancient artifacts, and enjoy collecting and displaying them. Some collectors believe their collections represent a contribution to science. They are unaware that the act of collection actually destroys much of the archaeological record, since the existence and locations of artifacts in sites, and the relationships among artifacts, provide more data than the artifacts themselves.

Although some pothunters are fully aware of the destructive aspect of their activity, others are simply ignorant of the consequences of their hobby, having been persuaded by friends and recreational magazines that theirs is a healthy, harmless, and fascinating interest. These people often have great potential for making genuine contributions to their state's cultural heritage. They often display remarkable dedication and interest in legitimate archaeological research once they have become aware of the destructive consequences of relic collecting. Such people often study archaeology out of interest and become extremely knowledgeable. Once they learn how much more can be accomplished through well-done research than through pothunting, they frequently join amateur or avocational societies (see Appendix C) or seek university training (see Appendix D). Well-intended relic collection is the form of vandalism most likely to be combated effectively through education.

The Archaeology of California was written in part to help alert the public to the fact that California's archaeological resources are culturally valuable but endangered and desperately in need of protection. The book was also written as a general introduction to the state's archaeological record, especially for non-archaeologists. It is intended to interpret the record from an understandable, unified perspective that makes sense to the nonspecialist. This framework should also allow scholars who study the archaeology of other parts of the world, particularly other areas of North America, to compare more readily California's archaeological record with that of their own areas of research. Finally, the book summarizes current understandings about the course of California's past as seen archaeologically and points to directions for future research.

The book owes its existence to the farsightedness of the U.S. Forest

Service, which perceived the utility and suitability of such a study to its growing program in public archaeology. The book's inception owes much to Donald S. Miller, Regional Archaeologist for the Forest Service in California, and to Richard Hubbard of the Pacific Southwest Forest and Range Experiment Station of the Forest Service, who helped conceive the project and obtained support for its development. Benjamin Spada of the Experiment Station oversaw the book's development, and Alice Ohara of the Station's staff administered the funding for the project.

We are glad for the opportunity to thank these agencies and people, without whose kind support the book could not have been developed. Others also deserve thanks and recognition. At the head of this list must be William W. Carver, Jean Doble McIntosh, and the staff of Stanford University Press, who with skill, dedication, and the kindest forbearance have seen the project reach fruition in far better shape than it began. We are equally grateful to our teacher and reviewer, Clement W. Meighan, whose editing through several revisions has contributed signally to the results.

Several agencies have kindly allowed us to use photographs from their collections. We thank especially the Lowie Museum of Anthropology of the University of California at Berkeley (James J. F. Deetz, director), the Michigan State University Archives and Historical Collection (Frederick Honhart, director), and the California Region, U.S. Forest Service (Donald S. Miller, Regional Archaeologist). The Department of Anthropology, Michigan State University, also earns our gratitude for its extensive support. We gratefully acknowledge, as well, the help given us by the following agencies, whose particular contributions directly aided the development of the book: Berkeley Public Library; California Department of Parks and Recreation, History Division; Department of Anthropology and Museum of Anthropology, California State University, Chico; Department of Anthropology, California State University, Hayward; Department of Anthropology and Treganza Museum of Anthropology, California State University, San Francisco; Department of Anthropology, California State University, Sonoma; Contra Costa County Library; Coyote Hills Regional Park; El Cerrito Public Library; Los Angeles County Museum of Natural History; Marin Miwok Museum; Michigan State University Library; Richmond Public Library; San Francisco Public Library; Southwest Museum; Department of Anthropology, University of California, Berkeley; Archaeological Survey, University of California, Los Angeles; and University of Michigan Library.

Finally and most particularly, we have benefited from the help and guidance of dozens and dozens of colleagues. What is known of California's archaeological record stems from lifetimes of devoted research by many scholars. We hope they will accept this book as one small increment in the great body of knowledge they have developed.

J.L.C.
K.K.C.

CONTENTS

6. CONCLUSIONS

APPENDIXES

TABLES AND MAPS

TABLES

MAPS

THE ARCHAEOLOGY OF CALIFORNIA

CHAPTER ONE

Introduction

Today, more than 25 million people live in California. Few of these people are aware that all around them, literally beneath their feet in many cases, is one of California's greatest resources and certainly one of its best-kept secrets: its archaeological record. Not wealth, in the traditional sense, but rather a wealth of information, this record traces and illuminates the full course of human experience in California from the earliest bands of Pleistocene hunters and gatherers to the suburbanites of the twentieth century.

Archaeologists have been exploring this record for more than a hundred years at thousands of localities throughout the state. Yet, despite the fact that archaeology is a subject of almost universal appeal, many Californians are completely unaware that any archaeological research has been conducted in their state at all. Part of the reason for this situation is that so little research has been made available to the public in a popular, easily understood form (see the Preface for a more complete discussion of this problem). This book represents an attempt to correct this situation by bringing to the general public and specialist alike a synthesis of what archaeologists have learned during a century of inquiry into California's past.

The archaeological record is that body of material remains deposited on or in the earth as the result of peoples' past activities. It is the sum of all the material evidence left behind by former cultures. It is a legacy left to those of the present to preserve because it is a cultural treasure that can never be replaced, since the cultures which created it have themselves disappeared. It is also a resource from which we of today can learn about the past. It forms a nonrenewable cultural resource that constitutes a major part of the state's heritage.

Archaeological records are created by the actions of people: actions that involve changing the physical form of the earth where they live and work. Many of the things people do leave a record in the soil. The houses and communities they build, the foods they eat and the raw materials they use, the ashes from their fireplaces and the trash from their workshops, the tools they employ and the toys with which they amuse themselves, all are eventually discarded, enter the soil, and become archaeological remains. Where such remains occur, they are cultural additions to the earth. Even the chemistry of the earth itself can be changed by such disposals. All such remains taken together form a region's archaeological record.

Among the regions of North America, California has a particularly compelling archaeological record. Its record may have one of the most ancient beginnings on the continent; its earliest traces may have been laid down 30,000 years ago or earlier. It may have as many or more sites than any other comparable part of the continent; researchers have already discovered more than 100,000 localities yielding remains. This large number of sites reflects the fact that from prehistoric times on, no part of the continent from northern Mexico to the Arctic Sea held more people than the region we now call California. What makes this achievement particularly remarkable, at least during prehistoric times, is that it was attained for all intents and purposes without farming. In almost all other cases in which prehistoric cultures grew to become so large and complex, farming was a necessary element of the economy. The state's archaeological remains also reveal a fascinating range of diversity, from tiny campsites to elaborate prehistoric settlements, as well as more-recent urban centers, all relics of important chapters in the state's past.

As notable as this record is, it remains remarkably little known to the general public. Many schoolchildren become more familiar with the archaeological remains of other parts of the country than they do with those of their own state. Many people go out of their way to visit ruins in the Southwest or Midwest, unaware that remains of considerable interest also exist in California. Corresponding to this lack of awareness is the fact that comparatively few of California's important archaeological sites have been made accessible to the public.

Few Californians are also aware that archaeology has things to say not just about the more remote past but about the recent past as well. The great historical transformations that shaped the state—from the building of the missions and Mexico's independence through the Gold Rush to the development of modern agriculture, mining, logging, transportation, and industry and the rise of the state's large cities—have contributed to its archaeological record. California's rich ethnic heritage is also reflected in this record, as each people has added new elements.

In part because so little is generally known or appreciated about it, much of the state's archaeological legacy has already been destroyed. Urban expansion, agricultural development, highway and reservoir construction, logging, mining, military activities, recreation, and vandalism have caused the destruction of tens of thousands of prehistoric and historical sites. During the past century archaeologists were able to conduct research on relatively little of what has been lost, giving us the barest hints of the wealth of the legacy that has been destroyed. Yet a considerable amount of California's archaeological heritage has managed to survive, mainly in the more isolated parts of the state, and from it archaeologists have pieced together the general course of California's past. For reasons discussed in the Preface these results have not yet been drawn into a coherent picture of the state's archaeological record as a whole, in a form that can be readily understood, nor have they been adequately related to the progress of prehistory elsewhere in North America. The aim of this book is to present a general overview of what archaeologists currently understand about California's archaeological record and what it has to say about the past. We hope that the archaeology of California will no longer remain so obscure.

THE VALUE OF THE ARCHAEOLOGICAL RECORD

California's archaeological record can be appreciated because of its antiquity, diversity, and uniqueness. It can be valued because it is the state's cultural heritage. It is useful to know, however, that there are other reasons for studying the state's archaeological record.

First of all, the archaeological record is the only record left behind by prehistoric peoples. Prehistory refers to that period of human development that predates writing. Since writing was developed or acquired at different times in different places, the beginning and ending dates of prehistory vary considerably from one part of the world to another. In the Near East, for example, the first prehistoric settlements began about a million years ago, and prehistory ended there about 5,000 years ago, when the practice of writing was developed for, as far as we know, the first time in the world. In California, on the other hand, prehistory began perhaps as early as 30,000 years ago and came to an end only in 1539 when Europeans recorded their first impressions of California in writing. The archaeological record indicates that California's prehistoric occupations reach farther back in time than those of almost any other part of the Americas. Thousands of years of development saw the creation of a complex of sophisticated Native California Indian cultures, beautifully and successfully adapted to their unique environments. We know from archaeology that, long before the advent of the Europeans and the written record, California Indians had achieved mastery of the technologies they needed in order to flourish, becoming along the way among the world's finest basketmakers. Archaeology has shown how the enormously productive economies of these people, based on hunting, fishing, plant gathering, and trade, supported a larger and denser population prehistorically than did those of any other region in the continent: one-tenth of all the Indians north of Mexico lived in California. But only through the study of the archaeological record can these cultural achievements be studied and understood.

The archaeological record, however, also includes remains left behind during the historical era, or the period ushered in by the advent of the written record. Although this period is most often studied through historical documents, written records can be incomplete or inaccurate. The archaeological record has proved of value in learning about those aspects of the past not well represented in documents. It happens that many dimensions of the historical past were never recorded in written form, or were recorded incorrectly, or reflected the distorting biases of the recorder. Until recently, for example, the literature of history has been the history of prominent adult White males, largely leaving out any consideration of the poor, the young, the female, and the non-White. In addition, many of the mundane aspects of daily life that are unimportant historically but enormously revealing culturally simply have not been reported in documents. Archaeology, then, can be seen as a way to complement and enlarge the written record, while correcting some of its biases, by providing kinds of information not found in the written record.

Archaeology has explored the physical record of a succession of colonizing cultures in California: the Spanish, Mexican, Russian, Anglo-American, and Chinese, for example. It has studied the economic activities these groups pursued—ranching, farming, mining, logging, and commerce—and the resulting growth of urban centers. The study of the archaeological record has also told a story all but unknown to many Californians today: what happened when these colonizing cultures encountered the native cultures, and what the subsequent fate of the native cultures has been.

The study of the historically known cultures in the state, a discipline called ethnography (see below), has also benefited from the archaeological record. Working with contemporary Native Californians, ethnographers have learned what these Indian cultures were like in their more recent stages of development. Since these cultures lack earlier historical records, archaeology provides ethnographers with the means to extend this knowledge into the past. The archaeological record allows ethnographers to reconstruct the paths of development taken by different cultures and to understand the processes that shaped them as they evolved toward their historically known forms.

There are other reasons for an interest in California's cultural past. Today's California is the product of its past. One way to understand why present-day California has taken the form it has is by understanding what happened to it in the past. California has become one of the most ethnically complex regions in the world, as well as America's most populous state and the home of several of the nation's larger urban centers. Through archaeology, Californians can come to know and appreciate more of the contributions different cultures have brought to the state, not only those of California's more than 100,000 Native Americans, but also those of Welsh coal miners, Hawaiian gold miners, Mexican ranchers, Russian trappers, Swiss farmers, Scandinavian loggers, Chinese railroad workers, New England sailors, or British traders. Telling their tales can help to create a sense of appreciation and shared experience with which to bind Californians together. And archaeology provides a way to study how these different groups of people came in contact with each other, and what the consequences were for their lives afterward.

There are other uses to which archaeological research might be put. Archaeology reveals, for example, what environmental variations and changes occurred in the past and how different societies responded to them. California's environments are diverse and have changed continually. Rainfall and temperature vary over the centuries as well as from year to year. Long periods of cool, wet weather that produced excellent plant growth were followed by periods of hotter, drier conditions. Lake beds in the desert filled and evaporated repeatedly over thousands of years. Sea levels rose and fell. Coastal lagoons formed as seas rose, only to disappear when sea levels stabilized or dropped. Beaches appeared and disappeared, and rivers changed their courses. Archaeology helps teach these facts of change, and points to their consequences for cultures. It can remind planners and developers that the environments they regard as unchanging have, in fact, shown a good deal of change over time, sometimes in very short periods. The environment is often regarded as a backdrop for human activities, but archaeology shows that cultures surviving over long periods interacted with the environment and accommodated themselves to it. Today's Californians, with no historical memory, continue to be amazed when chaparral and forests burn, when periodic flooding sweeps away highways and bridges, when cliffs erode and houses slide into the sea, or when mudslides bury houses and cut communities off from contact with each other.

Earlier cultures gained experience in adapting to California's environmental realities. People today have the opportunity to learn from the problems faced by earlier cultures, and to see how those experiences might be applied to comparable situations today. Archaeology can provide information about long- and short-term environmental changes and peoples' reactions to them, information that can be used to plan better for the state's development and growing population.

Given so much existing and potential interest in California's archaeological record, it is surprising that so few popular works interpret this record for the public and for professional archaeologists. The public has turned to other parts of the nation or world to satisfy its curiosity about the past, and professionals elsewhere treat California as an enigmatic exception to the general course of New World prehistory. Let's look first at what archaeology in California actually is and is not.

ARCHAEOLOGY IN CALIFORNIA

Archaeology (from the Greek *archaiologia*, or the study of antiquities) is one of the ways we may study the past. All archaeologists study the physical remains of past cultures. Wherever in the world archaeology is undertaken, and on whatever time period, the methods and techniques used are essentially similar. But there are different kinds of archaeologists, depending on the orientation of the researcher and the purposes for which the research was undertaken. What is meant by the term "archaeology" varies from place to place in significant ways, and thus it is useful to indicate what archaeology has come to mean in California.

Many people view archaeology in terms of popular images. One such image depicts the archaeologist, wearing pith helmet and khaki shorts, directing armies of laborers or crawling through the dusty tombs of pharaohs. This image has some basis in fact, but it is very different from archaeology as it is practiced in California or the rest of North America.

The pith-helmet caricature is based on a popular view of the *classical archaeologist*. Classical archaeology is the study of the remains of the great classical civilizations—ancient Greece, Rome, Egypt, Mesopotamia, and their immediate predecessors—that are known to scholars from ancient writings. Although classical archaeologists use the methods common to all archaeology in the excavation of their sites, the field is most closely allied to the study of ancient history and the classics. Excavators tend to focus on monumental art and architecture, and the art styles of ornaments and decorated pottery, turning less attention to the lives and livelihoods of the general population. Although American universities do employ many classical archaeologists, the practice of the discipline is, understandably, limited for the most part to the Old World. Its roots lie in European fascination with ancient history and Biblical studies, and it still owes much of its orientation to European scholarship. The focus of classical archaeology, toward the understanding of the development and nature of the great civilizations, has placed it within the sphere of history, art history, and ancient history.

Archaeology in North America, on the other hand, represents a much different tradition. In the United States, archaeology has emerged primarily as a branch of anthropology, one of the social sciences. Anthropology is the science of culture, the study of those aspects of human behavior that are learned rather than biologically inherited, behavior that is the shared practice of communities rather than the idiosyncrasies of individuals. Anthropology has traditionally dealt with cultures of the nonliterate world, ranging from tiny hunter-gatherer bands to pre-Columbian civilizations lacking written records, and with the peasant cultures of developing nations. It is also a comparative discipline, using studies of all cultures to develop general principles of human behavior. Anthropology has stressed the idea of cultural relativism, which means that the actions of people from other cultures must be understood in terms of the cultural setting in which the actions occur, rather than using the cultural values of the observer as a universal standard (Pearson 1974: 174).

Archaeology as pursued in America developed within anthropology largely because both fields were studying the cultures of the American Indians. The archaeological record in America had been largely created by the American Indians and their predecessors, whereas anthropologists studied the remnants of American Indian cultures still relatively intact in some parts of the country. Since Indian cultures had been nonliterate, archaeology was drawn to anthropology rather than history. Anthropologists felt that the form and character of contemporary Indian cultures could be understood more fully if their earlier stages of development could be revealed, and archaeology offered the means to do so. At the same time, archaeologists saw the descriptions of contemporary Indian cultures being compiled by anthropologists as a means to interpret earlier prehistoric cultures for which there were no written descriptions. The two fields thus found mutual benefit in their relationship.

As American anthropology developed into a formal academic discipline in the 1880's and 1890's, archaeology was made a part of it, and three other major branches—sociocultural anthropology, physical anthropology, and anthropological linguistics—came to be distinguished.

Sociocultural anthropology is the study of present-day and historically known cultures, based on intensive field study by specially trained observers. The description of cultures by sociocultural anthropologists is known as ethnography, and the comparative analysis of many cultures for the development of theories about culture in general is called ethnology. The term ethnography is often used as a shorthand reference to the corpus of cultural descriptions compiled by anthropologists over the last century.

Physical anthropology represents a link between cultural studies and human biology. It treats human anatomy, genetics, and physiology as they relate to cultural behavior. Physical anthropologists also study the biological history of humans through fossil evidence, a specialty called human paleontology. The specialty called primatology concerns the biology and behavior of our nearest animal relatives, the apes, monkeys, and other members of the zoological order Primates. Physical anthropology also inquires into human genetics and heredity, racial variability, human physiology, environmental adaptation, nutrition, and disease.

Anthropological linguistics deals with the languages of different cultures, the nature and development of language, and the relationship of language to other aspects of cultural behavior. Studies of language history often provide archaeologists with ideas about the prehistoric relationships between different ethnographic groups that spoke related languages. Linguists also work with physical anthropologists to understand the biology of speech and the speech potentials of other species of primates.

Despite these divisions, anthropologists view their field as holistic, meaning that these components of anthropology interact with each other and affect each other to produce an overall view of humanity and human behavior. Early in the history of the field, anthropologists were expected to be expert in all four branches of anthropology (see

Appendix A for a review of the history of California archaeology in relation to American anthropology generally). The enormous growth in anthropological knowledge and technical training has since made specialization in one of these subdivisions necessary.

American archaeology, as a division of anthropology, is primarily the study of past nonliterate cultures, taking its reconstructions of past lifeways from excavated data and, whenever available, from ethnographic descriptions of comparable cultures. In California, where Europeans began to seriously disrupt Native American cultures only about two hundred years ago, ethnographers were able to record many aspects of traditional cultures that had persisted from prehistoric times, producing a literature that has had considerable impact on what the archaeologist has to say. Basically, most archaeologists working in North America consider themselves to be cultural anthropologists who happen to deal with the cultures of the past instead of the present. They seek to apply anthropological principles to their understanding of past cultures and their changes over time, and to use their own data to extend the general body of anthropological knowledge.

Anthropologically oriented archaeology itself has several subdivisions. Most archaeology in the United States is usually called *pre historic archaeology*, which is the study of cultures as they existed prior to their contact with European cultures and the written record. *Paleolithic archaeologists* specialize in the study of the most ancient forms of human culture, those of the Paleolithic or Old Stone Age (generally before 10,000 B.C.). These scholars study pre-modern humans, as well as the early modern humans who are so ancient that they have no historical or ethnographic counterparts. Paleolithic archaeologists draw heavily on physical anthropology to augment their own studies.

At the other end of the time spectrum is a fairly new specialty, *historical archaeology*. This discipline deals mainly with the expansion of Europeans throughout the world during the last five hundred years and the effect of this expansion on the cultures they encountered (Deetz 1977: 5). But it focuses on other modern, literate societies as well. Despite the fact that most historical archaeologists are trained primarily as anthropologists, the field draws especially heavily on historical documentation and folklore studies, providing something of a bridge to the field of history.

Most of the archaeology in California has been done by anthropologically trained prehistoric archaeologists. Their studies of California have dealt primarily with lifeways that are now virtually extinct. California archaeologists have been able to join with ethnographers in developing reconstructions that go far toward explaining how people lived in prehistoric times, and how these cultures developed into the ethnographically known cultures of the historical period. Archaeology has enlarged upon and sometimes corrected the ethnographic record, besides adding the dimension of time to a more complete view of California anthropology.

Historical archaeology and Paleolithic archaeology have increased in popularity in California in recent years. Historical archaeology traces its origins in California to the Great Depression, when excavations began at some missions; in recent years it has burgeoned into a major interest. Within the last decade or so, material on the California Paleo-Indians has been compared with that of Eurasian Paleolithic cultures, and California scholars have begun using many of the same research methods as Paleolithic scholars.

Finally, California archaeology has been shaped by the very nature of the data (see Appendix B for a discussion of the data of California archaeology). Because prehistoric California had no great urban civilizations, an interest in monumental art and architecture did not develop as it did in Mesoamerica and Peru. The materials used by the California societies in their structures were perishable compared to, say, those of the prehistoric pueblos of the Southwest or the earthen mounds of eastern North America, so it is not surprising to find that California archaeologists have put less emphasis on the excavation of structures. Since many California sites are rich in shell and bone, California archaeology has emphasized faunal analysis (the study of animal remains in sites). And whereas pottery is lacking or very rare in most California sites, industrial stone tools are common; accordingly, the emphasis in California has been on the study of stone-tool technology and use. And because California sites have tended to lack the obvious stratigraphic layering found in large sites of other regions, California archaeologists have led in the development of many excavation techniques designed to extract other kinds of evidence about the age and development of sites. These distinctions have given California archaeology a somewhat unique flavor within American archaeology and an important place in the historical development of the discipline.

ASSUMPTIONS AND EXPLANATIONS

In preparing this book, a number of decisions had to be made about the way the material should be organized and presented. In our view, archaeological data require interpretation in order to be given meaning, and the interpretation can vary considerably depending on what is assumed and emphasized. Our interpretation represents something of a departure in the field's literature, so it is especially important to make clear our approach. The reader will be better able to understand our interpretation by knowing how we decided to organize the data. We feel that these features require discussion: (1) the area the study covers; (2) the framework for breaking time into manageable units; (3) how past lifeways are reconstructed; (4) the presentation of the archaeological evidence; and (5) an explanation of change (or the lack of it) in time and space.

California Archaeology and the Idea of a California Culture Area

This book looks at the archaeology of the modern state of California. Most scholarly studies that deal with California archaeology do not follow this practice, and instead focus on a few parts of the state where the most elaborate prehistoric cultures appeared. Since our practice is divergent, an explanation is in order.

Most of the books that deal with North American archaeology in general devote a section to California (see, for example, Jennings 1974, 1978: 133–46; Jennings & Norbeck 1964: 117–48; Snow 1976: 154–76; Taylor & Meighan 1978; Willey 1966). But a survey of these works quickly shows that the area they study under the name "California" is not the area defined by the political boundaries of the modern state. They leave out a great deal of the state, and the different coverages vary a good deal from one to another (Heizer 1978c: 2). This is because archaeologists, including California archaeologists (for example, Baumhoff 1963; Elsasser 1978a; Heizer 1964; C. King 1978; Meighan 1965), follow the cultural-anthropology practice of recognizing a California culture area (see Map 1), which differs from the modern political unit of California. When this book was conceived, it was necessary to decide whether it should deal with the archaeology of the California culture area or with that of the modern state. There are good reasons for either choice.

The concept of culture areas goes back to nineteenth-century European geographers, who divided the peoples of the world into groups of similar cultures sharing a common geographical region. They believed that each region had been originally settled by a colonizing group, which not only brought a particular way of life to the environment, but was in turn influenced by the environment to produce something distinctive to that region—a culture shaped by and appropriate to its environment.

Over time, so the theory went, the descendants of the original group spread out, filling the entire region with people who shared cultural traits. The peoples who occupied the center of such a culture

Map 1. The California culture area according to Philip Driver (1961). Anthropologists and cultural geographers developed the concept of culture areas in the last century as a way of organizing the cultures of a region that were neighbors and shared similar lifeways. Scholars recognized that neighboring peoples sharing similar habitats often developed similar economies, had similar patterns of social organization, shared similar ideologies and technologies, and in most respects had similar cultures. Authorities differed, however, on the causes of these similarities. German cultural geographers, for example, stressed the impact of the environment. American anthropologists, by contrast, tended to emphasize historical relationships. They held that shared cultural patterns occurred because a group of neighboring cultures descended from a single parent or ancestral culture. Because all cultures differ from each other in certain respects even while sharing other factors in common, the definition of any culture area depends on which traits are regarded as most important by each authority. As Heizer (1978c: 2–3) shows, the California culture area has been defined in many different ways, and there is no consensus about which cultures belong in the California culture area. Driver's version, shown here, reflects a fairly median interpretation of the California culture area's boundaries.

area were regarded as "core cultures" and those at the margins were "peripheral cultures." The core cultures were thought to express the purest and truest forms of the ancestral culture and to have the fullest array of the original cultural traits. The peripheral cultures were regarded as diluted because of their secondary genesis, their distance from the center of the culture area, and their marginal environment. Each peripheral culture was thought to differ from the others to the extent it retained a different set of traits from the original founding culture.

In this theory, cultural innovation or change was felt to take place at the core or center, not among peripheral cultures. When a cultural innovation occurred, the new trait spread from the center to the periphery like a ripple on the surface of a pond. The culture-area idea offered a way for early anthropologists to explain the similarities and differences they found among cultures from various parts of the world.

A. L. Kroeber, founder of anthropology in California (see Appendix A), was highly influenced by the basic idea of culture areas, and he and his colleagues began to apply it to American Indian cultures, including those of California. The Native Californian cultures of the Central Valley, the San Francisco region, and the southern coast were regarded as belonging to a California culture area, distinct from the cultures of the surrounding areas. Different scholars over the years included different ethnic groups in the California culture area and recognized different core cultures (Heizer 1978c: 2–5). However the California culture area was defined, though, its boundaries never coincided with those of the modern state, and between a third and a half of modern California was omitted from the culture area.

This idea of a California culture area was an ethnographic idea, but it was adopted and adapted by archaeologists. Kroeber had trained many of California's most important archaeologists, and his ideas were very influential. In addition, California's archaeology is tied even more closely to ethnography because of the state's particularly rich ethnographic literature and its recent emergence from prehistory. Also, until recently, most archaeological research in California has been conducted near the modern population centers, which happen to lie within the California culture area as it is usually defined. To a large extent the California culture area was defined by the aboriginal cultures that had been the largest and richest, and the environmental factors that helped make them so also influenced the growth of modern population centers.

When we began this study, we organized it along the lines of the

California culture area. As time went on, however, a number of considerations arose that eventually led us to discard it in favor of treating the modern political region as a whole. Since this approach runs counter to much established practice in California archaeology, a word of explanation may be helpful.

The California culture area has referred in practice only to a part of the archaeological record—the period when Europeans first arrived and the few thousand years before. Most of the archaeological remains of the earliest times of prehistory are found between the coast and the Colorado River, from Baja California to Mono Lake. This region crosscuts the California culture area as it is usually defined, instead of coinciding with it. Furthermore, with the coming of the Spaniards and the beginning of the historical period, the California culture area became less and less relevant to the archaeological record. Because Spanish settlement was concentrated along the coast, the weight of culture contact fell very unevenly across the culture area. After 1846 the boundaries of the modern political state became increasingly important, as is reflected in the distribution of archaeological remains from this period. In short, since the boundaries of the California culture area would have had to be redefined for each time period, excluding or including different parts of the state, the more encompassing political boundaries of the modern state were chosen as the easiest way to define the area under study.

Another reason for this choice is the fact that government archaeological programs are conducted largely within modern political boundaries. Much of the research funded by the federal and state governments has used the state's present boundaries as the administrative unit. These programs are conducted throughout the state regardless of the boundaries of the California culture area. The same is largely true of college and university research programs, owing partly to the scattering of the locations of campuses around the state and partly to the needs of state and federal funding agencies.

The result has been that archaeologists identify themselves as *California* archaeologists if they work within the state's borders, whether or not they work in the California culture area. Since archaeologists themselves tend to think and work in terms of such boundaries, since the state forms a precisely and permanently delimited administrative unit (and the culture area is inconsistently delimited), since it forms the area covered by professional journals devoted to California archaeology, and since the Society for California Archaeology draws its membership from it, the advantages of considering the state as a whole are considerable.

Furthermore, Native Californians have increasingly come to think of themselves as California Indians. The state's modern borders had no meaning for traditional Native Californian cultures, but the political, social, cultural, and educational perceptions of California Indians, in terms of sharing common problems and having to deal with state and federal administrations, have created a statewide consciousness. And since the remainder of the state's present-day residents also identify themselves as Californians, it makes sense to treat the archaeology of the state as a whole rather than just that of the California culture area.

The California Chronology

Archaeologists divide the past into periods, to emphasize the features shared by cultures at one age and their differences from cultures of other ages. These divisions, symbolic of all the characteristics of life in different eras, provide an easily understood framework by which to organize the continuum of the past. There has been little agreement about the best way to divide California's archaeological record into units (or periods, eras, stages, etc.) that would not only mark changes over time but also be consistent over the entire state. Current regional schemes often fail to deal with the whole of the archaeological record even in their own areas. They are also difficult to relate to the chronologies used by archaeologists for the rest of the continent.

We have tried to overcome these problems by using a simple chronological framework that can be imposed over the entire archaeological record, a framework comparable to those used in other parts of North America. The scheme must cover 13,000 years or more of cultural development, and must be able to include societies ranging from tiny bands of Paleo-Indians to the urban dwellers of the twentieth century.

The framework used in this study divides California's cultural past into four major time periods: Paleo-Indian, Archaic, Pacific, and Historical. Three of the periods are further subdivided into three or more units in order to make the divisions more manageable and more representative of change occurring within each period. We did not subdivide the Paleo-Indian Period because we felt that the existing data did not allow for a reliable breakdown. All the periods have been recognized and defined in terms of shared lifeways (or adaptations to the environment) that are distinctive of the cultures inhabiting the state at those times, and different from those of earlier or later periods.

Our concept of periods should nonetheless be taken as an organizing device and not as a model of evolutionary stages of development like that of Gordon Willey and Philip Phillips (1957). Our periods highlight times of shared traits, of shared trends toward particular styles of adaptation. We do not think of them as being bounded by revolutionary changes in the archaeological record.

These choices should make it easier to integrate California's archaeology into the archaeology of the rest of the United States. Three of the four periods we identify for California's past—the Paleo-Indian, the Archaic, and the Historical—are used by archaeologists throughout most of the rest of the continent to mean substantially the same things they do here (see Chapters 2, 3, and 5 for definitions). We coined the term Pacific Period for the purposes of this book, however, and it does not appear elsewhere. But as we have defined the period, it is comparable to periods of the same general age that have been defined in other areas, such as the Pueblo Period in the Southwest or the Woodland Period of the Great Lakes. In this way, California archaeology may be viewed in more general terms, while still recognizing the traits that make it unique.

The Reconstruction of Past Lifeways

The reconstruction of past cultures is one of the most difficult tasks archaeologists face. Not a great deal of it is done in most archaeological reports. We feel that the goal of reconstruction is especially important if archaeology is to illuminate our understanding of culture and human behavior as well as the shape and age of artifacts.

In an effort to further this goal, we have introduced each of the book's major chapters with a scenario, or brief reconstruction, of the everyday life of the peoples living in the time the chapter takes up. These reconstructions are based, of course, on actual archaeological research and environmental studies, but they go somewhat beyond them in an attempt to bring vitality to the people who might actually have lived in the past, the people who created the artifacts and sites that are the more common subjects of archaeological inquiry.

In most cases the reconstructions characterize the way of life typical of the period at its maximum level of development. The scenarios were therefore taken from later in each period rather than earlier. We have tried to include scenarios that depict life in different parts of the state at different times, and most major regions have been represented at one point or another.

The Presentation of Archaeological Evidence

Studies of the physical data of archaeology lie at the heart of any reconstruction of past ways of life. Students of archaeology need to master this technical literature, but the general public is more likely to find that such studies impede their understanding and appreciation. The terminology and even the purpose of technical literature, the emphasis placed on such things as the details of artifact types, make these studies generally irrelevant to the interests of the nonspecialist. We have not shrunk from a discussion of the archaeological evidence embedded in this literature, but since our audience is intended to include the general reader, we have minimized the use of technical terms in this material.

Following this concern, though we do discuss basic types of artifacts associated with different eras, we do not explore the analyses on which artifact typology rests. We also do not try to present a comprehensive summary of all the data of California archaeology. Instead, we try to summarize periods and their salient features, illustrating with appropriate examples.

Our discussions of data, especially of artifacts, are limited to the descriptions needed to present a reconstruction of a past lifeway. This approach accords with our emphasis on cultural reconstruction over the description of the details of the archaeological record. In this regard, we present the complex of artifacts, features, and sites characteristic of each time period. These complexes are described as "archaeological traditions." Each tradition embraces the archaeology of a large part of the state for a considerable period of time, and during that span of time the archaeology reflects continuity in social structure and adaptation even when details may vary from site to site. Other terms more commonly used in California archaeology—phase, horizon, complex, facies—tend to refer to more limited spans of time and space and to sites that have similar details and are found in similar habitats. Since a particular society may create a wide variety of sites in different environments, and since similar sites do not always reflect similar cultures, we felt that the "tradition" approach provided a more useful means of associating archaeological data with past lifeways.

Explanations of Change and California Archaeology

We subscribe to the notion that when archaeologists reconstruct the past, they also explain how and why past cultures looked the way they did by drawing attention, at least implicitly, to those features that they feel influenced the course of cultural history. Though archaeologists may agree about the data of a particular area or period, they frequently disagree about the factors that produced the data. In this study we suggest the elements we feel were most influential not only in shaping the past cultures of California, but also in producing change in them over time. We have tried to make these explanations consistent for the entire archaeological record, from the earliest Paleo-Indian settlement through the Historical Period, by combining environmental features, conscious or unconscious strategies of adaptation to the environment, and changes in technology and the organization of labor. We focus on the kinds of survival and subsistence problems faced by cultures in each period, the varying patterns of adaptation they developed to surmount those problems, and the consequences of the choices that were made.

We hope that, in doing so, this study will make the archaeological record more interesting and understandable than it might otherwise be. Through it all, then, we ask readers to remember that even though the data of archaeology are stones and bones, the goal of all archaeology is to understand the way people behaved in the past, and perhaps how they thought and felt. California's archaeological record was, after all, made by people, not by potsherds or projectile points. The present-day residents of California include descendants of earlier settlers, whether they be Native Americans, Europeans, Asians, Africans, or Latin Americans. The archaeological record created by these real, flesh-and-blood human beings is part of California's cultural heritage. It is a remarkable heritage, left to us by earlier Californians whose accomplishments we can all appreciate, a heritage from which we all can learn and be enriched, whether we are descendants of these earlier peoples or just their admirers.

CHAPTER TWO

The Paleo-Indian Period

Imagine a setting 12,000 years ago in what are now the deserts of southern California: a broad desert playa, ringed by distant mountains, with alluvial fans emptying out of every mountain canyon in a series of gentle slopes from the hills down to the playa's edge. This playa, however, owing to the wetter conditions prevailing during the late Pleistocene, is filled with shallow, brackish water, forming a lake several miles across.

The shores of the lake are more gravel than sand or mud. The lake's shallows are thick with cattails, tules, and other water plants. The surrounding terraces are carpeted with bunchgrasses and dotted with mesquite, creosote, and other shrubs adapted to a semiarid environment. Lining the larger streams in the canyons are cottonwoods and other larger trees that need to cluster around permanent water sources and escape the extremes of sun and wind.

Despite conditions that are wetter than today, this country is nonetheless relatively dry, with high summer temperatures, high rates of evaporation, and low rainfall on the valley floor, but it is not yet the desert it will become in time. Because more rain falls in the mountains, stream runoff can replenish the lake waters lost through evaporation. Thus the lake persists, and the plant and animal life found in the valley is varied and abundant.

Herds of camelids (native North American relatives of the camel), antelope, and horses are found on the valley floor; sloths browse at the brushy trees; bison and mammoths occasionally can be seen drinking at the lake; and deer range in the surrounding hills. Large numbers of waterfowl stop at the lake each spring and fall on their migrations along the Pacific Flyway, and a few waterfowl stay at the lake the year around to feed on the lake's fish and other life in the shallows. Turtles bask on rocks and logs, and any sudden noise can send hundreds of frogs plopping into the waters to hide. Lizards scurry over the terrace gravels, and snakes take refuge from the intense midday heat under rocks and bushes. Coyotes, owls, and bobcats hunt at night, and the early-morning hours may see a cougar from the mountains slip down to the lake-shore to drink. During the daylight hours vultures and hawks patrol overhead while wading birds poke among the reeds.

The valley is nearly 30 miles across, and in the entire valley only one spot is occupied by people: a hunters' camp on a gravel terrace near the lakeshore. The camp consists of a few simple brush shelters clustered around a pair of stone-ringed fire hearths. A dozen people live at this camp: an old man, his elderly sister, his grown son, the son's wife, and their children. The children include two teenage boys and a teenage girl, four younger children, and an infant. All are native to the valley except the wife, who came from the next valley to the north.

Every five to ten days the camp's meat supply begins to run low. On this particular morning, the two adult men and the teenage boys leave the camp with their spears and head toward one of the canyons to hunt. Within an hour, they locate a small herd of horses and begin to stalk it, creeping slowly into the breeze. The stalkers lie still whenever the sentry starts to look their way. At last the hunters get within a spear's cast of the nearest mare. The boys' father rises suddenly and in the same motion hurls his spear. The horses freeze momentarily and then bolt, but not before the spear strikes deeply into the mare's side.

The spear is harpoon-rigged. Its point is hafted to a foreshaft that has been set into a socket in the end of the spear shaft. When the spear strikes the horse, the foreshaft is dislodged from the shaft's socket, but a leather thong ties the two parts together, so that the fleeing wounded mare drags the spear shaft after her. The two teenagers run to cut off the mare's retreat into a nearby canyon while the men begin to trot after the animal. Steadily the hunters force the horse toward the lakeshore. Within a few miles the mare, already weakened by shock and loss of blood and hampered by the dangling spear shaft, is backed against the edge of the lake. The two boys run forward and use their own spears to complete the kill. The four then set to work butchering the carcass. The old man collects stone cobbles and prepares several chopping tools for dis-membering the skeleton while the others use their stone knives to begin clean-ing the horse. The mare is soon gutted and bled. The body is too heavy to carry back to camp whole, but camp is close enough that there is no need to move the other people to the kill site. The hunters skin the body and start to lay meat cuts on the hide. Three of them will carry part of the meat to camp. Then, while the women are slicing and drying the meat, the men will return to the carcass and drag the rest of the meat back to camp on the horsehide. One of the boys stays with the carcass to drive off the vultures. Almost every part of the car-

cass has a potential use: the meat and bone marrow for food, the hide and sinew for tools and household items.

While the men hunt, the women of the camp are at work at other tasks. The wife and her oldest daughter collect firewood in the brush not far from camp. The old aunt sits holding the infant and watching the younger children play around the huts. The women have to spend an hour or so almost every day collecting firewood. When a camp is newly founded, wood is plentiful and close at hand. As time wears on, however, the women have to travel farther and farther to find fallen twigs and branches. Eventually the difficulty of finding firewood is one factor among several that persuade the group to move their camp, but on this particular day firewood is still reasonably plentiful near the camp. After the women bring loads of wood back to their camp, they walk down to the lakeshore to gather edible plants and armloads of reeds to be used in weaving mats.

When the three hunters have brought their first load of meat from the horse kill, they return to the kill site, and the women begin to process the meat. For the next several hours they cut the meat into strips and hang it on stick racks to dry in the sun. When more of the horse is dragged back to camp, the men will join the women in processing the meat.

Part of a day's work has brought the camp enough food and raw materials to last for several days. Much of those days will be spent in relaxation and conversation while the adults carry on the production of household items needed in the people's daily lives. The long bones of the horse are left out in the brush at the edge of camp for the insects to clean. The women stake out the horsehide and scrape and work it into usable leather. While the men sit and talk, discussing the hunt, they cut up strips of reed and roll the strips together along their thighs to form rope and string. This cordage finds many uses in camp, from the making of sandals and the knotting of net carrying bags to the lashing of hut frames and the tying of thatch to the frames.

The day after the hunt, the old man goes out from camp to the bank of a nearby stream channel. The stream channel is dry at this time of year, and the old man glances along the channel bottom, looking for good quartzite cobbles. The ones he discovers he collects and carries back to camp. He sits down at one edge of camp with the cobbles, picks up one and begins to strike large flakes from it with another. He takes an antler that he carries in his kit and, using it as a soft hammer, goes on to strike off smaller flakes. He turns the piece over and over as he removes flakes, finishing both sides and straightening the edges, until he has produced an oval chipped-stone knife. This particular knife he makes for his daughter-in-law. Her last knife, made several months earlier, has been resharpened and damaged too many times to be useful any more. The old man rises from the litter of waste flakes he has created and walks to the fire where the young woman sits nursing her baby. He gives her the knife. After *she finishes nursing, she carries her baby and the new knife to her hut and sits down with her baby next to her on a reed mat. She takes up her digging stick and uses the new knife to resharpen the point and shave a rough spot on its handle. Finishing that task, she takes up a bundle of the recently collected reeds and uses the knife to trim them to uniform lengths. She slits the reeds lengthwise into strips, and pounds them lightly with the flat side of the knife to make the strips flatter and more pliable. The aunt walks over to the young woman's workplace to sit and chat, and plays with the baby while the young woman weaves the reeds into a new floor mat for her home.*

While the woman works plaiting a mat, her husband walks beyond the camp to the now-dessicated horse skeleton. He removes a leg bone and carries it to his workplace near the hearth. Using a rock as a hammer, he raps one end of the bone while bracing the other end against bedrock. He then twists the bone shaft in opposite directions until it fractures lengthwise in a long, spiral break. Using the stone hammer again, he breaks off a long splinter of the bone. He then grinds the edge of the splinter against a piece of sandstone, gradually smoothing the splinter's ragged edges and shaping one end into a sharp point, forming an awl. He sticks the new tool into his hair, where it is handy for use as a dagger, punch, scribing tool, or emergency flaking hammer.

While their parents work, the younger children play about the camp. A good deal of their play involves mimicking their parents' activities. The children practice stalking lizards, armed with sharpened sticks for spears, and bear their prey to camp for their father's approval. They take sharp-edged flakes from their father's flaking area and cut their own reeds, which they use to make their own sleeping mats to put inside a shelter they are building. And they pick green plants to use for a pretend meal, following the fashion of the adult women of the camp.

The family will live at this camp for several weeks, until food and firewood become too hard to find nearby. Then they will break camp and walk ten or fifteen miles around the lakeshore to another beach terrace where the resources are more abundant. Since this sort of move is made several times during the year, the few material possessions of the group tend to be light and portable. The wife carries her baby on her back in a sling, freeing her hands to carry her household tools. In one hand she holds a woven net bag, which contains the stone and bone tools she uses for such jobs as scraping and cutting hides, slicing plant stalks, and stripping bark from twigs. In her other hand she carries the long stick she uses to help her hike and to dig for bulbs and roots.

Because the wife is still nursing her baby and must carry it around with her from camp to camp, she is not yet able to care for another infant. She is therefore abstaining from sexual relations with her husband to keep from getting pregnant again until her baby is old enough to be weaned and to hike with the group when it changes camp.

This couple has already lost some of its children—death is fairly frequent during childbirth and infancy. Accidents take a further toll: three years earlier one of their teenage sons died when a wounded animal knocked him down and kicked him in the head. He was carried back to camp and buried nearby in a shallow pit that his father and brother dug with digging sticks and the shoulder blade of a camelid. Immediately after the burial ceremony the family broke camp and moved, never again to revisit that campsite as long as the memory of the boy's burial remained.

Less-serious accidents also affect the group. The year before, one of the children fell into the campfire. Although she survived, she was badly scarred, and a year later it was still difficult for her to walk or do any work. Even if she lives into adulthood, it is unlikely that she will ever marry and have her own family.

Infectious diseases, on the other hand, are rare. With groups so small and spread so far apart, there are few people to catch or spread illnesses.

The sort of life led by this family ages people quickly. Though young adults are healthy and strong, they are middle-aged by thirty and old by their mid-forties. Not many people live into their fifties or sixties.

The family keeps a close watch on the progression of the seasons. They follow the passage of time by noting the points on the horizon where the sun rises and sets in conjunction with the solstices and equinoxes. They are particularly careful to note the fall equinox. Food is most abundant at that season, which allows the family to cross the hills into the next valley and join camp with their relatives there. Counting the days is one of the responsibilities of the grandfather; at the equinox the family will cross to the valley to the north, where the family of his son's wife lives, and the family of his own late wife will also join them there.

The fall meeting is the time for the year's most important religious observances. It is also a time for feasting, games and gambling, the exchange of news, and visiting with friends and relations. Marriage agreements are made and weddings held most often at this time. Since there are no eligible marriage partners within a family, and since young people rarely meet anyone except their own family members during the rest of the year, only when several families meet can parents find eligible partners for their teenagers. Because most spouses come from nearby valleys, each family has kin in several adjacent valleys.

This scenario, based on archaeological, ethnological, and ecological evidence, gives some idea of what life must have been like in California's early prehistory. A consideration of this evidence is intended to show the basis for the interpretations made from it, and the kind of reasoning lying behind it. The terms used for such a discussion need to differ somewhat from the language used in the reconstruction above. The reconstruction depicts people in the act of expressing their culture, whereas the archaeologist must rely on material remains produced by past behavior to infer what the behavior must have been, rather than on directly observed behavior. For that reason, archaeologists have developed concepts of "archaeological cultures," called *traditions*. Traditions are descriptions of the archaeological remains characteristic of particular times and places, combined with inferences about the kinds of cultural behavior that archaeologists believe produced the remains. This chapter presents the tradition characteristic of the oldest period in California's prehistory, the Paleo-Indian Period.

Paleo-Indian is the term many archaeologists use to refer to the people who first entered the New World. These earliest Americans spread over much of the Western Hemisphere before the end of the Ice Age some 11,000–12,000 years ago (9000–10,000 B.C.). Some of these Paleo-Indians became the first settlers of California. All current scientific evidence agrees that before the Paleo-Indian migrations there were no human beings living anywhere in the entire Western Hemisphere. Then, at some point in the past, people began to trickle into North America from Asia across what is now the Bering Strait.

Archaeologists disagree widely about the time when these migrations began. Some feel that immigration did not begin until the Ice Age was almost at an end, around 12,000–13,000 years ago (10,000–11,000 B.C.). A few argue that the migrations began at least 80,000–100,000 years ago. A good many others, taking a middle ground, feel that the first settlement began 15,000–30,000 years ago. Which of these positions will prove to be correct awaits newer and more conclusive evidence (more about that question shortly). Archaeologists are agreed, though, that humans had settled many parts of the New World by the time the Ice Age came to its end. Somewhere along the way, people entered into California for the first time.

Who were the Paleo-Indians? What were they like? Where did they come from? When did they arrive in California? How did they get here? How did they live? What happened to them? Archaeologists need to learn a great deal more about the Paleo-Indians before these questions can be answered to our total satisfaction, but research suggests some possible answers.

THE SETTLEMENT OF THE NEW WORLD

To understand where California's first settlers came from and how they arrived, it is necessary to view them in terms of the settlement of the New World as a whole. Scientists are certain that *Homo sapiens*, or biologically modern humans, did not originate or evolve independently in the Americas (Laughlin & Wolf 1979: 1–2). That development took place in the Old World, and the peopling of the New World was through the migration of fully evolved humans. Today's fossil evidence indicates that our ancestors first appeared in Africa several million years ago. By a million years ago they had begun to spread into Europe and Asia, although at that time they were not yet fully modern biologically. Ancestral, primitive members of our own species may have developed from these *Homo erectus* forebears by perhaps 250,000–300,000 years ago. Fully modern humans did not emerge until about 40,000 years ago, however (for discussion, see Campbell 1976: 363–90). The earliest well-documented examples are known from Africa and Asia, though future discoveries might change this picture. Between 40,000 and 20,000 years ago, biologically modern humans from eastern Asia began to colonize the large islands of the western Pacific—Australia, Borneo and New Guinea, and perhaps Japan, Taiwan, the Philippines, Java, and Sumatra as well. Many archaeologists feel that the first settlement of the New World may have been part of this same expansion. In any event, there is no unquestioned fossil evidence to indicate that anyone other than fully evolved human beings ever set foot in the New World (Lampl & Blumberg 1979: 115–18). A few writers, however, argue that one or two ancient skulls found in California exhibit some traits suggestive of Neanderthal ancestry (e.g., Carter 1980: 292–94).

The recognition of Neanderthal traits in early New World skeletons is as important as it is controversial. If all New World skeletons are modern in their traits, and if modern humans did not appear until about 40,000 years ago, it would not be possible for New World skeletons to be older than 40,000 years. If, however, some early New World skeletons are related to the Neanderthals, who lived in the Old World from about 80,000 to 40,000 years ago, the earliest settlement of the New World might be much more ancient than 40,000 years. Of course, even if Neanderthal-like traits do appear on some early California fossils—a point not accepted yet by most scholars—the fossils still might not be as ancient as the real Neanderthals. Even among living people today it is possible to find individuals who have one or two traits similar to those of the ancient Neanderthals. Only the entire complex of Neanderthal traits as a whole is older than 40,000 years. Under the circumstances, then, most scientists view with a great deal of caution claims for New World sites dating to more than 40,000 years ago (Laughlin & Wolf 1979: 8–10).

What many archaeologists believe to be the earliest known archaeological site in the New World for which there is a reasonably secure

Fig. 1. Carved caribou tibia from the Old Crow Flat Site in eastern Alaska. Split, beveled, notched at one end and definitely man-made, it may have been a flesh-scraping tool. With a C-14 date of 27,000 B.C., this tool might be the oldest human artifact in the New World. Bone at widest part just under 3 cm.

date lies along the Old Crow River, a tributary of the Yukon River in eastern Alaska and western Canada. Artifacts found in deposits there have yielded a series of radiocarbon dates that go back to 27,000 years ago (25,000 B.C.) or more (Bonnischen 1979; Irving & Harington 1973). The earliest dated specimen is a tool made from the leg bone of a caribou, an artifact possibly used to clean animal hides (see Fig. 1). If the Old Crow date is substantiated, it suggests that settlement of the New World began sometime between 40,000 years ago, when modern *Homo sapiens* first appeared in the Old World, and 27,000 years ago, the earliest date from Alaska. The Old Crow Flat Site's location suggests that the migration route into the New World was by way of northeastern Asia, an inference suggested long ago because there the two continents almost touch. Supporting the conclusion is the fact that Soviet archaeologists have found sites in eastern Siberia that are quite similar in age and form to those reported from Alaska and western Canada (Butzer 1971; Canby 1979; Chard 1975; Jennings 1974).

The Beringia Route

Even though America and Asia almost touch at the Bering Strait, Alaska and Siberia are still separated today by a water gap 36 miles wide (58 km). The Diomede Islands lie in the Strait, and presumably a traveler could use the islands as stepping-stones, but anyone crossing from the Old World to the New there would have to cross at least 20 miles of frigid Arctic water. The historical Eskimos built watercraft capable of making such a voyage—kayaks and umiaks—but those highly sophisticated and specialized types of boats did not exist 40,000 years ago. It might have been possible to cross the water gap on rafts, or by whatever kinds of primitive watercraft were used at that time to reach the western Pacific islands, but crossing the frigid waters of the Bering Strait still would have been a perilous undertaking.

Although such a crossing could have been made, in all likelihood it was not necessary. For during the Pleistocene, when glaciation was at its peak, much of the world's seawater was locked up in vast ice sheets that covered parts of the northern continents to depths of 3 miles or more (5 km). World sea levels fell as the area covered by the ice sheets grew. Many times during the past half million years sea levels have dropped 300 feet or more (90 m) below today's level. Since the floor of the Bering Strait is only about 200 feet (60 m) below the present level of the ocean, there must have been times when, as glaciers reached their maximums and sea levels dropped, dry land was exposed to connect Siberia to Alaska (see Map 2). This connection has been named

Map 2. Beringia, or the Bering Land Bridge. Exposure of shallow seafloors around the Bering Strait is hypothesized to have occurred many times during periods of extreme glacial conditions in the Pleistocene. Geologists refer to the exposed land area as Beringia. The emergence of Beringia as shown here joined Asia and North America into a single continent. Blockage of cold Arctic Ocean currents would have yielded a mild environment along the subcontinent's southern coast. The shaded area indicates land exposed when sea levels were at least 300 feet lower than today.

Beringia, or the Bering Land Bridge (see Haag 1962; Hopkins 1967).

The term "bridge" is somewhat misleading because, when sea levels were lowest, Beringia was more than a narrow neck of land connecting two continents. It was a subcontinent of its own, up to 1,300 miles wide (2,090 km)—more than the distance from Tijuana, Mexico, to Vancouver, British Columbia. Beringia was a broad, low plain. Its emergence blocked cold Arctic ocean currents from reaching the northern Pacific, and the mild Japan Current, flowing north along the Asian coast, warmed Beringia's southern shore and gave it an unexpectedly warm climate (Hopkins 1979). Grasslands and forests developed, and were filled with herds of woolly mammoths, mastodons, horses, bison, and other grazing animals, as well as the beasts that preyed on them, such as Alaskan lions and dire wolves. These animals were able to enter and cross Beringia from either direction. The horse, for example, which evolved in the New World, entered the Old World via the land bridge during the Pleistocene.

Whenever Beringia emerged, human hunters could also have crossed, knowingly or unknowingly, from Asia into North America. The fact that Asia was already populated by hunters, while the North American game lands to the east were uninhabited, may have been enough to channel some of these nomadic peoples along the path of least resistance and on into the New World. Or, they may have simply followed the migrating herds of animals they hunted. We can only speculate about the motives that led people to cross Beringia, but the best current evidence indicates that sometime during the last 30,000 years of the Pleistocene they began to do so, and entered Alaska.

Once Alaska was reached, some groups began to migrate south and east into the rest of the continent. When and by what routes they did so are matters of passionate debate among archaeologists. The lowering of sea levels and the exposure of the Bering Land Bridge also coincided with the maximum development of glaciers in Canada and Alaska. Did this mean that the way into the interior of the continent was blocked by ice? Was there an ice-free route through or past the ice? Did the migrants travel along the coast, following routes that have since been drowned by higher sea levels? Conflicting evidence gives partial support to all three possibilities (Griffin 1979).

The Ice-Barrier Hypothesis

Beringia was exposed to its greatest extent during glacial maximums. During the last 50,000 years or so, glacial maximums occurred in North America at 49,000, 44,000, 30,000, 24,000, 16,000, 14,000, and 11,800 years ago (Hopkins 1967). During this time, the land bridge was exposed twice for relatively long periods: from 52,000 to

Map 3. Presumed maximum extent of the glacial barrier separating Asia from the interior of North America (after Flint 1957). By this construct, the migration route for humans from Asia into North America is blocked during periods of glaciation.

42,000 years ago (50,000 to 40,000 B.C.) and from 30,000 to 11,000 years ago (28,000 to 9000 B.C.). Although these long exposures created the best opportunities for hunters to migrate from Siberia into Alaska, some scholars argue that the very conditions that produced the bridge also blocked access past Alaska into the heart of the continent (see Map 3). The build-up of ice sheets across North America at these times not only hindered travel but also eliminated the food, shelter, and firewood that travelers would have needed along the way (Bryan 1969: 339–41).

Following this line of reasoning, it is argued that the only time hunters could have both crossed Beringia and gained access to the interior of the continent was when the ice sheet had just begun to form or had nearly disappeared, and when sea levels were still low enough to expose the land bridge. These conditions occurred during the two thousand years or so at the beginning and end of Beringia's two longest exposures, creating rather brief periods when migration could have taken place: between 52,000 and 50,000 years ago, between 42,000 and 40,000 years ago, between 30,000 and 28,000 years ago, and between 13,000 and 11,000 years ago. The site at Old Crow Flat in Alaska may provide evidence of just such a migration.

The Ice-Free-Corridor Hypothesis

Other scholars have argued that even when glaciation was at its maximum, an *ice-free corridor* always existed into the interior of the continent (see Map 4). This corridor is believed to have extended up the Yukon and Kuskokwim rivers from western Alaska into western Canada, and then southward along the Mackenzie River and the eastern flanks of the Canadian Rockies onto the northern Great Plains (Reeves 1973: 13–14). If this school of thought is correct, migration from Asia could have occurred at any time Beringia was exposed. The Old Crow Flat Site, since it is located on a tributary of the upper Yukon River, might have resulted from migration along this corridor rather than from movement into the interior during brief periods of retreat of the ice barrier.

The Coastal-Route Hypothesis

Both the ice-barrier and the ice-free-corridor hypotheses assume that the first Americans, once they gained the continent, crossed Alaska and Canada and emerged onto the Great Plains. But what if they followed another route? Such a proposition could replace both the ice-barrier and the ice-free-corridor hypotheses, and there are archaeologists who argue for just such a case. They believe that the earliest migrants crossed the Bering Land Bridge sometime after 40,000 years ago, perhaps when it reemerged 30,000 years ago. They then moved south, hugging the Pacific coastline, which was probably always free of ice (see Map 5). Their way into the continent would have been blocked between Alaska and southern California by glaciers on the Cascades, Sierras, and Rockies, but if they reached southern Cali-

Map 4. Hypothesized ice-free corridor through the glacial ice barrier. If it did exist, as some evidence suggests, a route into North America from Asia would have lain open during glaciation.

fornia their way eastward into the continent would have been wide open. This migration route, and the sites that might have produced evidence for it, would have been largely drowned by rising sea levels after the end of the Ice Age (Bickel 1978a: 8–10; Fladmark 1979: 58–64). There are a few places along the coast where deep, sheer cliffs drop off the shore to the sea, so that even when sea levels were at

Map 5. Western coast of North America from Alaska to California, showing area of now-submerged land that would be exposed if sea levels were 300 feet lower than today. Shaded area covers a hypothesized ice-free coastal route from Beringia to California.

their lowest, migrants would have had to travel along the cliffs that still rise above the sea, and here would be the place—the only place —to look for signs of their passage. These spots lie in southern California at places such as Del Mar, and there are archaeological sites at some of these places that some excavators claim to be Paleo-Indian sites 20,000 or more years old (e.g., Carter 1980). Unfortunately, controversy and uncertainty surround the dates of every one of these sites. Though they may support the coastal-migration hypothesis, it is also possible that they do not. Furthermore, it is possible that the three hypotheses are not mutually exclusive. More than one migration route may have been taken in the peopling of the New World. At the present time, however, the dates and direction of the first migrations into the Western Hemisphere remain uncertain, and as a consequence, so does the first settlement of California.

THE SETTLEMENT OF CALIFORNIA

California is a good place to test these migration-route hypotheses (see Map 6). If, for example, people originally migrated south along the Pacific coast, California's Paleo-Indian sites should be older than those farther east. If, on the other hand, the Paleo-Indians migrated across Alaska and Canada and out onto the Great Plains, California would have been settled by people coming by way of the Great Basin. Then the earliest sites should be found on the Great Plains, the Great Basin sites should be somewhat more recent, and the California sites should be the most recent. If both routes were used, however, sites along the coast and in the Great Basin should be equally early.

In principle the question should be easily settled by a review of the evidence. Unfortunately, today's evidence from California is not sufficiently strong or clear to support a single position. For example, there are some very early sites in coastal southern California that would seem to support the coastal-migration hypothesis. The Arlington Canyon Site on Santa Rosa Island, the Del Mar, Texas Street, and Buchanan Canyon sites, and the Sunnyvale, Los Angeles Man, Laguna Woman, and Yuha Desert burials all have yielded remains claimed to be at least 20,000–30,000 years old (Bada, Schroeder & Carter 1974; Berger 1975; Canby 1979; Carter 1980).

Other archaeologists have challenged the early dating of these sites, however (e.g., Haynes 1969; Meighan 1978; Payen et al. 1978; Riddell 1969). In some cases, such as the Texas Street and Arlington Canyon sites, the ages of the sites have been determined by radiocarbon assays of the charcoal found in them. Although these radiocarbon measurements are believed to be accurate, there is some question about whether the charcoal used in the dating came from man-made campfires or from ash produced by natural brush fires (Cruxent 1962; Orr 1968). In other cases, such as the Del Mar, Sunnyvale, Los Angeles, Laguna, Scripps, and Yuha Desert sites, dates are based on an experimental technique called aspartic acid racemization or amino acid dating (see Fig. 2). Because this technique has been used to date

Map 6. Scholars have suggested three alternative routes by which the first Paleo-Indian settlers might have migrated into California: along the now-submerged coastal shelf, south through the Great Basin from the Columbia Plateau, or west from the southern Great Plains and across the American Southwest.

the human bones found in these sites, the human origin of the material being dated is not in question (Bada & Helfman 1975). The technique itself is still experimental, however, and many archaeologists are not yet convinced of its accuracy. In addition, at some of the sites the dates based on radiocarbon assays of charcoal differ significantly

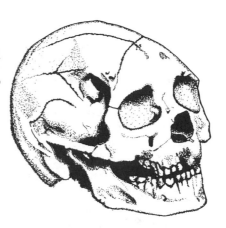

Fig. 2. Reported as a Paleo-Indian skull from San Diego County, the Del Mar skull was dated by the aspartic acid racemization technique to 48,000 years ago (Bada et al. 1974). Recent re-dating by three radiometric techniques has placed the age at only 11,000 years, casting doubt on its Paleo-Indian status and raising new questions about the accuracy of the technique of aspartic acid racemization (Bischoff & Rosenbauer 1981).

from those based on the aspartic racemization of bone. There have even been discrepancies when the two methods dated the same material, in this case, human bone (for a new variant of this problem, see Davidson 1981). Furthermore, in five of these sites the human bones used for dating were excavated long ago, and the original positions of the bones in the sites are uncertain. These problems cast even more uncertainties on the use of the bones in dating the sites (Berger 1975; Haynes 1973; Meighan 1978; Riddell 1969).

Many of the problems surrounding the question of California's earliest settlement are strikingly evident in the case of the Calico Site, claimed by its excavators to be the most ancient known site in the New World (Leakey et al. 1970, 1972). This site, in the Calico Hills of the southern California desert near Barstow, extends across a series of gravel terraces near a number of former springs. Excavators have discovered hundreds of fractured stones at the site, both on the desert's modern surface and buried in the terraces. On the basis of the geological dating of the terrace gravels and the radiocarbon dating of organic matter from some of the dried springs, the site has been claimed to have an age of 50,000 years or more. If this dating is valid, the Calico Site would not only represent the oldest archaeological site in the Western Hemisphere, it would also date to a time preceding the appearance of biologically modern humans in Asia. Such a finding would revolutionize ideas about New World prehistory as a whole, and would certainly have a radical effect on thought about human antiquity in California.

These claims have been widely challenged, however. Critics regard most of the fractured rock, claimed by the excavators to be human artifacts, as having been produced by accidents of nature (e.g., Haynes 1973; Wormington 1971). And although there are some unquestionably human artifacts from the site, almost all of them are surface finds that cannot be accurately dated and that are of styles that could have been employed at any time from the Pleistocene to as recently as the past thousand years. Furthermore, the radiocarbon samples that were used to obtain the very early C-14 dates come from buried springs hundreds of feet from the claimed artifacts, with no demonstrated connection between them.

In the face of these criticisms the proponents of the site nevertheless maintain that the weight of evidence is on their side. They argue, for example, that many of Calico's critics have not yet learned how to recognize some of the distinctive methods of tool manufacture used by Calico's Paleo-Indian occupants. Thus controversy continues to surround the Calico excavations and shows no sign of being resolved in the near future (see, for example, Davis et al. 1979).

If all the questionable early sites just discussed are eliminated from consideration, the case in favor of a coastal migration route at an early date becomes much less compelling. In fact, there would be no unquestionable evidence for humans in California before about 12,000–13,000 years ago (10,000–11,000 B.C.). That people first migrated to California across the Great Basin seems therefore as likely as that they migrated along the coast.

Is there any evidence to suggest that people used the eastern approach to California *instead* of the coastal route? Currently no sites from the Southwest or Great Basin have yielded reliable dates older than about 12,000 years, nor are there any Great Plains sites proved to be significantly earlier than Great Basin sites. Thus there is no good immediate evidence for the eastern route, but very little of our continent has been searched systematically for Paleo-Indian remains, and new evidence may turn up one day. Too, there are some sites farther afield that provide hints of early occupations in the continent's interior. Some examples follow:

The Meadowcroft Rockshelter in western Pennsylvania is a deeply layered cave site yielding several radiocarbon dates from intact remains. The dates, which get older as the deposits deepen, indicate that people lived there at least 14,000–16,000 years ago (Adovazio et al. 1978).

The Marmes Site, in southeastern Washington State, is another ancient rock-shelter with deeply layered deposits. Not quite as old as Meadowcroft, it shows that people were living on the Columbia Plateau by the end of the Pleistocene, around 12,000 years ago (Kirk & Daugherty 1978).

The Lewisville Site, in western Texas, has yielded stone tools, fire hearths, and the bones of extinct herd mammals. It *may* be as old as 40,000 years, but its age is still highly controversial (Canby 1979; Jennings 1974).

In central Mexico, the remains of apparently man-killed mammoths have been found, in some cases associated with stone tools or fire hearths, at Tlapacoya, Santa María Ixtapan, and Valsequillo, with radiocarbon dates up to 20,000 years old or more (Weaver 1972); and in the Ayacucho Basin of southern Peru MacNeish (1976) has reported stratified deposits in the Flea Cave Site going back to 22,000 B.C.

These sites are among the least controversial of all the ones claimed to show humans in the New World before 12,000 B.C. If the North American sites prove to be as old as claimed, they provide strong evidence for the use of the interior migration route into the continent, and would help make a case for the idea that California was settled from the east. If the Mexican or South American dates are correct, it means that people arrived in North America even earlier, a good deal earlier than most archaeologists have been willing to accept so far. It would also mean that people could have been in California for at least as long as in Mexico or Peru. The real meaning of these early dates is still unclear, however, and a great deal more research is needed before their relationship to the settling of California is known.

Some of the evidence concerning California's first settlement is controversial, and other evidence seems contradictory. Most of all, the evidence is simply scanty, poorly documented, or nonexistent. More sites with reliable dates need to be discovered and carefully excavated, not only in California but throughout the New World, although more substantial excavations at currently known but controversial sites could also resolve many uncertainties. Until such research is done, the questions about when the Paleo-Indians arrived in California and how they got there will remain largely unanswered.

In view of these uncertainties, what can be said about California's earliest settlement? In spite of problems with the present evidence, a few tentative conclusions can be offered. Although the the first settlement cannot be assigned a true date, most of the present evidence indicates that it took place after Alaska's early settlement of 25,000 B.C. Few scholars are willing to accept George Carter's recent claims (1980: 322) for a 100,000-year-old site in southern California, though his earlier claims (1957) for 20,000–30,000 years are no longer dismissed so readily. And since there are now several California sites with reasonably reliable dates between 11,000 and 12,000 years ago (9000–10,000 B.C.), the date of 12,000 years ago would be the youngest possible date for first settlement. Currently it seems that coastal and interior southern California were the first areas settled. Beyond that, we can turn to the archaeological evidence itself for a clearer picture of what the Paleo-Indians were like, how they lived, and what eventually happened to them.

THEMES OF THE PALEO-INDIAN PERIOD

Although a number of Paleo-Indian sites are claimed for the state, there has been little well-documented, extensive excavation. The state of research has been better in most of the other western states. We are forced, consequently, to use this more extensive body of data to generalize about Paleo-Indian life in general, and to fit the California data into the general picture as best we can (Hester 1980; Sivertsen 1980; Wilmsen & Roberts 1978).

Apparently, the cultures of the Paleo-Indian Period were broadly similar at any given time wherever in the Americas they appeared. Once past the Paleo-Indian Period, however, cultures became increasingly unique to their regions, and the sort of generalizations that can be made about Paleo-Indians become increasingly inappropriate.

The Paleo-Indian *Period* is the time of Paleo-Indian cultures; the Paleo-Indian *Tradition* is the aggregate archaeological manifestations of those cultures; and Paleo-Indian *Culture* is the actual, traditional, shared, learned behavior and beliefs of the Paleo-Indians. As noted above, Paleo-Indian culture cannot be observed directly. It must be inferred from the archaeological data of the Paleo-Indian Tradition, the remains that date to the Paleo-Indian Period (see Map 7).

The Paleo-Indian Period is more significant than just a block of time in prehistory, and more than just the first phase of California's archaeological record. It was a time when a way of life developed, a way of life successful enough to be pursued with little change for thousands of years. The form it took, its tremendous geographical spread, and its persistence through time may be best understood by considering three important themes that characterize the cultures of this period: pioneer settlement, focal economy, and universal technology.

Pioneer Settlement

Paleo-Indians were the first humans to live in California, so in that sense they were pioneer settlers by definition. But the term *pioneer settlement* refers to something more specific: the knowledge, skills, and technology that pioneers bring with them, and their ability or inability to use them in their new surroundings. Consider the situation facing the Paleo-Indians when they began arriving in California.

At some point in the distant past, people who apparently made

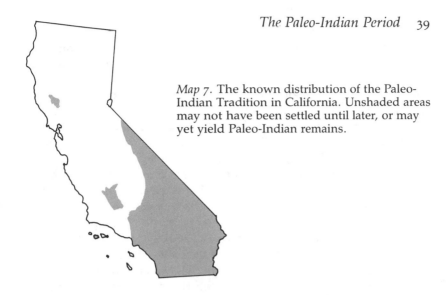

Map 7. The known distribution of the Paleo-Indian Tradition in California. Unshaded areas may not have been settled until later, or may yet yield Paleo-Indian remains.

their living primarily by hunting bison, mammoth, camelid, horse, ground sloth, or other big game began to move into California from neighboring parts of western North America. This migration was not the result of aimless wandering. The hunters may have been following the migratory patterns of their quarry, they may have been seeking a more hospitable environment, or they may have been slowly expanding into California as their own populations increased and competition for game intensified. Although we do not know the actual mechanics of their arrival, we do know a little of what happened to these settlers once they reached the state.

The first Paleo-Indians in California must have arrived in very small groups, perhaps of no more than one or two families. They must have had no detailed knowledge about the environment that lay ahead of them. As people who followed a highly nomadic way of life, they would have been able to bring only a few tools or other equipment with them. Under these circumstances, they probably did what all pioneers try to do: continue to follow, for as long as possible, their old way of life. They would have tried to make their living by using the kinds of plants and animals already familiar to them, with tools and techniques they already understood. They were simply unprepared to make use of resources that were new to them, for they lacked the proper knowledge and tools to do so. It is important to appreciate that this state of ignorance was not unique to the Paleo-Indians or their simple culture. It is common among pioneers to a new environment. Borland (1976: 42), for example, discusses the plight of the first English settlers at Jamestown. In three years 90 percent died of starvation or starvation-related diseases in the midst of plenty, because the settlers did not know the resources of the environment or how to exploit them.

In California, the acorn and the salmon were two rich resources that later became economic staples, but they were unavailable to the Paleo-Indians, who lacked the knowledge and means to harvest and use them. At the same time, the Paleo-Indians could not continue to rely on resources that they had used in their former home but that did not occur in California. As pioneer settlers they would have had to depend, at least at first, on resources that were common to both their old and new homes, and that could be developed with Paleo-Indian technology. Since Paleo-Indians were primarily big-game hunters, this meant concentrating on a moderate variety of animals that were found widely throughout the west during the late Pleistocene, including bison, horses, antelope, camelids, deer, sloths, and mammoths. Paleo-Indian pioneers relied on these species rather than on those that were unique to California, such as salmon or shellfish, regardless of their abundance.

The Paleo-Indians may have made some use of certain widespread species of small game—rabbits, lizards, and tortoises—and probably made use of widespread plant species that did not require specialized technology for harvesting or processing. So far there is not much evidence anywhere for small game or plant use by Paleo-Indians, which is why archaeologists believe they were primarily big-game hunters. Because every group of hunter-gatherers known to cultural anthropology makes use of at least some small game and plants, archaeologists assume that Paleo-Indians must have done so, too. If they did, they most likely would have drawn upon familiar, wide-ranging species demanding no special tools or knowledge, rather than the hard seeds or acorns more characteristic of California.

All pioneers face the problem of discovering which parts of their culture are still valid in a new environment. Because Paleo-Indians were in a constant pioneer-settlement condition as they moved across the New World, their lifeways were similar throughout the continent. That condition limits the things people can do in a new environment until they adjust to it and respond to its pressures for change. Until then, they are forced to maintain a general way of life, one that can be applied to a wide variety of situations, and one that is easily portable. Even when they begin to claim a region as their own and cease to be pioneers, their pioneering way of life can be expected to persist as long as it is even marginally effective.

When pioneers move into a new area, they select features or resources to exploit on the basis of their existing knowledge, not on the basis of the potential of the new environment. This can be seen in modern times in the failure of European-American settlers to make use of the plentiful food resources of California that Indians used so successfully. Millions of pounds of protein in the form of hard seeds and acorns, suitable for human or animal food at no cost to grow, go unused every year in spite of the fact that the knowledge of the resources exists and that Californians pay a great deal to buy human and animal food. The European-Americans, in other words, came to California as pioneers with a preset pattern and instituted it in the new land. Their adaptation remains significantly pioneer because circumstances have not yet required the newcomers to adapt themselves more closely to their new home. In the same sense the Paleo-Indians remained pioneer settlers in their new home until the end of the Ice Age, when environmental change forced them to adopt new approaches. By understanding the nature of the Paleo-Indian pioneer settlement and its limitations, we can better understand how these first Californians lived, where they lived, and why their lives took the form they did.

Focal Economy

The second characteristic pattern of the Paleo-Indian lifeway was a *focal economy*. According to Charles Cleland (1976), who developed the idea, a focal economy is one in which peoples' lives depend on relatively few resources, a couple of which become major staples. By contrast, in the next period, the Archaic, the economy would become *diffuse*, which is to say that people would come to exploit literally hundreds of kinds of animals and plants. People following a focal economy use far fewer types of resources than those following a diffuse economy; focal adaptations depend on key staples, whereas diffuse adaptations rely on diversity.

The Paleo-Indians, in their pioneer condition, concentrated on certain types of game. In California, they could move only into those environments that were familiar to them and offered the kind of game they were used to hunting. Thus restricted to certain species and habitats, they were unable, at least at first, to expand their economy to include the new resources they encountered.

The advantage of an economy focused on a few widely available species is that it is simple and highly mobile, easily adapted to new locations. Its disadvantage is that it severely limits the number of people it can support. For this reason Paleo-Indians lived in small, widely separated groups. Such dispersal allowed them to take maximum advantage of the game that formed their primary resource without competing with one another. These early settlers developed a very effective economy, given their small numbers, but one that did not place much pressure on them to change or increase their productivity. As long as people were still moving into new territories, as long as game remained available, and as long as human populations remained low, the Paleo-Indian economy remained essentially focal.

The climate also tended to favor focal economies. When Paleo-Indians began to settle in California, the continent was in the midst of the Wisconsin glacial period, the last major glaciation of the Pleistocene. When climatic conditions were most extreme, glaciers developed in the Sierra Nevada, the southern Cascade Range, the Klamath Mountains, and even in some parts of the Coast Ranges. The glaciated areas could not be occupied, and they reduced the area and variety of habitats available. There was simply not the range or variety of resources and environments available to the Paleo-Indians that there would be later (Alt & Hyndman 1975: 87–98).

In addition, the climate was changing repeatedly. Rather than a period of continuous glaciation, the Wisconsin was characterized by repeated periods of intense cold and ice (stadials) separated by milder episodes (interstadials). In just the past 30,000 years, stadials peaked at 28,000, 22,500, 18,000, 14,000, 12,000, and 9800 B.C. (Bailey 1966; Butzer 1971). These major warm and cold phases were themselves punctuated by smaller-scale temperature fluctuations. Complicating things even more, rainfall patterns changed more or less independently of temperature, so that the climate at turns was cold and wet, cold and dry, warm and wet, or hot and dry.

Ecologists find that when a climate changes rapidly and repeatedly, the numbers and varieties of animal and plant species stay fairly low (Odum 1971). That constraint helped ensure that Paleo-Indian economies remained focal. With constantly changing climates, most California Pleistocene environments did not become as rich or diversified as they have in more recent times, and the Paleo-Indians were therefore inhibited from developing subsistence patterns that were geared to any particular set of environmental conditions. In such a situation, the most effective economy for the long term is one that is highly flexible; in this case, that meant an economy focused on a small number of widely occurring species that had the ability to tolerate changing environmental conditions.

Universal Technology

The third major theme of the Paleo-Indian Period was *universal technology*, which refers to the generalized nature of the tool kit that

Paleo-Indians developed. Rather than having a separate tool for each specific task, the Paleo-Indians had few tool types, each designed for many tasks. Such a universal tool, something like a prehistoric Swiss Army knife, gradually took on a shape that made for maximum versatility. Such tools are very useful for people following a nomadic lifeway, who are unable to carry a large number of tools with them.

A universal-tool technology suited the migratory Paleo-Indian lifeway well. It also suited their pioneering status, since it allowed them to retain much of their technology and use it in many new environments. That these comparatively few, multi-functional tools were remarkably flexible and adaptable is demonstrated by the fact that the tool kit used by Paleo-Indian groups was similar throughout the continent. Designs were simple but well suited to their purposes, and with these few tools Paleo-Indians were able to perform all the basic functions their daily lives required: slicing, chopping, piercing, shredding, sawing, pounding, drilling, shaving, and making other tools.

By and large, the tools of Paleo-Indians found by archaeologists have been made of stone. Undoubtedly other raw materials were also used—wood and bone, for example—but these have not often been recovered from archaeological sites, owing to their perishability.

Figure 3 illustrates some of the tool forms associated with Paleo-Indian technology: chopping tools, core bifaces (which in some cases may be knives), flake scraping tools, and a few others (see Appendix B for a discussion of tool technology and types).

Some sites from the very end of the Paleo-Indian Period possess certain more-specialized tool forms, such as drills, gravers, and fluted projectile points (see Fig. 4). These artifact forms are closely associated with the cultures of the end of the Pleistocene. Why they appeared suddenly at that time is not at all clear. We treat them as a signal of the beginning of a transition from the Paleo-Indian way of life to something else, but other archaeologists may not agree.

The fluted projectile point is so firmly associated with the cultures of the end of the Paleo-Indian Period that it needs some comment. Fluted points are large stone artifacts that have been delicately retouched over their entire surfaces into a roughly triangular shape. Apparently used to tip spears or darts, they have been found in association with the bones of extinct Pleistocene mammals, proving both the association of the artifact with big-game hunting and the association of Paleo-Indians with the Ice Age. The points are called fluted because they exhibit shallow flake scars, or flutes, extending from the base of the point up each face for much of the point's length. The

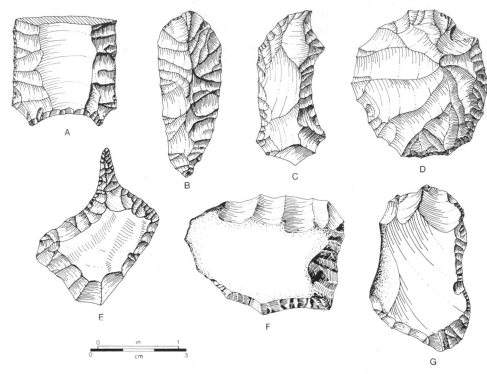

Fig. 3. Paleo-Indian stone tools: *a*, Folsom point base from Lake Mohave; *b*, biface (possibly a knife); *c*, Lake Mohave crescent (possibly a form of notched tool); *d*, keeled scraper or scraper plane; *e*, stone drill on a flake; *f*, core chopper; *g*, side scraper on a flake.

function of the flutes is debated; many writers think the flutes were made to help haft the point to a spear shaft (see Griffin 1979; Haynes 1964).

Named for the New Mexico site where the type was first recognized in the 1930's, the Clovis point, with an age range of 12,000 to 11,000 years ago (10,000–9000 B.C.), is the earliest form of fluted point. The Folsom point, another, slightly smaller form that is also named for a New Mexico site, has been dated between 11,000 and 10,000 years ago (9000–8000 B.C.), although one example has been dated to as recently as 9,500 years ago, 7500 B.C. (Hester 1980). Radiocarbon dating has shown that these fluted points, and all other forms of stone projectile points, occur no earlier than 12,000 years ago (10,000 B.C.) in the Americas, a fact that has important implications in the debate over the antiquity of settlement in the New World.

Archaeologists who believe that people entered the New World as early as 40,000 B.C. feel that the Americas were well populated long before stone projectile points appeared. What did these earlier hunters use for spear points? The answer is unclear, but perhaps bone. At the Manis Site in Washington State, a mastodon skeleton has been found with an apparent bone projectile point embedded in a rib (Kirk & Daugherty 1978: 28). Proponents of the early-settlement school of thought believe that the fluted Clovis point was developed by some unknown group of Paleo-Indians toward the end of the Ice Age, possibly in response to worsening hunting conditions, and that the idea of making these points spread rapidly throughout the continent. If so, the fluted point would either mark the end of the real Paleo-Indian Tradition or form an important exception to the universal-technology pattern.

Archaeologists of this persuasion accept the idea that there are pre-Clovis sites in the New World, and that pre-Clovis sites lack any stone projectile points. The term *pre-projectile-point horizon* (Krieger 1964) has been used to refer to such sites. Archaeologists, however, are not all convinced that the pre-projectile-point horizon exists. As with other claims for early settlement in the Americas, the sites claimed to represent this horizon present difficulties in dating. The artifacts of this horizon, lacking a definitive style, are characterized mainly by large size and crude workmanship. Since similar artifacts occur in

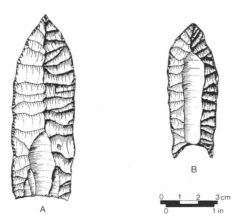

Fig. 4. Fluted Paleo-Indian projectile points: *a*, Clovis (10,500–10,000 B.C.); *b*, Folsom (10,000–9000 B.C.). These points, found widely across the Americas, date to the end of the Pleistocene. Were they left by the first settlers of the New World? Or did they signal the end of the ancient Paleo-Indian way of life?

sites thousands of years more recent in age, the validity of dating sites to a pre-projectile-point horizon remains uncertain.

For that reason, some archaeologists feel that Paleo-Indians did not enter the New World until around 12,000–13,000 years ago (10,000–11,000 B.C.). They regard the appearance of the fluted projectile point in archaeological remains as synchronous with the peopling of the hemisphere. They believe that the first migrants to North America either brought the Clovis point with them or else developed it shortly after reaching America, and carried it with them as they spread rapidly across the hemisphere. They view the spread of the Clovis point as a tracing of an actual migration of people rather than as a diffusion of an *idea* through a preexisting population (Aikens 1978; Canby 1979; Haynes 1964; Hester 1980; Jennings 1974; Wallace 1978).

Archaeologists who hold this view must, of course, deal with claims for the presence of earlier populations in the New World, such as the evidence provided from the dates at Old Crow Flat, Tlapacoya, Valsequillo, Flea Cave, and Arlington Springs. It is unfair to say that archaeologists of this view reject the possibility of earlier settlement in the Americas; they argue, rather, that all the evidence put forth for the existence of sites much earlier than about 12,000 years ago, anywhere in the New World, is suspect, so that the case for a pre-projectile-point horizon is still unproven. They take a wait-and-see attitude, joining other archaeologists in looking toward the day when more secure data will settle the matter.

The meaning of the Clovis and other fluted points is ambiguous in another respect. These stone points may have served more functions than seem apparent. Ethnographic descriptions suggest that recent peoples used the stone point as a multipurpose tool—a knife, scraper, drill, and small saw, for example. If so, the point is really more of a universal tool than it seems, and that may have been the case with fluted points. Archaeologists, still uncertain about the functional significance of fluted points apart from their association with big-game hunting, are awaiting more research and discoveries.

While it persisted, the Paleo-Indian universal technology seems to have been maintained because of its suitability to the focal economy of the pioneering settlers. Wherever Paleo-Indians lived, throughout the Western Hemisphere, they followed similar ways of life, hunted similar kinds of animals, and used similar kinds of tools. Pioneering conditions, fluctuating climates, tiny populations, and streamlined economies kept the Paleo-Indian way of life simple but effective century after century. At the end of the Pleistocene, however, the environment changed more than it had ever changed before, to be transformed eventually into something quite different. The great herds of grazing animals that had been the center of the Paleo-Indian economy dwindled, and many species became extinct (Martin & Wright 1967). Did the development of the fluted point stimulate this decline? Or was it a response to the decline? Did animals disappear because of environmental change or because of pressures from the growing number of Paleo-Indian hunters? The answers are still unknown. What does seem clear is that the world, as the Paleo-Indians knew it, had begun to change beyond limits their way of life could tolerate. Cultures in ancient California and elsewhere began to change in response, to evolve eventually into something quite different. For this reason we use the terminal Pleistocene date of about 11,000 years ago (9000 B.C.) to mark the close of the Paleo-Indian Period.

Since the fluted point is the most distinctive artifact type associated with Paleo-Indian technology, and the only type with a fully Paleo-Indian age, discussions of fluted points understandably dominate any review of Paleo-Indian artifacts. As indicated earlier, Paleo-Indians did not make very many other types of tools, and those artifacts that they did make were generally universal in nature.

Almost all surviving Paleo-Indian artifacts are made of stone, because artifacts of other materials have largely perished, owing to poor preservation conditions. As the bone spear point from the Manis Site indicates, Paleo-Indians did use other materials, but in most cases we can only infer what such objects might have been. The surviving stone pieces indicate that all Paleo-Indian artifacts were tools, rather than, say, jewelry or items of wealth. These characteristics reflect the Paleo-Indian way of life—nomadic and spare—in which all items were portable, and almost everything bore directly on survival. Furthermore, and again in keeping with the universal technology of the Paleo-Indians, almost all their tools reflect a generalized flake technology, rather than the more specialized blade-core technology associated with many Old World Upper Paleolithic cultures of the same age.

The actual number of surviving Paleo-Indian artifacts is not very large when compared to the remains left by later cultures. The generalized nature of the tools themselves necessitated the making of fewer tools, and the small number of Paleo-Indians meant that there were never many people making tools. The absence of decorative and wealth items, and the perishability of nonlithic artifacts, meant that fewer artifacts were deposited, and of those, even fewer survived. The nomadic lifeway also contributed to keeping the number of possessions low. Finally, the fact that most Paleo-Indian tools cannot be distinguished stylistically from later artifacts means that they cannot be reliably identified except in the context of an intact archaeological site. Paleo-Indian artifacts thus tend to be undercounted.

Paleo-Indian toolmaking technology relied heavily on percussion techniques (see Appendix B), more so than for later cultures. The large size of most tools, the deep embayment of flake scars, and the thickness of flakes suggest that the use of the soft hammer, or *baton*, for flake removal was uncommon. Pressure flaking was reserved for the manufacture of only a few artifacts, such as stone points and gravers—both of which are found normally only at the very end of the period.

Some late Paleo-Indian sites east of the Rockies show evidence that toolmakers manufactured specialized prismatic cores for the production of blades as tool blanks (Green 1963: 145–47). The evidence from California indicates that Paleo-Indians there made cores using unspecialized flaking techniques, using these cores both as tools and as sources of large flakes from which to make other tools. Unmodified cores and waste flakes thus make up substantial parts of California Paleo-Indian assemblages, whereas formally retouched tools make up only a small part of any representative Paleo-Indian collection. The hammerstones used to flake the cores and the flakes themselves are less often found (see, for example, Davis et al. 1979). Paleo-Indians had a greater preference for making tools out of cores than did most later peoples.

Choppers and chopping tools of widely varying forms were commonly made. Other core tools were worked around most of their edges and over both surfaces to form bifaces that may have served a variety of functions. Still other cores were unifacially retouched along an edge to create core scrapers.

Flakes were used less for tool blanks than in most later cultures. A number of Paleo-Indian flakes were so large and robust that they really served as core tools. Unifacially retouched scrapers were generally smaller than such robust flakes, though they tended to be larger than those made later on. The unifacially retouched flake tools form a series of scrapers that show a great deal of variability in both shape and edge form. Some scrapers had markedly serrate or denticulate edges; others had quite smooth edges. Edge curvature ranged from markedly convex to concave or notched. Paleo-Indian scrapers were virtually as varied in form as those of more recent traditions, but their workmanship tended to be less delicate.

Most known Paleo-Indian artifacts from California have been found on the surfaces of old desert-playa gravel terraces, where they have lain for 11,000 years or more. Over time, the surfaces of these tools have developed a patina called *desert varnish*. This patination is caused partly by the chemical reaction of gases in the air with the surface of the stone, and partly by a hundred centuries of sandblasting with windblown grit. This patina gives an artifact a somewhat polished, dark-colored surface with a modest sheen. Unfortunately, patination does not occur at a regular rate, so the degree of patination on a tool is not a reliable indicator of its age.

Although sites in other states have offered evidence for the use of bone and other nonlithic raw materials for making artifacts, Paleo-Indian sites in California have not yet yielded comparable evidence, and the use of nonlithic raw materials must be inferred from other evidence. The use of bone or antler appears not to have been too common among California Paleo-Indians because types of artifacts generally associated with bone working, such as burins and gravers for carving bone and grooved ground-stone slabs for sharpening bones to points, are rare or altogether absent from collections. The case for plant use is better. Specialized plant-processing tools such as mortars and pestles do not occur, but choppers, stone knives, serrate scrapers of flakes, and core scraper planes, which do occur in California Paleo-Indian sites, are often associated ethnographically with the harvesting and processing of bulk plant materials (see, for example, Gould 1977).

Evidence from early dry cave sites in other western states suggests what sorts of plant products might have been involved. The collecting of firewood must have been a major activity. The collection of fibrous plants to make cordage, used in the manufacture of nets, string bags, rope, sandals, and clothing, must also have been an important activity. Some sites yield bone needles with eyes, which may have been used in working with plant fibers for sewing. There is no evidence from Paleo-Indian times for basketmaking, though there is for the plaiting or weaving of mats, since some sites in Nevada and Oregon are located near what were then lakeshores rich in reeds and cattails, and since there is a very ancient use of mats in the western deserts (for evidence of cordage and weaving, see Fryxell et al. 1968).

The variety of sharp-edged scrapers among Paleo-Indian tool collections suggests that wood and leather may also have been worked, but so far no direct evidence has been found in California. The occurrence of spear points implies necessarily the manufacture of wooden spear shafts, and sinew is a good candidate for a hafting material if nothing else. It may be that the examination of stone tool edges under the microscope will shed new light on Paleo-Indian tool use, but such studies require collections from excavated sites, not surface collections whose tools have been too sandblasted to retain microscopic wear evidence. Since there have been very few excavations of Paleo-Indian sites in the state, this research will have to await new excavations.

THE PALEO-INDIAN ARCHAEOLOGICAL TRADITION

Some kinds of information about the life of the Paleo-Indians can be gained from the artifacts they left behind. Other kinds of information can be obtained by looking at their sites. Artifacts occur in sites, and the data of a site include the organization of artifacts and other remains in the site. Equally important is the physical setting of the site. The distribution of sites and their frequencies in different kinds of settings also tell us something about what was important to Paleo-Indian culture (see Map 8).

Compared with some other western states, not many Paleo-Indian sites are known for California, but the situation may be deceptive. Most of California's known Paleo-Indian remains come from the deserts of the southern part of the state, but relatively little research has been done there yet. Many more early sites in the desert may still be undiscovered, and others might have existed along the coast only to have been drowned beneath rising sea levels or obliterated by recent urban development.

Then again, California might well never have had as large a Paleo-Indian population as some other parts of the continent. If the state was simply unable to support the huge herds of big-game animals common to the Great Plains, for example, there would be fewer Paleo-Indian sites in California to find. It will take a number of systematic surveys to determine which of these alternatives is closer to the truth. In the meantime, enough sites have been discovered to indicate some variety among them (see Davis 1974, 1978a).

Site Types

Remains from the Paleo-Indian Tradition seem to be found in five types of location in California: occupation sites, workshops, butchering stations, burial sites, and find-spots of individual artifacts.

At *occupation sites* people lived in one place for some length of time. During the Paleo-Indian Period, such sites were temporary, not permanent, since people did not stay in them throughout the year. Occupation sites are identified by characteristic residues that resulted from certain kinds of activities, such as toolmaking, food preparation, craft activities, and garbage disposal. Fire hearths have also been found in some Paleo-Indian occupation sites.

Of the known Paleo-Indian sites in California, only a few have rea-

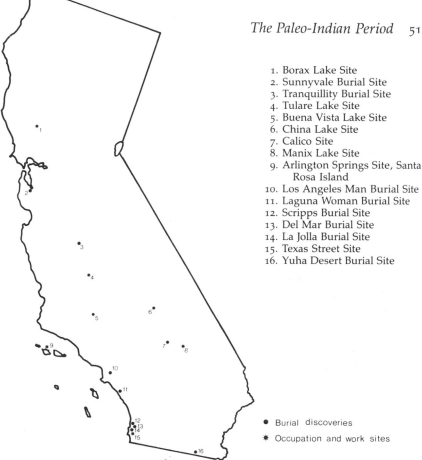

1. Borax Lake Site
2. Sunnyvale Burial Site
3. Tranquillity Burial Site
4. Tulare Lake Site
5. Buena Vista Lake Site
6. China Lake Site
7. Calico Site
8. Manix Lake Site
9. Arlington Springs Site, Santa Rosa Island
10. Los Angeles Man Burial Site
11. Laguna Woman Burial Site
12. Scripps Burial Site
13. Del Mar Burial Site
14. La Jolla Burial Site
15. Texas Street Site
16. Yuha Desert Burial Site

● Burial discoveries

✳ Occupation and work sites

Map 8. Reported Paleo-Indian sites. Paleo-Indian status is still widely argued for all but the Borax Lake, China Lake, and Manix Lake sites.

sonably well identified occupation remains. The China Lake, Lake Mohave, Borax Lake, and possibly Tulare Lake sites are among the best examples. Some of the sites of controversial dates, such as the Texas Street, Buchanan Canyon, and Arlington Springs sites, may also have been occupation sites.

Site location and the environmental setting of sites, both significant features, help to distinguish an occupation site from other site types, since different considerations were involved in locating different kinds of sites. Paleo-Indian occupation sites in California were located near what were then permanent water supplies, and the best-documented sites are found near the shorelines of Pleistocene lakes. Lakeshore lo-

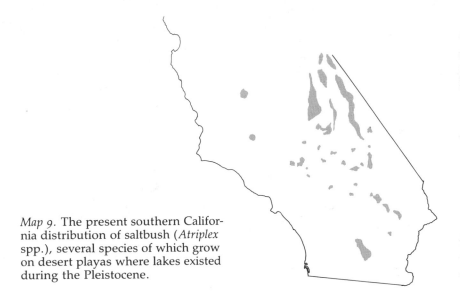

Map 9. The present southern California distribution of saltbush (*Atriplex* spp.), several species of which grow on desert playas where lakes existed during the Pleistocene.

cations were favored in part because humans needed reliable water supplies, but also because lakeshores attracted game animals, which came to drink and browse, and provided the sources for many economically useful plants (see Map 9).

Occupation sites contain a greater variety of stone tools than do other sites because a wider range of activities was carried on at such sites. One finds not only choppers, bifaces, knives, flake scrapers, and serrate flakes, but also the remains from the manufacture of these tools: waste flakes, discarded cores, hammerstones, and tools broken during manufacture. The Borax Lake Site in Lake County provides a good example of such an assemblage, but also an unusual one. Because the site is located at an obsidian flow near a Pleistocene lakeshore (Meighan & Haynes 1970), almost all the tools are made of obsidian (natural volcanic glass). Elsewhere obsidian is an unusual raw material for Paleo-Indian sites; quartzite, basalt, and metamorphic rocks were much more commonly used. The Tulare Lake Site in the southern San Joaquin Valley is more typical in this regard (Riddell & Olsen 1969).

Because the burning of campfires was an important element of Paleo-Indian occupation-site life, such sites generally feature considerable quantities of fire-cracked rock. Fire-cracked rocks at Borax Lake and Tulare Lake show that campfires had been maintained for considerable periods of time. Fires were important for warmth, protection, and cooking, among other things. At Lake Mohave, Borax Lake, and China Lake, the remains of several species of animals have been found, the apparent result of hunters bringing their kills back to camp (Campbell & Campbell 1937; E. Davis 1975; Meighan & Haynes 1970; Warren & Ore 1978).

Generally, when a site was used for many months, people's activities tended to cause the earth to become packed into hard surfaces that can be recognized archaeologically. And when people stay in one place for long periods, they often build fairly substantial houses that do not need to be rebuilt often. The absence of recognizable house remains or compacted surfaces in Paleo-Indian sites suggests that any shelters were so temporary they left no archaeological traces. Perhaps only of brush, similar to those of the Paiute Indians of the Great Basin (Kroeber 1925), they were most likely built to last for only a season or two.

The soils in these occupation sites are generally chemically homogeneous with the surrounding soils. Distinctions tend to be found in soils of permanently occupied sites because activities such as garbage disposal, the mixing of ash from fireplaces, and urination add concentrations of organic and inorganic chemical compounds to site soils in concentrations not found in surrounding soils. Although some compounds break down after a few centuries, others are long-lived. That Paleo-Indian occupation-site soils lack these distinctions is a further indication that the sites were not occupied for long periods.

Paleo-Indian occupation sites also tend to have small areas of tool concentration, reflecting the size of the groups that occupied them. The debris from such an encampment might be concentrated in an area of only a few hundred square feet. Size may also reflect the number of times a site has been reoccupied. A camp occupied only once would probably be quite small and shallow. If it were visited repeatedly over many hundred years, even on a temporary basis, it would tend to cover a much larger area. It would also often be deeper, as subsequent encampments deposited layer after layer of life's debris. Borax Lake, Tulare Lake, and China Lake are examples of Paleo-Indian occupation sites with long histories of repeated occupation. Most of the desert-playa occupation sites, however, such as the Little Lake Site (Harrington 1957), seem to reflect briefer occupations at any particular spot.

In fact, unlike the sites named above, it is difficult to identify most Paleo-Indian sites in California as having been definite occupation sites (see, for example, Glennan 1976; Payen & Taylor 1976). Most of the reported Paleo-Indian sites are desert surface scatters, and almost everything in them—except for artifacts made of stone—decomposed or disappeared long ago. In many cases these sites originally consisted of shallow deposits of cultural remains mixed with soil. The onset of desert conditions has meant, though, that over the centuries the soil has blown away, leaving perishable artifacts exposed on the surface. Very rarely has new soil been deposited that might have sealed a site and halted the erosion.

For sites occupied only once, the evidence of occupation is scanty at best, since even originally the sites were shallow and not very rich in artifacts. The high alkalinity of desert soils, followed by soil erosion and the exposure of artifacts to the air, led to the destruction of artifacts made of bone, plant fiber, or other organic materials, leaving only scatters or concentrations of stone artifacts on the eroded surface of the desert floor to mark the original campsite. Nevertheless, it is sometimes possible to identify some of these surface scatters as probable occupation sites, especially when stone tools found in them resemble tools found in the more evident occupation sites and differ from those found in other types of sites. Emma Lou Davis (1978a) has found a number of such small, temporary occupation sites around former desert lakes.

Other surface scatters are more difficult to distinguish from the more specialized types of sites, because the distinction between them is often only a matter of degree. For instance, if a group stopped to make stone tools at a place where the raw materials for the purpose were abundant, the resulting site would, at first, reflect the specialized activity of toolmaking almost exclusively. If, however, there was also a plentiful food supply nearby and the group maintained its camp for several weeks, gradually the remains would take on more and more of the characteristics of an occupation site.

For this reason, only the most evidently specialized sites are included in such distinctive categories as the *workshop*. Workshops are sites in which the main activity was the production of tools, generally stone tools. Workshops may occur as special activity areas within occupation sites, such as at the Borax Lake Site, or as separate sites located near sources of raw material. Malcolm Rogers (1929, 1968) described several such workshops from the Colorado Desert of southern California. At such sites the proportion of waste flakes, cores, and hammerstones is high compared to the assemblages from occupation sites, and the proportion of finished tools is low. In addition, the finished, identifiable types of artifacts found at workshops tend to include a high percentage of tools that were broken and discarded during manufacture. The percentage of finished, usable tools is very low, however, probably because they were normally carried away for use elsewhere.

In principle, one way to tell a workshop from an occupation site is by the microscopic study of tool edges. Tools discarded at occupation sites often display minute evidence of wear, especially along the working edges. In workshops, where tools are manufactured but rarely used, few tools display microscopic evidence of edge wear. It is usually not possible to study tools found on site surfaces, however, since 10,000 years of sandblasting have made them unreliable candidates for microscopic study.

Butchering stations represent another type of specialized site found in Paleo-Indian times as well as later. Butchering stations are locations at which large animals were killed and dismembered. Some of these animals were so large that their carcasses could not be carried back to camp, presenting hunters with two choices: they could bring their families to the kill site to camp temporarily while the meat was eaten on the spot, or they could cut off the most desirable parts and carry or drag them back to camp in one or more trips. In the former case, a butchering site would be hard to distinguish from an occupation site.

The most distinctive features of a butchering site are the stone tools associated with heavy butchering, such as choppers, cleavers, knives, and large flake scrapers; the waste from making and renewing these tools; and, when preservation conditions are good, portions of skeletons of the butchered game. A butchering site generally has bones of only one kind of game, in contrast to a normal occupation site. Only a few butchering sites have been identified for California, even though in other parts of the west they are more common. Emma Lou Davis has found an apparent butchering site at what she calls Post 15 near the edge of former China Lake. There she found part of a mammoth skeleton in terrace gravels near an assemblage of butchering tools (1975). Phil Orr found the bones of dwarf mammoths on Santa Rosa Island. He believes the mammoth bones show signs of having been butchered with stone tools, but he has had difficulty convincing many other archaeologists of his interpretation (1968).

Burial sites represent another type of specialized site that Paleo-Indians apparently produced. Burial sites are those in which the chief feature is the interment of human skeletal remains. So far, six California sites have been claimed to represent Paleo-Indian burials (see Map 8). Each site contains a single skeleton or part of a skeleton, and none is associated with an occupation site. Whether any or all of these burials date to Paleo-Indian times is a matter of debate, and the dating problems discussed earlier represent only part of the problem (see Bischoff & Rosenbauer 1981). In most cases it is not known where in the site the skeleton came from, or even where the site is. The so-called Los Angeles Man (actually a woman), for example, was discovered in the 1910's during the excavation of a sewer line, at a depth of about 80 feet (24 m) below the present ground surface; its precise location in the deposit is unknown. Only the skull was recovered, and neither the rest of the skeleton nor any associated site or artifacts was ever found.

Another example is the Laguna Woman burial. Another isolated skull find, it was reportedly discovered in the 1930's during construction of a house on a sand dune in Laguna Beach. The skull was shipped to Europe where it stayed for many years before being returned to the United States, and archaeologists have never been able to relocate the site from which it came (Berger 1975; Berger et al. 1971).

A more recent discovery is the Yuha burial from the Yuha Desert near the Mexican border (Bischoff, Childers & Schleman 1978; Bischoff et al. 1976; Childers 1974; S. Rogers 1977). This burial included a nearly complete skeleton found beneath a massive cairn of rocks. The basis for assigning it to the Paleo-Indian Tradition is a radiocarbon date of organic materials scraped from the rocks overlying the burial, which many archaeologists deem unreliable (Payen et al. 1978). In addition, the burial style is unlike any other known for the Paleo-Indian Tradition, and similar to burials made within the last few thousand years by more recent desert cultures in southern California (Wilke 1978). In fact, all the purported Paleo-Indian burials in California suffer from similar problems of location or age.

Some or all of the claimed burials might prove to be genuinely Paleo-Indian, however. If so, they suggest things about the culture that produced them. None of the burials occurred in the context of an occupation site, and no Paleo-Indian occupation site has yet yielded a burial. It appears that Paleo-Indians, unlike later peoples, did not bury their dead in their camps. With so few burials to go by, and considering that most possible occupation sites are surface scatters today, this conclusion must be regarded as tentative.

A more definite conclusion is that none of the burials is known to have been accompanied by grave offerings. Burials from later periods, by contrast, are almost always accompanied by artifacts. Their absence may reflect the relatively small numbers of material items the Paleo-Indians possessed, or were in a position to contribute to the dead. It may also reflect the fact that most of the reported burial sites were finds of individual skulls, discovered by amateurs who did not identify the site as a whole, much less make a systematic collection of the remains. In any event, burials from later periods are almost always found with grave goods of some sort, so it may be that some fundamental change in burial customs took place after the end of the Paleo-Indian Period. In addition, it should be noted that none of the purported Paleo-Indian burials was associated with other burials. Paleo-Indians apparently were not buried in collective cemeteries, but individually, perhaps close to the place of death. Such a practice would not be surprising for a people who changed camp frequently as a part of their nomadic way of life (Krieger 1964).

In addition to these types of living, working, and burial sites, a number of isolated Paleo-Indian artifacts have been found around the state (see, for example, Glennan 1971: 29–31; Wallace 1978: 26). These *find-spots*, or discoveries of isolated artifacts that are not associated with any other kind of site, are actually rather common. There is a problem in assigning such finds to the Paleo-Indian Tradition, however. Most isolated artifacts cannot be directly dated, and very few artifact types are unique to the Paleo-Indian Tradition; fluted points are the most important exception. Artifacts that are large, crudely flaked, or heavily patined are often called Paleo-Indian but might in fact belong to later times (see, for example, Campbell & Campbell 1935). The most reliable way to determine an artifact's age is to find it in association with other artifacts in a datable context such as a charcoal-filled fireplace or with the bones of an extinct Pleistocene animal. Since such associations are precisely what find-spots lack, many authentic Paleo-Indian artifacts have probably gone unrecognized.

Since the fluted point is an exception to this general rule, the finds of isolated fluted points tell us important things about where Paleo-Indians went and what they were doing (for fuller discussions of fluted points, see Davis & Shutler 1969; Haynes 1964; Judge 1977; Wormington 1957). As Map 10 indicates, isolated fluted points have been found mainly where occupation sites also occur. Some points have been found in the foothills of northern California, however. They suggest that toward the end of the Paleo-Indian Tradition hunters began to expand their range from the southern California foothill habitats into similar environments in other parts of the state. No other kinds of Paleo-Indian sites have shown up yet in the Sierra, which may mean that only individual hunters wandered up that far, but more likely means that richer sites lie there awaiting discovery.

1. Samuel Cave
2. Big Meadow
3. Borax Lake
4. Tracy Lake
5. Ebbetts Pass
6. Tulare Lake
7. Buena Vista Lake
8. Tehachapi Mountains
9. Owens Lake
10. China Lake
11. Panamint Valley
12. Death Valley
13. Pilot Knob Valley
14. Tiefort Basin
15. Fossil Springs
16. Lake Mohave (Silver and
    Soda lakes)
17. Baker
18. Arlington Canyon, Santa
    Rosa Island
19. Christy's Beach, Santa
    Cruz Island
20. Cuyamaca Park Pass
21. Pinto Basin

Map 10. Finds of Paleo-Indian fluted projectile points, dating to 10,500–9000 B.C.

Site Locations

Even though reasonably well confirmed Paleo-Indian sites in California are small in number, they indicate patterns of distribution that tell us more about Paleo-Indian life. For example, most of the Paleo-Indian occupation and working sites are found on the playas of interior southern California desert valleys; a few are located in similar environments to the north. As we have seen, in Pleistocene times these playas were shallow lakes situated on broad valley floors. These lakes were fed mainly by runoff from the surrounding mountains rather than by rain that fell directly on the lakes. Almost all the valleys of interior southern California are and were interior-draining: the rainfall drained into the central playa, rather than feeding rivers that ran to the sea (see Fig. 5). Pleistocene rainfall was more plentiful than today, so that enough rainfall drained into the playas to compensate for evaporation, and permanent, shallow, broad lakes formed. Although

Fig. 5. A desert valley near Baker in eastern California, showing a dried lake bed, or playa. In Paleo-Indian times such lake beds held permanent water and supported lush vegetation in their shallows, which attracted game animals to drink and browse. Paleo-Indians camped along the lakeshores to exploit the plants and animals and to enjoy the permanent water supply. They ranged into the nearby hills, which were nearly as dry then as now, to take advantage of the region's ecological diversity. (U.S. Forest Service Photo)

Fig. 6. Dry lake bed near El Centro, Imperial County; the foreground is a typical setting for a Paleo-Indian occupation site. This 1937 photograph shows a plant association, dominated by the ocotillo at the left, that may be only slightly changed from the valley terrace vegetation of the late Pleistocene. In the last 30 years this terrace, like many in southern California's deserts, has been badly disturbed by all-terrain recreational vehicles, and the Paleo-Indian sites there have been damaged in the process. (U.S. Forest Service Photo)

somewhat brackish, they supported fish and amphibians, as well as abundant water plants, and attracted migratory waterfowl. Because of these lakes, the area was able to support the kinds of large game favored by the Paleo-Indians. Rainfall was just enough more abundant in the valley bottoms than today to support grasslands which, though not nearly as rich as those of the Great Plains, still attracted large herbivores. The topography and resources of this region were similar to those occurring all over the west during the late Pleistocene, and the lakes provided a permanent water supply in a land where many streams were dry for much of the year. These conditions offered a favorable environment in California for the Paleo-Indian way of life, and it is therefore not so surprising that most Paleo-Indian sites have been found in such settings (see Fig. 6).

This sort of environment was found during the late Pleistocene in California from the coast to the Colorado River and from the Mexican border north into the Great Basin. On the coast, animals grazed on the coastal terrace grasslands and drank from springs, ponds, and marshes; Paleo-Indians hunted them. There is no indication that coastal residents of this period made use of any of the ocean's resources. Instead, they seemed to have followed a way of life very similar to that of their inland relatives (see, for example, Minshall 1976; Moriarty, Shumway & Warren 1959).

Lakeshore environments also occurred in several other parts of the state, and several sites indicate that these areas were also occupied by Paleo-Indians. The Borax Lake Site near Clear Lake in the North Coast Ranges is an example. Clear Lake is a Pleistocene lake that has survived to the present, and the Borax Lake Site, which was first occupied about 12,000 years ago (10,000 B.C.), features artifacts made of obsidian, a natural glass resulting from local volcanic activity. The presence of fluted points, augmented by radiocarbon dates and obsidian hydration measurements, have helped to date the earliest part of this site to the Paleo-Indian Period (Harrington 1948; Meighan & Haynes 1970).

Other examples of early sites are located in the southern half of the San Joaquin Valley, around Buena Vista Lake and Tulare Lake. Because of the geological development of the San Joaquin Valley, its southern half is interior-draining most of the time, creating shallow lakes in the valley bottoms much like desert-playa lakes. Archaeological sites around the shores of these lakes reflect a lakeshore way of life that had emerged toward the end of the Paleo-Indian Period (Riddell & Olsen 1969). Some archaeologists, however, suspect that the sites are not quite that old (Aikens 1978; Wallace 1978).

These central California sites notwithstanding, at least two-thirds of the known or suspected Paleo-Indian occupation, workshop, and butchering sites occur in interior southern California. By contrast, all but one of the claimed burial sites are found along the southern California coast. No one is sure why this concentration should occur, but there are many possible explanations. For example, it may be that, owing to the erosion and exposure of many desert-playa sites, burials there may have been lost. Or it could be that the claimed Paleo-Indian burials actually belong to later periods, and that there is no concentration along the coast. Certainly the sample is so small that it is not possible to draw any firm conclusions yet about distribution.

The distribution pattern of fluted points, as noted earlier, is more straightforward than that of burials (see, for example, Glennan 1971). The fact that fluted points occur in central and northern California even though they are concentrated in interior southern California suggests that Paleo-Indians may not have been as restricted to lakeshore habitats as we maintain.

Economy

Even though the evidence is scanty, archaeologists have some ideas about the economy of California's Paleo-Indians. The first Californians relied completely on hunting and gathering for their livelihood. They apparently focused on the hunting of medium-sized and large game: deer, antelope, camelids, horses. There is no evidence that mountain sheep were killed, probably because Paleo-Indians did not hunt regularly in the higher mountains. In contrast with their contemporaries on the Great Plains, California's Paleo-Indians apparently hunted bison, mammoth, and giant ground sloth only occasionally. Since California could not support herds nearly as large as those in the vast grasslands of the Great Plains, we understandably find no evidence that the early residents practiced the mass-hunting techniques of the Plains, such as driving whole herds over cliffs or into arroyos. In the American West, including California, big game occurred mainly in the vicinity of lakes, so it was for the game that Paleo-Indians lived around lakes, not for the lakes' own aquatic resources. We do find occasional site-associated bones of some smaller creatures, such as rabbits and tortoises, but not those of fish and waterfowl, even though they were available where the Paleo-Indians lived.

The same pattern holds true at Paleo-Indian sites elsewhere in the country. At the Naco and Lehner sites in Arizona, the McLean and Miami sites in Texas, the Dent Site in Colorado, and the Clovis Site in New Mexico, hunters who lived between 12,000 and 11,000 years ago (10,000–9000 B.C.) made Clovis fluted points. Their game included bison, camelid, mammoth, horse, and tapir, and the only indications of smaller game are bones from a turtle and possibly a deer at the Dent Site (Jennings 1974: 81–84).

No evidence of Paleo-Indian plant-food use has been positively identified from California sites, but archaeologists believe that plant foods must have been important to these early hunters. For one thing, all the ethnographically known societies that followed a way of life comparable to that of the Paleo-Indians made considerable use of plants for food, fuel, and raw materials. For another, many of the kinds of flake and core tools made by Paleo-Indians were also made by historically known California Indians, who used some of them to process plant materials as well as for hunting. Many archaeologists, believing that the image of Paleo-Indians as specialized big-game hunters is overdrawn, suggest that wild fruits, berries, greens, and bulbs were probably eaten. Equally likely is that Paleo-Indians used pliant plants for craft materials. Although no evidence suggests an extensive Paleo-Indian basketry industry, the production of matting, cordage, nets, and bags is probable. Even more certainly, the Paleo-Indians relied on harder woods for firewood and spear shafts, and if any woodworking was done, possibly other things were crafted from wood as well. The microscopic study of stone tool edges offers one of the best potential avenues for the further study of Paleo-Indian crafts.

Society

Although we have some evidence on which to base ideas about Paleo-Indian technology and subsistence, only sparse data exist about the kind of social organization characteristic of Paleo-Indian culture. Much of the evidence is negative—no signs of permanent houses or sedentary villages, no evidence of large populations or elaborate technology. Under such circumstances, archaeologists often make use of *ethnographic analogies* to reconstruct the more nonmaterial aspects of culture. That is, archaeologists examine the cultures of present-day or historically known peoples who are suspected of leading lives similar to that of the archaeologically known people under study. The ethnographic cultures are used as sources of ideas about how the prehistoric peoples might have behaved. In the case of the Paleo-Indians, analogies might be drawn to the Shoshone Indians of the Great Basin, the Seri of western Mexico, the !Kung of southwestern Africa, the Ituri Forest hunters of Zaire, the Birhor of southern India, the Andamanese of Indonesia, the Arunta of central Australia, the Caribou Eskimo of Canada, or other hunter-gatherer groups. From such ethnographic examples are drawn ideas about the behavior of hunter-gatherers in general, and the ethnographic groups that most closely resemble the Paleo-Indians in material remains and environment are used as analogies for understanding the nonmaterial aspects of Paleo-Indian culture that do not leave direct archaeological evidence. The archaeologist then looks for evidence in his excavated data to confirm—or reject—such a model (Binford 1967).

Using ethnographic analogies, archaeologists have developed ideas about the nature of Paleo-Indian social organization that can be applied to California. Our current model posits small, widely separated groups of people, each group probably amounting to no more than an extended family: a husband with one or more wives and their children as the family core, plus additional relatives who cannot maintain autonomous groups of their own, such as an aged parent, aunt, or uncle, a newly married son with his wife and baby, an orphaned cousin, or a widowed sister. Anthropologists call this sort of group a *micro-band*. The micro-band is a very appropriate form of society for small populations living under demanding circumstances. It has no formal organization in the normal sense, beyond the structure of the family itself; structure and role relationships are provided solely by kin relationships. There is no chief or other formal leader. Rather, the head of the household is the head of the group, though all the adults participate in decision making, and authority extends no further than the micro-band itself.

Micro-bands do not have formal bodies of law. They rely instead on customs that have been worked out over generations, and on constraints imposed on people by the reality of their environment and their way of life. Such groups practice a truly democratic and egalitarian form of social life: only personal abilities distinguish individuals, and everyone's opinions are valued equally. The divisions of labor normally practiced among such peoples follow age and sex lines. Ethnographers find that among hunters and gatherers—people who subsist without farming or herding—males tend to be the hunters, and females tend to have the primary responsibility for the collection of plant foods, raw materials, and fuel. Food is shared throughout the group, a practice that maximizes the survival chances of the group as a whole, and therefore of each individual who makes up the group, since none could survive long in isolation (see T. Kroeber 1959 and her discussion of the fate of Ishi in isolation). The few pieces of personal property that micro-band members own are also widely shared, normally on request, with the tacit understanding that group members always have the right to call on each other for help when needed. In societies with such sharing ethics, it is difficult for an individual to accumulate personal wealth: the more a person has, the more his kin will borrow from him. Thus, few economic distinctions arise within such groups.

Micro-bands cannot be wholly isolated from each other, for if nothing else young people would find it difficult to find suitable marriage partners. Marriage within a family invariably leads to genetic abnormalities among offspring, and in any event small groups rarely have enough young people to serve as potential mates for each other. The incest taboo works strongly in micro-bands, leading young people to marry individuals from neighboring bands. Neighboring groups tend to get together periodically, and these meetings provide opportunities for young people to become acquainted, for marriages to be arranged, and for kin members separated by prior marriages to visit with their relatives and in-laws. Such gatherings are also usually marked by celebrations, religious observances, gambling, and perhaps some economic activities.

Marriage creates ties of kinship and cooperation between groups, ties that are reinforced by periodic visits and later marriages among children. Typically, hunters and gatherers follow the practice of *patrilocal postmarital residence*: when a couple marries, the woman leaves her parents' group and goes to live with the group of her husband's parents. It is not clear why this practice is so common among hunting peoples, but some anthropologists think that male hunters need to live in a region for a long time to learn its characteristics well enough to be effective hunters, and that the degree of local expertise needed for plant collecting—usually a female responsibility—is not as great. It is therefore more efficient for the wife to move to the husband's group than vice versa.

There are exceptions to the rule, however. Sometimes the couple stays with the wife's micro-band, especially if it has fewer hunters than it needs. In other cases, the new couple may go off after some time to found a new micro-band in some unoccupied region, especially if their parents' micro-bands suffer from relative overpopulation for their environments. If a family has several sons and all of them grow up, marry and have large families, the group has to break up. Often the stress and crowding that accompany such growth lead to the increase of interpersonal friction, which promotes the division of the group.

In any event, one net effect of marriage is the creation of kinship ties between micro-bands. These ties improve the survival chances of all the groups involved, providing a wider network of mutual assistance and a sort of safety valve. During times of famine or drought, or when a personality conflict threatens to disrupt the tightly knit group, relatives in other groups can be visited temporarily until local conditions improve. By creating options for meeting stressful conditions, kinship ties among micro-band members of different groups help reduce the chances that adverse circumstances will lead to the extinction of any individual group.

Archaeologists feel that this model of ethnographic hunter-gatherer social organization is a reasonably accurate depiction of California Paleo-Indian lifeways. The micro-band, with the family as the basic unit of economic production, was a successful way of organizing people in a pioneer situation. And, as pioneer conditions gave way during the end of the Paleo-Indian Period, it provided the building block upon which a new way of life was founded.

Terminal Pleistocene Extinctions

One of the most remarkable aspects of the end of the Pleistocene was the relatively sudden disappearance of many types of animals.

Extinction is a natural process, but its rate during the last 10,000 years of the Pleistocene appears to have been more than a hundred times what would have been normally expected, and this sudden upsurge of extinctions makes the subject an important one for scientific inquiry. Because extinctions in North America coincided with the appearance of Paleo-Indians, archaeologists have joined the inquiry and considered the possible relationship between the terminal Pleistocene extinctions and Paleo-Indian culture (Butzer 1971).

The last 10,000 years or so of the Pleistocene saw the extinction of hundreds of species of animals—more than 200 genera worldwide, including more than 35 genera in North America alone (Martin & Wright 1967). Most of them were *megafauna*, or large mammals. Present data suggest that small mammals, birds, insects, reptiles, amphibians, fish, plants, and other forms of life were relatively unaffected. Most of the animals that became extinct were mastodons, mammoths, giant ground sloths, and other herbivores. Several types of carnivores that preyed upon the megafauna also became extinct, including the Alaskan lion, the dire wolf, and the saber-toothed tiger.

In some cases extinction meant the disappearance of a species from a continent, but not its total eradication. For example, the tapir, which lived in North America 20,000 years ago, died out there by 10,000 years ago but survives today in South America. Similarly, the jaguar, which used to range as far north as Nevada, is now found no farther north than southern Mexico. The horse, which evolved in North America and was widespread until 12,000 years ago, disappeared from the continent. In the meantime, however, it had crossed into Asia at one period when the Bering Land Bridge was exposed, and it survived there after it disappeared from North America. (Ironically, the horses so effectively employed by the Plains Indians later were not of New World stock but rather descendants of the Arabian horses brought to the New World by the Spaniards.)

In other cases, the species did not become extinct, apparently, but underwent rapid selection for a smaller form. The giant bison, for example, was replaced about 12,000 years ago by the modern bison, and paleontologists believe that the smallest, most agile bison of the day (within the range of variation of herds of giant bison) were able to survive when their larger relatives perished. During the Pleistocene, great size and strength were apparently advantageous traits, but as the Ice Age ended, those traits became liabilities, and only the smaller, quicker animals within herds were successful in reproducing. The average size of animals shrank rapidly, and the descendants were enough different from their ancestors to appear to be a different species; thus the giant bison only appeared to have become extinct. The same thing seems to have happened to the dire wolf, a giant Pleistocene wolf that was quickly replaced by the modern prairie wolf.

Most of the disappearances were true worldwide extinctions, however. The most significant North American extinctions of this sort included the mammoth, mastodon, giant ground sloth, four-pronged antelope, North American camelids, Alaskan lion, and saber-toothed tiger.

In trying to determine the causes of the terminal Pleistocene extinctions, investigators have been presented with a series of fascinating puzzles. If climatic change is cited as the only cause, why were there not comparable numbers of extinctions at the end of the previous glaciation (the Illinoian), roughly 200,000 years ago, when climatic changes were just as great? Some scholars have suggested that a wave of diseases may have carried off the megafauna. But if so, why did these diseases arise suddenly, and why did they not do as diseases do today, leaving some naturally resistant survivors to repopulate the continent? Why would only the megafauna have perished, and not other forms of life? What role, if any, did humans play in the process? After all, humans, as relative newcomers to the Western Hemisphere, represented perhaps only 10,000–50,000 hunters armed with handheld spears against tens of millions of animals. Hunters had ranged over the Old World for a million years or more without bringing on waves of extinctions, so why should the migration of small numbers of hunters bring on the complete extinction of 35 genera of megafauna from the continent? Archaeologists feel that humans must have played some role in the extinctions, however, at least in North America, although the exact nature of this role is still much debated (see E. Davis 1978b; Martin & Wright 1967).

Arguments about the relationship between extinctions and the Paleo-Indians are intertwined with discussions about the age of human colonization of the Americas. Archaeologists who believe that New World settlement began toward the end of the Pleistocene, around 12,000–13,000 years ago (10,000–11,000 B.C.), view the Paleo-Indians as a wave of highly skilled, specialized big-game hunters, armed with spears tipped by fluted points, who swept across the continent with ease over a few short centuries, slaughtering the abundant animal life the way the buffalo were slaughtered a century ago. In fact, archaeologists have excavated sites, such as the Lindenmeier and Olsen-Chubbock sites in Colorado, where numbers of mammoth and bison were slaughtered at one time. There is no evidence, however, for killings of a magnitude that could account for extinction.

If, on the other hand, people first colonized the New World some-time between 20,000 and 40,000 years ago, Paleo-Indians must have hunted megafauna for thousands of years without making a serious impact on their numbers. Then, as the Ice Age drew to a close, environmental factors, including climatic change, began to cause populations of megafauna to decline. In this view, Paleo-Indian hunting is seen as just one more pressure. The development of the fluted point at the very end of the Pleistocene may not have been a cause of the extinctions so much as a reaction to them. From this perspective, it is felt that Paleo-Indians coped with the decline in their meat supply by developing more effective tools and hunting techniques, and that the additional pressure of this intensified focus only upset the deteriorating balance between megafauna and environment even further, hastening the extinctions.

The appearance of the fluted point signaled the end of the pioneering condition of the Paleo-Indian and marked the beginning of a move away from a universal technology. Whether Paleo-Indians entered the New World at the end of the Pleistocene or much earlier, by 11,000 years ago (9000 B.C.) they had spread over much of the hemisphere and had begun to adapt to their new environments. As the ending of pioneer settlement brought forth a technology more closely adjusted to the features of local environments, Paleo-Indian life itself began to change.

End of the Paleo-Indian Tradition

We do not know whether any one or a combination of these models might prove to be most accurate. We do know that the environment did change, and it reshaped the world to which California's Paleo-Indians had become adapted. The beginning of the Holocene (Recent) brought warmer conditions to the desert valleys and less precipitation to the surrounding mountains. With just slight increases in evaporation and decreases in rainfall, or just the decline of rainfall in the mountains, many of the lakes began to lose water faster than it was being replaced, and the lakes gradually dried up. Other sources of water also became less available, and California's ability to support the larger game animals was sharply curtailed. But whereas the megafauna became extinct, relatively smaller animals survived; antelope, mountain sheep, deer, and others were able to range from the mountains and foothills down into the valleys in search of food and water.

All these changes had serious implications for the Paleo-Indians: meat and water sources were declining; the lakeshore plants, so useful for animal food, human food, and craft materials, were vanishing with the lakes. And although the lakes did not dry up suddenly, or all at the same time—in fact, some playas are temporarily filled by rainfall even today (Lake Elsinore rose 20 feet, or 6 m, in the winter of 1979–80, and the Salton Sea rose from rainfall every winter from 1977 to 1980)—the environment as a whole inexorably lost its ability to support the Paleo-Indian economy. Ancient Californians responded by developing new ways of life better suited to the new environment. The Paleo-Indian Tradition gradually gave way to the Archaic way of life.

CHAPTER THREE

The Archaic Period

Imagine a scene set at the edge of the Central Valley among the foothills of the Sierra. At the mouth of a broad, grass-covered valley, a small river winds toward the marshlands of the great valley to the west. The valley floor is dotted with oak groves. The river meanders quietly westward, its swift mountain flow slowed as the gradient of its bed flattens. The valley floor constricts a few miles to the east where several creeks descend from out of the foothills to join it.

On one particular oak-capped terrace above the river four campfires flicker. A small encampment has been built in a clearing within the grove. Not far from each fire stands a beehive-shaped brush shelter, measuring eight or nine feet high and perhaps a dozen feet across. Each shelter is home to a family of up to eight to ten people. The camp includes 36 people in all. The four families to which they belong make up the band that occupies this valley. Like the micro-bands of Paleo-Indian times, each family includes a man with his wife or wives, their children, and one or two unmarried, widowed, or aged relatives. In this particular band, an older man heads one household; his two grown sons head two others, and the son of his late brother heads the fourth.

It is autumn. Despite the clear day there is a chill in the air. People are warming themselves around their campfires. This is the first week the whole band has been together since last spring. All summer, each family hunted and foraged by itself through the hills and mountains, living in temporary camps. During that time none of the families saw each other. Now, sitting together at the fires, they tell each other about their summers: the places where they camped, how abundant various plants and animals were, how many bears and cougars were seen, what injuries were suffered, and the rest of their experiences.

Each family has brought back a few baskets of seeds and acorns to supplement local food supplies while they last. For the moment, however, there is no worry about having enough to eat. Acorns are still abundant in the oak groves near camp, some kinds of grass seeds are still available, salmon are in the river, and deer can be found in the hills nearby. Two boys rise and, borrowing their fathers' three-pronged spears, go down to the river. They return in less than an hour with five silver salmon—enough meat for the entire camp.

Nearby, one of the women kneels at a milling slab, working a mano, or handstone, in circles to grind handfuls of seed into flour. The large stone slab has been sunk partly into the ground to keep it from moving while in use. As a handful of seeds is ground into meal, she carefully sweeps the meal into a basketry tray using a small brush of plant fibers. Then she takes another handful from a storage basket and spreads it on her milling stone.

Another woman is cracking acorns on a milling slab. She dumps the nutmeats into a nearby mortar to be pounded into meal with her pestle. Later, after leaching the meal with water to remove its tannins, she will mix the leached meal with fresh water in one of her large cooking baskets. She will cook this gruel by dropping heated stones into it, stirring rapidly with a stick to keep the stones from burning the basket.

Her husband sits nearby, splitting a deer leg bone into splinters so he can make bone awls and needles. His wife will use these tools during the coming months to make baskets, mats, and clothes. The man uses a small grooved cobble to sharpen the splinters into the proper form. He rubs the end of each splinter back and forth in the groove, abrading the bone into a point.

The old man sits at the edge of camp with two of his grandsons. He is teaching them how to produce round, thin flakes from stream cobbles to use for cleaning fish. The previous day, when the boys were looking for rabbits in the brush along the river, they happened upon a sizable piece of jasper in a dry creek bed. Since they knew it was a good material for making stone tools, they carried it back to camp. Now the old man sits with them, showing them how to remove the desired shape of flakes and how to prepare the edges with an antler tine to produce the proper scraping edge.

Another boy runs into camp carrying the carcass of a ground squirrel he has just caught in a snare. The boy approaches the old man and asks for a sharp waste flake from the pile of chipping waste the old man and his grandsons have been creating. He is given a large flake with a thin, sharp edge. He uses it as a knife blade to skin and gut the rodent. He casts aside the used flake and takes the squirrel carcass to his mother, who drops it in her mortar and pounds it with her pestle to a jellylike consistency. She adds the mashed carcass to the gruel in the cooking basket for the midday meal.

Two of the women have begun to weave baskets as they sit and talk. During the summer, as their families moved from camp to camp, the women collected bear grass, redbud root, sugar-pine root, maidenhair fern, and other basketry materials. Now the people will be staying in winter camp for several months, and there will be plenty of time for the women to make baskets and teach basketmaking to their daughters. These baskets will be used in several ways. A few will be given as gifts. A few will be saved for grave offerings for the next death in the band. Some will be used in trade or to hold trade goods. Most, however, will be used in the household to replace worn-out baskets. While autumn lasts, the women will collect bark and make matting to cover the frames of their houses. Otherwise, by the time the rainy season starts, around the winter solstice, the brush coverings on the huts will be too flimsy to keep out the weather.

Though each adult is engaged in a task, most sit close enough to each other that they can chat while they work. Some occupations are more solitary, however. One man sits quietly under a nearby oak tree. He is preparing to leave the next day to go into the nearby chaparral to hunt deer. He is fasting and meditating to cleanse himself in preparation for the next day's hunting trip. As part of his meditation, he holds a phallus-shaped stone, a "charmstone" carved by a younger brother who is stone carver, doctor, and shaman for his band.

This younger man does not often join in the band's casual social life. He sits off at some distance, working at carving soapstone. During the past summer he visited a soapstone quarry in the mountains, and brought a considerable amount back to the winter camp. He is now carving one piece into a religious talisman, a plummet-shaped charmstone for one of his brothers to wear. His next work will be the bowl of a pipe. He saves small pieces of the soapstone to make later into beads and pendants.

This man has always seemed different from everyone else in the band. He has never married, for one thing, and still lives in his father's household. Some believe he has special power, power that he can put into the charmstones to aid and protect the owner. Some even believe he can change himself into a bear. No one wants to insult him, for no one wants to meet a bear when alone out on a trail—and it is strongly suspected that this is exactly what would happen. No one feels entirely comfortable around him, yet everyone respects him for his abilities. His charmstones are known to be effective, and he knows more about healing and medicinal herbs than anyone else in camp. Although he is somewhat feared, he is never unwelcome. He does not have to hunt often, for the other men see to it that he has a share of whatever food there is.

Within the month, the band expects to be visited by kinsmen from a camp twenty miles downstream, in the Central Valley. The two bands meet every fall, when acorns and salmon are most abundant. Then the groups feast, visit, play games, gamble, and hold religious ceremonies together. Over the years, a number of marriages have united families in the two bands. This year there are no marriages to be conducted, but future marriages may be negotiated.

A little trading may also be conducted between the families of the two bands. The visitors may bring olivella and abalone shells, which they themselves obtain by trade with other bands living closer to the sea. The people value shells highly because of their attractiveness and because so few shells ever reach them. In order to have something to offer in exchange for the shells, the band has accumulated things from the mountains that the valley group has a harder time getting, such as steatite (soapstone) and chippable stone. The women are able to collect some basketry materials that valley women cannot find, so a few baskets may change hands. One or two visitors may negotiate with the carver for charmstones.

One of the reasons the people want seashells is to make beads for grave offerings. Sometimes in the summer a group member too ill or weak to go back up into the hills is left behind in camp. But it is a rare winter when one or two people do not die, sometimes even more, and only rarely does the entire group survive. Snow and rain make the mountains inaccessible, plant life dormant, and game hard to find. By winter's end there is never enough food, and the weakest—the elderly, the children, and the ill—suffer even more than the rest. When someone dies, the body is buried in a long, narrow grave along with the band's ancestors, and the survivors will conduct a proper burial with suitable offerings of baskets, food, and shell beads and pendants to go along with any possessions the person might have had. When an old person dies, the ceremony befits the person's status in the band.

The band plans to remain in camp throughout the winter, surviving on whatever they can find in the vicinity of the camp. For the survivors, spring will return, marked by budding trees and new grass, and the band will once more divide into family groups and disperse into the hills.

This scenario depicts a California culture thousands of years after the end of the Paleo-Indian Tradition. Some features found in Paleo-Indian times remained. People still followed a seasonally migratory way of life, still depended on hunting and gathering, still relied on a stone-tool technology, and still lived in small groups. Yet important differences arose: group size became several times larger; economies became correspondingly more productive; big-game hunting dwindled, whereas the use of plant foods became much more important; base camps were occupied for several months; seasonal migration came to extend across several kinds of environments rather than within one; and trade and new toolmaking technologies appeared.

We have seen that the world the Paleo-Indians knew had begun to change as the Pleistocene drew to a close. These changes were many and varied. The climate shifted as temperatures rose, glaciers melted, and precipitation patterns changed. Sea levels rose while inland-lake levels fell. Distributions of plant species changed; some forms became locally extinct, others became widespread. The distribution of herbivorous animals shifted along with the plants, and some animals, particularly the megafauna, became extinct. Megafaunal extinctions, in turn, made it harder and harder for Paleo-Indians to maintain a focal economy based on big game. In response, a new cultural pattern gradually developed, not only in California, but throughout the hemisphere. Archaeologists call it the *Archaic*. The Archaic Period lasted for about 7,000 years in California. Ultimately Archaic cultures developed a much broader subsistence base than had ever been the case during the Paleo-Indian Period. Marked by the spread of settlers into new parts of the state, the Archaic Period is also characterized by a considerable growth in population size and social complexity compared to Paleo-Indian times.

THEMES OF THE ARCHAIC PERIOD

The Archaic Period in California began about 11,000 years ago (9000 B.C.) and lasted until about 4,000 years ago (2000 B.C.) (Wallace 1978: 25). There is no dramatic change to mark its boundary with the Paleo-Indian Period. Differences between late Paleo-Indian sites and early Archaic sites are so slight that any distinction between them is arbitrary. Yet the Archaic Period does mark the start of a new way of life, and, although changes were slow and modest, they were to affect the course of prehistory. By the end of the Archaic, the economies that had developed in California (and elsewhere throughout the New World) were far more complex and sophisticated than they had been in Paleo-Indian times, and could support far more people (Meighan 1959a).

The Archaic Period, like the Paleo-Indian Period, is characterized by certain themes, themes that define it and contrast with the periods that came before and after. These are a diffuse economy, a specialized technology, and the penetration of new ecological niches.

Diffuse Economy

A *diffuse economy* is one in which people make use of a great many kinds of resources, no one resource being the single most important staple (Cleland 1976). Much different from the focal economy practiced by the Paleo-Indians, this system arose in response to the deteri-

oration of the Paleo-Indian resource base at the end of the Pleistocene. In the absence of any other large single-food source comparable
to big game, people were forced to diversify, increasing the array of
species they exploited. This change was accompanied by a shift toward a greater reliance on plants for food, medicine, and craft materials. By the height of the Archaic (5,000–4,000 years ago, or 3000–2000
B.C.), people were using literally hundreds of plant species and dozens of animal species.

A diffuse economy involves more than just enlarging the resource
base, however, because the very act of doing so affects many aspects
of people's lives. Paleo-Indians tended to restrict themselves to a
single kind of environment. Archaic peoples, in order to increase and
diversify their resources, had to become familiar with several kinds of
environments. They had to learn how to exploit many more kinds of
resources, especially various species of plants, which were much more
affected by seasonal availability than the megafauna had been. The
Paleo-Indians had moved camp only as local resources were exhausted, and only to a different part of the same environment, regardless of season.

By contrast, Archaic people had to learn to schedule their movements to correspond with the seasonal availability of many kinds of
resources in several different environments. Such scheduling, based
on knowledge of the content of each environment and of the natural
history of every species used, rested on experience accumulated during generations of residence in an area. Scheduling meant that, rather
than following the Paleo-Indian pattern, Archaic peoples practiced
seasonal migration, in which their camps were moved from one environment to another, as part of a carefully scheduled *annual round*.

In California, the nature of this annual round was determined in
part by the many mountainous areas (see Map 11). Since the particular environment, or life zone, varies with altitude, Archaic people in
many parts of the state could arrange their annual round simply by
moving uphill or down with the seasons. In the most typical Archaic
pattern, people spent the winter in a camp at a lower elevation, migrated to higher elevations in the spring, and returned to the winter
camp in the fall. This migration pattern allowed a group to reach several different life zones to take advantage of the resources of each,
and to adjust the timing of their migrations such that they could be in
each life zone when its most important seasonal resources were
ripening.

Coastal populations generally lacked access to great mountain
ranges. They developed a seasonal migration pattern that took them

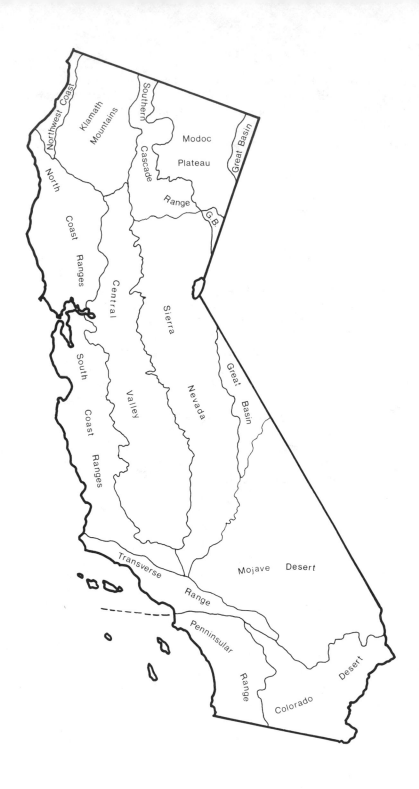

from base camps or winter camps on the coast to summer camps in the interior hills and valleys. The ecological differences between coast and interior provided much the same contrast in life zones and resources that inland peoples enjoyed by migrating up and down mountainsides.

Often the winter base camp was home for several families who came together in the fall when resources were most abundant but split up in the spring, each family going alone to a different part of the mountains or interior to subsist. This pattern of seasonal congregation and dispersal allowed groups to adjust their local population densities to the quantity of seasonally available resources and differed markedly from the Paleo-Indian migration pattern.

Specialized Technology

The exploitation of the many different kinds of resources that Archaic peoples encountered during their annual round was enhanced by the development of a *specialized technology*. Although it is possible to use many different kinds of plants and animals with a simple, non-specialized tool kit (as we saw in the Paleo-Indian Period), there is a limit to the flexibility and efficiency of such a technology. It is possible, for instance, to collect shellfish without a specialized tool, but if one is harvesting a lot of shellfish, it helps to have the sort of knife that can be used to pry open the shells of bivalves. One can collect and eat nuts without specialized tools, but the job is more efficient with collecting baskets and milling or pounding tools. The collecting, processing, and storage of chaparral and grass seeds is greatly enhanced by the use of seed beaters, collecting baskets, winnowing trays, milling tools, and storage baskets. Paleo-Indians may have used some of these same resources, but never systematically or to any great extent, for they lacked the technology that would have allowed them to do so. Archaic peoples advanced beyond their Paleo-Indian predecessors by developing the technologies necessary to using these many local species effectively.

One way the Archaic peoples specialized was to elaborate and re-

Map 11 (facing page). The major geomorphological provinces of California. Each province is a region with a distinctive land surface, underlying geological substratum, and history of development. The setting and topography of a geomorphological province give it a characteristic climate and particular habitats filled with associated plants and animals. These provinces are useful for understanding the nature and distribution of prehistoric cultures that made their living by hunting and gathering wild resources.

fine the generalized tools used by Paleo-Indians. For example, the Paleo-Indians had only a few basic forms of flake scrapers, which they used for many jobs, but Archaic people developed more than a dozen types of scrapers, most of which had rather specific uses. The same sort of proliferation and specialization took place with bone tools.

Specialization also inspired the creation of entirely new kinds of tools, using techniques with which Paleo-Indians were largely unfamiliar. For example, although Paleo-Indians made sandals and simple mats, they did not weave baskets. Archaic people not only learned how to weave baskets, but developed several specialized forms of basketry. Neither did Paleo-Indians make stone tools by the techniques of grinding, pecking, polishing, and abrading. Archaic peoples developed a ground-stone industry using these techniques to design milling tools and other specific forms that helped them perform particular subsistence tasks more efficiently. This trend was expressed in other items as well, such as ritual objects and personal ornaments, so that the Archaic artifact assemblage is much larger and more elaborate than that of the Paleo-Indians.

Penetration of New Ecological Niches

The third theme characterizing the California Archaic, the *penetration of new ecological niches*, is the adaptation that enabled the Archaic peoples to develop the characteristics of a specialized technology and diffuse economy. Because they had begun to learn how to use the resources unique to California, they were no longer confined to the ecological niche occupied by the Paleo-Indians, the pan-western big-game hunting niche. These unique resources distinguished the character of the California Archaic from the Archaic of the rest of North America. Although the Archaic everywhere shared the three themes of diffuse economy, specialized technology, and penetration of new ecological niches, California was unusual in having so many varied habitats in such close proximity to each other. The number and variety of habitats, the abundance of their resources, the uniqueness of some of those resources, and the marked seasonality of many species caused the California Archaic to become distinctive and particularly diverse.

Perhaps the easiest way to illustrate the diversity of Archaic subsistence is to consider the variety of California habitats that became important to Archaic economies and the resources within them that were exploited. The following divisions are not necessarily those of an ecologist (e.g., Bakker 1971) because they emphasize the particular

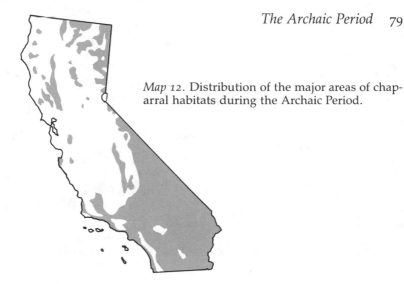

Map 12. Distribution of the major areas of chaparral habitats during the Archaic Period.

features that were most important to Archaic peoples rather than the plant and animal communities and their environments per se. These habitats include the chaparral, the coastal littoral, the coastal and interior valley parklands, the Transition Zone oak-pine-grass associations, the montane coniferous associations, the interior lakeshores, the playa deserts, and the riverine associations (Baumhoff 1978).

The Chaparral (Map 12). Chaparral is a generic term for associations of brushy, drought-resistant plants (Jepson 1963). Several dozen species are included in the term, among them the sages, mountain lilacs, chamise, salal, manzanitas, chinquapin, buckthorns, mountain mahogany, and scrub oaks. Many of the chaparral species produce large quantities of small, hard seeds, rich in protein. There are many species of flowering plants within the chaparral association and, prehistorically, several species of seed-bearing perennial bunchgrasses. The leafy vegetation, grasses, and cover provided by chaparral are very attractive to several kinds of game animals, most notably deer, rabbits, hares, quail, and, in some areas formerly, Roosevelt elk (Brown & Lawrence 1965; Ingles 1965).

Three major types of chaparral associations occur in the state. True chaparral occurs in higher hills and mountains, especially around the Central Valley and in interior southwestern California (Fig. 7). Northern coastal and foothill scrub chaparral occurs from Monterey County north and tends to include lower brush and more grass (Fig. 8). It is adapted to cooler, wetter conditions and is not as rich in hard seeds. Coastal-sage scrub chaparral occurs south of Monterey County and on the Channel Islands (Fig. 9). Dominated by sages and tending to

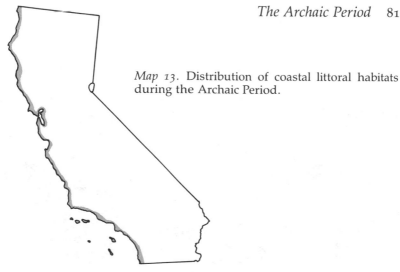

Map 13. Distribution of coastal littoral habitats during the Archaic Period.

have lower shrubbery than even the northern coastal scrub, it is also poorer in hard-seed production and hosts significantly fewer birds and mammals (Brown & Lawrence 1965: 12–13). Chaparral associations are generally classified as belonging to the Upper Sonoran Life Zone. Although ecologists distinguish among them, these three varieties of chaparral share many traits, and Archaic people needed only one basic pattern of exploitation to make use of this niche wherever they encountered it.

The Coastal Littoral (Map 13). The littoral is the strip of land found along the coast (Fig. 10). California has more than a thousand miles of coastline, made up of a series of microenvironments unique to the lit-

Fig. 7 (facing page, top). Mountain chaparral association, North Coast Ranges of Mendocino County. Although the landscape and dense brush made movement difficult, Archaic people made extensive use of the hard seeds and rich supply of game found here. (U.S. Forest Service Photo)

Fig. 8 (center). Northern scrub chaparral, Del Norte County. The brushy plants of this habitat are smaller and less dense than those in the more southern chaparral associations. This habitat does not hide game animals (or hunters) as well as the richer chaparrals, nor is it as hard to move through, but its seeds, acorns, and leafy vegetation still support abundant wildlife. The major game animals of this zone include mule deer, elk, and black bear.

Fig. 9 (bottom). Southern scrub chaparral, northwestern San Diego County, Mount Palomar in the background. Sage (*Artemisia*) and mountain lilac (*Ceanothus*) dominate, but more than 25 species provide the richest land habitat for people and game animals in southern California. (U.S. Forest Service Photo)

toral habitat: sandy and rocky shores, sea cliffs, salt- and freshwater lagoons, tidepools, river-mouth estuaries, bays, gravel bars, marshes, and grassy terraces (Fig. 11). In some places, coastal chaparral or forests also form part of the littoral (Fig. 12). Each of these features has its own complex of fish, shellfish, mammals, land- and waterfowl, and potentially useful plants. Of these, the most dramatic are the great profusion of shellfish, the seals and sea lions, and the whales that periodically become stranded or washed ashore (Bakker 1971; Ricketts & Calvin 1968; Yocum & Dasmann 1965).

Fig. 10 (facing page, top). Coastal littoral, Point Lobos, Monterey County. The coastal strip compresses many microenvironments into a narrow life zone. Here, coastal scrub chaparral blanketing the terrace is dwarfed by wind and weather. A rocky beach, hidden from view by the terrace, separates the land from an offshore rocky outcrop colored white by the guano of the California brown pelicans that nest there. A more distant, dark outcropping is a rookery for a sea-lion colony. Sand builds up in pockets protected from the downcoast ocean currents by the jutting point of land. Where streams cut through the terrace to the sea, small estuaries develop. These diverse microenvironments support different varieties of shellfish, fish, birds, and mammals, and the once-rich offshore fisheries add to the environment's wealth. These resources began to draw human settlement to the central California coast during the Archaic Period.

Fig. 11 (center). Coastal littoral, San Diego County sandbar. Over time, the mouth of each of the hundreds of streams and rivers that cut through coastal terraces to the sea undergoes repeated changes. Here a sandbar has developed, blocking the fresh water of the San Dieguito River in the foreground from the salt water of the distant ocean. While the sandbar is low, tides carry salt water across the bar and create a saline lagoon. As the sand barrier is built higher by tides and currents, the lagoon gradually becomes fresher, and its plants and animals change accordingly. Eventually a violent storm cuts through the sand bar or causes the river to erode the bar and scour the channel. Salt water floods in and a saline estuary is created, with yet different plants and animals. Then natural processes begin to create a new sand barrier. Thus, whereas the life of the terraces above remains constant, the life of the estuary continually changes. At any time, different nearby streams will be at different stages of the cycle, providing a diverse array of resources for coastal settlers.

Fig. 12 (bottom). Coastal littoral, Newport Bay. Large, permanent bays occur at several places along the California coast. Less subject to evolution than estuaries, bays remain in the tidal zone and are only slightly less saline than the ocean. Their calm waters and miles of protected shoreline create habitats very different from those of the open coast shown in Fig. 10. Starting in the Archaic Period, literally hundreds of shell-mound sites began to develop around the rim of this bay. In general, earlier sites were located on higher terraces, and later sites were situated nearer the water, reflecting the increasing importance of aquatic resources over time.

Fig. 13. White-oak parkland habitat, Glenn County. A young deer watches from the shade of a massive white oak. Although the wild oats that today blanket much of the state are a European import, native bunchgrasses provided a similar function in prehistoric times. The seeds produced by the grasses and the acorns of the oak groves were important summer and autumn food sources for people during the Archaic Period.

Fig. 14. Blue-oak parkland habitat. The blue oak occurs mainly in northern California's foothills, in contrast to the valley habitat of the white oak, but the blue oak's zone also qualifies as parkland because of the open grasslands within which the oak groves occur. Though not as rich a producer of acorns per tree as the white oak (about 200 lbs/year vs. 400–500 lbs/year for the white oak, or 75 vs. about 170 kg/year), the blue oak tends to grow in larger groves, and is thus a significant acorn supplier as well as an important deer habitat for much of the year. In this part of western Tehama County, sheep grazing has denuded much of the valley and hillside of brushy vegetation, which has not been able to restore itself since nineteenth-century farmers and stockmen cut down the chamise and other chaparral species that once added to the richness of the environment.

Map 14. Distribution of the major areas of coastal and interior parkland habitats during the Archaic Period.

The Coastal and Interior Valley Parklands (Map 14). The great Central Valley, as well as smaller valleys that enter the Central Valley or occur along the coast, feature a *savanna* habitat: grassy parklands dotted with groves of oak trees (Figs. 13 and 14). The dominant oak varies from one part of the state to another. In the Central Valley it is the California white, or valley, oak; in the coastal valleys, the coast, or California, live oak; in the lesser interior valleys, the interior live oak; and in the foothills, the blue, or Douglas', oak. These oaks provided Archaic gatherers with abundant supplies of acorns, and the grasses —today driven almost to extinction by hardier European competitors such as wild oats—were sources of edible seeds (Figs. 15 and 16). Antelope, tule elk, deer, rabbits, quail, and other animals were attracted to this environment, as were the people who hunted them (Bakker 1971: 105–22).

The Transition Zone Oak-Pine-Grass Associations (Map 15). Except for the barren ranges of the southeastern deserts, most of the mountainous areas of California have marked zones of plant and animal life that vary according to altitude (Figs. 17 and 18). Upper Sonoran associations, such as chaparral, tend to be found on the lower slopes of most ranges. Above the chaparral is the Transition Zone. In many parts of the state, particularly around the Central Valley, this zone formed a habitat important to the Archaic way of life. Much of the zone consists of hilly grasslands, dominated at lower elevations by groves of blue oak and buckeyes, and at higher elevations by groves of black oak and digger pine. The nuts and acorns of this zone, plus many other kinds of plants useful as food, medicine, or industrial raw

Fig. 15 (left). Coastal live-oak parkland habitat, Point Reyes National Seashore, about 5 miles (8 km) inland. California has nearly a dozen species of oaks, many of which occur in parkland settings. The coastal live oak is found from Sonoma County southward behind the littoral on hillsides, on sheltered terraces, and in open canyons. This ecological niche is rather similar to the parklands dominated by white and blue oak in terms of its abundance and diversity of animal and plant life.

Fig. 16 (right). Coastal oak parkland with chaparral, Santa Barbara County. Oak-parkland habitats frequently lie close to other habitats. This 50-year-old photograph shows a grove of live oaks in a parkland setting bounded by hillside chaparral. The proximity of two such rich habitats allowed Archaic peoples to exploit both zones from a central campsite. (U.S. Forest Service Photo)

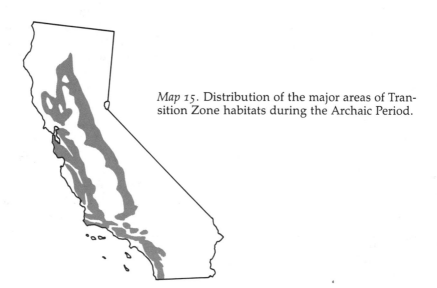

Map 15. Distribution of the major areas of Transition Zone habitats during the Archaic Period.

Fig. 17. Transition Zone mosaic of blue oak and digger pine, North Coast Ranges. Because this life zone supports the richest concentration of deer in northern California, it was a preferred habitat for hunters from the Early Archaic on. Archaeological evidence found in the vicinity of this Lake County scene shows that this life zone has been important to hunter-gatherers for the past 10,000 years. Even today, recreational deer hunters crowd these hills every autumn, drawn by the same ecological conditions that attracted prehistoric peoples.

Fig. 18. Transition Zone mosaic in the central Sierra. This Tuolumne County digger pine is surrounded by blue oak, chaparral, pockets of grassland, and other conifers. High species diversity, rich seed and nut yield, and abundant leafy vegetation made the Transition Zone the life zone in northern California with the greatest quantity of usable food for the Archaic way of life. (U.S. Forest Service Photo)

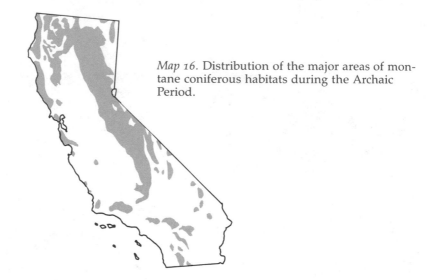

Map 16. Distribution of the major areas of montane coniferous habitats during the Archaic Period.

Fig. 19. Montane coniferous association, eastern Tuolumne County. Most of the higher mountain habitats are dominated by dense stands of such conifers as Ponderosa pine, red fir, lodgepole pine, Douglas fir, Jeffrey pine, sugar pine, white fir, western pine, and incense cedar. Although these montane coniferous habitats are high in biomass, the biomass consists mainly of cellulose (wood), which is not a useful food for humans or for the animals humans hunt. In addition, access to the higher mountains is hampered by the snows that blanket them for much of the year. Archaic use of these habitats was sparse and developed later here than in most other California environments.

Fig. 20. Piñon-juniper association, southern Cascades in eastern Tehama County. In some of the state's more arid mountain regions, the habitats occurring above the Transition Zone are dominated by such important nut-bearing trees as the piñon. Pine nuts formed an important food source for many groups and also attracted game animals. Exploitation of this habitat occurred earlier in the Archaic and with greater intensity than in most other montane coniferous habitats. (U.S. Forest Service Photo)

material, made this habitat an important one. This zone was also an excellent hunting territory for deer, rabbits, and rodents (Brown & Lawrence 1965).

The Montane Coniferous Associations (Map 16). Lying above the Transition Zone in ranges throughout the state is a zone featuring associations of pine and fir (Fig. 19). Although sugar pine and some other species produce edible nuts, the primary use of pine and fir was as material for various crafts and industries. Clearings in the coniferous forests, however, are frequently filled with seed- or berry-producing plants, and a number of kinds of wildflowers useful for their edible bulbs or their medicinal or craft properties can be found there (Fig. 20). Deer range at these elevations in the summer, and in the northern mountains, bear and Roosevelt elk were abundant. Many species of smaller mammals are found in these mountains as well. Archaic people were able to make use of these forests from midsummer to early fall; in this season game was most available, plants were flowering and fruiting, the snow was gone, and the climate was the most favorable (Brown & Livezey 1962).

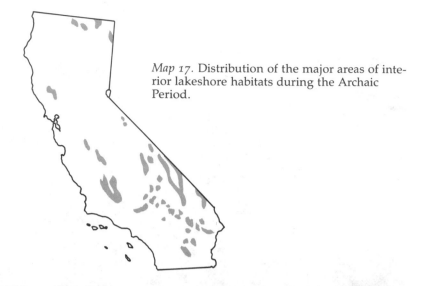

Map 17. Distribution of the major areas of interior lakeshore habitats during the Archaic Period.

Fig. 21. Interior lakeshore habitat, Lake County. Many lakes survived well into the Archaic Period; and some, like Clear Lake (shown here) in the North Coast Ranges, still exist. Archaic peoples made extensive use of lakeshore plants and hunted or trapped animals that came to drink. The shoreside strip of lakeshore resources added variety to the surrounding environment, making the habitat valuable for diffuse Archaic economies. But Archaic people rarely took advantage of the seasonal bounty of the lakes: the millions of waterfowl that stop to rest during their migrations along the Pacific Flyway. Successful exploitation of such seasonal abundance would wait until subsistence and work practices changed during the subsequent Pacific Period.

The Interior Lakeshores (Map 17). The lakeshore habitat, described in the preceding chapter, began to disappear from southeastern California during the late Paleo-Indian Period and the early Archaic (Fig. 21). Some lakes in this area, such as Mono Lake and Crowley Lake, did endure through much of the Archaic and supported small Archaic populations. Clear Lake in the North Coast Range, and Buena Vista and Tulare lakes in the southern San Joaquin Valley, also persisted during the Archaic. This type of habitat, with its seasonal and permanent waterfowl, many useful food and industrial plants, and animals attracted to the lakes by food and water, remained regionally important throughout the Archaic (Bakker 1971: 137–38).

The Playa Deserts (Map 18). In the basin and range country of southeastern California, nearly sterile salt pans were left behind by the drying Pleistocene lakes (Fig. 22). As most of the lakes disappeared, their former shorelines, beaches, and alluvial fans became host to an arid-land vegetation now typical of the Lower Sonoran Life Zone. The playa bottoms are dominated by brushy creosote, ocotillo, yucca, agave, saltbush, smoke tree, and sages. The surrounding terraces are covered by sagebrush desert plants, mostly brushy sages not too distantly related to the sages of the true chaparral (Benson 1969: 57–63). Although aridity forces these plants to maintain relatively low numbers and densities, they often produce useful seeds, beans, and fruit, as well as craft materials. Chief among the most useful species are mesquite and screw bean.

Many of the ranges surrounding the valleys are too arid to support the rich, stratified bands of life zones found in the western Sierra, but some of the larger ranges, such as the eastern Sierra, the slopes west of the Salton Sea, and the White Mountains, do support on their upper slopes zones of arid-land associations, such as chaparral and the piñon-juniper zone (Mooney 1973: 7–14). Some deer are found in the hills, antelope range many of the valleys, and rabbits thrive in several life zones. Useful plants occur in canyons and arroyos where seasonal streams and springs create oasis conditions, and where moisture-retaining silts, aided by the canyons' protection from sun and wind, allow some species to flourish. These conditions allowed small numbers of Archaic foragers to survive in the desert regions (see Fig. 23) even after most of the lakes had disappeared (Bakker 1971: 223–97).

The Riverine Associations (Map 19). California features several major river systems, most notably the Sacramento–San Joaquin system, which drains the Central Valley, and the Klamath system of the northwest (Fig. 24). A number of smaller rivers drain from the western

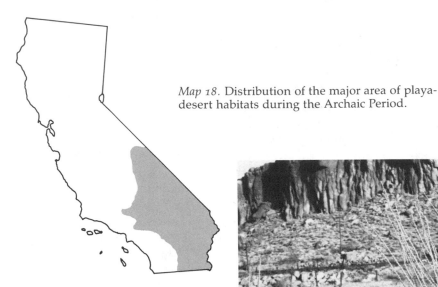

Map 18. Distribution of the major area of playa-desert habitats during the Archaic Period.

Fig. 22 (right). Playa desert, Inyo County. Dry playa floors host such Sonoran desert plants as the ocotillo and cactus, forcing the Archaic peoples who exploited them to live in small, widely spaced groups and to follow a highly nomadic existence.

Fig. 23 (below). Interior southern California valley. Valley terraces and surrounding hills supported seed-bearing scrub and grasses, not in abundance, but enough to allow a subsistence pattern to be practiced by small numbers of people from the Early Archaic onward. (U.S. Forest Service Photo)

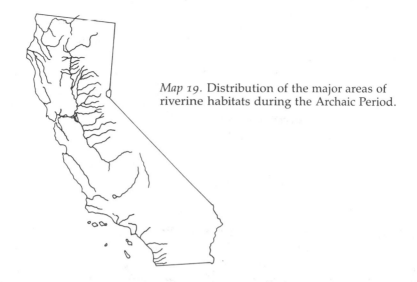

Map 19. Distribution of the major areas of riverine habitats during the Archaic Period.

Fig. 24. The Klamath River, one of the major salmon streams of western North America, was the focus of subsistence activities among some of California's most complex prehistoric cultures.

slopes of the Coast Ranges. From Monterey north, most of the rivers host (or did prehistorically) great numbers of *anadromous fish* (fish that are born in freshwater rivers and streams, migrate when young to the sea to grow to maturity, and then return to their home rivers to reproduce during annual spawning runs), including the king and silver salmon, steelhead trout, and the Pacific lamprey eel. The main spawning runs are in the fall, but lesser runs occur in spring and winter. In addition, much smaller numbers of fish, such as perch, sunfish, and speckled dace, permanently reside in most of the streams. A great many industrial, medicinal, and food-bearing plants grow alongside the rivers and streams. Many creeks and rivers draining mountainous areas tend to run swiftly through narrow valleys, but the Sacramento and San Joaquin rivers meander slowly though broad floodplains until meeting at the delta that has formed east of the San Francisco Bay. The margins of both the swiftly moving streams and the meandering rivers have their distinctive plant and animal associations (Fig. 25). Prehistorically, the delta and the marshy floodplains of the Central Valley were particularly notable for large areas of cattail and tule reeds, plants important to the settlers' livelihood that at one time also provided the principal habitat for the tule elk (Fig. 26). A remnant of the once-extensive tule marshes of San Francisco Bay can be seen at Coyote Hills Regional Park near Fremont. These habitats still provide seasonal stopping places for millions of waterfowl migrating along the Pacific Flyway (Brown & Lawrence 1965: 7–9, 20–21).

Few of these habitats, in isolation, could provide enough resources throughout the year to support even small populations of hunters and gatherers permanently. The Archaic annual round functioned to allow people to take advantage of resources available in adjacent habitats at different times of the year. As in our scenario, a group might have spent the winter based in a valley, surviving off the nearby riverine, parkland, and chaparral habitats. In the spring, they could have traveled to the Transition Zone above the chaparral. In the summer they could have ranged throughout the montane coniferous forests. Fall would have brought them back downhill, through the Transition Zone, where they would begin to harvest the late summer and fall crops of those habitats, and eventually back to their winter camp in the valley. The fact that most California deer herds follow similar migration patterns may have helped establish the development of this particular annual round (Ingles 1965: 425–30).

As the Archaic Period progressed, people began to exploit more kinds of resources than ever before, particularly those species that

Fig. 25. Grapevine thicket in a streamside habitat, Butte County. This tangle of undergrowth conveys some feeling of the lushness of the streamside habitat and the contrast it formed with the surrounding parkland habitats (e.g., Fig. 16). In parts of the Central Valley, this growth was so dense as to be essentially impenetrable. Indians were forced to travel along trails made by grizzly bears in these areas, always with the fear of meeting one of the dangerous beasts face to face.

Fig. 26. Riverside tule thicket, northern Contra Costa County. Riverside tules and similar reeds grew abundantly in many parts of prehistoric California. The plants were important raw materials for several crafts: mat weaving, clothing manufacture, house building, and even boat construction. The tule marsh was also an important habitat for game ranging from ducks to the tule elk.

TABLE 1 *Sequence of Traditions During the Archaic Period*

Regions	Early Archaic			Middle Archaic			Late Archaic		Early Pacific	
	9000 B.C.	8000 B.C.	7000 B.C.	6000 B.C.	5000 B.C.	4000 B.C.	3000 B.C.	2000 B.C.	1000 B.C.	
Desert	······· SAN DIEGUITO ——— LAKE MOHAVE ——————————————— PINTO BASIN ———→									
Coastal Southern California	——— SAN DIEGUITO ——— ENCINITAS — La Jolla/Pauma — Topanga Culture — Millingstone Horizon — Oak-Grove Culture ——— CAMPBELL ——→									
San Francisco Bay Area	······· Santa Clara Valley ······· BART, Stanford ——— West Berkeley, University Village ——→									
Delta, Central Valley	······· Buena Vista, Tulare Lakes; Tranquillity ·······									
North Coast Ranges	······· Borax Lake Post Pattern ······· BORAX LAKE ——— WINDMILLER (Early Horizon) ——— Mendocino Complex ——→									
Northeastern California	NORTHEASTERN CALIFORNIA ARCHAIC ——————— ······· Menlo Phase ······· ——— Bear Creek Phase ——→									

NOTE: Major traditions are in small capital letters, local phases or manifestations in lowercase letters.

were especially characteristic of California or of certain parts of the state. They began to move into more parts of the state that had never before been permanently settled. They developed adaptations that were more localized as well as more diversified—adaptations that depended on their growing knowledge of the potential and limitations of the land. They were no longer the pioneer settlers of Paleo-Indian times.

Diversification was not unique to California, however. It characterized the Archaic of North America in general and, in a larger sense, was a worldwide phenomenon as well: the result of cultures facing the dramatic environmental changes that occurred at the end of the Pleistocene. One writer has called it the "Broad-Spectrum Revolution" (Flannery 1968). In some parts of the world, but not in California, this "revolution" was part of the process that eventually led to the development of agriculture.

ARCHAEOLOGICAL TRADITIONS OF THE ARCHAIC PERIOD

The scenario at the beginning of this chapter depicts a way of life followed by people in California about 4,500 years ago, well into the period we call the Archaic. That lifeway was the result of more than 5,000 years of development after the end of the Ice Age. Archaeological evidence from different times within this period reflects the fact that this development took place gradually for the most part, and at somewhat different paces in different parts of the state (see Table 1). There were no sudden breaks in the archaeological record caused by dramatic cultural or statewide environmental changes that might be used to subdivide the Archaic.

Yet the Archaic Period, unlike the Paleo-Indian Period, did witness considerable change over time. During the Paleo-Indian Period there was so little variability that one archaeological tradition could characterize the entire period. Archaeologists have defined several traditions within the Archaic Period, however, each reflecting different stages in the development of cultures as they became increasingly unlike Paleo-Indian society.

Along with variability across time, California's Archaic cultures also displayed growing variability across space. Through the course of the Archaic, people increasingly adapted to the specific varieties of resources found in each part of the state. Each area saw the development of somewhat different combinations of specialized tools, different patterns of seasonal migration, different kinds of resources, and different places in which to locate camps. This variation is reflected in the fact that the archaeological remains from this time period look somewhat different from one part of the state to another. Archaeologists have dealt with this fact by recognizing that there were not only different traditions within the state over time, but also different traditions throughout the state at any one time. This is a useful practice as long as one does not let the differences between traditions obscure their basic similarities.

The modernization of California's environment during the Archaic makes the recognition of traditions somewhat more complicated, however. We have noted that it took more than 5,000 years for the environment to change from Ice Age conditions to more or less modern ones (see Table 2), and this is the time period in which the Archaic was evolving. Environmental change did not occur uniformly around the state; in fact, its effects were often very localized. For example, San Francisco Bay did not exist during the late Pleistocene, but was created from 11,000 to 9,000 years ago when rising sea levels flooded the area. Similarly, many coastal lagoons and estuaries developed and in some cases disappeared as modern environmental conditions emerged (Bickel 1978a,b). These changes had important consequences for the Archaic peoples who lived in the area—consequences that must be understood in order to interpret the archaeology of an area—but their impact was localized and did not change the basic course of Archaic cultural development.

In recognizing both the changes that took place over time during the Archaic, and the differences that developed among Archaic cultures in different parts of the state, archaeologists have defined more than a dozen traditions that fell within this period. Recognition of this variability may make it difficult to perceive the common threads of development that ran through the various traditions (Warren 1973). In order to emphasize these common patterns, we have organized the traditions of the Archaic into three successive developmental phases: the Early Archaic (11,000–8,000 years ago), the Middle Archaic (8,000–6,000 years ago), and the Late Archaic (6,000–4,000 years ago).

We emphasize that these divisions are arbitrary and serve to highlight times for which trends are evident rather than to mark major breaks in California prehistory. Other authors, such as Wallace (1978) and Aikens (1978), place their emphasis on the continuity within culture periods and the differences between them, rather than on transitions and gradual changes over time. Consequently, other authors may define period boundaries at different points than we do. Wallace, for example, makes a division at 3000 B.C., whereas we choose 4000 B.C. (Wallace 1978).

Each developmental phase in our scheme reflects the refinement of the basic Archaic strategy, with differences between the cultures in different parts of the state growing greater as the Archaic progressed. We characterize the three developmental phases below, and in doing so briefly sketch six traditions, each manifesting a development of the Archaic strategy at a different time or in a different part of the state. This will help to place these traditions, which are featured prominently in the archaeological literature, within the general scheme we have imposed on them. Although we do not describe these traditions in nearly the detail used to describe the single Paleo-Indian Tradition, the details highlighted will serve to give the reader some idea of the archaeological evidence for our model of the Archaic way of life. Further information can be found by consulting in the bibliography the works cited in the description of each tradition.

The Early Archaic (9000–6000 B.C.)

The *Early Archaic* witnessed the decline of the Paleo-Indian desert-lakeshore way of life and the shift to other ways of life in different microenvironmental settings. In the desert regions of southeastern California, the Early Archaic descendants of the Paleo-Indians continued to subsist around lakeshores wherever possible. Pleistocene large game had become extinct by 11,000 years ago, however, so that people had to shift to other game, particularly deer, pronghorn antelope, mountain sheep, hares, and rabbits. Because these animals ranged the hills as well as the playas and canyons, Early Archaic peoples systematically ventured farther afield than had their predecessors. They also relied on a wider range of plant species. In doing so, they developed a larger tool kit with some more specialized forms, better suited to the brushy habitats they were beginning to utilize more fully.

Those Early Archaic peoples living close to the southern California coast used the chaparral zone more completely than did their inland contemporaries, and from this adaptation evolved a new cultural complex, known archaeologically as the San Dieguito Tradition.

The San Dieguito Tradition (Map 20). The San Dieguito is perhaps the earliest truly Archaic culture to be recognized as a distinct tradition, and is also the most thoroughly researched tradition in the archaeological record of the Early Archaic. It takes its name from the San Dieguito River in northwestern San Diego County, where its remains were first excavated (M. Rogers 1929). According to Warren (1967, 1968), the San Dieguito Tradition was widespread in southern California and, in certain cases, in other parts of California and the Southwest between 10,000 and 8,000 years ago. Other scholars define

TABLE 2 *Post-Pleistocene Climatic Sequences*

					Regions			
Years ago	Western North America[a]	Coastal southern California[b]	Channel Islands, ocean[c]	Lower Klamath[d]	Central Sierra Nevada I[e]	Central Sierra Nevada II[f]	Western Great Basin[g]	Western Great Basin[h]
500		Warm, moist						
1,000	Medithermal (warm and arid to semi-arid)		Warmer than today	Cool, moist	Relatively cool	Warm, dry / Cool, wet		Cool, moist
2,000			Cooler than today			Warm, dry		Warm, dry
3,000 (1000 B.C.)		Hot, dry	Warmer	Warm, dry		Cool, wet	Less hot, somewhat wetter	Cool, moist
4,000 (2000 B.C.)			Cooler than today		Warmer	Warm, dry		Warm, dry
5,000 (3000 B.C.)			Cool, moist	Cool, moist		(no data)	Very hot, very dry	(no data)
6,000 (4000 B.C.)		Warm, moist	Warmer than today		Cooler	Cool, wet		

Date				
7,000 (5000 B.C.)	Altithermal (very hot, very dry)			Hot, dry
8,000 (6000 B.C.)		(no data)	Warmer	Warm, dry
9,000 (7000 B.C.)	Anathermal (warm and semi-arid to arid, with warmth increasing over time)			
10,000 (8000 B.C.)				Warm, wet

[a] From Antevs (1948), cited in O'Connell (1975); based on geomorphology.

[b] From Heusser (1977); based on pollen core data.

[c] From Pisias (1978); based on fauna from varved ocean-floor sediment deposits. Note that these values refer to surface water temperatures. Cooler surface water temperatures are correlated with increased precipitation on land; warmer surface water temperatures are correlated with less precipitation because precipitation increases with evaporation, which increases when the differential between water and air temperatures increases (Pisias 1978: 379).

[d] From Grayson (1976), cited in O'Connell (1975); based on faunal analysis.

[e] From Adam (1967), cited in O'Connell (1975); based on pollen.

[f] From Curry (1971), cited in O'Connell (1975); based on glacial analysis.

[g] From Benson (1978); based on plant macrofossils and sediment analysis.

[h] From Davis & Elston (1972), cited in O'Connell (1975); based on geomorphology.

Map 20. Distribution of the San Dieguito Tradition (after Warren 1967).

the San Dieguito Tradition in a more limited way and apply it to the Early Archaic societies in the chaparral zone of southwestern California (Wallace 1978: 27).

San Dieguito people lived mainly on the chaparral-related resources of mule deer, rabbits, and plants, although they did not collect hard seeds, which are a feature of chaparral plants. They lived in very small groups—of perhaps ten to twenty people—and moved often as they exhausted local resources. Much of their movement took place within the chaparral zone itself, rather than from major life zone to major life zone. Some moved from the coast to the interior and back, however, and to and from the slopes of the coastal Peninsular Range of western San Diego County, so some degree of environmental variability may have been involved in the migration strategy (Warren, True & Eudey 1961).

San Dieguito people made distinctive, large, rather coarse chipped-stone tools, including several forms of knives, choppers, and heavy scrapers (Fig. 27). Evidence for basketry is associated with the end of the San Dieguito Tradition, when bone awls and needles used for basketmaking first became common (M. Rogers 1968; Warren & True 1961). During most of this tradition, apparently neither basketry nor bone tools formed much part of the San Dieguito technology.

In many ways the San Dieguito Tradition was not far removed from the Paleo-Indian lifeway, but the shift from big game to chaparral-related game, the location of sites in different habitats, and the development of new and more specialized tools separate the San Dieguito as an Archaic tradition.

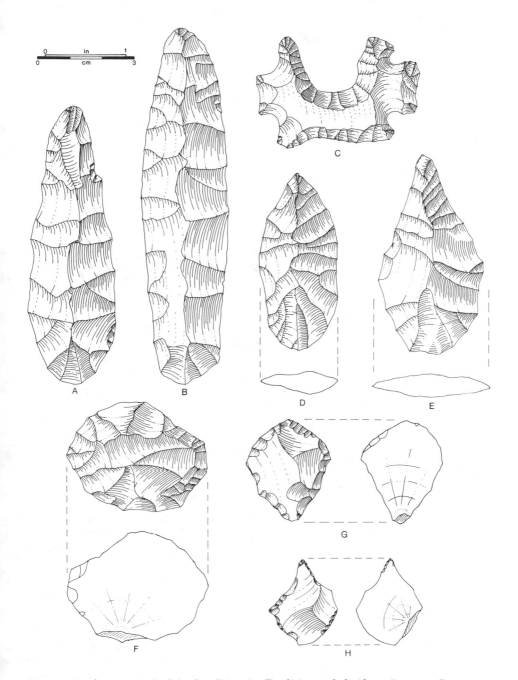

Fig. 27. Artifacts typical of the San Dieguito Tradition: *a,b,* knife; *c,* "crescent" (possible notched scraper); *d,* convex side scraper; *e,* pointed scraper; *f,* side scraper; *g,* flake scraper; *h,* graver. (After M. Rogers 1929, 1968; Warren & True 1961.)

Map 21. Distribution of the Lake Mohave
Tradition.

One of the areas occupied by the San Dieguito people was the coastal chaparral zone of southern California. A few sites in this area from late in the San Dieguito show that people had begun to collect shellfish and hard seeds to supplement their diets. There is some evidence to suggest that the first attempts to settle the southern Channel Islands occurred by the end of this period. These expansions into new ecological niches foretold the emergence of the more developed Middle Archaic (Davis, Brott & Weide 1969; Hudson 1976).

The Lake Mohave Tradition (Map 21). The Lake Mohave Tradition reflects the first adjustments to deteriorating environmental conditions made by peoples of the interior southern California deserts. In lifeways the Lake Mohave Tradition reflects a good deal of similarity to the San Dieguito Tradition just described. Warren (1967, 1968), in fact, regards Lake Mohave as simply a regional variant of San Dieguito. Other writers, however, such as Donnan (1964) and Wallace (1962a, 1978), feel that Lake Mohave represents a distinct tradition adapted to a different environment.

The abundance and variety of projectile points in the Lake Mohave tool kit, called the Playa Industry in some papers (e.g., M. Rogers 1939), indicate a continued emphasis on hunting in an era when the big-game mammals had virtually disappeared from interior southern California, the desert lakes were drying up, and plant foods were beginning to become more important. The tradition is named for the type site where it was first recognized, an occupation site on the shores of former Lake Mohave. A shallow Pleistocene lake, which once covered 75 square miles (194 km^2) and had a maximum depth of perhaps 40 feet (12 m), Lake Mohave lasted into the Early Archaic and has refilled temporarily on occasions since then—most recently within the past 60 years (at the site of Silver Lake and Soda Lake beds). While it lasted, the lake provided an attractive habitat for early Archaic hunters and gatherers.

In general, Lake Mohave tools became increasingly specialized as the subsistence base gradually grew more diffuse (Fig. 28). Wallace (1962a: 174) suggests that fishing may have begun at this time. Assemblages from Lake Mohave, Pinto Basin, Owens Lake, Silver Lake, and other playas occupied during the Early Archaic lack the milling tools of later times that would indicate a heavy reliance on hard-seed resources, but they include stone choppers and scrapers in some abundance, suggesting that plant resources were more important than in Paleo-Indian times.

Lake Mohave sites reflect temporary occupation by small groups. The number of habitats exploited during a year by such a group may have been greater than in Paleo-Indian times, but camp movement seems to have taken place mainly within a single major habitat, the valley floors and edges surrounding the dwindling lakes. The Lake Mohave way of life seems to have persisted until well into the Middle Archaic, with the importance of hunting gradually shrinking and the importance of plant resources gradually increasing as the general trend toward modern environmental conditions ground on. Some writers (e.g., Antevs 1952) have argued that the Lake Mohave Tradition was punctuated by an abnormally hot, dry period—the Altithermal—around the end of the Early Archaic. Others (e.g., Warren 1967) regard the Altithermal as something that either happened only in some areas or did not occur at all. The preponderance of evidence indicates that the southern California deserts did not experience heating and drying in a simple, gradual trend, but underwent, instead, a great deal of variation from place to place and several fluctuations over time, and that these fluctuations influenced the specific lifeways of groups in different valleys.

The Middle Archaic (6000–4000 B.C.)

The Middle Archaic represents a period of increasing diversification. People began to exploit the local resources of different parts of the state more systematically, resulting in greater regional differences among traditions. On the southern California coast, traditions such as the Encinitas are marked by great mounds of discarded shells, suggesting that people were systematically harvesting the coastal shellfish. Milling tools appeared in coastal chaparral sites for the first time, indicating that large quantities of hard seeds were being processed

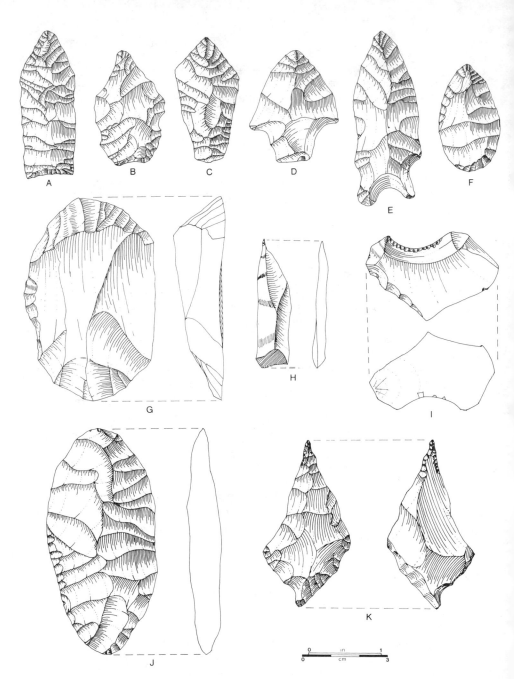

Fig. 28. Artifacts typical of the Lake Mohave Tradition: *a*, Yuma-like projectile point; *b*, Silver Lake projectile plant; *c*, Lake Mohave projectile point; *d*, stemmed projectile point; *e*, concave-base projectile point; *f*, round-base projectile point; *g*, pointed scraper; *h*, graver or piercer; *i*, notched scraper; *j*, oval bifacial knife; *k*, drill. (After Donnan 1964; Rogers 1939; Wallace 1962; Warren 1967.)

Map 22. Distribution of the Encinitas Tradition.

(Wallace 1955; Warren, True & Eudey 1961). And the settlement of off-shore islands during this period must have required the development of effective watercraft (Bryan 1970; Meighan 1959b, 1978).

Other parts of the state saw similar developments. The Borax Lake Tradition emerged in the Coast Ranges from San Francisco Bay to the Klamath River as a way of life that combined generalized hunting and gathering with the exploitation of hard-seed-bearing chaparral plants (Frederickson 1974a; Meighan & Haynes 1970; E. G. Stickel, pers. comm. 1980). In northeastern California, the early sequences at Surprise Valley and the Nightfire Island Site reveal an economy based on the hunting of bison, deer, mountain sheep, and antelope supplemented by diversified plant collecting (O'Connell 1975).

Since several regional cultural traditions arose during the Middle Archaic, we have selected four examples to illustrate the ways in which environmental variation produced cultural distinctions within the general Archaic framework.

The Encinitas Tradition (Map 22). Encinitas, a Middle and Late Archaic tradition of coastal southern California, flourished between 8,000 and 4,000 years ago (6000–2000 B.C.). Warren (1968) has defined the Encinitas Tradition as a synthesis of several more localized cultures, whose names are the commonly known terms of the region's archaeological literature, including the La Jolla Culture of coastal San Diego and Orange counties (M. Rogers 1939, 1968; Shumway, Hubbs & Moriarty 1961; Warren & Pavesic 1963); the Pauma Culture of inland western San Diego County (Crabtree, Warren & True 1963; Warren, True & Eudey 1961); the Topanga Culture of the Santa Monica Mountains (K. Johnson 1966; Treganza & Bierman 1958; Treganza & Mala-mud 1950); the Millingstone Horizon of coastal southern California (Curtis 1959; C. King 1962, 1967; Peck 1955; Ruby 1961; Wallace 1955); and the Oak-Grove Culture of Santa Barbara and Ventura counties (Greenwood 1969, 1972; Harrison & Harrison 1966; Olson 1930; Owen 1964; Owen, Curtis & Miller 1964; D. Rogers 1929).

Encinitas people exploited the hard seeds of the chaparral and the resources of the coastal littoral, as well as continuing to use the game and plant resources developed by their San Dieguito predecessors. Since they developed a wider resource base than the San Dieguito people had, they were able to support more people. Groups were larger, averaging 20–50 people, and more numerous. Encinitas people lived wholly in the chaparral zone or along the coast, or they traveled seasonally between the two. Encinitas people were the principal colonizers of the offshore islands. The ocean resources they used consisted mainly of shellfish and sea mammals. There is little evidence that they caught fish, either along the coast or in the offshore deep waters, and they seem to have hunted seals and sea lions at rookeries ashore, rather than by boat. Theirs was an expanded land-based economy, which began to take in resources from the coast that required the least amount of technological or behavioral change. Only later would the rich potential of ocean resources be realized more fully.

Encinitas artifacts are more varied than San Dieguito tools, though the basic heavy-duty choppers, scrapers and scraper planes of the Early Archaic continued to be made (Fig. 29). Encinitas people made well-formed projectile points, indicating that hunting was still important. They also made large numbers of milling slabs, which were used to grind hard seeds. It is in Encinitas sites that archaeologists find numbers of formal burials for the first time, suggesting that people were staying in base camps for long enough periods to formalize their burial places. Also for the first time, Encinitas people began to make items to which no utilitarian use can be easily assigned, such as gearlike "cogwheels" and stone disks. These artifacts suggest that the Encinitas way of life was richer and more elaborate than the earlier San Dieguito Tradition had been.

The Encinitas Tradition can be seen as an elaboration of the San Dieguito Tradition and a logical outgrowth of it. Evidence indicates that the elements of the Encinitas Tradition, after appearing piecemeal at different times and places, slowly coalesced into a tradition that was distinct from its predecessor. Thus the break between San Dieguito and Encinitas seems more an arbitrary midpoint to this trend of change than a true cultural boundary. Similarly, the Encinitas had no abrupt end. It was a way of life so well attuned to its environment that

Map 23. Distribution of the Borax Lake Tradition.

it persisted for several thousand years, well beyond the arbitrary end of the Middle Archaic.

The Borax Lake Tradition (Map 23). Borax Lake lies in the Coast Ranges north of San Francisco, in the vicinity of Clear Lake. A long archaeological sequence is found there, beginning in Paleo-Indian times and continuing for 12,000 years (Harrington 1948; Meighan & Haynes 1970). Since the lake never dried up, a similar way of life could be maintained year-round, allowing for a gradual decrease in the importance of large-mammal hunting.

The Early Archaic remains at Borax Lake bear a strong resemblance to the San Dieguito of southern California: a generalized hunting-and-gathering tool kit, lacking in such Paleo-Indian diagnostics as fluted points or such specialized plant-processing tools as milling stones and manos. It was during the Middle and Late Archaic that a more fully fledged Archaic way of life was established in this region: the Borax Lake Tradition (Frederickson 1974a). This tradition was widespread, as shown by the occurrence of distinctive Borax Lake projectile points throughout the North Coast Ranges from less than 8,000 years ago (Fig. 30). Very few Borax Lake Tradition sites have been excavated, so archaeologists still turn to the type site at Borax Lake to define this tradition's artifacts.

Apart from the distinctively square-stemmed Borax Lake points, Borax Lake assemblages include a variety of heavy-duty scrapers, scraper planes, unifacial knives, and bifaces. Milling stones and manos occur in some number, indicating that North Coast Ranges peoples had begun to exploit hard seeds systematically by the Middle Archaic.

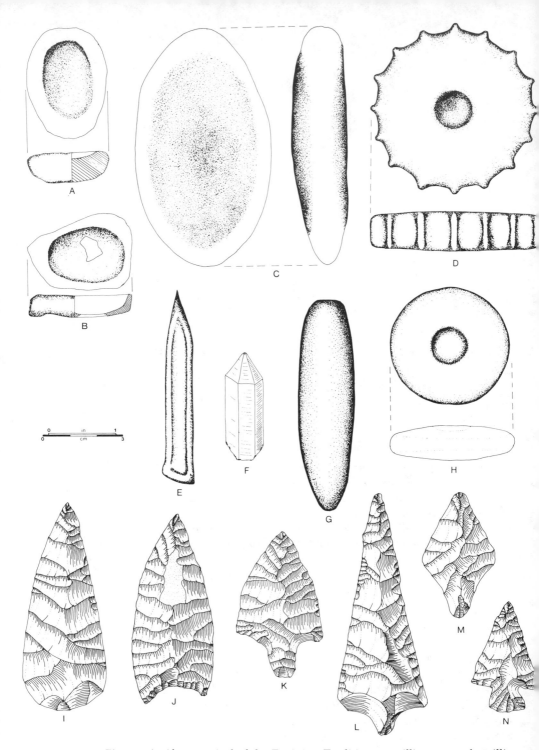

Fig. 29. Artifacts typical of the Encinitas Tradition: *a*, milling stone; *b*, milling stone with bottom "killed," or deliberately broken (frequently done when used with burials); *c*, double-sided mano; *d*, "cogwheel" (stone disk); *e*, bone awl; *f*, quartz crystal; *g*, "charmstone" (tapered ground-stone cylinder); *h*, "doughnut stone" (stone disk); *i*, convex-base projectile point; *j*, concave-base projectile point; *k*, contracting-stem projectile point; *l*, corner-notched projectile point; *m*, contracting-stem projectile point; *n*, expanding-stem

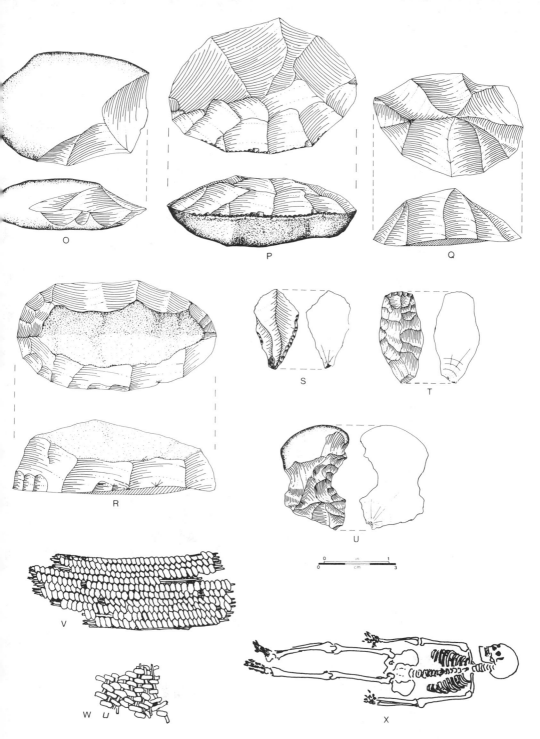

projectile point; *o*, bifacial chopping tool on a core; *p*, unifacial chopping tool on a core; *q*, keeled scraper on a core; *r*, plano-convex scraper or scraper plane on a core; *s*, side scraper on a flake; *t*, end scraper on a flake; *u*, notched scraper on a flake; *v*, coiled basketry from a rock-shelter site; *w*, twined basketry from a rock-shelter site; *x*, typical burial position. (After Curtis 1959; Greenwood 1969, 1972; Harrison & Harrison 1966; K. Johnson 1966; M. Rogers 1939; Wallace 1955; Warren & Pavesic 1963; Warren, True & Eudey 1961.)

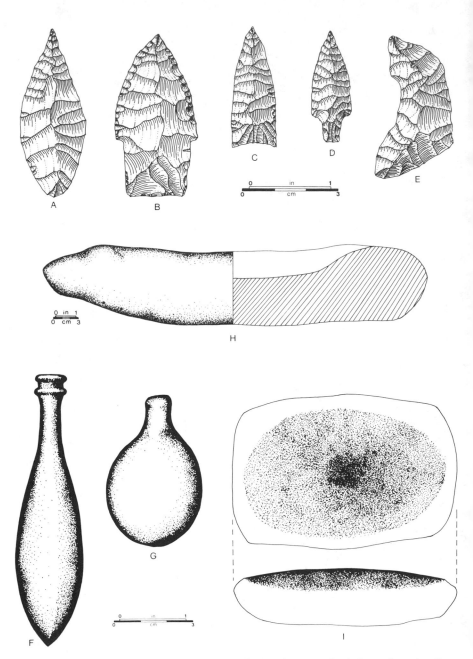

Fig. 30. Artifacts typical of the Borax Lake Tradition: *a*, leaf-shaped projectile point; *b*, wide-stem projectile point; *c*, concave-base projectile point; *d*, contracting-stem projectile point; *e*, crescentic tool (possibly a notched scraper); *f*, plummet-shaped charmstone; *g*, bulb-shaped charmstone; *h*, milling stone; *i*, mano (stippled area is worn surface). (After Frederickson 1974a; Harrington 1948; Meighan & Haynes 1970.)

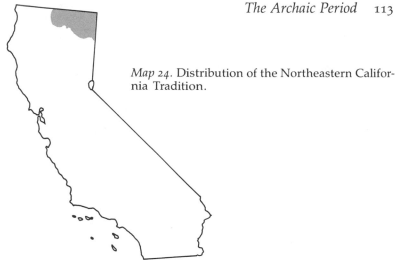

Map 24. Distribution of the Northeastern California Tradition.

Deer hunting and generalized plant-food use were also significant (Frederickson 1974a: 44–48; Meighan 1955: 27–28; Meighan & Haynes 1970: 1220).

Many Borax Lake sites are known from surface finds, and they suggest a preference for settlement locations at the edges of alluvially filled valleys. These locations may represent the shores of remnant Pleistocene lakes, or the preference of the settlers for access to two adjacent environments by making camp at the border between them. The distribution of Borax Lake points shows less association with a habitat and indicates that hunters, at least, ranged through a number of life zones. There is some basis for thinking that Borax Lake people followed a seasonal migratory round up and down the mountains, moving from the edges of the valley parklands through the chaparral, and then through the Transition Zone of oak and pine into the coniferous forests. Archaeological sites suggest that Borax Lake people lived in small groups, perhaps of no more than a few families. Most of their camps seem to have been temporary sites, perhaps occupied for no more than a few weeks at a time.

The Borax Lake Tradition economy was more diverse than its predecessors had been, but the limits of ecological diversity in their environment limited the size of the population their economy could support. Their subsistence was akin to the chaparral exploitation of the Encinitas people without the added benefit of the littoral's resources, which probably explains why this area was unable to support as large or elaborate a way of life.

The Northeastern California Archaic Tradition (Map 24). Archaic settlement in the northeastern part of the state began permanently during

Middle Archaic times, about 7,000–8,000 years ago (L. Johnson 1968; O'Connell 1975). There some aspects of the Paleo-Indian way of life were perpetuated under favorable environmental conditions. Northeastern California, physiographically a part of the Great Basin, is a land of interior-draining basins and arid mountain ranges. Many of its basins contain lakes that have endured to the present, or at least far into the Archaic Period. Lakeshore habitats survived longer there than in the deserts of southeastern California. Though the megafauna disappeared from this country at the end of the Pleistocene, some sizable game animals survived, including mule deer, antelope, bison, and mountain sheep.

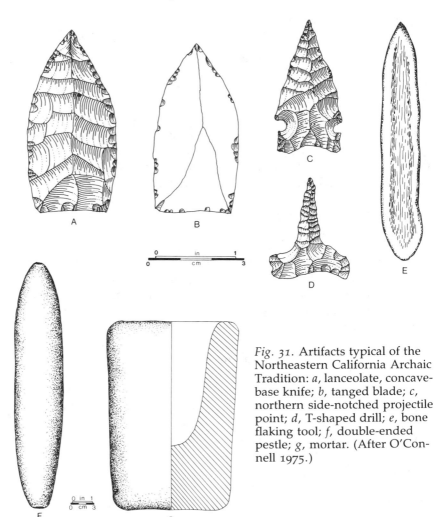

Fig. 31. Artifacts typical of the Northeastern California Archaic Tradition: *a*, lanceolate, concave-base knife; *b*, tanged blade; *c*, northern side-notched projectile point; *d*, T-shaped drill; *e*, bone flaking tool; *f*, double-ended pestle; *g*, mortar. (After O'Connell 1975.)

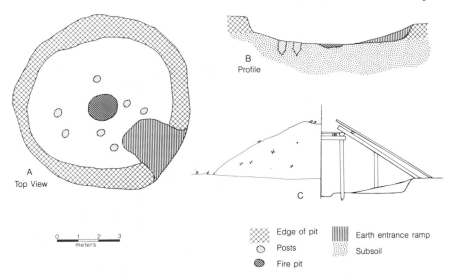

Fig. 32. Menlo Phase house from the Northeastern California Archaic Tradition: *a*, top view of the floor plan; *b*, profile of the floor; *c*, split profile showing support timbers and entrance ramp on the right, with earth covering on the left. (After O'Connell 1975.)

These environmental features are reflected in artifacts made by people of the Northeastern California Archaic (Fig. 31). The importance of hunting is indicated by their large, well-made projectile points and knives. Bone and antler flaking tools indicate the vigor of their chipped-stone industry. But like other Middle Archaic peoples, they also began to make systematic use of the hard-seed resources of the arid brushlands in their environment. Well-made mortars and pestles appear in the region for the first time with this tradition.

Mammal hunting and hard-seed collection provided the mainstays of this tradition's subsistence. Toward the end of the period, seasonal waterfowl were harvested at the Nightfire Island Site north of Weed (L. Johnson 1968). Hunting was productive enough in Surprise Valley that Archaic people there were able to build substantial semi-subterranean pit houses and stay in one place for most of the year (Fig. 32). During the Late Archaic, however, many of the northeastern California lakes began to shrink or dry up, and people had to shift away from a predominantly hunting life to one more dependent on a broad array of small animals and many plants (T. Hester 1973; O'Connell 1975). In most parts of this region, the end of the Northeast California Archaic Tradition saw people following a way of life more nearly akin to the Lake Mohave Tradition of southeastern California.

The Late Archaic (4000–2000 B.C.)

Some Middle Archaic traditions persisted into the Late Archaic, but this period saw the emergence of some distinctive traditions of its own (see Table 1). The trend toward diffuse economies that began earlier became even more pronounced during the Late Archaic. People enriched their diets by refining their system of seasonal migration and by adding even more resources to the list of species being utilized. The annual round reached its maximum development during this period. Late Archaic people perfected techniques of leaching the poisonous tannins from acorns so that this protein-rich food could be used, and a similar method of leaching buckeyes may also have been discovered at this time. Late Archaic people were the first to make significant use of salmon as a resource. Archaeologists believe that, even in the Late Archaic, however, people were still using these resources only seasonally and had not yet developed the practice of gathering large surpluses and storing them for future use (Wallace 1978).

The Late Archaic is also marked by the permanent settlement of more parts of the state than ever before. The earliest settlements are recorded at this time for the northern Sierra, the southern Cascades, and northwestern California (Gould 1966, 1972; Ritter 1970). Middle Archaic people had developed the exploitation of the chaparral, littoral, lakeshores, and playa deserts. Late Archaic people refined the use of these and additional habitats: the coastal and interior valleys, Transition Zone, and coniferous forests. The additional sources of food and raw materials recovered there allowed people to expand even further into new parts of the state.

Population increase and settlement expansion produced more cultural variety than ever before. In many parts of California variation grew as Middle Archaic traditions elaborated and diversified, for example, in the Encinitas and Borax Lake traditions (Kowta 1969; Olsen & Wilson 1964; Riddell 1951). Elsewhere, expansions into areas that previously had not been permanently settled led to the establishment of new traditions (Nelson 1909, 1910; Ritter, Hatoff & Payen 1976; Uhle 1907; Wallace & Lathrap 1975). The most significant new tradition, and the best known archaeologically, is the Windmiller Tradition from the Delta region of central California (Ragir 1972).

The Windmiller Tradition (Map 25). When Lillard, Heizer, and Fenenga (1939) first described the sequence of prehistoric cultures in central California, they defined three successive phases, which they called the Early, Middle, and Late Horizons. These names have been used widely in the state's archaeological literature (see, for example,

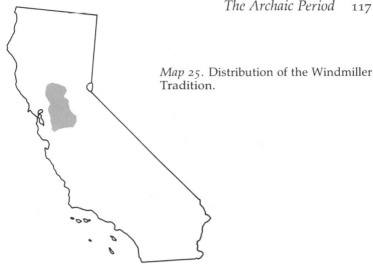

Map 25. Distribution of the Windmiller Tradition.

Beardsley 1954; Elsasser 1978a; Heizer 1964; Meighan 1965) but over time have come to mean different things to different writers. In some cases the terms have been used to refer to just the Sacramento River Delta area, but in other cases they have referred to several parts of the state. Partly to overcome this confusion and to establish a firmly local set of terms, Ragir (1972) suggested a set of terms for the Delta area that were based on the names of sites where various phases were first defined. The oldest culture she named after the Windmiller Site, and following her practice we identify the phase as the Windmiller Tradition.

The Windmiller Tradition represents the earliest permanent oc- cupation of the Delta region in central California. It appeared early in the Late Archaic, sometime between 4,500 and 5,500 years ago (2500– 3500 B.C.), and lasted until between 3,000 and 3,500 years ago (1000– 1500 B.C.; Elsasser 1978a: 37–41). Most of our information about Windmiller comes from a series of burial sites found on natural knolls within and near the riverine floodplain. Even though most of the Windmiller artifacts that have been found were originally grave offer- ings, we can use the more utilitarian offerings to give us some idea of what everyday life must have been like (Fig. 33).

Windmiller people spent part of the year in the Delta region of the riverine floodplain, close to the valley-oak parklands and chaparral of the lower foothills. Archaeologists presume that they spent the rest of the year in the foothills of the adjacent Sierra, living in the chaparral, Transition Zone, and coniferous forests. They hunted deer and other mammals for meat and hides, and caught salmon in limited numbers

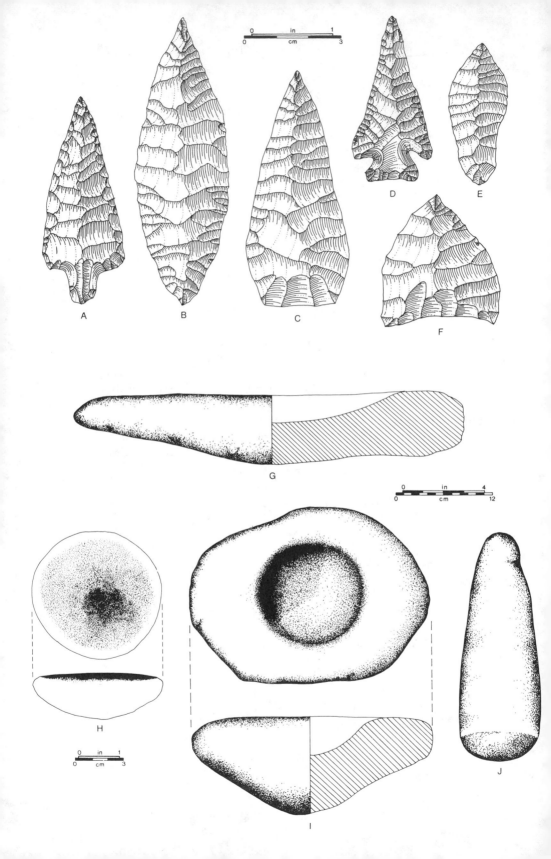

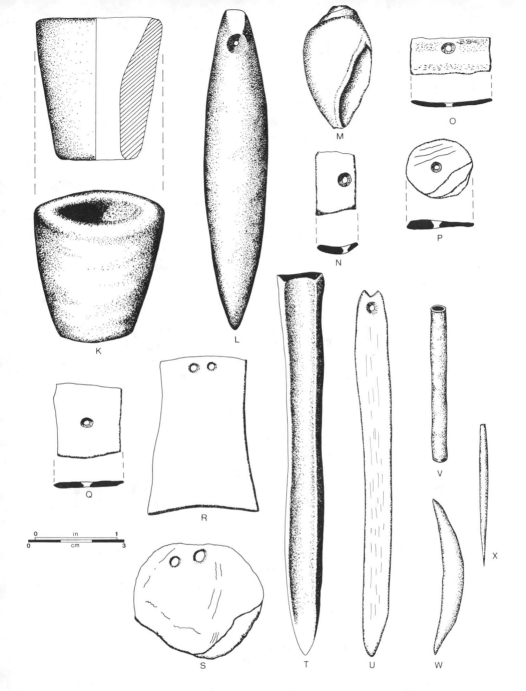

Fig. 33. Artifacts typical of the Windmiller Tradition: *a*, stemmed projectile point; *b*, leaf-shaped, or lanceolate, projectile point; *c*, flat-base projectile point; *d*, corner-notched projectile point; *e*, convex-base projectile point; *f*, concave-base projectile point; *g*, milling stone; *h*, mano; *i*, mortar; *j*, pestle; *k*, ground-stone pipe bowl; *l*, ground-stone charmstone pierced with biconically drilled hole; *m*, spire-lopped *Olivella*-shell bead; *n*, square-cut *Olivella*-shell bead; *o*, rectangular *Olivella*-shell bead; *p*, abalone disk bead; *q*, square-cut abalone bead; *r,s*, abalone pendants; *t*, split-bone tool; *u*, bone bangle; *v*, bird-bone-tube bead; *w*, bipointed bone toggle; *x*, bone needle. (After Beardsley 1954; Lillard, Heizer & Fenenga 1939; Ragir 1972.)

during the fall. Another potentially valuable riverine resource, the river mussel, was rarely used. They gathered an abundance of hard seeds from the nearby grasslands and chaparral, and made milling slabs and manos to grind the seeds. They also made stone mortars and pestles in limited numbers, and apparently were the earliest people in California to master the techniques of acorn leaching (Wallace 1978: 31–36).

A number of Windmiller cemeteries have been excavated. Most often the deceased was buried in the extended supine position, on his back in a long, narrow grave (Fig. 34). Windmiller burials were commonly accompanied by grave offerings or burial goods, including industrial tools such as manos and pestles in female burials, and projectile points and knives in male burials. In many cases these implements may have been the possessions of the deceased; in others, contributions from relatives.

Windmiller burials also contain some ornaments. Beads and other ornaments of olivella and abalone shell suggest that Windmiller people were involved in trade to some extent, since these shells originated at the coast. Other ornamental artifacts include pipe bowls and charmstones carved from steatite (soapstone), alabaster, schist, diorite, and similar materials. The charmstones hint at the origins of the historically known shamanistic ritual traditions of central California (Ragir 1972).

Some authorities suggest that the Windmiller people are the ancestors of the five groups of Indians known from historical times in the Central Valley and adjacent coast of California: Yokut, Miwok, Maidu, Wintun, and Ohlone or Costanoan (Elsasser 1978a). This interpretation is based primarily on linguistic evidence (Shipley 1978). These five peoples spoke closely related languages, which linguists have grouped together under the name *Penutian.* It is believed that the Penutian languages descended from a common ancestral language, *Proto-Penutian,* which may have appeared in California 3,000–4,000 years ago. Since the Delta area is the center of that part of the state

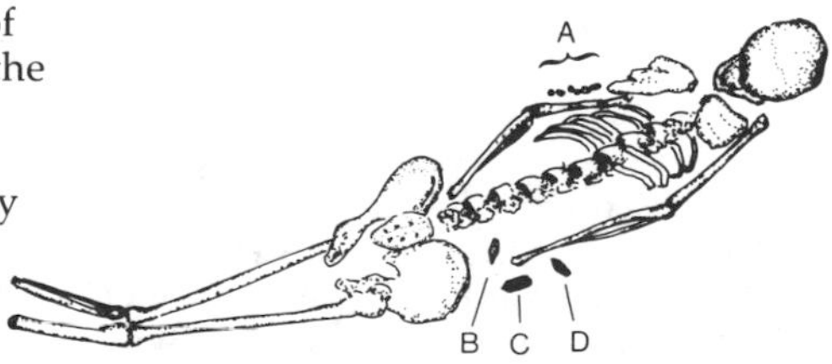

Fig. 34. Typical burial position of the Windmiller Tradition, with the body extended face down, the head oriented toward the west, and the remains accompanied by grave offerings: *a,* shell beads; *b,* charmstone; *c,* quartz crystal; *d,* projectile point.

Map 26. Distribution of the Pinto Basin Tradition.

occupied historically by Penutian speakers, linguists feel that ancestral Proto-Penutian speakers may have been the original settlers of this area.

Some archaeologists have taken these inferences one step further. Noting that the Windmiller Tradition is the earliest tradition in the Central Valley, they have argued that the appearance of the Windmiller Tradition resulted from the immigration of Proto-Penutian-speaking people from some other part of the continent to the vacant Delta ecological niche. If so, their archaeological remains provide a record of one of the longest and most successful subsequent developments of a cultural tradition in America.

The Pinto Basin Tradition (Map 26). An outgrowth of the Lake Mohave Tradition, the Pinto Basin Tradition emerged in the Late Archaic (Donnan 1964; C. Hunt 1975; Wallace 1962a, 1978). The tradition is named for the type-site locality in the Pinto Basin, in northwestern Riverside County, where occupation had begun in Paleo-Indian and Lake Mohave times (Campbell & Campbell 1935). The remains show that Pinto Basin people had had to adjust to the final disappearance of the Pleistocene lakes and of the animals and plants that the lakes had supported. They adjusted by increasing their reliance on hard seeds and other arid-lands plant resources, by developing an annual round that covered mountain, foothill, valley springs, and arroyo habitats in addition to the playas and playa terraces, and by hunting both larger and smaller desert game animals.

Pinto Basin assemblages are invariably marked by numbers of distinctive projectile points, generally with thick stems of varied forms

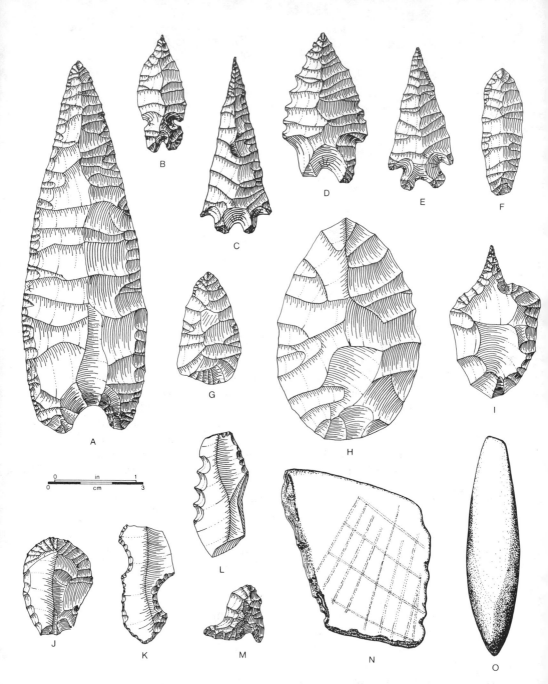

Fig. 35. Artifacts of the Pinto Basin Tradition: *a,* concave-base projectile point; *b,* side-notched projectile point with basal indentation; *c,* corner-notched projectile point with basal indentation; *d,* contracting-stem projectile point with basal indentation; *e,* corner-notched projectile point with basal indentation; *f,* leaf-shaped projectile point with convex base; *g,* convex-base projectile point or knife; *h,* oval biface or knife; *i,* drill; *j,* thumbnail or end scraper on a flake; *k,* flake scraping tool with double notches; *l,* denticulate flake scraper; *m,* eccentric retouched piece; *n,* incised slate tablet or piece; *o,* charmstone. (After Donnan 1964; C. Hunt 1975; Wallace 1962a, 1978.)

(Fig. 35). The size and shape of these points suggest the continued importance of the spear and spear-thrower and, by implication, the persistence of hunting as a major subsistence activity (Donnan 1964: 9). The spear-thrower, or atlatl, allowed the hunter to fire darts with greater range and power than could be achieved with hand-thrown spears (see Appendix B). Manos and milling stones, though not abundant in Pinto Basin sites, are common enough to show a significant use of chaparral-zone hard seeds, and possibly mesquite beans and screw beans. The abundance of choppers, hammerstones, scrapers, and scraper planes attests to the importance of plant resources in Pinto Basin adaptation—for fuel and craft materials as well as for food (Wallace 1962a: 175). Pinto Basin tool kits are more varied than those of their Lake Mohave predecessors, but not as varied as other Late Archaic assemblages found in lusher parts of the state.

Evidence of Pinto Basin architecture is still scanty. Perhaps the best-known examples come from the Stahl Site at Little Lake in southwestern Inyo County. Harrington (1957: 24–37) describes the uncovering of seven structures clustered in the shelter of a lava extrusion overlooking the playa. The structures each consist of a roughly circular enclosure of posts (Fig. 36). Most enclosures contain a fire hearth; several also con-

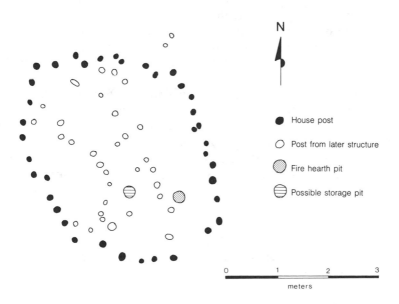

Fig. 36. House floor plan (Stahl Site, House 6), Pinto Basin Tradition. (After Harrington 1957.)

tain storage pits. These structures, as substantial as most known from later desert architecture, indicate a marked increase in relative sedentism compared to earlier, Lake Mohave times. It may be that during the Pinto Basin Tradition winter base camps gradually emerged like those that had appeared somewhat earlier in less arid parts of the state.

Although the Pinto Basin Tradition was first defined more than 40 years ago, its true age is still unclear, mainly because few substantial excavations have been made of Pinto Basin sites. The consensus is that the tradition emerged by the middle of what we call the Late Archaic, no later than 5,000 years ago (3000 B.C.). It is understood to have lasted into what we call the Early Pacific Period (2000–500 B.C., or 4,000–2,500 years ago) and possibly into the Middle Pacific Period (500 B.C. to A.D. 500, or 2,500 to 1,500 years ago). In our view, the Pinto Basin Tradition reflects part of a continuum of desert adaptation, and illustrates the benefits—for both adaptation and population density—to be gained from carrying the Archaic strategy to its logical conclusions in a demanding environment.

THE ARCHAIC WAY OF LIFE

The Archaic way of life evolved slowly over 7,000 years toward ever-greater levels of social, economic, and technological complexity. Despite this trend toward greater variety and distinctiveness in the details of local resource exploitation and artifact style in different parts of the state, there was a fundamental similarity among all contemporary Archaic cultures. These common features allow us to talk about Archaic culture as a whole.

The following discussions explore several aspects of archaeological evidence from the Archaic and inferences drawn about Archaic culture, in order to characterize the period's archaeological record and distinguish it from that of its predecessors and successors. We review kinds of sites, features, and artifact technologies that appeared or matured during the Archaic, and what these remains indicate about Archaic life. This material provides a basis for exploring the nature of Archaic economy and society.

Site Types

Some types of sites characteristic of the Paleo-Indian Period continued to develop during the Archaic; others were no longer used. Still other types of sites originated during the Archaic.

All Archaic traditions include *occupation sites*, and in most cases they were more substantial than those of the preceding periods because Archaic groups were larger, stayed in their camps for longer spans of time, and reoccupied the same spots repeatedly. By the Late Archaic, if not earlier, *base camps* were being used, sites that people occupied over and over again for relatively long periods of time (see Map 27). Pursuit of the annual round also led to the development of *seasonal exploitation sites*, where people camped briefly at the source of some resource during the period of its seasonal availability.

Although sites consisting of individual burials are found in the Archaic as well as in the Paleo-Indian Period (for example, Stanford I and II, the BART Site, Farmington, and Tranquillity; see Bickel 1978a and Henn, Jackson & Schlocker 1972), Archaic people developed California's first *cemeteries* (for example, Bear Creek, Glen Annie, Malaga Cove, Parker Mesa), where numbers of burials were concentrated in one place (see C. King 1962; Olsen & Wilson 1964; Owen, Curtis & Miller 1964). Cemeteries were initiated by the larger, more sedentary populations; perhaps because they stayed for longer periods at their major campsites, they had more dead to bury in one place.

Some cemeteries are found associated with base camps, or as part of them, as in the Encinitas Tradition. These base camps were inhabited during the winter, a particularly bleak time of year for Archaic peoples, when many children and older people apparently died of starvation or starvation-related illnesses. In other cases, cemeteries show few signs of association with occupation sites, as in the case of the Windmiller Tradition. The treatment given to the dead in both types of cemeteries indicates that Late Archaic societies were egalitarian, since there are no significant differences in the worldly goods buried with the community members.

Kill and butchering sites, characteristic of the Paleo-Indian Period, were not characteristic of Archaic traditions, since the large animals that had earlier occasioned the establishment of such sites had disappeared by the end of the Ice Age. Nor did Archaic peoples make intensive use of specialized quarry sites, where useful types of rock were quarried for processing and export in large quantities. There are some examples of Archaic occupations at quarry sources—Clear Lake and Mammoth Creek obsidian sources, for example—but the scope of the use of the raw materials at such sites was modest and does not indicate the development of specialized quarrying operations. At Mammoth Creek, for example, the Archaic occupation of the site seems to have revolved around the harvest and milling of seasonally available seeds and pine nuts. The obsidian work done at the site during the Archaic reflects the use of available material to make the tools needed during the camping period, not the systematic production of

1. Borax Lake
2. Arcade Creek
3. Stanford
4. Santa Clara 178
5. Mono Lake
6. Tranquillity Site
7. Tulare Lake
8. Diablo Canyon
9. Buena Vista Lake
10. Owens Lake
11. Panamint Valley
12. Death Valley
13. China Lake
14. Oak Grove sites of the
    Santa Barbara region
15. Lake Mohave (Silver and
    Soda lakes)
16. Parker Mesa
17. Topanga Canyon (e.g.,
    Tank Site, lower level)
18. Malaga Cove
19. Pauma
20. Agua Hedionda Lagoon
21. C. W. Harris Site
22. La Jolla
23. Chemehuevi Wash
24. Pinto Basin

Map 27. Selected sites of the Early and Middle Archaic periods (9000–4000 B.C.).

large numbers of export artifacts, which would be the case in later periods (Sterud 1964).

Some *bedrock mortar sites* and *bedrock milling-slab sites* were in use by the end of the Late Archaic in central and southern California, although such sites would become much more important during the Pacific Period (Chartkoff, Johnson & Miller 1976). The same may be said for *rock-art sites*. Some examples of rock art may be as old as the Archaic, but they are few in number and relatively insignificant compared to the later burgeoning of the craft (Heizer & Clewlow 1973).

Site Locations

The distribution or location of Archaic sites differed from the Paleo-Indian pattern in two ways. First, sites were distributed across more than one major habitat, presumably reflecting an annual round. And second, new parts of the state were colonized, as more and more habitats were utilized.

That the development of diffuse economies took a long time is shown by the locations of sites at different times. Early Archaic traditions, such as the San Dieguito, have site distribution patterns similar to those of the Paleo-Indians but situated in different habitats. San Dieguito people tended to limit their adaptation to one kind of habitat, the chaparral, and to move within it as local resources became scarce. Though some of their movements were from the coast to the interior, the same general resources were exploited in both areas. By Middle Archaic times, such traditions as Encinitas and Borax Lake show that people had learned to draw on the resources of more than one habitat, and to move seasonally from one habitat to another. By Late Archaic times scheduled seasonal rounds allowed even more diversified adaptations.

This pattern took different forms in different parts of the state. In the Central Valley, for instance, people migrated in late spring from the lowlands up into the surrounding mountains. They shifted habitats by moving uphill or down. Along the southern California coast, the mountains do not provide as much vertical separation of habitats as does the Sierra, so the pattern differed. People migrated from the coast to the interior valleys, crossing the low coastal hills or staying in the hills for short periods. In the deserts of interior southern California, mountain ranges were more barren and could not support people for as long periods. Desert people tended to visit mountains for shorter periods to collect specific resources, confining more of their movements to the playas and the canyons of the surrounding ranges. But in all cases, people of the Middle and Late Archaic followed the practice of migrating among different habitats to take advantage of particular resources available at different seasons.

The colonization of different parts of the state also progressed through the Archaic. Most of the state's population in the Early Archaic lived in southern California. On the coast, people lived along the many small rivers and creeks and around the bays and estuaries that cut through the chaparral. In the interior, people with similar cultures lived around the playas that had formerly been permanent lakes, such as Lake Mohave, Panamint Valley, Pinto Basin, Silver Lake Basin, and Manix Lake Basin. Other groups with comparable cultures lived at the southern end of the San Joaquin Valley near Buena Vista Lake and Tulare Lake, and in the Coast Ranges valleys in Lake and Santa Clara counties (Frederickson 1974a; E. G. Stickel, pers. comm. 1980; Warren 1967; Warren & Ore 1978).

By Middle Archaic times, settlement in southern California had spread north along the coast beyond Santa Barbara, and out to several of the Channel Islands (Bryan 1970; Meighan 1959b; Meighan & Eberhart 1953). An occupation site near San Jose, and some burials in San Mateo and San Francisco counties, shows that people had begun to live around San Francisco Bay (Bickel 1978a; Henn, Jackson & Schlocker 1972). Middle Archaic people spread throughout the North Coast Ranges and into the Klamath Mountains (Bickel 1979; Chartkoff & Chartkoff 1979; Frederickson 1974a). The valleys of northeastern California were also first occupied at this time (O'Connell 1975).

The Late Archaic saw the continuation of occupation and an increase in population density in the areas already settled (see Map 28). In those areas, Late Archaic traditions grew, with few significant changes, out of Middle Archaic cultures. The Late Archaic saw the settlement of the last remaining large lowland in the state: the Central Valley. The earliest sites of the Windmiller Tradition in the Delta date to this time (Ragir 1972), as do the central and southern Sierra foothill occupations in the Yosemite area (Elsasser 1960; Fitzwater 1962, 1968) and at Buchanan Reservoir (Moratto, King & Woolfenden 1978), and such sites as the Wurlitzer Site in the northern Sacramento Valley (Chartkoff, Johnson & Miller 1976). By the end of the Archaic, the only parts of the state apparently not permanently occupied were the higher mountains, the northern California coast, and the Klamath River Valley.

Technology

Our reconstruction of Archaic culture was based partly on the types and distributions of sites, and partly on the artifacts archaeologists find in those sites. They show that basketmaking, stone grind-

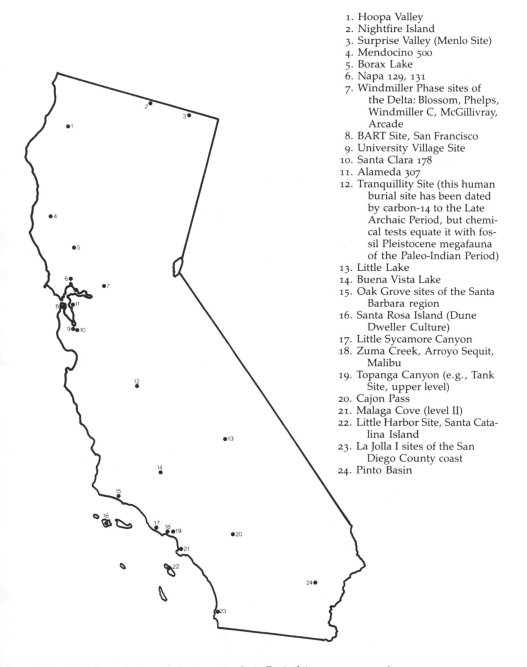

1. Hoopa Valley
2. Nightfire Island
3. Surprise Valley (Menlo Site)
4. Mendocino 500
5. Borax Lake
6. Napa 129, 131
7. Windmiller Phase sites of
   the Delta: Blossom, Phelps,
   Windmiller C, McGillivray,
   Arcade
8. BART Site, San Francisco
9. University Village Site
10. Santa Clara 178
11. Alameda 307
12. Tranquillity Site (this human
    burial site has been dated
    by carbon-14 to the Late
    Archaic Period, but chemi-
    cal tests equate it with fos-
    sil Pleistocene megafauna
    of the Paleo-Indian Period)
13. Little Lake
14. Buena Vista Lake
15. Oak Grove sites of the Santa
    Barbara region
16. Santa Rosa Island (Dune
    Dweller Culture)
17. Little Sycamore Canyon
18. Zuma Creek, Arroyo Sequit,
    Malibu
19. Topanga Canyon (e.g., Tank
    Site, upper level)
20. Cajon Pass
21. Malaga Cove (level II)
22. Little Harbor Site, Santa Cata-
    lina Island
23. La Jolla I sites of the San
    Diego County coast
24. Pinto Basin

Map 28. Selected sites of the Late Archaic Period (4000–2000 B.C.).

ing, shell working, and other new techniques brought new materials into Archaic technology and increased the range of artifact forms being created. At the same time, Archaic craftsmen continued to use techniques practiced by their Paleo-Indian predecessors, such as stone flaking and bone working, but they used these techniques to develop a larger number of tool types, with more specific functions, than ever before (see Appendix B).

One of the most important components of Archaic technology was basketry (Wallace 1978). Ancient Californians were to become among the world's most skilled basketmakers, and although the roots of basketmaking may be traced back as far as the end of the Paleo-Indian Period (for example, bone needles were found at the Marmes Rockshelter in Washington), evidence seems to show that basketmaking did not become fully developed until Archaic times. Because baskets are so perishable, few survive in archaeological sites as old as the Archaic. But we do find tools from that time, such as bone awls and needles, that are known to have been used to make baskets in historical times.

In California, basketry served many of the functions that pottery did elsewhere. Baskets were used for cooking, serving, storage, and transporting burdens. Beaters for seed collection, seed collection trays, and winnowing trays all were made of basketry. Fish traps and weirs (which may not have appeared until the subsequent Pacific Period) were made with basketry techniques. Basketmaking methods were used to make matting to cover house floors and walls and to make clothing and footgear. Some basketmakers wove baskets so tightly that they could hold water; others waterproofed their baskets by lining them with pitch or asphaltum.

The presence of large quantities of burned and fire-cracked rock in Archaic sites indicates that the stone boiling method of cooking was developed at this time. By this method, heated rocks were dropped into large baskets filled with water and the raw food—usually a gruel of acorn meal or seed meal. Like many other Archaic innovations, this method of cooking was still being practiced by California Indians in historical times.

One common but interesting artifact type from Late Archaic sites in central California is the baked clay ball. Presumably, these balls were used instead of rocks in the stone boiling method of cooking (Ragir 1972). Apparently the clay balls were heated in the fire and then dropped into a liquid-filled basket. The absence of suitable rocks in the Delta area is presumed to have led Archaic people to develop the pottery substitutes.

To test the usefulness of the stone boiling method, we did some experiments. If potato-sized rocks are heated in a fire and then dropped four or five at a time into a metal bucket containing two gallons of water, the water rapidly comes to a boil, sometimes within 120 seconds. When baskets are used, the heated rocks can burn holes in the baskets unless the rocks are moved about with stirring sticks. Ethnographic records show that wooden sticks or tongs were used to lift rocks in and out of baskets and that stirring sticks and paddles were used to keep the heated rocks moving within the basket (Kroeber 1925). The crafting of wooden implements is thus assumed to be a part of the technology of the stone boiling method.

Clay boiling "stones" are not the only example of pottery from the California Archaic. Clay figurines and some crude pottery vessels were made during that period, especially in the Windmiller Tradition. But for reasons still not adequately understood, pottery never became very important in California, whereas basketmaking reached technical and artistic levels unsurpassed in the New World (Drover et al. 1979).

Milling tools, which also emerged during the Archaic, played an important role in Archaic and later economies. These tools were made of stone that was shaped by pecking and abrading rather than by flaking (see Appendix B). Milling tools took two basic forms: the mortar and pestle, and the milling stone and mano. The mortar and pestle were used primarily for pounding nuts, acorns, and the carcasses of small animals, and the milling stone and mano were used primarily for grinding hard seeds. Manos and milling stones appeared earlier and were more numerous in Archaic sites than mortars and pestles. The latter became common during the subsequent Pacific Period when acorn processing grew in importance.

Although technically portable, mortars and milling slabs were so heavy that they were probably left at campsites when people moved. Discarded, worn-out, or deliberately broken milling slabs were frequently used to cover burials. Toward the end of the Archaic, some communities began to make additional mortars and milling surfaces on large rock outcrops. These bedrock mortars and grinding slicks are found most often at campsites near oak groves and streams of the canyons and foothills.

Many of these innovations emphasize the increasing importance of plants in the Archaic economy, but hunting techniques also reflected technological specialization. Archaic hunters developed pronged spears, or leisters, for spearing fish, as well as nets, toggles, hooks, and traps. Nets were also used during rabbit drives and for bird snares. The spear-thrower probably also appeared for the first time in California during the Archaic. And, since the offshore islands were colonized during the Archaic, some sort of watercraft must have been developed by that time.

Chipped-stone tools of the Early Archaic in California are distinguishable from their Paleo-Indian precursors not by better craftsmanship, but by the appearance of more-specialized forms. Distinctive types of chipped-stone knives began to appear, and scraper planes were produced in great numbers. In addition, projectile points for spears and darts were made in a variety of sizes and shapes. Archaic knappers used several kinds of raw materials to make chipped-stone items, including chert, jasper, chalcedony, obsidian, basalt, andesite, and rhyolite. Most of these materials were locally available, but a few were imported from considerable distances, early evidence of trade.

By the height of the Archaic, a variety of specialized stone tools was being made. Many of them, such as the milling tools, were made by abrading techniques rather than flaking. Ground-stone weights were produced for use with hunting and fishing nets. Stone pipe bowls, stone beads, pendants, plummet- or phallus-shaped charmstones, and other nonutilitarian objects were also made of ground stone. Steatite, sandstone, alabaster, and schist were among materials favored for these items.

There is little direct evidence of architecture in Archaic sites. One of the most impressive structures of those examples in the state known from the Archaic is in Surprise Valley in northeastern California (O'Connell 1975). There the combined resources of the lakeshore, valley, and surrounding mountains allowed people to maintain a camp for six to eight months of the year. Because they stayed at one camp for so long, they apparently found it worthwhile to build substantial houses. Excavation put the floors of these houses one to three feet (up to a meter) into the ground, and the roofs were held up by thick posts and covered with mats and earth (see Fig. 32).

Nowhere else were Archaic houses so sturdy or elaborate, probably reflecting the fact that most people did not stay in their camps as long, so the effort needed to make such constructions was not considered worthwhile. At Buchanan Reservoir in the southern Sierra foothills, for example, houses found at base camps were not built over excavated pits. They probably took instead the shape of a cone, tepee-style, with a framework of poles tied together at the top and covered with bark slabs (Moratto, King & Woolfenden 1978). The houses at the Stahl Site in Pinto Basin had similar shapes but their frames were probably covered with mats or brush (see Fig. 36). Anything constructed at the temporary or seasonal camps could have been no more than very simple shelters at best, since no archaeological evidence of any sort survives in such sites.

Another aspect of Archaic technology for which little archaeological evidence remains is clothing. As a result, archaeologists have turned to the ethnographic literature of the California Indians for ideas about what Archaic dress might have been like. In traditional California cultures women customarily wore aprons in front and back or skirts. In most areas the skirts were made of plant fibers, such as shredded bark. Skirts of leather are also reported, most often as dress for ceremonies or other special occasions. Men went without clothes in many cases, except perhaps for a thong around the waist to carry things or for a skirtlike wrap. Children generally went naked. In cold weather, people wrapped up in animal skins or fur blankets. Some groups made rain ponchos from plant fibers. People often went barefoot, although plant-fiber sandals were made in some cases. Tailored clothing and leather moccasins were not characteristic of California dress (Heizer 1978a; Kroeber 1925). Archaeologists suspect that Archaic people dressed in fairly similar ways. The small quantity of beads and ornaments from Archaic burials and campsites suggests that Archaic people did not have as much jewelry or ornamentation as later people did, and may not have developed the elaborate ceremonial costumes found in ethnographically known California cultures.

Economy

In adapting to a wider range of habitat types, Archaic peoples began to use many of the same resources that were to be developed during the Pacific Period. Archaic economies were not as intensively specialized, however, and resources were largely used when they were available, rather than being gathered and saved for use later in the year.

In the Early Archaic, although people were still dependent on hunting to a large degree, they had shifted their reliance from large to smaller game. By the end of the Early Archaic, coastal people had also begun to add shellfish to their diet. Starting in the Middle Archaic, however, game became a less-important part of the diet as people began to rely more heavily on plants for food. Milling stones and basketry, plus the location of sites in habitats where plant resources were abundant, testify to the fact that Archaic peoples were relying on plants for food and for raw materials to a much greater degree than Paleo-Indians had. An important discovery of Middle Archaic times was how to make use of the vegetable proteins available in the hard seeds of chaparral plants and grasses. Equally important, Late Archaic peoples discovered how to remove the tannins from acorns, converting them into a useful food. This new emphasis on plant foods not only resulted in a broader and improved diet, but also enabled people to live in more parts of the state than ever before. The effect was an increase in the size and distribution of Archaic populations.

The shift from meat to plants as sources of nourishment was not simply a shift in food preferences. That it served to multiply the available food supply as well can be shown by considering an ecological model of a simple food chain (Odum 1971). In such a model, energy comes to the earth in the form of solar radiation, which is transformed into useful energy by photosynthesis in green plants. Herbivorous animals obtain energy by eating green plants; carnivores accomplish the same thing in turn by eating the herbivores. With each step from plant to herbivore to carnivore, however, about 90 percent of the potential energy is lost. This means that the number of organisms that can be supported at higher levels in the chain is much smaller than at lower levels.

Paleo-Indians were more heavily reliant on meat than Archaic peoples, who became increasingly herbivorous over time. All else being equal, Archaic peoples had several times as much potential energy available to them as did the Paleo-Indians. Whatever the actual figures might have been, populations did in fact expand during the Archaic. And since California has many more species of plants than game animals, this model also explains why economies became less focal and more diffuse over time as the Archaic peoples became more plant-oriented.

Another aspect of Archaic economy was trade. The exchange of raw materials and finished artifacts appeared in California during the Archaic Period. Archaeologists recognize the presence of trade by the discovery of materials not native to a site area. Cultural anthropologists have established the importance of trade among the ethnographic cultures of California (J. Davis 1961; C. King 1978), and archaeologists have pushed its study back into prehistoric times.

Besides the durable items that archaeologists might expect to find in sites, ethnographic records show that many items of a perishable nature were also traded. The use of ethnographic analogy helps to illuminate those dimensions of trade not preserved archaeologically. Of the more durable materials, such as obsidian, many can be traced to their points of origin by analyzing the particular combinations of trace elements found in them and matching them to those of possible sources. In this way, the direction of ancient trade can be reconstructed, and estimates made of the nature of goods flowing in different directions. The resulting trade patterns suggest the volume, direction, and quantity of perishable goods, such as feathers or bearskins, that might also have been traded.

Examples of artifacts whose sources can be traced turn up occasionally in Early and Middle Archaic sites. E. G. Stickel, for example, found a few pieces of obsidian in a Middle Archaic occupation site near San Jose. The obsidian can be traced to Clear Lake, more than 120 miles (190 km) to the north (Stickel, pers. comm. 1980). But such discoveries are rare, and it is apparent from the paucity of trade items in earlier sites that trade was irregular at best before the Late Archaic. By and large, people of Early and Middle Archaic cultures seem to have made utilitarian artifacts primarily, and made them of locally available raw materials. The uneven distribution of needed raw materials may have kept some parts of the state from being occupied, and might also have required many Archaic groups to maintain very large territories in order to have access to enough needed resources. The larger the territory needed by one group, the fewer territories there can be in a given region, and consequently the fewer groups. Most likely, the development of trade was a major factor in allowing Late Archaic population sizes and densities to increase above Middle Archaic levels.

The archaeological record shows that the movement of raw materials over considerable distances increased markedly during the Late Archaic. For example, Windmiller Tradition burials have yielded numbers of plummet-shaped charmstones made of materials that originated in the Sierra 50, 100, or more miles away (80–160 km or more). For example, steatite, a common raw material for charmstones, is found in several outcrops in the Sierra. Although no one has identified an Archaic Period steatite quarry yet, the fact that steatite is found in Archaic burials shows that it was being quarried and exported. Presumably, steatite was collected by groups having outcrops in their territories, and then traded to other groups that lacked direct access to the material. The largest steatite source in the state was in southern California, on Santa Catalina Island, and the trading of Catalina steatite began during the Late Archaic. Other lithic materials traded either as raw materials or as finished artifacts included alabaster, chert, diorite, jasper, serpentine, slate, amphibolite schist, and obsidian (Wallace 1978: 33).

At least two kinds of seashells were also traded during the Late Archaic: abalone and olivella shells. These shells have been found up to a hundred miles (160 km) inland from their coastal sources. Pieces of abalone shell were ground into square, circular, or rectangular shapes for use as beads or pendants, and some beads were cemented onto steatite artifacts as ornaments. Olivella shells were either used whole as beads or cut into rectangular pieces to make flat beads. The amount of trade in shells was small, however, compared to what it would become in the subsequent Pacific Period.

Late Archaic peoples also traded crystals, which prehistoric peoples apparently regarded as the spiritually most powerful of all native materials (Levi 1978). Quartz and tourmaline crystals were traded north from San Diego County, and quartz crystals from the Sierra were traded into the Central Valley. This early trade also suggests that the tradition of shamanism in California had its origins at this time.

Trade began very slowly during the Archaic, but not until the Late Archaic did it become well enough established to leave behind the evidence that could later be used to reconstruct regular trade routes. The growth of trade parallels the expansion of Archaic cultures into more and more ecological niches and the development of more complex societies. Although the amount of trade in the Archaic was not very large by later standards, it served three important functions: it provided objects for personal jewelry and ornamentation; it provided exotic goods for use as grave offerings; and it provided some of the objects used in the shamanistic religion. What trade there was rearranged the distribution primarily of relatively rare, nonutilitarian objects, rather than any substantial quantity of raw materials used for everyday life. Nor did trade involve any sort of money system. In this way it differed from the trade of later periods, in which craft materials, money, and subsistence all figured importantly. However, as we shall see in the next chapter, once the mechanics of trade were worked out, this orderly exchange of goods became an important stimulus for transforming Archaic cultures into different, more-sophisticated forms.

Society

We have already seen that there is not a lot of direct archaeological evidence for the kind of social organization that seems to have characterized the Paleo-Indian Period. The same may be said of the Archaic, although to a somewhat lesser degree, since there are many more—and more-extensive—sites known for this period. Even with this additional information, archaeologists rely on ethnographic analogy to understand the nature of Archaic society. The Archaic comes much closer in time and character to the historically known cultures of California than did Paleo-Indian culture. Consequently it is felt that analogies of the Archaic to these ethnographically known cultures are more relevant and reliable than would be similar analogies to the Paleo-Indian Period. Therefore, whereas Paleo-Indian analogies were drawn from historically known hunter-gatherer micro-bands in many parts of the world, the principal basis for the reconstruction of Archaic social organization comes from the ethnographies of the more than a hundred historically known cultures of Native California.

The earliest Archaic societies were probably not much different from those of the late Paleo-Indian Period, but by the time the Archaic had matured, between 6,000 and 4,000 years ago, a different lifeway had emerged. The economy was so much more productive that permanent groups of 25–100 people could be maintained, forming what anthropologists call true *bands* (Service 1975: 47–55; Steward 1938: 9–20). Similar to micro-bands, bands are larger and somewhat more complex. Such a group contained several nuclear families, with the adult males, in most cases, related by common descent from parent or grandparent. Like micro-bands, bands tend to draw mates from other groups (exogamy), which creates kinship bonds between groups. Bands can usually send their members to other groups in times of stress. And, although the band has an organization as a whole, it is not a rigid organization. Individual families have the basic responsibility for their own subsistence, and households can leave bands to join others if they have relatives to receive them. Membership in bands is consequently even more fluid than in micro-bands.

Bands, like micro-bands in being essentially egalitarian, are dissimilar in having slightly more structure and social differentiation. Because they include several nuclear families, there are several household heads. Commonly, a band has a headman, often a respected older male, who leads discussions and acts as a mediator in disputes. The headman rarely has binding or arbitrary power, which means that he often has to rely on his charisma, as well as the respect accorded his position, to effect decision making. Band headmanship can be inherited, but if a new headman proves unpopular or inept, he can be deposed and replaced. The powerful sharing ethic found in micro-bands is also found in most true bands, so that differences in wealth rarely occur, and society is correspondingly democratic.

In addition to the headman, there is one other exception to the egalitarian status of band members: a medical and religious specialist, often called a *shaman*. Shamans appear in ethnographically known band-level societies around the world, generally combining the features of a medical practitioner and a religious authority. Medicine in band-level societies tends to combine practical treatment, such as bone setting, tooth drilling, minor surgery, and herbal doctoring, with spiritual treatment based on ritual and belief. Such cultures tend to mix religion thoroughly with all other aspects of life, and to interpret events as effects of combined spiritual and secular forces. The shaman, therefore, works to promote both the spiritual and physical well-being of his fellow band members.

Shamans in band-level societies are not usually full-time specialists. Although they may be compensated for their services, they often must provide for at least some of their own needs, since many bands may not be able to fully support such an individual. Shamanism sometimes also acts as a means of providing deviant personalities with an acceptable place in society. Since shamans tend to be feared or set apart because of their mastery of religious knowledge and magic, they frequently do not maintain "normal" households. They are, therefore, as dependent on the help of normal households for many of their everyday needs—such as preparing meals—as the band members are on them.

Archaeological evidence suggests that shamanism appeared during the later part of the Archaic. Excavations in some Late Archaic sites have yielded charmstones, quartz crystals, cog stones, and other artifacts that suggest shamanistic practices (Levi 1978: 49–50). If this interpretation is correct, the roots of shamanism, an important aspect of life in later times, can apparently be traced to this period in California's past.

The Archaic way of life succeeded in overcoming the ecological crisis faced by the Paleo-Indians. Solid figures are not available, but it is clear that there are several times more Archaic than Paleo-Indian sites in California. Many archaeologists feel that, by the end of the Archaic, populations were at least ten times larger than they had been at the end of the Ice Age. Populations might have become even larger had it not been for the limiting factors of mobility and seasonal food shortages.

The Archaic lifeway required people to change camp frequently during much of the year, a necessity that helped to limit population growth. Infants could not march with the group until they were three to four years old. In the meantime they had to be carried by their mothers, who also had to carry household tools and equipment. This tended to limit the numbers of infants that the band could support at any one time. In addition, the mortality rate must have been very high, since those not able to travel had to be left behind to fend for themselves.

Seasonal food shortages provided the other limit to population size. During the late winter and early spring little wild food was available. As a result, Archaic populations could grow no larger than the number of people who could be fed during this lean period. X-ray studies of skeletal material indicate that Archaic people frequently suffered from late-winter starvation (Peter Schultz, pers. comm. 1970). The young, the aged, and the ill often died at this time of year, and the survivors often suffered from loss of growth and reproductive ability. The Archaic subsistence pattern failed to deal with this problem very well. More dramatic population growth could not occur in California until adjustments were made, in the subsequent Pacific Period, to handle just this problem.

CHAPTER FOUR

The Pacific Period

A low, grassy terrace faces the ocean along the Santa Barbara Channel. The terrace parallels the shore and slopes gently upward away from the beach. A rocky point of land juts out into the water to the west of the beach, sheltering it from the prevailing winds and currents. East of the beach, a stream descends from the nearby coastal mountains and cuts across the terrace, where it empties into the sea. At its mouth is a sizable tidal estuary and lagoon. Shorebirds wade in and out among the thickets of reeds and cattails. Cries of the gulls that wheel above the sandbar sound through the rolling of the surf beyond. Behind the lagoon, oaks line the sides of the small canyon through which the stream drains, and chaparral blankets the slopes of the hills beyond. A ridge of coastal hills rises to define the horizon to the north; southward out to sea the spines of the distant Channel Islands punctuate the ocean's line.

A village settlement spreads out over the sloping terrace. There are perhaps 30 huts in all, grouped in several irregular clusters. Most of the huts are about 15 feet across and built almost wholly above ground, but in the center of the settlement is a much larger structure, almost 30 feet across. The common huts are made with frames of saplings lashed into beehive shapes and covered with layers of reed mats and thatching for their walls and roofs. The larger hut, though outwardly similar, requires the support of several heavy posts set into its subterranean floor to support its roof beams.

At one edge of the settlement, near the creek, stands a large roofless enclosure whose interior is a bare earthen floor. Not far from it, but much closer to the beach, is a small, low-roofed, semi-subterranean structure, in front of which are heaps of ashes. A thatched hut stands at the opposite end of the vil-

lage, so small that only a few people can enter it at a time. Along the beach, above the high-tide mark, a half-dozen plank canoes are drawn up onto the sand.

Nearly 250 people live in the village. A family lives in each hut, and the groups of huts represent four different lineages. It is spring, past the rainy season and warm enough for outdoor work. In the morning hours the women of most households are doing chores at the hearths next to their huts. At this time of year houses are used mainly for sleeping, as shelter during foul weather, and to store the family's belongings. Now that winter has passed, the indoor fireplace, used for cooking and heating, has been cleaned out in each house, and the food preparation and cooking are done at the outdoor hearths. Women and older girls move back and forth among the houses, visiting, carrying firewood or bundles of reeds, hauling water in basketry canteens, bringing acorns from the granaries, or tending babies. Children run around the settlement. Dogs can be seen prowling between the houses, looking for discarded bits of fish and meat.

The low-roofed, semi-subterranean structure near the beach is the village sweathouse. Smoke rises from the sweathouse's smoke hole. Some of the older men have stoked a fire inside, in which they are heating rocks. When enough stones have been heated, the men will spread them around the hearth. The men will lie on the floor, perspiring from the heat that radiates from the stones. After soaking up all the heat they can bear, the men will crawl out through the sweathouse's low door, hurry down to the creek, and complete their bath by plunging into the chilly water. While they are inside the sweathouse, the only sign of activity visible from the outside is the column of smoke rising from the smokehole, and the fresh pile of old coals, ashes, and fire-cracked rocks outside the door.

Along the beach several of the older boys dig for clams in the sand. One young man has swum offshore from the rocky point and dives in search of abalones on the channel bottom. Several other boys clamber along the rocks at the point to harvest mussels from the boulders in the splash zone. A young woman with her baby in a carrier on her back can be seen making her way along a path up the terrace to a small spring above the village where she can collect some spring greens.

Several plank canoes are rounding the point and making for the shelter of the estuary mouth where they can be drawn up onto the beach. A number of men from the village went out to sea before dawn to hunt schools of skipjack and yellowfin. Now they are returning. Each of the 30-foot-long boats rides low in the water, burdened by the sodden nets, stone net sinkers, and piles of fish. The bearskin cloaks of the boat captains glisten with spray. Bailers have worked steadily throughout the voyage to remove the water that leaks in between the canoe planks, since even the best-fit boards are never completely *watertight in spite of their sewn lashings and caulking of asphaltum. The pad-dlers have to work especially hard to bring the heavy craft to shore. Tired boat crews pull their nets onto the beach to stretch them out to dry. Later, each net owner will have his wife or the village netmaker repair any damage to the net-ting he owns.*

The fish from each boat are laid out above the beach. Here they will be gutted and scaled. Women come down from their houses to meet the boats and help with the catch. Several groups begin to process the fish, while others set up green-wood drying racks, under the direction of senior boat captains. The cleaned fish will be laid out on the racks to be dried or smoked. When the pro-cessing is complete, the catch will be divided according to shares. Each crew member gets a share, with extra shares going to the helmsman, captain, and owner of each boat. The day's catch can feed the village for more than a week, as well as providing a surplus to feed the community and visitors during fu-ture festivals. As the fish cleaning proceeds, some women begin to bring down piles of firewood that the headman had asked them to collect for the smoking racks.

The headman walks down from his large house in the center of the village to watch the landing of the boats. He directs the cleaning operation, calling on people to work well and take care. His house dominates all others, as befits his station. He is the most important figure in his village, and this village is the largest and politically most important for several miles in each direction along the coast. His village dominates this district and the dozen other settlements in it, making him the richest and most important individual in the entire area. In the village, his position is symbolized by the fact that the doorways of all other houses face his house, even though he belongs to only one of the four lineages in the village. Each of these kin groups has relatives who live in sur-rounding settlements, or even on the offshore islands, for most of the wives in the village were born elsewhere and were brought here by their husbands.

The headman asks one of his children to hike up the terrace out to the point to watch for another canoe. This canoe has carried a trading party to the area now known as the Palos Verdes Peninsula. One of the headman's younger brothers heads this expedition. It left two weeks before to trade for steatite, a highly desirable raw material used for the manufacture of stone cooking pots, frying griddles, beads, pipes, pendants, funeral offerings, and religious items. Santa Catalina Islanders quarry the rock, carving some pieces into finished artifacts and leaving some in rough, unfinished form. They then export their products by canoe to the great trading port villages around the Palos Verdes Peninsula, where they exchange the steatite with village headmen for shell money and goods. The headmen in turn trade with delegations from all over southern California. Some traders come from as far away as Arizona, bring-ing pottery and turquoise to exchange for the steatite, abalone shell, as-phaltum, and other coastal products.

The canoe trip to Palos Verdes from the village normally takes four or five days. Stops are made along the way to visit kinsmen and engage in some small-scale trading. The canoe left the village packed with goods to exchange for the steatite: baskets filled with lumps of asphaltum, blocks of Monterey chert and fused shale (flintlike rocks used for toolmaking), bundles of pismo clam shells, and bales of sea-otter pelts acquired from villages farther up the coast. The trade goods had to be protected well during the voyage, so the canoe had to be bailed continually and beached during heavy seas.

The headman is starting to be concerned about the canoe's return, because it has been away a day or more longer than might be expected. The trading crew might be expected to have stayed at Palos Verdes for two or three days, since trading is an occasion for feasting and negotiations are not completed in haste. Expeditions are invariably risky, however, and delayed returns cause concern.

Trading trips are made in spite of the risks. Steatite is highly prized for its many uses and ease of carving. No other available material can substitute for it. Its acquisition makes the time, effort, and dangers of the trading trips worthwhile, and the trips offer chances for profit as well. Those who contributed the most to the trading expedition will be best rewarded when the canoe returns and the headman divides up the steatite. He himself will keep a larger share as compensation for having organized the expedition and for backing it with supplies from the resources stored in his house.

The headman is well respected for having organized a number of expeditions and for having rewarded his supporters with proceeds from the trips. His main source of prestige has been his skill and valor as the village's war leader, however. Only the year before a party of raiders attacked the village one morning before dawn to steal a woman. The headman led his fighters across the mountains after the raiders. His war party launched a revenge raid against the raiders' settlement, burning it to the ground, rescuing the kidnapped woman from her would-be husband, and killing two enemies. Since then the village has been peaceful and the headman's stature as a war leader has become widely known along the coast.

Not all the villagers are at work cleaning fish. In the tiny hut at the village outskirts, a young girl is in seclusion in commemoration of her first menstrual period. She is fasting while being prepared for her initiation into womanhood. She has been isolated in the hut for nearly three weeks now, and during that time she has worked to make her initiation costume. She has also received many long hours of instruction from her older female relatives on the proper conduct of a person in her new status.

Later in the day, the large, roofless ceremonial house near the sweathouse will be the scene of a comparable activity for boys. Here, the village shaman and some of the senior men in the religious society of the community are training a group of boys for the rituals that mark their entry into manhood, teaching them the extensive bodies of lore and ritual they must memorize before their circumcision ceremony. Even though they come from all the different kin groups in the village, the boys who go through their circumcision experience together will share lifelong bonds.

As some of the heavier work of the fish cleaning comes to a close, the headman directs a team of young men to another part of the beach, where a partially dismembered whale skeleton lies. Since the whale was beached during a storm the previous fall, the villagers have long since removed the meat. During the winter, the skeleton was cleaned by scavengers. The work party will now cut out some of the whale's ribs and carry them to the village. Some of the ribs will be used as support posts for new house construction. Others will be cut into sections and carried to the village cemetery to be used for tombstones and grave covers.

Village life will continue in this fashion throughout the year. The village will never be totally abandoned at any time. During the summer, some families will camp in the nearby coast ranges for a few months to hunt and to gather the resources peculiar to that area. But other families will remain in the village, along with people too old or ill to travel and mothers with newborn babies. If the village were left unoccupied, someone might steal or destroy the ritual costumes stored there that are necessary for the proper conduct of the village's ceremonial life. Such a calamity would have terrible consequences for the well-being of every member of the community.

During the year, groups will make trips into the surrounding hills to collect particular resources. Ten or twelve men might go out for a week to quarry fused shale from an outcrop in a particular canyon. Several kinswomen might travel to the ridge crest for three or four days to gather basketry materials. Autumn is a good time for teams of men to cut trees in the hills and drag the logs back to the village to be split into planks for more canoes. Early autumn is also the time for groups of women and children to go into the hills and canyons to collect acorns. People will spend much of the late summer and fall filling the granaries near their houses with acorns, storing them for the rest of the year. Seeds, collected during the summer, will also be stored in baskets kept in each house. Extra trips will be made to fill the headman's granaries, so that he can host and sponsor ceremonies. When a headman is famed for his hospitality, he brings prestige to his kinsmen and village.

By excelling in war and ritual, the headman has become almost as notable as his father, who was headman before him. The memory of his father is still honored. When the father died, his funeral was one of the most lavish in memory. Representatives came from all the surrounding villages to attend the ceremony, bringing with them gifts to contribute to the burial offerings. To mark his high status, his grave was excavated in an area of the village cemetery separate from the ones regularly used by each kin group. After preparation, the body was placed in the grave fully extended; the bodies of ordinary people were prepared for the grave by being drawn up and tied into a fetal position. More than 200 strings of shell beads accompanied the body of the former headman. Other contributions included carved steatite bowls inlaid with shell and filled with food, and two dozen baskets filled with food and shell ornaments. The headman's ceremonial costumes and finest weapons were placed in the grave with him. A whale scapula was placed over the grave before it was covered with dirt, and a long section of whale rib was stuck upright at the head of the grave. It still stands there, bleached white by the sun and turning chalky from the elements.

The funeral was accompanied by more than a week of feasting. The old headman's widows mourned in public, singeing off their hair and smearing themselves with soot. Nearly a year later, they still wear ashes in respect and tribute to their husband. Now his son, the new headman, is rising to similar prominence. His valor in war has confirmed the judgment of the village elders that he should succeed his father. Since then his generosity in hosting feasts, his piety in leading ceremonies, and his skill in helping lead the village have brought prestige to him, his family, and the whole village.

This scenario of life in a late prehistoric village along the southern California coast describes a way of life that embodied the climax of several thousand years of development away from the Archaic pattern. Archaeologists have recognized climaxes of this sort in many parts of the state but have not agreed on a term to embrace them all. Since we feel that the climax cultures around California have many general features in common, we have decided to create a general term to refer to them. The last four millennia of prehistory we have called the *Pacific Period.*

Starting between 3,500 and 4,500 years ago, California's cultures began to evolve beyond the Archaic pattern (Elsasser 1978a; Wallace 1978). The beginning of the change is not marked by a definite boundary but by the recognition that some new features of subsistence, technology, and society had begun to appear piecemeal in different parts of the state. Archaeologists elsewhere have recognized similar post-Archaic developments, including the Formative in Mesoamerica, the Woodland east of the Mississippi, and the Basketmaker/Pueblo of the Southwest (see, for example, Jennings 1974; Willey 1966).

In offering the term Pacific Period we should point out that archaeologists have no commonly accepted rules for creating period names. "Formative" refers to a perception of a stage in the evolutionary development of Mesoamerican cultures toward civilization (Fitting 1973; Warren 1973; Willey & Sabloff 1974). "Woodland" refers to both a geographical region and a kind of habitat. "Basketmaker" and

"Pueblo" refer to distinctive, important technological developments that marked their periods.

Our intention is to characterize the development of cultures throughout the state and over the whole post-Archaic period of prehistory with a single term. We chose "Pacific Period" partly to draw attention to our thesis that the kinds of cultural developments taking place elsewhere were also occurring along the Pacific Coast at the same general time. We also chose it as a geographical term to emphasize the importance of maritime resources at this time compared to the Archaic Period.

Like the Archaic, the Pacific Period was not initiated by dramatic events, but rather by gradual change on a small scale. These changes began to appear at somewhat different times in different parts of the state, so the date of 4,000 years ago (2000 B.C.) is an average figure for the period's beginning—an average for dates in different parts of the state at which archaeologists can detect new developments. Throughout the state a new approach to subsistence was emerging, an approach that drew on new principles to solve the problems that Archaic peoples faced but could not resolve.

The Pacific Period may have begun undramatically, but it ended climactically, when contact was made between Native Californian cultures and the Europeans, a contact that was to disrupt the native cultures permanently. Although contacts had begun by the 1540's, we use the date 1769 to mark the end of the Pacific Period, because that was the date of the establishment of the first permanent European settlement—the mission at San Diego.

From about 4,000 years ago (2000 B.C.) to 1769, cultures in California underwent a transformation from small groups of seasonally wandering hunters and gatherers to large groups in sedentary settlements, with a form of cash economy and the beginning of larger political organizations. This transformation is the story of the Pacific Period.

THEMES OF THE PACIFIC PERIOD

The onset of the Pacific Period cannot be linked to environmental change, since essentially modern conditions had arrived by the Late Archaic. Nor can change in the Pacific Period be explained as the result of the colonization of new habitats, as was the case with the Archaic Period. As we note below, Pacific Period peoples did penetrate new ecological niches, but this fact alone cannot account for most developments of the period. Furthermore, there is no evidence to suggest that a new phase of cultural history was launched by the immigration of new peoples into the state or by the coming of a radically new mode of subsistence such as agriculture. What sets the Pacific Period apart is the mode of organization of people and the full expression of traits already in existence. Pacific Period societies took certain practices begun in the Archaic Period and refined them to extraordinary degrees, which ultimately transformed their whole way of life.

In previous chapters we discussed distinctive themes characteristic of each period. Those for the Pacific Period include the development of a new approach to focal economy, the rise of complex societies, and the penetration of new aquatic ecological niches.

A New Approach to Focal Economy

The concept of a focal economy was introduced in Chapter 2 in our discussion of the Paleo-Indian way of life. We used Cleland's concept (1976) to refer to a subsistence pattern in which people exploited relatively few species, making some of those species important staples. As the Paleo-Indian Period gave way to the Archaic, subsistence practices began to evolve away from the focal emphasis on hunting toward reliance on a greater diversification of species.

The Pacific Period marked a return *toward* a more focal subsistence economy, but the pattern differed considerably from the Paleo-Indian approach. Although the Pacific Period economies concentrated on a few staples, none made use of as few species as did the Paleo-Indians. Pacific subsistence actually involved the use of more species than in Archaic times, though many of the species were used for craft materials, medicines, and rituals, rather than for food. Even so, virtually every California ethnographic group made use of as many as 200–300 species of plants and animals.

Within this diversity, however, each group relied heavily on just a few species as staples. Desert peoples used mesquite and screw-bean pods as staples. Valley groups relied heavily on acorns, deer, and hard seeds. Coastal groups harvested offshore schooling fish, seeds, and acorns. Mountain groups relied on pine nuts and venison. People of the northeastern California lake country used the wokas bulb (*Nymphaea*) as their staple. Riverine peoples relied heavily on salmon and acorns. In each region, two or three food crops served as staples. Other species were proportionately much less important, serving as supplements or as standbys in case the primary staples failed some year.

It is this concentration on selected species as staples that makes Pacific economies focal compared to Archaic economies. Most of the species that were Pacific Period staples were also used in Archaic times, but only seasonally and for a few weeks. Pacific groups learned to support more people by collecting certain crops in great surplus, saving the surpluses for other seasons when less food was available. Thus Pacific groups could exceed the limits that the leanest season would impose on population size. The collection, storage, and redistribution of surpluses allowed Pacific cultures to raise the carrying capacity of their environment. In every case, the species used for staples were ones that occurred in great abundance at one season and could be collected and stored readily. Since virtually every part of California had at least two or three kinds of plants and animals that could become staples of this sort, the Pacific strategy could be followed everywhere from the desert to the coast. The actual population size that could be supported varied from place to place according to the nature and abundance of the staples species, but the strategy remained the same. As the Pacific Period wore on, societies became increasingly effective in following this strategy. Population densities and group sizes accordingly became much larger than in Archaic times, and the cultures that emerged were comparable to those of rich farming areas elsewhere in North America.

Two other features contrasted the Pacific focal economy with that of the Paleo-Indian Period, and with the Archaic's diffuse economy. One was a much greater emphasis on cooperative labor, which had the effect of increasing the yields from harvesting, hunting, and processing the most important species. The other was the introduction of specialized labor, particularly for the development of species used for supplementary foods, medicines, and materials for crafts.

Why did a focal economy, even in this new form, reappear during the Pacific Period? The reasons can be seen in the conditions that obtained at the end of the Archaic Period. By intensifying the labor of unorganized and nonspecialized individuals, and through the complex organization of seasonal migrations, Archaic peoples had reached notable levels of population size and density. The same thing happened in other parts of the continent as well. The peoples who reached high population levels through these strategies found themselves with few alternatives when food limits occurred, as they did both seasonally and periodically during lean years. In many other parts of the world people turned to animal and plant domestication to overcome these shortages. Why this did not happen in California is still not fully understood. A critical factor apparently was the unique combination of resources in the region, which allowed an unusually high potential for a nonagricultural lifeway. These resources were seasonally abundant, of high nutritional value, and capable of supporting large populations once the proper social and technological adjustments had been made to permit their intensive exploitation.

Using cooperative group labor, Pacific peoples learned how to harvest great amounts of such resources, how to store a surplus for use throughout the year, and how to move resources from one environment to another. Added to these achievements were technological advances that enhanced the efficient harvesting of the resources: oceangoing canoes, fish dams, and the bow and arrow.

The Rise of Complex Societies

The high productivity of the Pacific focal economy was essential to the rise of large and complex societies in prehistoric California. This rise is the second theme of the Pacific Period. During this period at least a dozen settlements arose with populations of 1,200 people or more, and at least two dozen others had populations of 500–1,200 (C. King 1978). Archaic settlements in the state rarely if ever held over a hundred people, so by Archaic standards this increase was a remarkable achievement. Eventually Pacific populations throughout the state grew to be as large as ten times those of the Archaic Period. Size alone was not the only difference between Pacific and Archaic communities, however, as Pacific communities were socially more complex. Although Pacific peoples did not develop the kinds of complex intergroup political systems that arose in some other parts of the Americas—such as tribes, chiefdoms, kingdoms, or states—Pacific communities did achieve higher degrees of social complexity than had their Archaic predecessors (Bean & King 1974).

As Pacific communities grew in size, it became more and more advantageous to organize the community into smaller, more manageable groups. These units served to formalize relationships between people in a world in which people no longer personally knew every member of the community as fully as Archaic people had. Furthermore, since there were no formal laws to regulate activities, such groups presented a way to direct people's movements that relied less on the informal contact characteristic of a smaller community. One of the most important bases for defining group membership was kinship. Descendants from a common ancestor regarded themselves as sharing special affinities with one another, and often organized their work, recreation, and ritual life accordingly. Kin relationships among people gave them avenues for interaction with each other, obliging them to provide mutual help. Members of several different kin groups might live in a single, large community, and even distant kinsmen in other communities could call on each other for support, so that lines of kinship provided an important means of organization both within and between Pacific communities. In fact, kinship was the single most important basis for organization among Pacific societies.

Other kinds of organizations also appeared, however, based on other relationships. Location of residence, age, sex, and voluntary associations of friendship or interest were also bases for organizations. Such organizations, whatever the basis, performed a wide range of special tasks and functions. Many groups were temporary, organized for specific jobs and abandoned once the job was completed. Other task groups might have been organized at regular intervals, such as a fish-dam construction party or a rabbit-drive team that was organized for a few weeks every year. Still others might serve special functions on a permanent basis, such as a religious society. In many parts of the state, most of the men in a settlement belonged to a secret society that was both religious and economic in nature, and which also took on some governmental functions. In such cases, the man who led the secret society was also the most important political figure, the most important religious leader, the trade negotiator for the whole village, and often an informal judge. By contrast, the person leading a temporary or special task group such as a war party or a rabbit drive might have no other social importance in the community.

These organizations helped unite people who otherwise had little basis for unity—no overall symbolic leader, no bonds of universal kinship, no sense of nationhood, not even necessarily residence in the same community. They helped Pacific people to accomplish tasks efficiently and productively in a way that Archaic people could not, since in Archaic times the individual household was virtually the only unit of production. And, whereas Archaic communities had been largely egalitarian, social distinctions began to emerge during the Pacific. The need for leadership, the development of trade, the evolution of a money system, and the emergence of specialists in medicine, religion, trade, craftwork, navigation, war, and administration led to differences in wealth and social status. Some Pacific communities even developed forms of slavery for individuals who fell into debt or were captured in war. The resulting communities were simply stratified: slaves, commoners, the elite, and a headman or "big man" leader.

Archaeologists recognize these developments partly from studies of historical California Indian societies (see, for example, Bean & Blackburn 1976; Bean & King 1974; Kroeber 1925; Landberg 1965; Merriam 1955; Pilling 1978) and partly from excavations of settlements and cemeteries (see, for example, Chartkoff & Chartkoff 1980; Frederickson 1974b; Heizer & Mills 1952; C. King 1978, 1980; L. King 1969; T. King 1974; Stickel 1968). In Archaic times, when communities were egalitarian, all families lived in houses of similar size and design, owned more or less the same amount of tools and luxury goods, and were buried with more or less the same degree of ceremony. During the Pacific Period, these conditions began to change. By Late Pacific times, important families often lived in houses that were markedly larger and more elaborate than others (see, for example, Chartkoff & Chartkoff 1980), owned considerably greater amounts of luxury goods, and were buried with notably greater amounts of grave goods (see, for example, T. King 1971; Orr 1943). Burial evidence indicates that many villages were occupied by several kin groups at the same time, that different kin groups in the same community enjoyed different degrees of wealth and prestige, and that marked differences in wealth and prestige attended individuals within the same kin group (see, for example, Holman, pers. comm. 1980; C. King 1980; L. King 1969; Orr 1943). Some individuals enjoyed high social standing by virtue of their kin relationship to other important people, rather than because of their own accomplishments (T. King 1974). All these developments resulted in archaeological remains that differ markedly from those of the Archaic Period.

Penetration of New Ecological Niches

The third characterizing theme of the Pacific Period derives from a process begun in the Archaic: the full development of the many and varied resources of California, including for the first time riverine fish and acorns. Another niche entered systematically for the first time during the Pacific was the deep-sea waters beyond the littoral.

The Riverine Niche (Map 29). Although river fishing for salmon

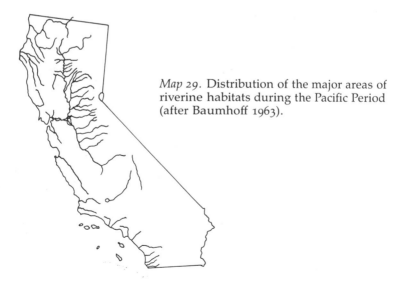

Map 29. Distribution of the major areas of riverine habitats during the Pacific Period (after Baumhoff 1963).

Fig. 37. A Karok man stands at a narrows on the Klamath River to net salmon during the fall spawning run. Although this net uses modern materials, such as stainless-steel poles and nylon netting, the form of the net is traditional. This spot, where fish are forced into a narrow channel by the constriction of the river, has been in use since the Late Pacific Period as a favored fishing place. The rights to the use of such important resource-harvesting places were held by families as a form of Pacific Period wealth.

began in the Archaic Period it did not become extremely important until the Pacific (see Fig. 37). At this time, prodigious numbers of fish were made available to Pacific peoples through the organization of specialized task groups of fish crews, by the innovation of nets, traps, weirs, and dams, and by the development of effective methods of preserving and storing the fish (see Fig. 38). This more systematic exploitation of the riverine niche is also shown in the collection of freshwater mussels for the first time by Pacific peoples.

Fig. 38. This historical photograph shows two traditional Yurok canoes on the Klamath River near Weitchpec. These bluff-ended dugouts, carved from Douglas-fir logs, provided an important means of travel during the last thousand years or more in this land of rugged mountains, where the river became a highway for trade and travel. Skillful boatwrights and navigators were highly esteemed. Canoes also increased fishing capabilities. (U.S. Forest Service Photo)

Map 30. Distribution of the major areas of valley-parkland and Transition Zone habitats during the Pacific Period.

The Valley Parkland and Transition Zone Niches (Map 30). Acorn collection was another form of resource use begun by Archaic people but not developed to its fullest capacity. As part of their focal emphasis on key resources, Pacific peoples greatly increased the size of the autumn acorn harvest, developed storage facilities for the surplus, and transformed acorns into an important year-round staple (see Figs. 39 and 40). The appearance of specialized processing sites at this time is another indication of the much greater importance of this resource (see Fig. 41).

The Littoral-Offshore Niches (Map 31). As early as 4000 B.C. (6,000 years ago), Archaic people ventured out to sea as far as San Nicolas Island, 90 miles offshore (145 km). The watercraft of that time were adequate to allow the colonization of all the major islands (leaving aside the still-controversial evidence that Santa Rosa Island had been settled by Paleo-Indians). Enough traffic occurred between the islands and the mainland to allow a modest amount of trade. Archaic people apparently did not practice deep-water fishing, however (Meighan 1959b). Remains of the kinds of fish that inhabit deep waters are rarely, if ever, found in Archaic sites.

Pacific peoples developed the necessary skills, tools, and knowledge to fish offshore. In this they were amply rewarded, because certain parts of the California coast were extraordinarily rich in offshore schooling fish. Huge schools of bonito, albacore, skipjack, yellowfin, jack mackerel, and bluefin were drawn to coastal waters, especially in southern and northwestern California, attracted by the teeming populations of smaller fish such as the northern anchovy and the Pa-

Fig. 39. This Pacific Period village site, in the foothills of the North Coast Ranges of western Glenn County, dates to the Late Pacific Period (A.D. 500–1500). It was situated near permanent springs at the base of hills blanketed with black oak (*Quercus douglasii*). The village may have held a hundred people; several of the dozen pit houses identified can be seen as shallow depressions marked by stakes (for mapping purposes). The rich acorn crops of the hillside oaks served as a primary food staple; the hard seeds of the grasslands and chaparral (eliminated historically by sheep) provided another important crop; and the salmon from a stream beyond the hill and the deer that wintered in the chaparral offered additional staples. By the Late Pacific Period, most important settlements were located to give access to such important seasonal staples.

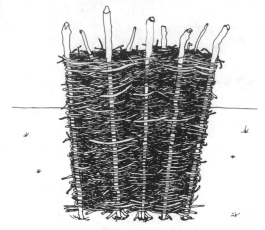

Fig. 40. Pacific Period acorn granary, Point Reyes National Seashore, Marin County. This replica, built in the style of the Coast Miwok by the Miwok Archaeological Preserve of Marin, represents an architectural feature that became common by Late Pacific Period times (A.D. 500–1500) throughout most of California. Granaries allowed the storage of acorns, pine nuts, mesquite beans, screw-bean pods, chaparral seeds, and other seasonal wild-plant foods. Earlier peoples used the same crops, but only on a daily basis when the crops were ripe. The practice of storage permitted the collection of surpluses, which could be kept throughout much of the rest of the year to increase the total available food supply for the settlement, particularly during late winter and early spring when few foods were available for harvest. Typically, each house had a granary next to it, but in many larger settlements the headman managed a larger granary for the benefit of the community.

cific sardine. Rich beds of kelp near Santa Barbara made that region the most productive prehistoric fishery on the coast. Because of the schooling habits of the larger fish, fishermen with large nets could harvest great quantities of fish at one time (Yocum & Dasmann 1965).

In the process of developing the offshore niche, Pacific peoples also learned to make better use of the littoral. The California littoral boasted many sea-mammal rookeries in prehistoric times. Seals and sea lions of six species lived at least seasonally on the mainland coast and on offshore rocks and islands (see Fig. 42). Sea otters, fifteen species of whales, four species of porpoises, and five species of dolphins were found at least occasionally in the littoral or just offshore (Ingles 1965). Though not nearly as numerous as schooling fish, sea mammals provided considerable amounts of food. Seals and sea lions could be hunted in their rookeries without special weapons or boats; the other species were hunted by boat.

Archaic people occasionally happened upon a stranded whale or killed a seal or sea lion. Hunting for these animals did not begin in a systematic way, however, until the early Pacific Period. In the Santa

Barbara region, for example, the "Hunting Culture" named by David Rogers (1929) represented the transformation of the chaparral-valley-littoral adaptation of the Late Archaic people into a Pacific-style focal emphasis on sea-mammal hunting (Harrison & Harrison 1966; Olson 1930). As the Pacific Period developed, coastal groups and inland groups with access to the coast began to kill seals and sea lions in substantial numbers. In northwestern California, later Pacific groups went offshore in canoes to harpoon migrating whales, dragging the mortally wounded animals to shore or waiting until their bodies were

Fig. 41. Except in the northwest, bedrock mortars have been found in most parts of the state, usually in streamside settings in association with oak groves. Some examples may be older, but the practice of making bedrock mortars belongs to the Pacific Period. The meaning of the different sizes and depths of the mortar holes is not fully understood. Large, deep mortar cups may have resulted from longer use than shallow, smaller holes, or the different sizes may have been created deliberately for different purposes. A less-common, even more ancient phenomenon is the "grinding slick," a bedrock exposure used as a milling stone, which was used throughout the Pacific Period. Sometimes bedrock mortar cups and grinding slicks occur on the same outcrop, suggesting that different kinds of resources were processed at the same site. Bedrock mortars and grinding slicks were often located next to seasonal occupation sites where food surpluses were processed. Fifty years ago many such mortars still had pestles sitting in them, tools left where they were needed rather than carried back to base camps. (U.S. Forest Service Photo)

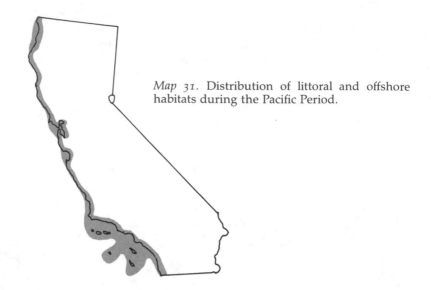

Map 31. Distribution of littoral and offshore habitats during the Pacific Period.

Fig. 42. Rookeries along the coastal littoral. A number of birds and sea mammals make homes on rocky outcrops along the coast and on coastal rock stacks and islands. The outcrop in the foreground is a nesting site for pelicans, and sea lions occupy the small island beyond it. The proximity of these resources allowed Archaic hunters to extend their land-oriented subsistence practices to ocean resources that could be harvested using the same techniques. This extension began to appear toward the end of the Early Archaic Period in some San Dieguito Tradition sites. As the Archaic wore on, the oceanic niche began to be exploited more and more. Gradually, new techniques were developed to exploit those resources that could not be harvested with land-oriented procedures. The development of trends toward intensification began to appear by 2000 B.C., marking the evolution into the Pacific Period.

washed ashore by the coastal currents. Because of favorable currents, a modern coastal whaling station was maintained at Crescent City in northwestern California until a few years ago (Elsasser & Heizer 1966; Gould 1966; Loud 1918; Pilling 1978). Southern California people appear not to have used boats to systematically hunt most of these animals, except sea otters. Porpoise and dolphin bones do show up in sites, however, suggesting that the animals occasionally may have become tangled in fishing nets. The migration routes of several species of whales pass close to the southern California coast, and whales are stranded or washed ashore with some frequency (Ingles 1965). This happened often enough that Late Pacific communities were able to use whalebone as an important resource for house supports, grave coverings, and tombstones. Sea otters, the only sea-mammal species hunted regularly from boats, were a significant source of pelts and meat for some communities in the Morro Bay region.

Coastal populations began to harvest shellfish in Archaic times, but the practice reached its peak during the Pacific. As a result, Pacific communities created great mounds of discarded shells around their villages. These *shell middens* are among the most distinctive archaeological sites in California. The greatest middens are 30 feet or more deep (9 m) and may be over ¼ mile across (400 m; for examples of shell-midden excavations, see Curtis 1959; J. Davis 1960; Davis & Treganza 1959; Loud 1924; Nelson 1909, 1910; Peck 1955; Schenck 1926; Uhle 1907; Wallace & Lathrap 1975; Wallace et al. 1956).

The size of shell middens suggests that there was a focal emphasis on shellfish. In many cases this impression is misleading. The amount of meat in most shellfish is small, so a great mass of shell represents less food than it might seem. In addition, ethnographic evidence indicates that shellfish were not a preferred food source for most groups, but were used as supplements to the diet or as backups when preferred foods were not avaialble (Baumhoff 1978). Shellfish use was further restricted by toxicity during the summer, owing to seasonal infestation with a dinoflagellate. The remains of as many as 30–40 species of shellfish have been found in some sites, but the use of most species was sporadic, and normally only a few species contributed most of the shells. The popularity of species changed over time, owing to cultural choice and to changes in the microhabitats near a site, since the abundance of each species depended on the size and distribution of the microhabitats it preferred (see, for example, Koloseike & Peterson 1963: 446).

The area where shellfish became most nearly a focal food source was the San Francisco Bay region, where analysis has shown that shellfish were the single most important source of meat (Elsasser

1978a). Another kind of emphasis on shellfish occurred in north-western California, where mussels were collected in the summer—while poisonous—because their meat was prized as a surgical anesthetic (Arnold R. Pilling, pers. comm. 1979). Shellfish were also focally important on the offshore islands because there were so few food resources on the islands themselves (Reinman 1964).

Concentration on these key resources allowed Pacific people to become settled in permanent villages, to expand their populations, and to develop the complex societies and cultures known ethnographically from throughout the state. The result was a way of life far different from the simple, nomadic band life of the Archaic.

ARCHAEOLOGICAL TRADITIONS OF THE PACIFIC PERIOD

Pacific Period traditions differed from one another even more than did Archaic traditions (see Table 3). This was because Pacific peoples increasingly adapted to particular environments and their unique resources. Despite this, we must emphasize that the three themes just outlined characterize the whole of the period to a greater or lesser extent, so there were fundamental similarities among all the different traditions. What differed was the increasingly localized *expression* of these themes.

The Pacific Period lasted from about 4,000 years ago (2000 B.C.) to around the end of the eighteenth century, two hundred years ago. During that period, California cultures underwent many changes that are reflected in the archaeological record. Although a particular change never occurred throughout the state at exactly the same time, its occurrence and spread can be more easily understood if the Pacific Period is subdivided into smaller units. In order to characterize the differences between cultures at different times, we divide the Pacific Period into four parts: Early, Middle, Late, and Final.

The Early Pacific (2000-500 B.C.)

The *Early Pacific Period* represents the transition from the Archaic way of life to a more productive focal adaptation (Map 32). In the Santa Barbara region, for example, the "Hunting Culture" of this period (D. Rogers 1929) reflects the shift from Archaic diffuse subsistence to a more focal emphasis on the hunting of deer and sea mammals. Some researchers, such as William and Edith Harrison (1966), have joined Rogers in interpreting the "Hunting Culture" as an immigrant culture brought to the Santa Barbara coast from the northwestern coast. We join other writers in regarding the "Hunting

1. Point St. George (DNo-11)
2. Nightfire Island
3. Surprise Valley
4. Redding District (Sha-20, -47;
   Teh-58; Tri-58)
5. Round Valley
6. Mendocino 187, 500
7. Karlo Site
8. Kingsley Cave
9. Wurlitzer, Llano Seco
10. Oroville District
11. Borax Lake
12. Nevada 15
13. Martis (Pla-5)
14. Auburn Reservoir (Pla-101)
15. Sacramento 43, 60, 66, 73, 151
16. Napa 1, 32
17. Sonoma 299
18. McClure (Mrn-266)
19. San Francisco 7
20. Contra Costa 14, 30, 151,
    259, 295
21. Alameda 307
22. Alameda 328
23. University Village and Santa
    Clara 1
24. Middle Horizon foothill
    burial caves
25. Monterey 281, 282
26. Yosemite Valley
27. Buchanan Reservoir
28. Cambria Pines
29. Rose Springs
30. Twichell Reservoir
31. Buena Vista Lake (Krn-39,
    -40, -41, -42)
32. Stahl Site (Little Lake)
33. Aerophysics Site and
    Glen Annie
34. North Channel Islands sites
    (e.g., Frazer's Point)
35. Big Sycamore Canyon, Little
    Sycamore Canyon, Deer
    Canyon
36. Century Ranch
37. Zuma Creek, Parker Mesa,
    Arroyo Sequit
38. Malibu Canyon, Corral
    Canyon
39. Topanga Canyon,
    Mulholland
40. Chatsworth, Big Tujunga
41. San Nicolas Island
42. Little Harbor (Santa Catalina
    Island)
43. Malaga Cove
44. La Jolla sites of San Diego
    County coast
45. Cuyamaca Rancho State Park

Map 32. Selected sites of the Early
and Middle Pacific periods
(2000 B.C. to A.D. 500).

TABLE 3 *Regional Manifestations of Pacific Period Cultures*

Regions	Late Archaic	Early Pacific	Middle Pacific	Late Pacific	Final Pacific	Ethnographic groups[a]
	2000 B.C. — 1500 B.C.	1000 B.C.	500 B.C. — 0	A.D. 500 — A.D. 1000	A.D. 1500	
Southeastern deserts[b]	PINTO BASIN		AMARGOSA		Rose Spring / SHOSHONEAN	Paiute, Chemehuevi, Mohave
Coastal southern California[c]		CAMPBELL		YUMAN		
San Diego County[d]		La Jolla II	La Jolla III	CANALIÑO / San Luis Rey I	Cuyamaca / San Luis Rey II	Diegueño (Ipai, Tipai), Luiseño
Los Angeles, Orange counties[e]	Malaga Cove II / Millingstone Hzn., Little Harbor, Topanga Culture		Malaga Cove III / Intermediate Period	CANALIÑO / Malaga Cove IV	Malaga Cove V	Gabrielino, Juaneño, Fernandeño
Santa Barbara, Ventura counties[f]	Oak-Grove Culture		"Hunting Culture"	CANALIÑO		Chumash
San Francisco Bay Area[g]		Early San Francisco Bay Complex / University Village Complex		Late San Francisco Bay Complex / Lower Emeryville	Patterson Mound	Costanoan or Ohlone and Coast Miwok
Central California[h]		WINDMILLER / Early Horizon	COSUMNES / Middle Horizon	HOTCHKISS / Late Horizon I	Late Horizon II	Miwok, Nisenan, Patwin
Sacramento Valley[i]		Wurlitzer Phase	Llano Seco Phase	Patrick Phase		Konkow
Southern Sierra[j]			CHOWCHILLA	RAYMOND	MADERA	Yokuts
Central Sierra[k]		Crane Flat Complex	Tamarack Complex		Mariposa Complex	Miwok
High Sierra[l]		Martis Complex		King's Beach Complex		Washo
Southern Cascades, Northern Sierra[m]		MESILLA	BIDWELL	SWEETWATER	OROVILLE	Maidu
North Coast Ranges[n]		Mendocino Complex / Middle Archaic	Upper Archaic	Clear Lake, Shasta complexes / Emergent		Pomo, Nisenan, Yuki
Trinity Alps[o]					Trinity, Shasta, Whiskeytown complexes	Shasta, Wintu
Northeastern California[p]		Bare Creek Phase / Nightfire Island III	Emerson Phase / Nightfire Island IV	Alkalai Phase / Nightfire Island	Bidwell Phase	Northern Paiute, Modoc
Northwestern California coast[q]		Point St. George I	(Hiatus)		Tsurai I–IV / Patrick's Point, Gunther Is.– Point St. George II	Tolowa, Yurok, Wiyot
Klamath River[r]	....	Hupa Valley			May Site / Iron Gate Reservoir / Elk Valley	Karok Shasta Yurok, Hupa

NOTE: Major traditions are in small capital letters, local phrases or manifestations in lower-case letters.

[a] The ethnographic groups named here are described most fully in Heizer (1978a) and Kroeber (1925).

[b] Lanning (1963) is the site report on the Rose Spring excavations; see also Bettinger (1977); Bettinger & Taylor (1974); and C. Hunt (1975). Early descriptions of Amargosa are found in Campbell & Campbell (1935); and C. Hunt (1975). Early descriptions of Amargosa are found in Campbell & Campbell (1935). M. Rogers (1945), and Harrington (1957). See also Hester (1973) and Wallace (1962a, 1977).

[c] The basic scheme is from Warren (1968); see also Meighan (1965, 1978) and Wallace (1955).

[d] Malcolm Rogers defined the basic sequence for the San Diego coast; see, for example, M. Rogers (1968); see also Meighan (1954); and Crabtree, Warren & True (1963). The definition of the more interior Cuyamaca sequence owes much to D. L. True's research; see, for example, True (1968) and True, Meighan & Crew (1974). See Heizer (1978a); 550–63 on the Luiseño, 592–609 on the Ipai and Tipai, known in Kroeber (1925) and most other literature as the Diegueño.

[e] See, for example, Curtis (1959), Peck (1955), and Wallace et al. (1956). B. Bryan (1970), Meighan (1959b), and Reinman (1964) are examples of research for this period on the southern Channel Islands, which are aligned culturally with the Los Angeles–Orange County coast to some extent. Interpretations of the relationships between inland and coastal settlements at this time vary; see, for example, Galdikas-Brindemour (1970), Glassow (1965), King, Blackburn & Chandonet (1968), Leonard (1966), Rozaire (1960), and Ruby (1966). Kowta (1969) describes an interior manifestation allied both with the earlier Millingstone Horizon of Wallace (1955) and with the more specialized, focal resource uses of the Pacific Period closer to the coast.

[f] The basic sequence was established in D. Rogers (1929) and Olson (1930). Harrison & Harrison (1966) has an important, more recent analysis of a Hunting Culture occupation. Orr (1943) is a major reference for the Canaliño, but see also Harrison (1965) and Stickel (1968). Glassow (1977) and Orr (1968) describe the contemporary archaeology of the northern Channel Islands. Susia (1962) offers an example of an inland manifestation of the Canaliño Tradition. (Susia, incidentally, is cited from the mid-1960's to the mid-1970's as Margaret Weide; subsequently as Margaret Lyneis.) The San Luis Obispo County area is circumstantially allied with the Santa Barbara area, but publications for it are less widely circulated. The papers of the San Luis Obispo County Archaeological Society are devoted largely to this area; see also McKusick & Watson (1959). Smith (1961), Smith & LaFave (1961), Wallace (1962c), and Wire (1961).

[g] The Bay Area was among the first parts of the state to be studied archaeologically. Key early excavations are described in Nelson (1909, 1910), Schenck (1926), Uhle (1907), and oth-ers. The period from the mid-1950's to the mid-1970's saw salvage archaeology of most of the remnants of Bay Area shell mounds; see, for example, J. Davis (1960), Davis & Treganza (1959), Gerow (1974), and Gerow & Force (1968). Frederickson (1968) is an example of archaeology in the greater Bay Area up the channel to the Delta. Riddell (1955) offers a picture of the archaeology of the Farallon Islands outside the Golden Gate. T. King (1971, 1974) and Slaymaker (1977) are examples of research in the north Bay Area; see also Heizer (1953). A good deal of excavation has been done on the coast north from the Golden Gate, but most is difficult to find in print; see Meighan & Heizer (1962) for an example. Meighan (1955) and Frederickson (1974a) extend into the northern hinterlands of the Bay Area. The coast south to Monterey and beyond is less well represented in print, as are the South Coast Ranges of Monterey and San Benito counties.

[h] The Delta is the diagnostic area for central California's sequence. The basic sequence was defined by Lillard and Heizer in a series of now-rare papers in the late 1930's: see, for example, Lillard, Heizer & Fenenga (1939). They introduced the Early, Middle, and Late horizons scheme, which Beardsley (1954) updated and refined. Ragir (1972), in further updating the sequence, introduced the Windmiller, Cosumnes, and Hotchkiss concepts. See also Heizer (1964, 1978b) and Meighan (1965, 1978). The adjacent foothills are discussed under notes i and k below.

[i] There is no widely accepted sequence for the Sacramento River Valley above Marysville, but it is not identical to the Delta's sequence. Keith Johnson found Early Pacific materials at the Wurlitzer Site near Chico and Middle Pacific remains at the nearly Llano Seco Site (see Chartkoff & Chartkoff 1968; and Chartkoff, Johnson & Miller 1976). Late and Final Pacific remains are typified in the alluvial fan by the Patrick Site (Chartkoff & Chartkoff 1980), and along the Sacramento River by the Finch Site (Chartkoff & Chartkoff 1968). A large number of unpublished excavations and surveys describe the west side of the valley, along with a few published or accessible sources; see, for example, Chartkoff & Childress (1974) and Treganza, Heickson & Woolfenden (1966). The sequence for the San Joaquin Valley is still less fully developed; most excavations have been in the foothills, owing to reservoir projects. For examples of Valley studies, see Olsen & Payen (1968), Pendergast & Meighan (1959). Riddell (1951), Riddell & Olsen (1965), and Warren & McKusick (1959).

[j] The southern Sierra is best described in print in the Buchanan Reservoir project. See especially Moratto (1970) and Peak (1976). Olsen & Payen (1968) is also germane.

[k] The definitive works in this area are Bennyhoff (1956) and Elsasser (1960); see also Heizer & Elsasser (1963). Fitzwater (1962, 1968) elaborated and refined the sequence. J. Johnson (1967, 1970) reports on studies in the northern and central mother-lode country; Moratto (1971) discusses Tuolumne River research; Rasson (1966) reports on a Yosemite Valley excavation; and Payen & Boloyan (1963) describes work near Volcano and Jackson.

Notes continued overleaf

Notes continued

[l] The basic sequence for the high Sierra is presented in Bennyhoff (1956) and Elsasser (1960). See also Riddell & Pritchard (1971), Elston (1971), and Elston et al. (1977) for the sequence as it ranges eastward into Nevada. Sterud (1964) is one source for the eastern side of the Sierra.

[m] Ritter (1970) has developed the most complete sequence for this area on the basis of his research in the Oroville Reservoir; see also Jewell (1964) and Olsen & Riddell (1963). Pritchard et al. (1966) describes a rock-shelter occupation in the Konkow ethnographic area, and Baumhoff (1955) describes the type site for the Final Pacific in the Yana ethnographic area. The publication series of the Museum of Anthropology at California State College, Chico, probably provides the fullest description of this area's archaeology. See also J. Johnson (1973).

[n] Harrington (1948) did the first major study in the North Coast Ranges. Meighan (1955) put together the first major sequence. Meighan had seen the Mendocino Complex as Middle Pacific, but by the time Frederickson (1974a) did his synthesis, C-14 dates showed Mendocino sites to range from Middle Archaic to Early Pacific. See also Meighan & Haynes (1970). The Middle Archaic, Upper Archaic, and Emergent sequence offered by Frederickson (1974a) is still the most thorough synthesis widely available in print, although a number of writers have argued about it.

[o] The mountains to the north of the Sacramento Valley were first described extensively in the archaeological literature in C. Smith & Weymouth (1952) following salvage excavations at the Shasta Dam. Treganza (1958a, 1959) and Treganza & Heickson (1960) extended this work with excavations at Whiskeytown Reservoir. K. Johnson (1976) and Johnson & Skjelstad (1974) did more recent work at Whiskeytown. This area is the territory of the ethnographic Wintu, and its archaeology extends to the fringes of the Sacramento Valley.

[p] The Surprise Valley sequence is the most complete for northeastern California; see O'Connell (1975). L. Johnson's research at Nightfire Island provided the first obsidian hydration sequence for the area (1968) and a nice contrast ecologically with Surprise Valley. Riddell (1960) offers a higher-elevation occupation report. See also Grayson (1976) for an example of data on adaptation.

[q] L. Loud provided the first significant excavations for northwestern California (1918); systematic research languished until the 1940's when Heizer initiated new fieldwork; see Elsasser & Heizer (1966), Heizer & Elsasser (1964), and Mills (1950). The site of Tsurai provided the first real sequence for the area (Heizer & Mills 1952), but it covered only the Final Pacific. Gould (1966, 1972) provided the first evidence of earlier material with his work near Crescent City. Hughes (1978), Bickel (1979), and Bickel & Salzman (1979) reflect more sophisticated recent work on problems of economics and microenvironmental adaptation within the general tradition.

[r] The interior of northwestern California may have been the last part of the state to be settled archaeologically. Late and Final Pacific archaeology on the Klamath River is described in Leonhardy (1961, 1967) and Chartkoff & Chartkoff (1973, 1975). Chartkoff & Chartkoff (1979) discusses data from the adjacent mountains and valleys.

This list is far from complete for the state's Pacific Period archaeology. We have tried to rely, as much as is practical, on archaeological reports that are reasonably widely available, though certainly many deserving reports have been left out. Also, try as we may, we are influenced by the areas whose literature we know better than others. Unfortunately, the great majority of research reports written during the last ten years are either rare or wholly unavailable to the nonspecialist.

Culture" as part of a more widespread trend in southern California. This focal emphasis on hunting, together with an increased emphasis on acorn harvesting and processing, appears to have spread during Early Pacific times southward toward San Diego and the Channel Islands in what Warren (1968) calls the Campbell Tradition.

Ragir (1972) has defined a similar trend in central California in what she calls the Cosumnes Tradition, which is generally comparable to the Middle Horizon defined earlier (Beardsley 1954; Lillard, Heizer & Fenenga 1939). The Cosumnes Tradition shows an early focal emphasis on salmon and acorns when compared to its predecessor, the Windmiller Tradition. Focal economies seem to have developed somewhat later in central California than they did in southern California, not becoming evident around San Francisco Bay until a little after 3,000 years ago (1000 B.C.; Elsasser 1978a). Indeed, the emergence of trends pointing toward the Pacific way of life appears at different times throughout the state.

The increased productivity of Early Pacific economies was coupled with the expansion of permanent settlement into some of the remaining parts of the state still unsettled or only seasonally occupied. For example, the earliest permanent settlements in northwestern California (the Point St. George I occupation at Crescent City; Gould 1966, 1972) and the northern Sierra–southern Cascades region (the Mesilla Tradition; Ritter 1970) date to this period. The earliest evidence for the regular use of the high Sierra, the so-called Martis Complex (Elsasser 1960), belongs to the Early Pacific, but it is not yet clear whether the Martis material reflects a separate culture or the summer-occupation phase of a seasonally migratory population whose winter base camps lay at lower elevations.

Archaeologists have recognized several separate traditions that can be assigned to the Early Pacific. Despite the apparent distinctions between them, distinctions based on local environmental differences, these traditions all provide evidence of the beginnings of an increasingly focal economy, and of the other Pacific features discussed earlier. We have selected two of the most significant traditions for illustration: the Campbell Tradition of coastal southern California and the Cosumnes Tradition of the Central Valley.

The Campbell Tradition (Map 33). The Campbell Tradition is an Early to Middle Pacific tradition found in coastal southern California. Some traces in the Santa Barbara region appeared as early as 4,800 years ago (2800 B.C.), toward the end of the Late Archaic, but in most areas it began about 4,000 years ago (2000 B.C.) and lasted until about 1,500 years ago (A.D. 500). Campbell Tradition sites were located mainly along the littoral on both the mainland and the offshore islands,

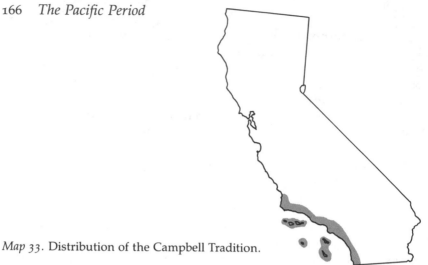

Map 33. Distribution of the Campbell Tradition.

though some examples are found on the mainland up to 50 miles in-land (80 km). They had, therefore, direct access to the resources of the littoral and the chaparral zone.

Although more concentrated than Archaic economies, the economies of Campbell Tradition people were not as fully focused as those of later Pacific peoples. We find that Campbell sites reveal an emphasis on several foods, rather than a real focus on one or two or a fully diffuse use of many. The Campbell people of the Santa Barbara region showed an early reliance on the hunting of deer and sea mammals (Harrison & Harrison 1966), whereas farther to the south the collection of hard seeds and acorns remained more important (K. Johnson 1966; C. King 1962, 1967; Kowta 1969; Ruby 1961). All the coastal Campbell people made use of shellfish, and began to develop the ability to fish offshore (Curtis 1959; Peck 1955; Warren & Pavesic 1963). The Campbell people were the first southern Californians to make acorns a staple, as shown by the facts that acorns were stored and that mortars and pestles became quite common for the first time in this area (see Fig. 43). Trade in steatite, shell, obsidian, and other

Fig. 43 (facing page). Artifacts typical of the Campbell Tradition: *a,* stemmed projectile point; *b,* side-notched projectile point with convex base; *c,* side-notched projectile point with concave base; *d,* knife or bifacially retouched tool; *e,* side scraper on a flake; *f,* compound scraper on a flake; *g,* notched scraper on a flake; *h,* bifacially retouched drill; *i,* steatite teardrop pendant; *j,* shell disk bead; *k,* incised-bone tube; *l,* charmstone; *m,* pestle; *n,* stone-bowl mortar; *o,* hopper mortar base. (After Curtis 1959; Harrison & Harrison 1966; Kowta 1969; Peck 1955; Warren & Pavesic 1963.)

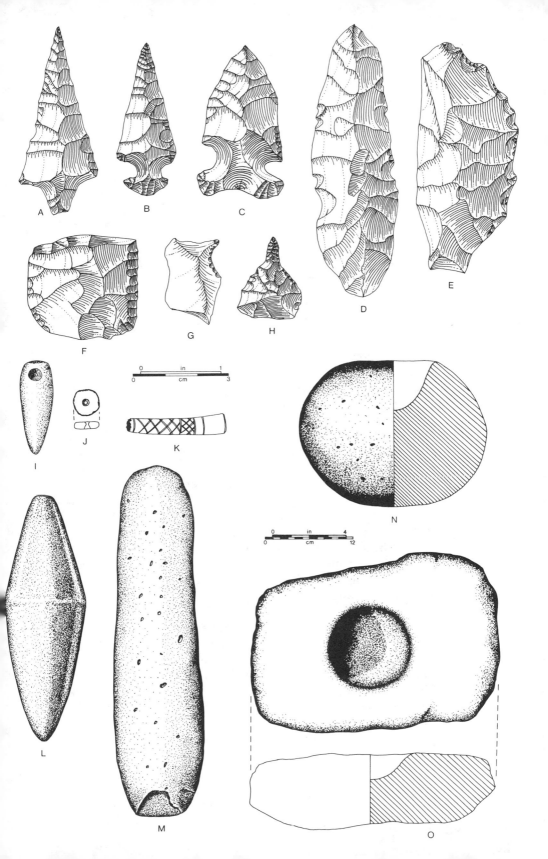

Map 34. Distribution of the Cosumnes Tradition.

natural resources also began to grow in importance during this period (Baumhoff 1978; Erickson 1977).

David Rogers (1929) and the Harrisons (1966) have speculated that the Campbell people of the Santa Barbara region were immigrants, perhaps coming from the Pacific Northwest, who replaced the earlier Late Archaic populations of the Oak Grove Culture and brought new ways of life to the region. Most archaeologists have not been persuaded that there is much evidence for such a theory, noting the lack either of any sudden, systematic change along the southern California coast to indicate a population replacement or of a wholesale change to mark the founding and spread of the Campbell Tradition.

The Cosumnes Tradition (Map 34). The Cosumnes Tradition is an Early to Middle Pacific tradition (3,700–1,500 years ago, or 1700 B.C. to A.D. 500) that developed in the Delta region out of the preceding Windmiller Tradition of the Late Archaic. Cosumnes people continued the Archaic practice of living in the Delta and near the lower San Joaquin and Sacramento rivers on knolls or other high points of land that placed them above the floodplain. They also lived along the grassy terraces lining the nearby tributaries that drained westward out of the Sierra: tributaries such as the American, Cosumnes, and Mokelumne rivers. They lived in the midst of the valley parklands, with rich supplies of seeds and acorns close at hand—as well as the resources of the rivers and marshes—and with the foothill chaparral close by.

Cosumnes populations were larger, and their settlements more numerous, than those of their predecessors. Salmon fishing and acorn harvesting grew in importance as the Early Pacific wore on. Cosumnes people made more milling tools than their predecessors, along with specialized fish spears and hunting gear. Trade apparently became more important, since burials contain much larger quantities of imported seashell and obsidian than in earlier times. Archaeologists have discovered that the skeletons in some Cosumnes burials have projectile points embedded in them. The implication drawn is that warfare was growing, perhaps as a result of increasing competition for food or trade goods (Fig. 44). Cosumnes people also developed more variability in burial styles than their Late Archaic (Windmiller) predecessors. For example, some foothill caves have been found that were apparently used as burial sites. Cosumnes people buried most of their dead in flexed positions, with the knees drawn up toward the chest, in contrast to the predominant Windmiller practice of burying people fully extended (Beardsley 1954; Lillard, Heizer & Fenenga 1939; Ragir 1972).

Although the Cosumnes Tradition was centered in the Delta, it had some relationship with cultural developments in the nearby San Francisco Bay region, into which the Delta's waters eventually drain. A number of the Bay Area's shell mounds were founded during the Early Pacific, and archaeologists have long speculated on relationships between the cultures of the two areas. Robert Heizer, one of the definers of the Cosumnes Tradition in the Delta, viewed that area as the core of central California's prehistoric cultures, and regarded the Bay Area's cultures as peripheral and derivative. Bert Gerow, who excavated in the Bay Area, regarded the Bay Area's cultures as autonomous and possibly even originating a little earlier than the Delta's cultures (Gerow 1974; Gerow & Force 1968; Heizer 1964). Though the problem of temporal precedence remains to be worked out, it is clear from existing data that contemporary sites in the Delta, the Bay Area, and the adjacent foothills reflect differences among the methods of subsistence depending on the kinds of resources locally available. At the same time, a wide variety of artifact and feature styles appear sporadically throughout the entire region, suggesting quite complex patterns of interaction that do not conform to the Bay/Delta dichotomy (see, for example, J. Davis 1961; Frederickson 1968; Lillard, Heizer & Fenenga 1939; Wallace & Lathrap 1975).

The Middle Pacific (500 B.C. to A.D. 500)

Although *Middle Pacific* cultures are distinct from Early Pacific cultures in matters of burial style (the replacement of extended or loosely

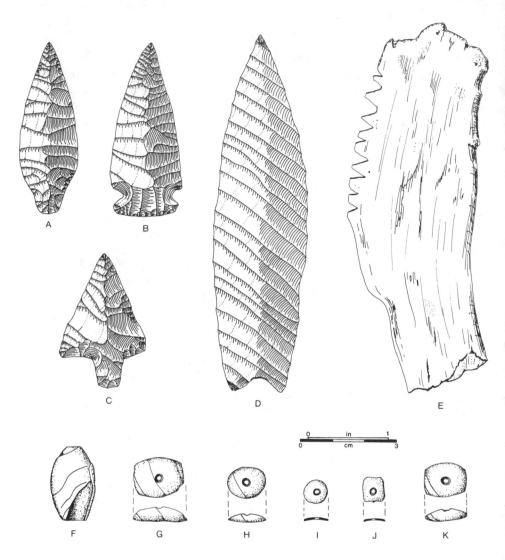

Fig. 44. Artifacts typical of the Cosumnes Tradition: *a*, convex-base projectile point with contracting stem; *b*, side-notched projectile point with convex base; *c*, stemmed projectile point; *d*, basal-notched projectile point; *e*, scapula-bone "saw" with serrate edge; *f*, whole, spire-lopped *Olivella*-shell bead; *g*, split, drilled *Olivella*-shell bead; *h*, *Olivella*-shell saucer bead; *i*, *Olivella*-shell disk bead; *j*, square-cut *Olivella*-shell bead; *k*, *Olivella*-shell saddle bead; *l*, *Mytilus*-shell disk bead; *m*, *Haliotis*-shell (abalone) disk bead; *n*, steatite (soapstone) tapered disk bead; *o*, *Haliotis*-shell disk ornament; *p*, *Haliotis*-shell pendant; *q*, steatite "claw" pendant; *r*, steatite "ear spool" tubular ornament; *s*, ground-slate flat pendant; *t*, deer-cannon-bone (metapodial) awl; *u*, pierced canine-tooth bead or ornament; *v*, bipointed bone toggle; *w*, pierced bone needle; *x*, bone-tube whistle; *y*, bone pendant; *z*, bone gaming piece; *aa*, charmstone; *bb*, bipointed pestle (used with wooden mortars). (After Beardsley 1954; Lillard, Heizer & Fenenga 1939; Ragir 1972.)

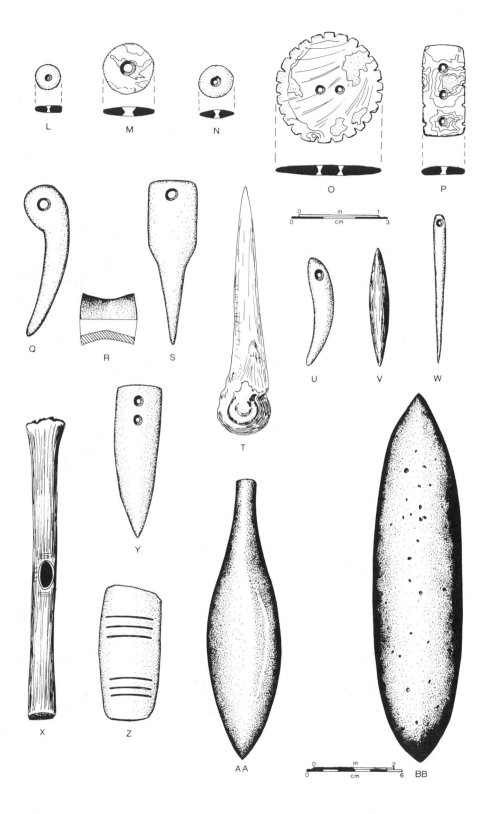

L M N O P

Q R S T U V W

0   in   1
0   cm   3

X Y Z AA BB

0   in   2
0   cm   6

flexed interments by more tightly flexed interments) and artifact styles (such as the appearance of small clamshell disk beads, barbed bone harpoons, shell fishhooks, and the bow and arrow), in terms of the themes we have been developing this period is a time of transition rather than one of dramatic change. The remaining unoccupied parts of the state were permanently settled for the first time, including the southern Sierra, the lower Klamath River, and the coast between Santa Cruz and Morro Bay. By the end of the Middle Pacific Period nearly all parts of California had been settled.

Middle Pacific cultures continued to increase their emphasis on anadromous fish, acorns, seeds, and to a lesser degree large animals. Population densities rose, and burial data indicate that a greater degree of social complexity began to emerge. Trade increased. Houses were built more substantially, suggesting a greater degree of sedentism than in the Early Pacific. The Middle Pacific saw the growing productivity of the Pacific way of life, the development of permanent communities in areas that previously were occupied only seasonally, and the consequent growth in size and complexity of populations.

Where Early Pacific traditions were well established, they evolved gradually into the Middle Pacific. The Cosumnes and Campbell traditions are examples. The Middle Pacific traditions described below, however, are chosen from three areas of the state not previously discussed, in order to illustrate what occurred in the rest of California.

The Bidwell Tradition (Map 35). Bidwell is a Middle Pacific tradition of the Oroville area in the southern Cascades (Fig. 45). Emerging around 2,000 years ago and lasting until about A.D. 1000 (1,000 years ago), during the Late Pacific Period, it shows an increasingly focal economy when compared to Early Pacific sites in the same area (known locally as the Mesilla Tradition). Bidwell sites were situated in the foothills overlooking the Feather River and its tributaries. Riverine, chaparral, oak parkland, and lower Transition Zone habitats are associated with these sites. Introduction of the bow and arrow during Bidwell times suggests that there was an increased focus on hunting compared with the Mesilla Tradition (Fig. 46). There also was an increasingly focal emphasis on seed collection and, to a somewhat lesser degree, acorn harvesting. Burials show the acquisition of more exotic materials, such as seashells and obsidian, suggesting a growing importance of trade. There is also evidence of a greater degree of village sedentism than earlier (Ritter 1970).

The Bidwell Tradition seems to capture a culture in the process of evolving toward a full expression of the Pacific way of life, describing Pacific institutions midway in their development from the preceding Mesilla Tradition to the subsequent Oroville. Similar developments

Map 35. Distribution of the Bidwell Tradition.

Fig. 45. The Bidwell Tradition, from the Middle Pacific Period, existed in the foothills of the southern Cascades near Oroville. This Bidwell site occupies a knoll overlooking the Feather River in an area now drowned by the Oroville Reservoir. The excavation unit in the foreground revealed a dark midden almost 3 feet deep (about 90 cm). Acorn processing was an important activity at the site, as shown by the quantity of ash, greasy soil, fire-cracked rock, carbonized acorn hulls, and fragments of ground-stone tools found there. Acorn use continued here through the rest of prehistory, but the settlements evolved from the seasonal campsites of Bidwell times to base camps for a montane culture by Late Pacific times.

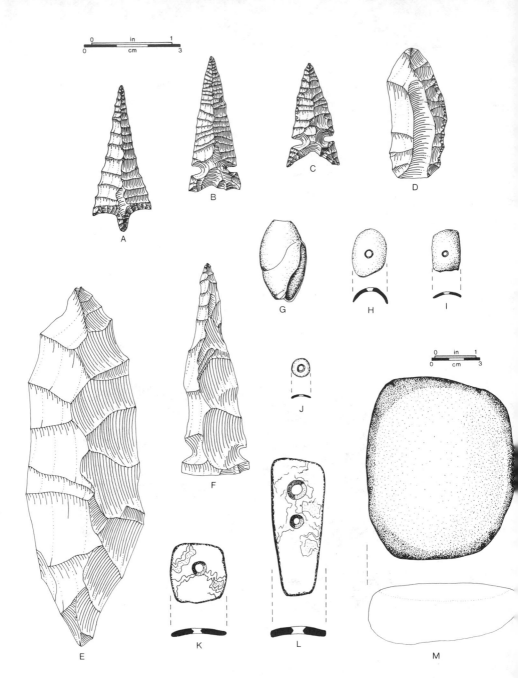

Fig. 46. Artifacts typical of the Bidwell Tradition: *a*, stemmed projectile point; *b*, side-notched projectile point; *c*, "desert side-notched" projectile point with basal notch; *d*, side scraper on a flake; *e*, basalt knife or bifacially retouched tool; *f*, basalt bifacially retouched drill; *g*, whole, spire-lopped *Olivella*-shell bead; *h*, *Olivella*-shell saucer bead; *i*, square-cut *Olivella*-shell bead; *j*, *Olivella*-shell disk bead; *k*, *Haliotis*-shell (abalone) bead; *l*, *Haliotis*-shell pendant; *m*, ground-stone muller or mano; *n*, milling stone; *o*, polishing stone; *p*, pecking stone; *q*, abrading stone. (After Jewell 1964; Olsen & Riddell 1963; Ritter 1970.)

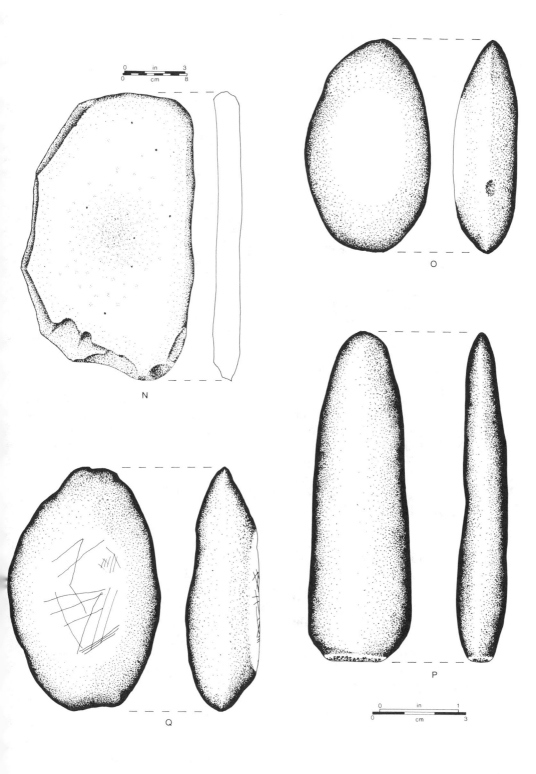

N

O

P

Q

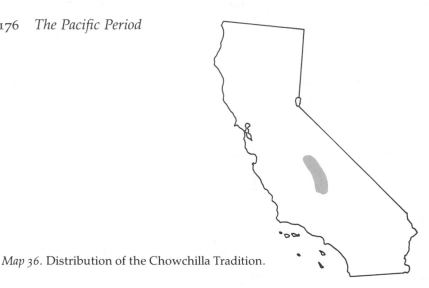

Map 36. Distribution of the Chowchilla Tradition.

were occurring farther south along the Sierra in comparable foothill environments. Bennyhoff (1956) and Fitzwater (1962, 1968) have defined a Crane Flat Complex in the Yosemite area, which began in the Middle Pacific and exhibited a focal orientation toward deer hunting and the use of hard seeds (see also Elsasser 1960). Acorn use, modest in early Crane Flat occupations, grew over time. Other similarities with Bidwell sites are still uncertain, owing to a lack of substantial excavations, but traces from tested sites indicate that the cultural developments of the two foothill regions were generally comparable. As the following discussion of the Chowchilla Tradition indicates, these similarities extended over an even wider area.

The Chowchilla Tradition (Map 36). Permanent settlement in the southern Sierra, begun during Middle Pacific times, is represented by the Chowchilla Tradition. The earliest C-14 dates for Chowchilla sites are about 2,200 years old (200 B.C.), and the tradition lasted until about 1,100–1,200 years ago (A.D. 800–900). Sites of this tradition are found in the lower valleys of Sierran rivers from Yosemite to Three Rivers. The sites show that people lived in fairly small settlements situated on terraces along the major streams. Milling tools and faunal remains in their sites indicate that their resources came primarily from seed collection, salmon fishing, and deer hunting—another example of a transitional adaptation (Fig. 47). Acorn processing was apparently not yet of major importance. The areas that the Chowchillans occupied—the valley-oak parklands adjacent to the chaparral and riverine habitats—provided plenty of acorns, but the absence of mortars, pestles, and acorn remains in sites indicates that Chowchilla

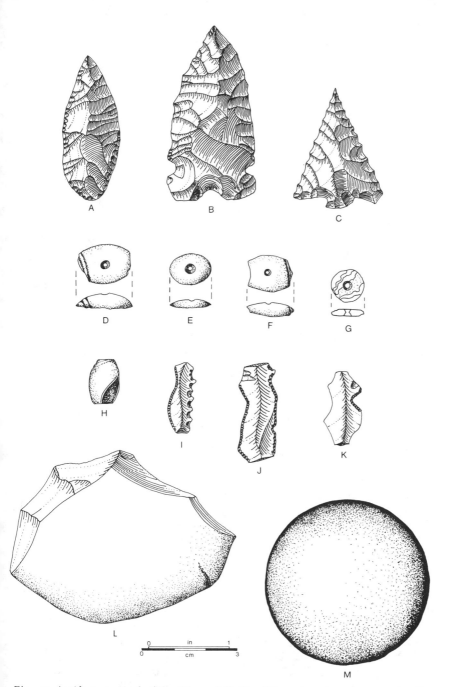

Fig. 47. Artifacts typical of the Chowchilla Tradition: *a*, convex-base projectile point; *b*, side-notched projectile point with concave base; *c*, stemmed projectile point; *d*, split, drilled *Olivella*-shell bead; *e*, saucer-shaped *Olivella*-shell bead; *f*, saddle-shaped *Olivella*-shell bead; *g*, *Haliotis*-shell (abalone) disk bead; *h*, whole, spire-lopped *Olivella*-shell bead; *i*, denticulate scraper on a microblade; *j*, compound scraper on a microblade; *k*, notched tool on a microblade; *l*, chopping tool on a basalt core; *m*, stone ball. (After Aikens 1978; Moratto 1971; Peak 1976.)

Map 37. Distribution of the Amargosa Tradition.

people did not take advantage of this resource. Studies of the descriptions of Chowchilla sites suggest that winter base camps were still used, and some aspects of the Late Archaic style of summer foraging in the mountains persisted in Chowchilla times (Aikens 1978; Moratto 1971; Peak 1976).

The Amargosa Tradition (Map 37). Amargosa is an arid-lands tradition associated with southeastern California's playas and ranges. It is generally regarded as having emerged by about 2,500–3,000 years ago (500–1000 B.C.) and to have lasted until around 1,000 years ago (A.D. 1000; Wallace 1962a). A number of manifestations of this tradition are scattered across the desert basins, but most of them cannot be dated very accurately. C-14 dating of the stratified, or multilayered, Rose Spring Site in Inyo County indicates that Amargosa belongs in the Middle Pacific as an outgrowth of the earlier Pinto Basin Tradition (which emerged in the Middle Archaic and persisted into the Early Pacific; Lanning 1963).

The bow and arrow was introduced to this area during Amargosa times, enhancing the Amargosans' concentration on hunting deer and antelope. Remnants of nets found preserved in caves suggest that collective hunts for antelope and rabbits began at this time; cooperative hunting characterized Pacific people in this area and to a lesser extent in the Great Basin to the east, where cultures continued to follow lifeways more nearly similar to the Archaic (Fig. 48).

In order to more effectively focus their economy on mesquite beans and screw-bean pods, Amargosans improved the milling tools that had been first introduced during Pinto Basin times. The desert and foothill environments of the Amargosans were not rich enough to permit the development of truly sedentary villages or even large communities, but the application of Pacific subsistence methods to desert resources allowed a greater degree of sedentism and larger and more complex societies than had been possible during Archaic times (A. Hunt 1960; C. Hunt 1975; Wallace 1962b, 1977).

Some climatic evidence suggests that severe high temperatures and aridity may have reduced populations in the desert regions, or driven them out altogether, during part of the Late Archaic; scholars are

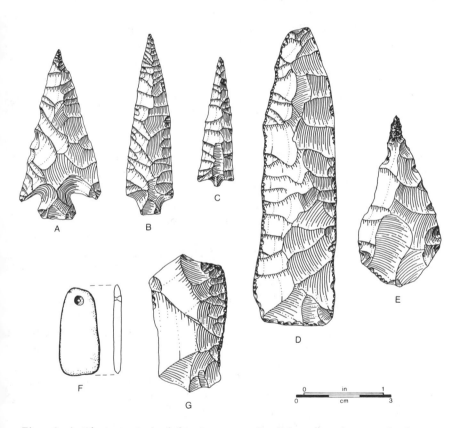

Fig. 48. Artifacts typical of the Amargosa Tradition: *a*, corner-notched projectile point; *b*, contracting-stem projectile point; *c*, corner-notched projectile point; *d*, knife on a bladelike biface; *e*, drill on a bifacially retouched flake; *f*, ground-slate pendant; *g*, side scraper on a flake. (After C. Hunt 1975; Lanning 1963; Wallace 1962b, 1977.)

divided about whether the region was truly abandoned, however (Aikens 1978; Hester 1973; Jennings 1974; Madsen 1978; Madsen & Berry 1975). After 4,000 years ago (2000 B.C.), however, environmental conditions became moderate enough that a Pacific style of subsistence could be introduced to the region.

The Late Pacific (A.D. 500–1500)

The *Late Pacific* is known in the archaeological literature as the Protohistoric Period because it was then that the historically known California Indian cultures took their final form (C. King 1978). During the Late Pacific, almost all the economic, technological, and social traits characteristic of the historical cultures were fully developed. Riverine and ocean fishing reached their greatest productivity. Population levels rose markedly and societies became increasingly complex. An increase in the variety and amount of trade was linked to the development of a shell-bead money system. Throughout the state, cultures increased their reliance on particular combinations of resources. The development of oceangoing canoes, fish dams, and specialized storage structures at this time demonstrates how focal these economies had become.

We should note that the growing richness of Pacific life did not occur equally throughout the state. The varieties and amounts of resources Pacific people were able to take advantage of differed from place to place. As a result, the size and complexity of Pacific societies differed. In the southeastern deserts, for instance, resources were too scant to permit the establishment of large, sedentary villages with complex social organizations. Pacific life in that part of the state could not become as elaborate as it became along the southern California coast, where resources were more abundant. In fact, one trend throughout the Pacific Period was the growing disparity in size and complexity among communities in different parts of the state. Nevertheless, people in regions of scantier resources still practiced Pacific-style adaptations during this period. They traded in regional networks, collected and stored seasonal surpluses, and organized work collectively. By doing so, they achieved greater population size, community sedentism, and social complexity than they would have in the same environment by the use of Archaic patterns.

Cultural traditions of the Late Pacific continued the trend toward regional differences and localized, intensified resource exploitation. To illustrate, we have selected examples from the southwestern, central, and northwestern parts of the state: the Canaliño, Hotchkiss, and Northwestern California traditions (see Map 38).

The Canaliño Tradition (Map 39). Canaliño is the name given by David Rogers (1929) to the late prehistoric cultures of the Santa Barbara
coast and the offshore islands along the Santa Barbara Channel. Similar cultures existed from the north side of Point Conception to Orange
County. From their homes along the coastal littoral, Canaliño people
made excursions both out to sea and inland, into the oak groves,
grasslands, and chaparral. They developed an extremely focal economy, based on two techniques: offshore fishing and sea-mammal
hunting using plank canoes, and the seasonal collection of acorns,
hard seeds, and shellfish (Grant 1978; Hudson 1976; Hudson, Timbrook & Rempe 1978; Landberg 1965; Orr 1943). Island populations
were not able to make use of significant amounts of land-based resources and consequently were even more focused on fishing, sea-
mammal hunting, and shellfish collection than were their mainland
counterparts (Glassow 1977; Meighan & Eberhart 1953; Orr 1968;
Reinman 1964; Ruby 1966). Canaliño sites in the interior of the mainland tend to lack much evidence of oceanic resources, but they do
show focal concentrations on acorns, hard seeds, and deer hunting
(Leonard 1966, 1971; Meighan 1954; Rozaire 1960; Singer & Gibson
1970). Some of these inland sites saw seasonal exploration by people
from coastal settlements who moved into the interior for portions of
the year; others may represent permanent inland populations who
varied their site use according to the seasons. The existence of an inland variant of the Canaliño tradition and the recognition of which
sites belong to it have been debated among archaeologists for years
(see, for example, Galdikas 1968; Glassow 1965; Leonard 1966).

Canaliño communities were large and socially complex, with up to
1,500 people living in one settlement (Blackburn 1974; Greenwood
1972; C. King 1978). The degree of social complexity varied with size
and situation; the most complex communities were large settlements
on the coast that served as trade centers and dominated surrounding
areas. Less centrally situated settlements appear to have been more
egalitarian (L. Bean 1974, 1978; C. King 1980; L. King 1969; Stickel
1968; Thomas & Beaton 1968).

The Canaliño developed a rich artistic tradition in stone, shell, and
bone (see, for example, Figs. 49 and 50). They were responsible for
some of North America's most noteworthy cave paintings, and their
basketry was among the continent's finest (Grant 1965, 1978). Their
economies were characterized by extensive regional and local trade
and the development of shell-bead money (Chagnon 1970; J. Davis
1961; Greenwood 1978; C. King 1974, 1978; Landberg 1965; Orr 1968).

During the span of this Late Pacific tradition, ancestors of the his-

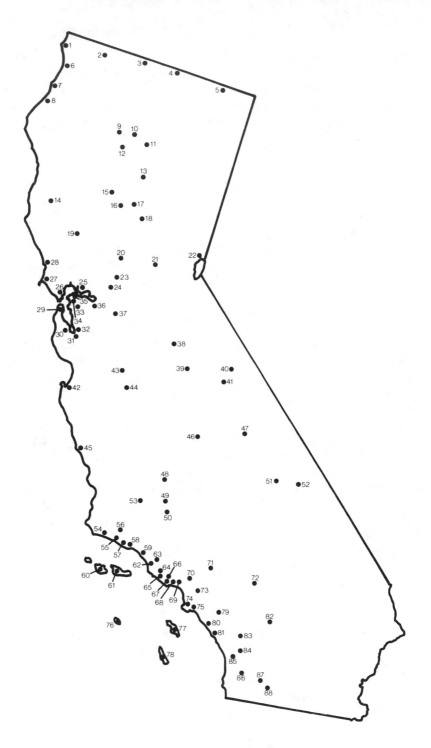

Map 38. Selected sites of the Late and Final Pacific periods (A.D. 500–1769).

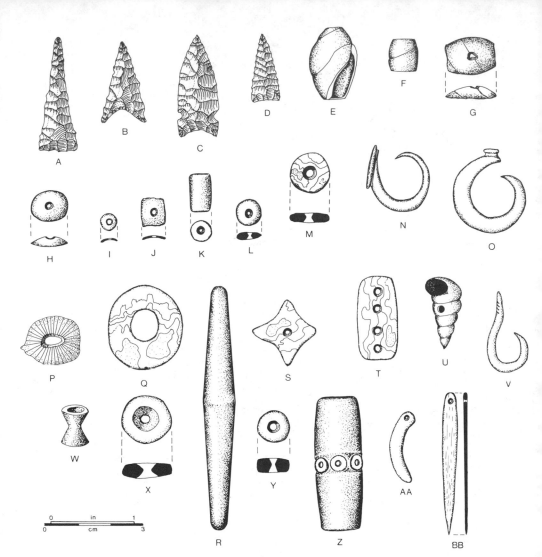

Fig. 49. Artifacts typical of the Canaliño Tradition: *a*, straight-base projectile point; *b*, concave-base projectile point; *c*, side-notched projectile point with concave base; *d*, straight-base projectile point; *e*, whole, spire-lopped *Olivella*-shell bead; *f*, barrel, spire-lopped *Olivella*-shell bead; *g*, split, punched *Olivella*-shell bead; *h*, saucer-shaped *Olivella*-shell bead; *i*, *Olivella*-shell disk bead; *j*, *Olivella*-shell rectangular bead; *k*, *Tivela*-shell tube bead; *l*, *Mytilus*-shell disk bead; *m*, *Haliotis*-shell (abalone) disk bead; *n,o*, *Haliotis*-shell circular fishhooks; *p*, keyhole-limpet-shell bead; *q*, *Haliotis*-shell disk (fishhook blank); *r*, sandstone reamer for making fishhooks; *s*, star-shaped *Haliotis*-shell ornament; *t*, *Haliotis*-shell ornament; *u*, *Cerithidea*-shell bead; *v*, bone fishhook; *w*, fish-vertebra bead; *x*, ground-stone serpentine disk bead; *y*, steatite (soapstone) disk bead; *z*, steatite tube bead inlaid with clamshell disk beads set in asphaltum; *aa*, steatite pendant (possible claw effigy); *bb*, pierced-bone needle; *cc*, ringed pestle; *dd*, ringed and incised steatite pipe; *ee*, stone-bowl mortar; *ff*, steatite bowl; *gg*, steatite *comal*, or griddle; *hh*, Canaliño adult-male burial position showing associated artifacts (typical of Late and Final Pacific periods; after Wallace 1962b). (After Glasgow 1965, 1977; Grant 1978; L. King 1969; Landberg 1965; D. Rogers 1929.)

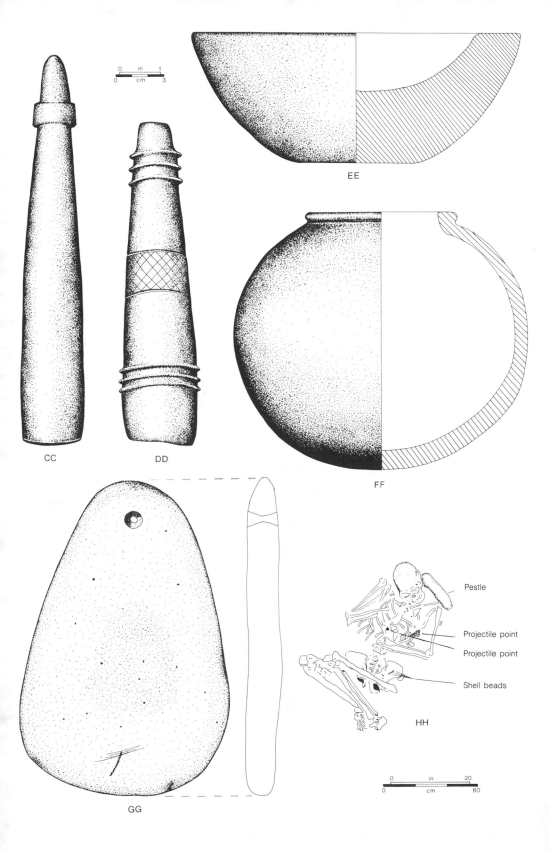

CC

DD

EE

FF

GG

HH

Pestle

Projectile point

Projectile point

Shell beads

Map 39. Distribution of the Canaliño Tradition.

torically known Shoshonean or Numic-speaking peoples (Gabrielino, Juaneño, and Luiseño) apparently migrated from the Great Basin and settled on the coast. Linguistic evidence places this migration between A.D. 500 and 1000, or 1,000–1,500 years ago. Some distinct new artifact complexes that appeared at this time seem to provide the archaeological support for this linguistically based hypothesis (Aikens 1978; Paul Chace, pers. comm. 1980; Shipley 1978; True 1966; Warren 1968). If this theory is true, these newcomers apparently adapted quickly to the Canaliño way of life.

The Hotchkiss Tradition (Map 40). This tradition represents the protohistoric cultures of the Delta region in central California. Its roots lie in the earlier Cosumnes Tradition of the Middle Pacific, but it had become a recognizable archaeological tradition of its own by about 1,500

Fig. 50. Canaliño steatite whale, inlaid with clamshell disk beads.

years ago (A.D. 500). Originally defined by Lillard, Heizer, and Fenenga (1939), Hotchkiss was first conceived as a historically distinct complex of artifacts from the Delta area and was termed the "Late Horizon" (Beardsley 1954; Heizer 1964; Meighan 1959a; Ragir 1972). The Hotchkiss Tradition lasted throughout the Late Pacific and Final Pacific, and was brought to a close only by the immigration of Europeans into central California.

During Hotchkiss times, acorns and salmon achieved paramount importance as foods, and deer hunting continued to be important. Hard seeds, waterfowl, and other resources were harvested but were not central to subsistence. Hotchkiss people lived in large, sedentary settlements spread along the lower San Joaquin and Sacramento rivers, along the lower river valleys east of the Delta, and in the Delta itself (see Fig. 51). Hotchkiss people had ready access to riverine, floodplain, oak-grove, grassland, and chaparral resources. Expeditions into the Sierra made Transition Zone and coniferous resources available to the settlements as well.

Compared with settlements of the Cosumnes Tradition, those of Hotchkiss times were larger, more numerous, and denser, reflecting significant population growth. Large pit-house villages had storage facilities and sizable semi-subterranean houses (see Fig. 52). Trade goods were abundant and varied, and burials reflect a large, wealthy, socially stratified society in the marked differences in the amount of wealth goods accompanying the burials. The pattern of tightly flexed burials, begun in Cosumnes times, continued during the Hotchkiss, but Hotchkiss people also began to cremate some of their dead in sig-

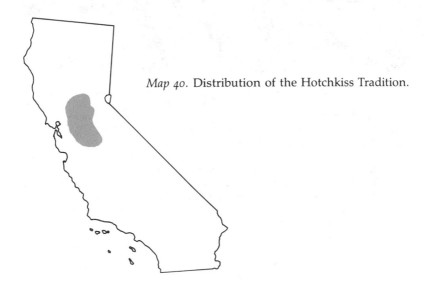

Map 40. Distribution of the Hotchkiss Tradition.

nificant numbers. The social significance of cremation versus interment of bodies is still not fully understood (Ragir 1972).

Hotchkiss artistry was exceptional, judging from surviving artifacts
of stone, bone, and shell (Fig. 53). Manufacturing tools such as mortars and pestles were particularly well shaped and finished. Projectile
points and certain other functional artifact forms are represented by
some large and fragile examples. These delicate artifacts almost certainly could not have been intended as implements, and more likely
were intended for wealth, status, or religious use and display. Hotchkiss people made a number of artifacts of bone. Some were utilitarian,
such as awls, needles, and barbed harpoon heads; others, such as

Fig. 51. A village of 40 Final Pacific pit houses, sheltered within a Sacramento
Valley oak grove. The oaks may have first drawn the settlers, but acorn use
probably helped the grove to grow. The site now covers 5 acres (2 hectares),
but aerial photographs and surface study show that it once covered 11 acres
(5 hectares) and may have included up to 90 houses. A larger house, 30 feet
across (9 meters), lies near the site's center; was it the headman's house? Perhaps 500–700 people lived here when the site was occupied 300–400 years
ago. In addition to acorns from the oaks, the people could harvest salmon
from the stream that ran by the village until Gold Rush miners diverted the
channel. The many resources of the Sierra foothills lay less than 2 miles away
(about 3 km), oak parklands surrounded the village, and the riverine floodplain lay only a few miles downstream.

Fig. 52. Site 4-Butte-1 (CA-But-1), near Chico in the Sacramento River Valley, occupied in Late and Final Pacific times. The floor of House 45 exposed here is typical of Final Pacific pit houses at this site. In the center of the dish-shaped floor of packed earth, excavators found a stone-rimmed fire hearth. The floor, about 18 feet across (5.5 m), is rimmed with a dozen stout posts that had held up the roof. Near the hearth, a combination mortar-and-milling stone made on a block of stone is set flush in the floor to serve as a kitchen appliance. To the left is an oval pit, apparently used for storage. Smaller holes are post-occupation rodent burrows. A cache of pestles and stone hammers in the left foreground had been abandoned when the house caught fire and collapsed. The pestles, of stones of different coarseness, may have been used to prepare particular foods of different textures. To the rear of the picture excavators have exposed an earlier house over which House 45 was built; a third house was built later. This sequence shows that although house function stayed the same from the end of the Late Pacific Period to the end of the Final Pacific Period, average house size increased by 50 percent in this village and roof structures became progressively sturdier.

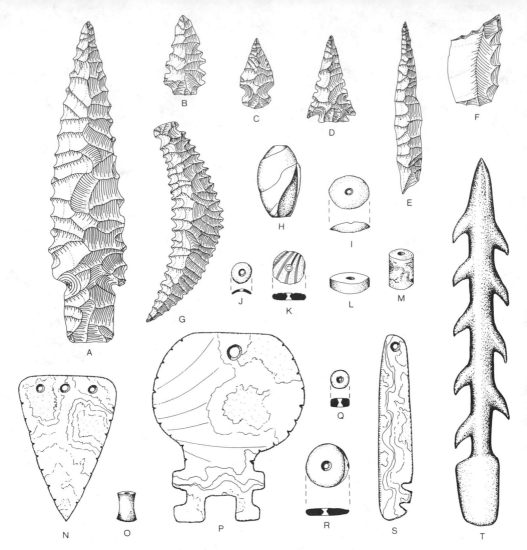

Fig. 53. Artifacts typical of the Hotchkiss Tradition: *a*, large, serrate, stemmed projectile point; *b*, serrate, corner-notched projectile point; *c*, side-notched projectile point with convex base; *d*, serrate, corner-notched projectile point; *e*, drill on a bifacially retouched flake; *f*, graver on a flake side scraper; *g*, "Stockton curve," a serrate, bifacially retouched curved piece, possibly used by dancers to represent bear claws; *h*, whole, spire-lopped *Olivella*-shell bead; *i*, saucer-shaped *Olivella*-shell bead; *j*, *Olivella*-shell disk bead; *k*, *Saxidomus*-clamshell disk bead; *l*, steatite disk bead; *m*, magnesite tubular bead; *n*, *Haliotis*-shell (abalone) ornament; *o*, steatite "hourglass" tubular bead; *p*, *Haliotis*-shell ornament; *q,r*, clamshell disk beads (possibly *Tresus* sp.); *s*, *Haliotis*-shell ornament; *t*, barbed bone harpoon; *u*, incised-bone whistle; *v*, incised-bird-bone tube; *w*, bird-bone tube (possibly a bit for a stone pipe bowl); *x*, serrate-rib "saw"; *y*, charmstone; *z*, arrow-shaft straightener; *aa*, steatite labret (lip-plug) or ear-plug fragment; *bb*, stone pipe bowl; *cc*, clay ball; *dd*, stone-bowl mortar; *ee*, cupule rock or rain rock. Cupule rocks were boulders or exposed bedrock surfaces on which dozens or hundreds of small depressions or cupules had been chipped and ground. In some parts of the state this type of artifact has been associated with rain-making ceremonies, but in other cases its purpose is unknown. (After Beardsley 1954; Heizer 1964; Meighan 1959a; Ragir 1972.)

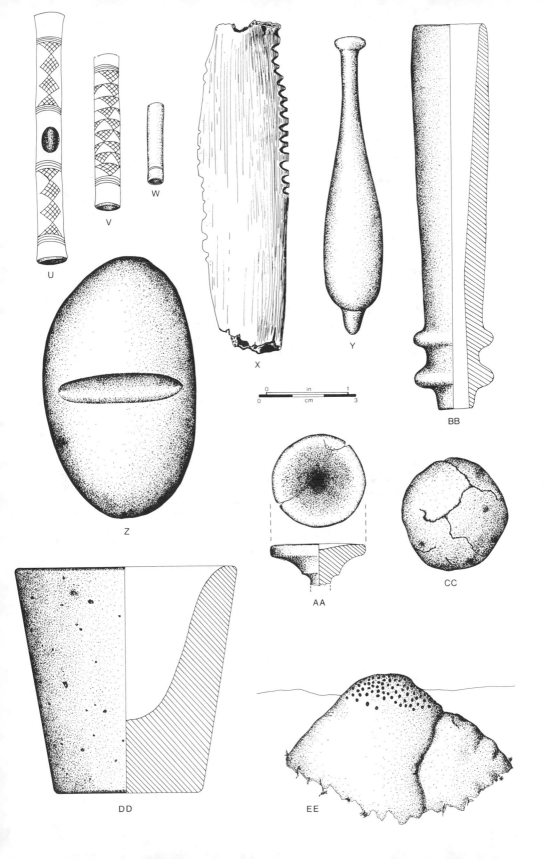

U

V

W

X

Y

BB

Z

AA

CC

DD

EE

Fig. 54. Unfired clay figurines from a Late Pacific site in Marin County. Although the use of them remains uncertain, the practice of making clay figurines became widespread through much of central California during the Pacific Period. Although these figures were unfired, some other clay artifacts were fired. In spite of their obvious familiarity with ceramic technology, Pacific groups in central California did not make pottery vessels. (Courtesy of the Lowie Museum of Anthropology, University of California, Berkeley)

Fig. 55. A baked clay bead (about an inch in diameter, or 2.6 cm) from a Late Pacific burial site in San Joaquin County. Hotchkiss Tradition burials from central California's Late Pacific Period tended to have greater varieties of grave goods than the earlier Cosumnes Tradition burials did. The use of ceramic technology in the making of beads was part of this diversity. (Courtesy of the Lowie Museum of Anthropology, University of California, Berkeley)

trimmed lengths of bird leg bone, were ornamental. The bird-bone tubes frequently were decorated with elaborate geometric patterns. A distinctive chipped-stone artifact was the "Stockton Curve," possibly a figure of a bear claw. Ground-stone charmstones were rarer than in earlier traditions, but ground-stone pipes were more common. Beads and ornaments of haliotis and olivella shell were particularly abundant. Hotchkiss people also did some work in fired and unfired clay, making beads, ornaments, and effigies (see Figs. 54 and 55).

As with earlier Delta traditions, Hotchkiss is known principally from cemetery excavations, and much of the ornamental art of this tradition is known from grave goods accompanying the burials. Much of our understanding of Hotchkiss lifeways comes from a wider pool of sites in central California. Although the specific constellation of traits that characterizes Hotchkiss tends to be concentrated in the Delta and surrounding areas, similar lifeways can be seen throughout the San Joaquin and Sacramento valleys and the San Francisco Bay Area, allowing for variations in local resources. The Bay Area, for example, had access to less salmon than the Central Valley but more shellfish and saltwater fish (J. Davis 1960; Davis & Treganza 1959; Gerow 1974; Gerow & Force 1968; Riddell 1955; Wallace & Lathrap 1975). Foothill resources were more accessible to the Sacramento Valley people than to the Delta people, owing to proximity, so the hard seeds of the foothills were used more for food staples in the Sacramento Valley; some evidence suggests that the proportion of milling stones and manos compared with mortars and pestles increases as one goes from the Sacramento River into the foothills (Chartkoff & Chartkoff 1968, 1980; Chartkoff, Johnson & Miller 1976). By comparison, Hotchkiss sites in the Delta are rich in mortars and pestles, but milling tools are rare or absent (Beardsley 1948).

Population densities in the San Joaquin Valley seem to have been somewhat lower than in the Delta or Sacramento Valley, even though lifeways were generally comparable. Environmental differences may have been responsible. The broad San Joaquin Valley is not as well watered as the Sacramento Valley, making salmon a somewhat less significant resource. Riverine resources were particularly sparse in the wide western half of the valley, which lies in the rain shadow of the Coast Ranges and is not drained by as many salmon-spawning streams as is the west side of the Sacramento Valley (compare, for example, Chartkoff & Childress 1974; Riddell & Olsen 1965; Treganza, Heickson & Woolfenden 1969). Consequently, focal economies in much of the San Joaquin Valley turned more to hard seeds, acorns, and deer than did Delta settlements of the Hotchkiss Tradition, and corresponding quantities of milling tools showed up in the valley sites.

Similar lifeways were pursued in the foothills of the Sierra, southern Cascades, and Coast Ranges, for the same basic reasons. In the foothills, riverine resources were less available (depending on the presence of salmon-carrying streams such as the Feather River or the American River), whereas chaparral, grassland, oak-grove, and Transition Zone staples were more accessible. These areas, lying adjacent to the Central Valley as they did, participated in trade relations

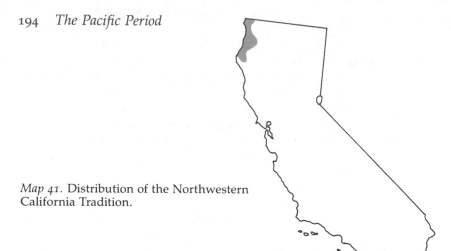

Map 41. Distribution of the Northwestern
California Tradition.

and other interactions. Understandably, a number of artifact styles and
other cultural remains of the Hotchkiss Tradition are found in sites of
these surrounding areas, but each area is characterized by its own
unique combination of artifacts (see, for example, Frederickson 1974a;
J. Johnson 1967; Meighan 1955; Olsen & Payen 1968; Olsen & Riddell
1963; Payen & Boloyan 1963; Ritter 1970; Treganza 1958a, 1959).

The Northwestern California Tradition (Map 41). There is no description of a Northwestern California Tradition in the archaeological literature, but several recent excavations along the northern California
coast reveal a distinctive Late Pacific cultural pattern. Major excavations at Patrick's Point, Trinidad, and Point St. George have been supplemented by smaller-scale studies in Redwood National Park and
several other localities. Combined with older studies done at Gunther
Island (near Eureka), they reveal that a distinctive maritime/riverine
culture revolving around fishing developed there some time after
1,500 years ago (A.D. 500; Bickel 1979; Bickel & Salzman 1979; Elsasser
& Heizer 1966; Gould 1966; Heizer 1951; Heizer & Elsasser 1964; Heizer
& Mills 1952; Loud 1918; Mills 1950; Theodoratus, Chartkoff & Chartkoff 1979). Anadromous fish, offshore schooling fish, sea mammals,
and deer provided a rich subsistence base. Coastal middens reveal
that these communities were large, complex, and generally sedentary,
and enriched by artistic traditions and elaborate trade networks. A
money system also arose in this area, based on strings of dentalium
shells imported from Puget Sound (see Fig. 56). On the basis of this
information, we have recognized a Northwestern California Tradition
for the Late Pacific Period (Hughes 1978).

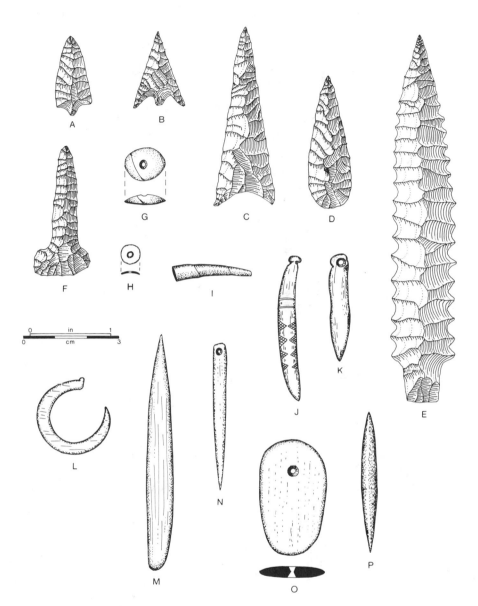

Fig. 56. Artifacts typical of the Northwestern California Tradition: *a*, contracting-stem projectile point; *b*, "Gunther Island Barbed" projectile point; *c*, concave-base projectile point; *d*, convex-base projectile point; *e*, serrate projectile point with stemmed base; *f*, drill on a bifacially retouched flake; *g*, saucer-shaped *Olivella*-shell bead; *h*, *Olivella*-shell disk bead; *i*, *Dentalium*-shell bead; *j*, incised-bone "head scratcher"; *k*, pierced deer-bone (metapodial) pendant; *l*, bone circular fishhook; *m*, bone awl; *n*, pierced-bone needle; *o*, pierced-bone disk; *p*, bone double-pointed toggle; *q*, barbed bone harpoon; *r*, steatite pipe; *s*, elk-antler wedge; *t*, slate zooform club; *u*, steatite dish or shallow bowl; *v*, large chert biface; *w*, chipped-stone net weight; *x*, ground-stone net weight; *y*, stone strigel; *z*, antler tine; *aa*, nosed scraper on a flake; *bb*, denticulate scraper; *cc*, burin; *dd*, teshoa flake. (After Gould 1966; Heizer & Elsasser 1964; Heizer & Mills 1952; Loud 1918.)

Continued

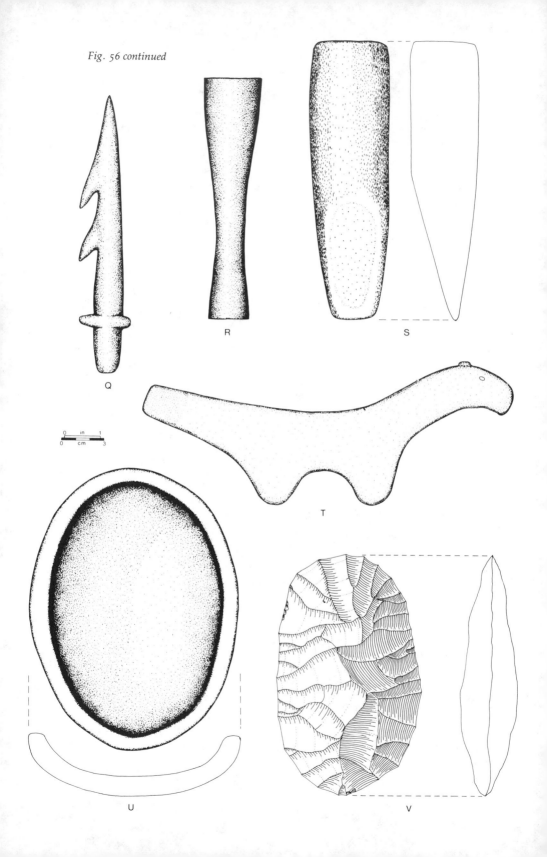

Fig. 56 continued

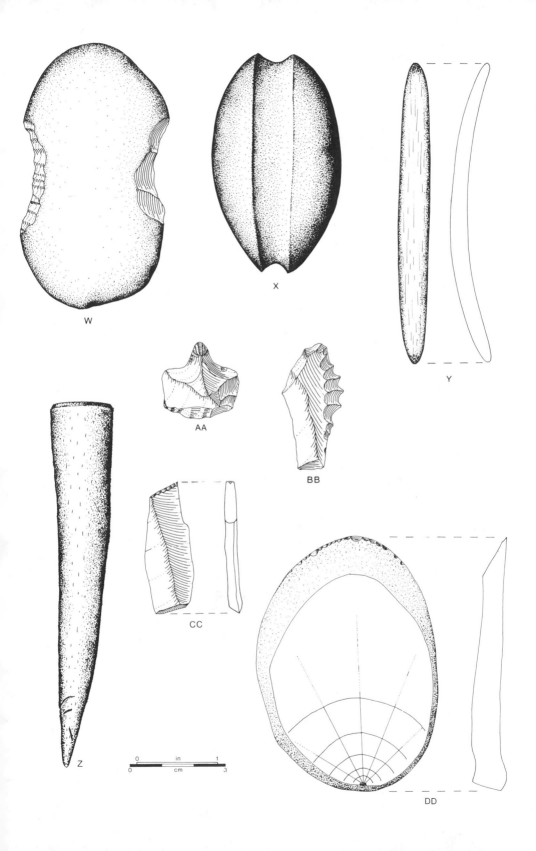

W

X

Y

AA

BB

Z

CC

DD

0   in   1
0   cm   3

The Northwestern California Tradition shares many traits with other Late Pacific traditions, such as a focal economy, social stratification, a money system, extensive trade, the storage and redistribution of food surpluses, and high-quality craftsmanship in chipped stone, ground stone, shell, and bone. Like a number of other Late Pacific traditions, this one produced an excellent basketry art. Along with the Canaliño the people of the Northwestern California Tradition manufactured oceangoing canoes, although theirs were dugouts rather than plank canoes.

At the same time, Northwestern California had features more in common with the cultures of the Pacific Northwest, such as rectangular plank houses, slavery, and wealth-display ceremonies (see Fig. 57). For this reason Kroeber set the Northwestern California area apart from the California culture area, regarding it as the southernmost extension of the Northwest Coast culture area (1939). More recent research shows that Northwestern California had a unique cultural florescence that, while it bore some resemblance to the Pacific Northwest, related at least as well to the rest of California. It should not be regarded as peripheral or marginal, but as a flourishing area in its own right. Its characteristics were shaped partly by its unique environmental setting in the coastal redwood zone and partly by its interactions with its neighbors.

The artifacts of this tradition include a number of distinctive forms (see Fig. 56). Among projectile points the "Gunther Island barbed" is most characteristic, but stemmed and concave-base points are also common. Obsidian is a particularly common material for point manufacture, and since none occurs in the region, imports from eastern Siskiyou County, Lake County, and southern Oregon were acquired through trade. Extremely large, delicate obsidian blades were items of great wealth. The maritime orientation of this tradition is seen in its variety of barbed and simple bone harpoon points, stone net weights, and curved shell fishhooks. Bone needles and awls indicate the importance of basketmaking, and elk antler wedges, stone adzes, and stone mauls suggest the great importance of woodworking. Stone and magnesite beads were part of the tradition's money and wealth complex, in addition to shell beads of olivella and dentalium.

Ground stone played a distinctive role in this technology, since milling tools were rare. In addition to well-formed pestles, stone-tool makers worked steatite to create a variety of bowls and platters. A number of slate zoomorphic "clubs" have been found (see Fig. 58). These clubs are often called "slave killers." The name appears to come from the Pacific Northwest, where the ritual killing of slaves was practiced, and where zoomorphic clubs were associated with the act.

Fig. 57. Yurok White Deerskin Dance. This 1923 photograph shows one of the public rituals of the great Northwestern California World Renewal ceremonial cycle. The ceremonies, which have been held since Late Pacific times, feature a line of male dancers displaying the hides of albino mule deer. Albinism is rare in deer, and the hides of albino deer were enormously valuable in traditional Northwestern California cultures. The public display of these treasures confirmed the wealth and prestige of their owners, while contributing to the ceremonies intended to keep the world in order. Families from dozens of different Yurok, Karok, and Hupa settlements traveled to attend these multi-day ceremonies. (U.S. Forest Service Photo)

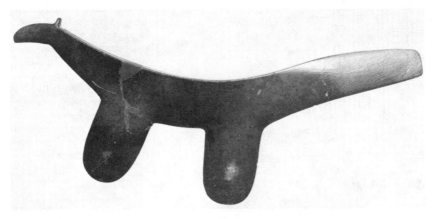

Fig. 58. This zooform serpentine club from the Eureka area in coastal northern California shows the excellence of stoneworking in the Late or Final Pacific Period. It provides one kind of evidence for the development of craft specialization or semi-specialization by Late Pacific times (A.D. 500–1500). (Courtesy of the Lowie Museum of Anthropology, University of California, Berkeley)

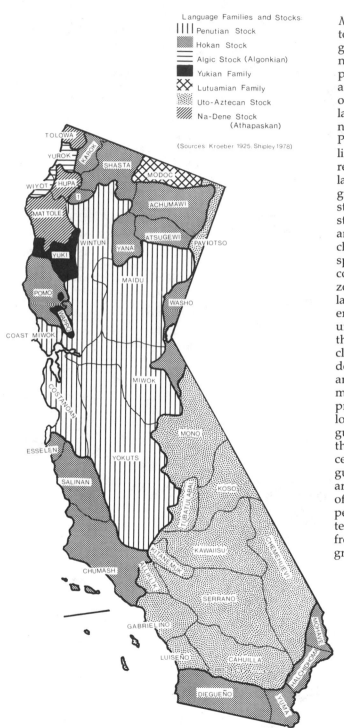

(Sources Kroeber 1925. Shipley 1978)

Language Families and Stocks:

‖‖‖	Penutian Stock
▨	Hokan Stock
≡	Algic Stock (Algonkian)
■	Yukian Family
⧓	Lutuamian Family
⠿	Uto-Aztecan Stock
⧄	Na-Dene Stock (Athapaskan)

Map 42. Distribution of historical languages and language stocks. By the late nineteenth century, anthropologists had discovered and mapped the distribution of almost all the aboriginal languages spoken in California (see Heizer 1978c: 2; Powers 1976). Subsequent linguistic analysis revealed relationships among some languages, which were grouped into families and stocks. Some families and stocks, such as Athapaskan and Algonkian, proved closely related to languages spoken elsewhere on the continent. The Navajo of Arizona speak an Athapaskan language, for example. Others, such as Yukian, seemed unique to California. Anthropologists assume that closely related languages are descended from a common ancestor. The linguistic method of glottochronology provides estimates of how long ago two related languages were separated from their presumed common ancestor language. Thus linguistic analysis provides archaeologists with models of past relationships among peoples, which can then be tested against artifactual data from prehistory. Numbered group: 1, Chimariko.

The name was apparently given to virtually identical artifacts found in northwestern California, although there is no evidence to support the contention that they were ever actually used to kill slaves (Kroeber 1925: 32–33; Pilling 1978: 141).

A fascinating aspect of Late Pacific prehistory in northwestern California is the apparent migration of several groups into the region. Linguistic evidence indicates that ancestors of the Algonkian-speaking Yurok and Wiyot, and ancestors of the Athapaskan-speaking Tolowa, Hupa, Chilula, Whilkut, Nongatl, Mattole, and Sinkyone, migrated into northwestern California between 1,100 and 900 years ago (A.D. 900–1100), to join the ancestors of the Hokan-speaking Karok already residing in the region (Baumhoff & Olmstead 1964; Hoijer 1956). Linguists feel that the Algonkian speakers originated in the St. Lawrence River area east of the Great Lakes, whereas the homeland of the Athapaskan speakers lay in western Canada. When linked with the hypothesized migration of Shoshonean speakers at a slightly earlier date, this linguistic evidence suggests that a number of long-range migrations across the continent took place over a considerable period of time. If these migrations occurred, they would add a new dimension of drama and complexity to the study of American prehistory (Map 42).

What is well established is that, regardless of their routes and dates of arrival, peoples with radically different languages had settled in northwestern California by around 1,000 years ago. In spite of language differences, these peoples soon came to share the same general social, political, economic, and religious traits. Kroeber states that the cultures of the Yurok, Karok, and Hupa are so similar that a description of one of their cultures can represent all three with only minor differences in detail (1925). Remarkably, in spite of these similarities and in spite of long traditions of intermarriage, these groups and their languages remained distinct (see Map 43; Elsasser & Heizer 1966; Heizer & Mills 1952; Pilling 1978 and pers. comm. 1978).

At the same time that new groups were apparently settling in northwestern California, the middle stretch of the Klamath River was apparently being settled for the first time—the last major part of the state to be permanently occupied. Radiocarbon dates from Iron Gate Reservoir and Seiad Valley indicate that the earliest settlement in this region began between 1,000 and 1,400 years ago, or A.D. 600–1000 (Helfin 1966; L. Johnson 1968; Leonhardy 1961, 1967; Theodoratus, Chartkoff & Chartkoff 1979). It is not clear why this region, rich in timber and supplied with abundant salmon runs along the Klamath, should not have been occupied earlier. One suggestion has been that

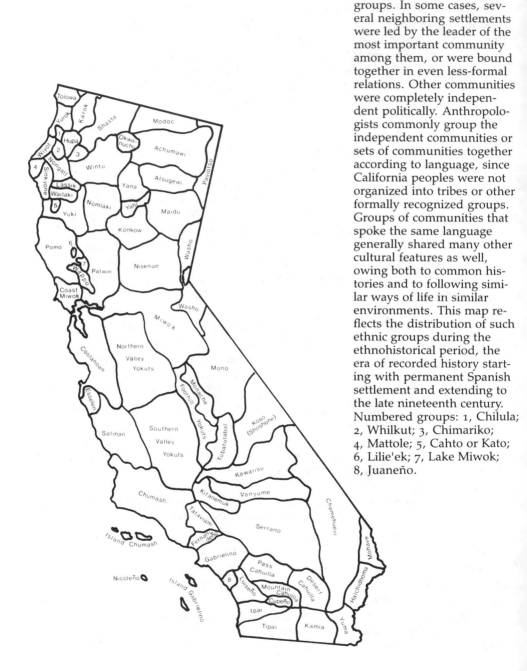

Map 43. Ethnohistorical groups. In some cases, several neighboring settlements were led by the leader of the most important community among them, or were bound together in even less-formal relations. Other communities were completely independent politically. Anthropologists commonly group the independent communities or sets of communities together according to language, since California peoples were not organized into tribes or other formally recognized groups. Groups of communities that spoke the same language generally shared many other cultural features as well, owing both to common histories and to following similar ways of life in similar environments. This map reflects the distribution of such ethnic groups during the ethnohistorical period, the era of recorded history starting with permanent Spanish settlement and extending to the late nineteenth century. Numbered groups: 1, Chilula; 2, Whilkut; 3, Chimariko; 4, Mattole; 5, Cahto or Kato; 6, Lilie'ek; 7, Lake Miwok; 8, Juaneño.

the region lacks useful stone for toolmaking and has few other food sources in any quantity. Permanent settlement may not have been possible until the Medicine Lake obsidian flow around A.D. 600 created a good supply of chippable stone, and the cultures downstream had perfected the practice of catching and preserving large surpluses of salmon (Chartkoff & Chartkoff 1973, 1975, 1979). An alternative is that the region, one of the least studied in the state, was settled as part of the same movement of peoples that brought the Algonkians and Athapaskans to the coastal area.

The Final Pacific (A.D. 1500-1769)

This period represents the final episode in the development of Native Californian cultures before the settlement of Europeans. During this period California cultures reached their greatest population levels and their most complex forms. The shell-bead money system became fully developed and trade reached its maximum importance. As far as archaeologists know, population distributions remained generally the same as in the preceding period, although some adjustments were made along the coast, around San Francisco Bay, in the Central Valley, and in the northeast (C. King 1978; see also Map 38).

We have not described any Final Pacific cultural traditions because these Indian cultures have already been well depicted by ethnographers (e.g., Forbes 1969; Heizer 1978a; Heizer & Whipple 1971; Kroeber 1925; Merriam 1955; Murray 1965; Phillips 1975; Powers 1976; Steward 1933). By the time of the Final Pacific, all the basic institutions of historically known California cultures had been developed; only their final elaboration remained.

Ethnographers found that California Indians had settled every part of the state. Kroeber recognized 104 separate language groups in California, derived from seven distinct language stocks, or families. Each of the 104 groups was associated with a cluster of settlements in which people spoke the same language, but no all-embracing political organizations (Bean & King 1974). Although several adjacent settlements were often allied to form what has been called a *tribelet*, every tribelet was a sovereign political entity, a grouping of several settlements in a loose federation dominated by the headman of the most important settlement (see L. Bean 1978; Heizer 1978c).

Normally all the communities in a tribelet spoke the same language, but the speakers of a particular language might be dispersed among as many as 40–50 tribelets. In fact, despite the existence of tribelets, individual settlements were fairly autonomous. Since there were no political bonds uniting all the speakers of a language, there was no political basis for recognizing cultures in California. The speakers of the same language generally shared many other cultural traits as well, however, so Kroeber used language as the basic means for defining the different groups in the state.

The Pacific Period saw the emergence and development of these many varied California cultures. Many anthropologists believe that the state's languages were originally introduced by waves of immigrants who entered California, became established in an area, and expanded to fully occupy a particular region. It is assumed that, as people filled a region, those living in more distant settlements developed distinctive dialects compared to those remaining in the area of original settlement. Linguists find that distance and isolation tend to lead to divergence of speech within a language. In time, these differences grew large enough that the dialects became mutually unintelligible, and different languages emerged from a common ancestral stock (Hoijer 1956). This seems to have happened especially where settlements occupied somewhat different habitats or where settlements were far apart. Thus, in the Sacramento Valley, the people of the east side were Maiduan speakers, and the people west of the river were Wintuan speakers, both languages having evolved from a Penutian tongue (Proto-Penutian) spoken by their common ancestors. Subsequently, the northwestern Maidu developed a language (Konkow) separate from that of the southern Maidu (Nisenan), and both languages were different from the one spoken by the Maidu who lived in the southern Cascades and northern Sierra (Maidu). Similarly, the ancestral Wintuan tongue that evolved from Proto-Penutian became separated into distinct northern, central, and southern dialects, which eventually became three separate languages: Wintu, Nomlaki, and Patwin.

This model of language evolution has been adopted by many archaeologists to suggest the course of cultural evolution in the state. Other scholars, though acknowledging the value and stimulation of these reconstructions, place less emphasis on them and point to difficulties in their use. Archaeologists are still struggling to relate specific types of artifacts to specific language speakers, so it has been hard to test many of these hypothesized reconstructions. As the case of the Yurok, Karok, and Hupa (see above) indicates, peoples can share virtually identical material cultures while maintaining completely separate languages.

The reverse can also be true. Speakers of the same language can show considerable differences in other aspects of culture; Island and interior Chumash are a case in point (Grant 1978; Greenwood 1978). Furthermore, some archaeologists feel that using migrations to explain changes in the archaeological record begs the question. Even if migrations did occur, to identify them does not explain why they occurred, what happened to people already living in the area, or why the archaeological record changed as it did. These scholars prefer to pay more attention to conditions in the local environment in order to understand what happened in the past. Thus, although language studies might not provide answers to archaeologists' questions, they can stimulate further research by providing insights and hypotheses.

During the Final Pacific, California's population rose to more than 300,000 (Cook 1976a, 1978). One out of every ten Indians in America north of Mexico lived in California, one of the country's most favorable environments then as now. That Final Pacific people achieved one of the greatest population concentrations in pre-Columbian North America is in itself a remarkable achievement. That such large and rich cultures were developed without agriculture (see "Settlement," below, and Chapter 6) is all the more remarkable, and testifies to the genius and sophistication of the Pacific way of life.

THE PACIFIC WAY OF LIFE

So far the discussion of archaeological evidence for the Pacific Period has concentrated on the features distinguishing the traditions of different times and places within the period. It is appropriate to also look at the kinds of evidence that characterize the Pacific Period as a whole and help distinguish it from the Archaic Period. This evidence can then be related to the theoretical themes that characterize the Pacific Period.

Site Types

Pacific Period cultures continued to produce the types of sites made during the Archaic, but developed several new types as well: rock-art sites, ritual sites, astronomical sites, quarry sites, trading sites, and permanent villages.

Rock-Art Sites. The major features of rock-art sites are designs or pictures rendered on exposures of bedrock. Rich in prehistoric rock art, California may have more such remains than any other state. Most rock art is very difficult to date, since styles are rarely associated with specific cultural periods and the art rarely occurs in association with remains that can be dated with existing techniques. The consensus of professional opinion is that most prehistoric rock art in the

Fig. 59. This pictograph in the San Bernardino Mountains probably dates to the Late or Final Pacific Period. The pigments have been protected from weathering by the sheer canyon walls. The specific purpose and meanings of such rock paintings are still largely unknown. Vandalism unfortunately threatens many of the surviving examples of this prehistoric art tradition. (U.S. Forest Service Photo)

Fig. 60. Petroglyphs in Mono County. These rock carvings, in contrast to the painted pictographs, are cut into rock by pecking, grinding, and incising. Some designs have recognizable animal forms, but most are abstract or geometrical; human depictions are rare. Tens of thousands of rock carvings have been recorded, from most parts of the state; most probably date from the Pacific Period, though few can be dated accurately. As with the paintings, the true meanings and purposes for making most petroglyphs are still unknown. (U.S. Forest Service Photo)

state was made during the Pacific Period (Clewlow 1977, 1978; Garfinkel 1978; Grant, Baird & Pringle 1968; Heizer & Baumhoff 1962; Heizer & Clewlow 1973; Smith & Turner 1975).

Pacific Period rock art includes paintings (*pictographs*; see Fig. 59) and carved or incised designs (*petroglyphs*; see Fig. 60). Some authorities believe they can recognize certain changes in rock-art styles over time, and certain examples have been attributed to the Archaic Period. More certain is the existence of several regional styles from the Pacific Period (see, for example, Garfinkel 1978). Examples of rock art have been found in most parts of the state except northwestern California. The deserts of interior southern California appear to contain the richest and most varied petroglyph art. One canyon has more than 20,000 glyphs covering more than 5 miles (8 km) of canyon wall. A state park in the Gold Rush country near Jackson (Indian Grinding Rock State Historical Park) contains one of the most accessible petroglyph sites in central California, set among what may be the largest concentration of bedrock mortars in western North America (see Payen & Boloyan 1963). The Santa Barbara area contains many examples of remarkable Chumash pictographs, as illustrated in Campbell Grant's *The Rock Paintings of the Chumash* (1965). This art tradition is among the finest expressions of rock painting in the Western Hemisphere. A well-protected example is open to the public at Chumash Painted Cave State Park.

A unique variant of rock art is the desert *intaglio*. The term refers here to designs made on the floor of the open desert by arrangements of rocks. California is one of several parts of the world with giant ground drawings. The few surviving examples in the state are found in the southeastern deserts (see Fig. 61), where the activities of off-road-vehicle drivers threaten to destroy them. That some figures may have been made in the historical period is suggested by the apparent horse in the photograph. Others cannot be dated accurately, but their styles are similar to some petroglyph designs of Pacific Period age.

Although California rock-art traditions are still only partly understood by archaeologists, intense scholarship in recent years is beginning to shed some light on many aspects of this enigmatic cultural tradition (see, for example, Clewlow 1977, 1978; Heizer 1978d; Lee & Horne 1978).

Ritual Sites. Ritual sites, created especially for the conduct of religious or ritual activities, are known from several parts of the state, particularly from the Late and Final Pacific periods. Some contain distinctive rock structures or other features (Chartkoff & Chartkoff 1979; see also Fig. 62). Others contain specialized structures, such as sweathouses, but not residential structures (Hudson & Blackburn 1978; see also Fig. 63). Still others are found where groups of people assembled to perform ceremonies, sometimes adjacent to villages and sometimes not (Kroeber & Gifford 1949; see also Fig. 64).

Often there are no distinctive archaeological remains to mark such spots, but they are known instead from ethnographic records (for example, Hudson & Underhay 1978). A number of these sites are still being used today by Native Californian communities, one reason for our not drawing attention to particular examples. Ritual sites were generally located well away from regular settlements because in many California cultures important rituals had to be performed in isolation.

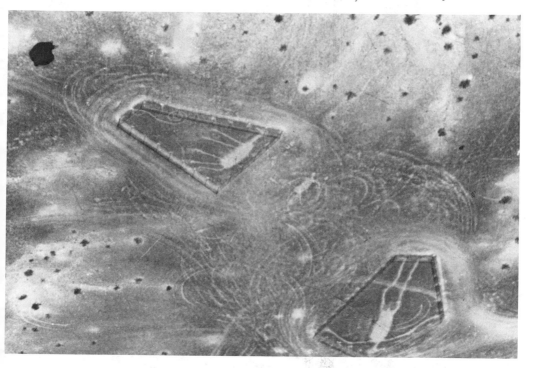

Fig. 61. Desert intaglios in the Colorado River region. These giant figures rendered on the desert floor are rare examples of an art tradition found across much of the desert west. The subjects are also unusual for Native Californian art: the depiction of humans is rare; and the four-legged creature may be a horse, also unusual in California Indian art. Since horses did not arrive in California until after Spanish exploration and settlement had begun, the four-legged figure, if a horse, would have been made during the Historical Period. Note the damage to the figures caused by the tire tracks of recreational vehicles. (Courtesy of the Lowie Museum of Anthropology, University of California, Berkeley)

Contact with people performing ordinary daily activities constituted a form of contamination to the ritual.

Astronomical Sites. A few astronomically significant sites have been identified in California. Archaeologists have only begun to learn how to recognize such sites, which may be more common than they now seem. Astronomical sites usually consist of rock alignments oriented toward important celestial points, such as the place on the horizon where the sun rises during the summer or winter solstice, or the point on the horizon where a distinctive constellation or star appears.

Fig. 62. Toward the end of the Late Pacific or early in the Final Pacific Period, Indians in northwestern California began to build semicircular masonry *tsektsels,* or "prayer seats," such as the one shown here from Del Norte County. The practice of building these structures and their use in religious observances have been continued by some traditionally oriented California Indians down to the present.

Fig. 63. This reconstruction of a Coast Miwok sweathouse, built by the Miwok Archaeological Preserve of Marin at Point Reyes National Seashore, shows features commonly found in many parts of the state. The structure is semi-subterranean, with a low roof and no smoke hole. The log roof beams are covered with wickerwork and earth to form a weathertight roof that keeps smoke from escaping. Rocks in the fireplace radiate heat to promote sweating. Over time they fracture; old ones are discarded (note the pile near the entrance) and new ones must be gathered from the nearby creek bed.

Fig. 64. A Karok Brush Dance, held at Orleans in the 1920's. The Brush Dance was one of the great public ceremonies of the World Renewal cycle (see Fig. 57), held among more than 200 communities of the Yurok, Karok, and Hupa peoples each year. Each dance was sponsored by a wealthy individual who earned great renown for a successful dance. The ritual specialist who directed the dance could also gain great prestige. (U.S. Forest Service Photo)

Ethnographic evidence shows that several groups of California Indians possessed considerable knowledge about the movement of various stars and visible planets. Computer analyses of rock alignments at such sites show systematic relationships between some alignments and the positions of certain stars and planets. Most of the astronomical sites now known have been found high in the mountains, far from occupation sites, where observation conditions are best. In some cases there appear to be relationships among astronomical, ritual, and rock-art sites, so the remote locations of astronomical sites may also be associated with the practice of rituals in remote places and the need for separation between ritual and everyday activities (Hudson & Blackburn 1978; Hudson, Lee & Hedges 1979; Hudson & Underhay 1978; Lee & Horne 1978; Levi 1978).

Quarry Sites. Quarry sites were not widespread until the Pacific Period, when people made expeditions to collect lithic raw materials in quantity at their source. Archaic people visited sources to get stone for toolmaking during their annual rounds, taking only enough for immediate needs and staying too briefly to leave many remains. In the Pacific Period, expeditions to quarries became a type of special ac-

Fig. 65. A small part of the Glass Mountain obsidian quarry source in eastern Siskiyou County, one of the three major obsidian sources in northern California. A ridge 500 feet high and more than half a mile long (150 meters high by 800 meters long) is covered with millions of nodules and boulders of volcanic glass. Over 1,800 chipping stations have been recorded around the base of the ridge. Obsidian from this source was traded to groups hundreds of miles away in California, Oregon, and the Great Basin. (U.S. Forest Service Photo)

tivity, often conducted by special task groups. The raw materials quarried were often collected in surplus for trade (Erickson 1977; see also Fig. 65).

The Mammoth Creek site in Mono County (the site has been destroyed by the construction of U.S. 395) exemplifies the nature of a quarry site. Located near an important obsidian source, it was visited in Archaic times by people who camped there while collecting pine nuts as part of their annual round. These collectors apparently stayed at the site for a few weeks at a time, using bedrock mortars to pound the nuts into meal, which they ate while they camped. While there, they used the obsidian to make items needed in their daily activities. Some obsidian tools may have been carried away when the group moved on.

By Pacific times, the camping and pine-nut-harvesting functions of the site had become very minor. The site was visited mainly to quarry obsidian for export, although some tools were used while the workers camped at the quarry. Some obsidian was taken away in natural blocks. A great deal more was fashioned into roughly worked, large, bifacially flaked forms called shipping blanks or preforms for easy transportation and eventual trade (Fig. 66). Still more was manufactured into large quantities of projectile points, knives, drills, scrapers, and other specific, finished forms. Obsidian from this source has been traced westward across the Sierra into the Central Valley, south to the Los Angeles area and east across the Great Basin. The amount of quarrying at the site was perhaps a hundred times greater during Pacific times than during the Archaic (Sterud 1964).

In addition to the approximately two dozen obsidian quarry sites known in California, Pacific people established quarries for many other kinds of rocks and minerals, including steatite, chert, asphaltum, salt, quartz crystals, andesite, rhyolite, jasper, chalcedony, ala-

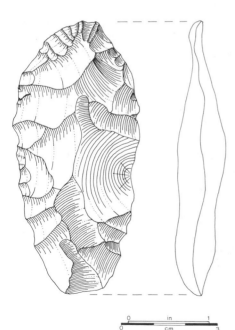

Fig. 66. Obsidian preform. This bifacially retouched, oval artifact was manufactured at an obsidian quarry site in Mono County, east of the Sierra Nevada. Such pieces were made by the thousands at the quarry workshop and in this form were transported by human packers to villages to the west, across the Sierra, to the south in southern California, and to the east across the Great Basin. The specimens are often called preforms by archaeologists because they are not tools but are made as easily transported blanks to be made into tools at their destinations.

0   in   1
0   cm   3

baster, fused shale, diorite, greenstone, and magnesite (Heizer & Treganza 1944).

Trading Sites. The rise of trade to a position of great importance during the Pacific Period led to the creation of trading sites—specialized sites where groups of people from different cultures met to exchange their goods. Most Pacific Period trade took place in settlements, but sometimes it was necessary to have a neutral trading spot, as when traders came from groups that were hereditary enemies. Such trading was often done at locations along the boundary between the two groups' territories. Neutral locations were also needed when the traders had traveled great distances from groups with no kin ties to the hosts. When traders from the Southwest came to the Pacific Coast, for example, the trading sometimes took place in isolated mountain locations that did not lie within the territories of any of the participants, so that none of the participants was at a political disadvantage or was threatened by a politically hostile population, and the trading was not disturbed by domestic activities.

Trading sites, though resembling temporary campsites, can sometimes be distinguished by their locations remote from normal occupation areas and by the abnormally high amounts of exotic goods. Otherwise, it is often necessary to rely on ethnographic accounts that designate a particular area as a trading site (J. Davis 1961; Erickson 1977; C. King 1976).

Settlement

All these site types reflect important aspects of the Pacific Period focal economy: the decline of the Archaic annual round, the development of permanent settlements, and the replacement of many temporary campsites in the hinterlands by special-function sites. The five kinds of sites just described are examples of special-function sites. They were used for particular purposes rather than for general camping; and they were used by special groups, rather than by the general population. The generalized, temporary campsites characteristic of the Archaic continued to be used in many parts of the state, but the trend during the Pacific Period was toward their replacement by special-function sites.

This trend was accompanied by the development of *permanent settlements*. Sedentism is a complex phenomenon attained by few non-farming cultures anywhere. Its role as a feature of Pacific Period cultures is therefore of particular interest to scholars.

Sedentism describes the practice of maintaining a permanent residence. Most hunter-gatherers cannot become sedentary because they cannot acquire enough food or other critical resources in one location to support themselves throughout the year. In almost all cases, cultures were able to become sedentary only when they began to farm and produce their food, rather than simply collecting it. The Pacific Period cultures in California, attaining sedentism through their extraordinary hunting, gathering, and fishing economies, constitute an important exception to this general rule.

The people of a particular society may display any degree of sedentism. Near one end of the scale are people who move camp many times each year, staying in any one place for only a few days or weeks at a time. Many Paleo-Indian communities were like that. At the other extreme people maintain the same homes throughout their lifetimes. Between these two extremes fall most of the cultures of the world, both past and present. Many Late Archaic societies, for example, had winter base camps they occupied for several months at a time. These settlements were relatively more sedentary than Paleo-Indian societies, but even the richest Archaic cultures in California could not support the high degree of sedentism reached in the Pacific Period. With few exceptions, Pacific cultures were more sedentary than their Archaic predecessors in the same environments. Many Pacific cultures were able to maintain fully permanent settlements, some of which were occupied over many centuries.

Archaic peoples, with their small groups, simple technologies, and diversified diets, had to move camp frequently because their reliance on available resources soon exhausted the key resources near any camp. Pacific cultures overcame the limits of this lifeway by developing more productive methods to harvest and store food. As these methods became more productive, the pressures to shift camps were lessened and Pacific groups could stay in camps for longer periods.

This success, however, created new problems. Economic success meant not just a more sedentary population but a larger one. Sedentism itself contributes to population growth, in part because it facilitates the maintenance of a large infant population. But growing populations place pressure on the people to harvest more food. There are limits to how far people could range in search of food without giving up sedentism or without running into some other group occupied in the same task. Rather, people had to increase their food supply by focusing even more intently on the few resources that were seasonally abundant and by organizing labor even more efficiently. Trapped by the consequences of their earlier successes, the sedentary peoples of the Pacific Period had fewer options for dealing with food supply limitations than had Archaic peoples. The growth of sedentism, therefore, should be seen both as a result of Pacific strategies and as a cause of their continued development.

Sedentism also allowed the elaboration of architecture and other technological aspects of life. Since Archaic people had to move frequently, they could not build structures requiring heavy investments of labor or materials. The costs would far exceed the gains, and the investments would have to be repeated at the many sites occupied during the annual round. Neither could they accumulate large numbers of tools and supplies in need of transport from camp to camp, or carry large crop surpluses with them on their moves. For sedentary Pacific groups, however, it was more economical to build substantial houses every few years than to replace temporary shelters every few weeks. Sedentism and permanent shelters allowed the accumulation of large tool inventories and food surpluses. These investments in turn made it less likely that settlements would be abandoned seasonally. The development of each element of the Pacific settlement system thus worked to reinforce the growth of the other elements in a pattern leading toward full sedentism (Flannery 1968: 67–75).

Archaeologists recognize sedentism by the remains they find in village sites. Permanent settlements, larger than seasonally occupied campsites, reveal more structures, and the structures are more substantial. There also are more *kinds* of structures, including such special-function buildings as dance houses, sweathouses, bachelors' huts, and menstrual huts. More than in temporary campsites or base camps, village sites created by sedentary populations also display larger amounts of artifacts, and these artifacts in turn exhibit a greater variety of functions. Storage facilities are also more likely to be found in sites occupied by sedentary groups, as are objects used for ornaments or rituals. Cemeteries tend to be larger and more elaborate. Food remains representative of all seasons of the year are found in such sites, whereas temporary camps yield food remains representative of only part of the year. Finally, items involved in trade are much more common in permanent sites than in temporary campsites.

Site Locations

A few parts of the state still had not been permanently settled by the end of the Archaic; all were settled to one extent or another during the Pacific Period. Current evidence suggests that the high Sierra was not occupied by distinct ethnic groups. Since mountains above 5,000 feet (1,500 m) were covered with snow for much of the year and therefore not habitable, groups living at lower elevations traveled to higher country during the summer to obtain the resources found there. In the most fully developed Pacific cultures, such trips were made by special task groups rather than by whole communities or family work units.

Permanent settlements were most extensive at locations where two or more of the key resources of Pacific focal economies were most abundant: along the southern California coast, around San Francisco Bay, around the margins of the Central Valley, on the northern California coast, and on the lower Klamath River. As populations grew in these areas, they tended to divide the area into smaller and smaller units, in a Balkanization of the regions around the permanent settlements.

Pacific economies were able to support two distinct ethnic groups in some locations where previously only one had been. For example, Archaic people living at the base of the Sierra needed both the Sierra and the adjacent part of the Central Valley for seasonal use, and there could be no separate Sierran and Valley populations as long as strict annual rounds were followed. Pacific people living in the same area were able to support separate groups in the valley and in the mountains because of their more productive economies. Separate patterns of site distribution developed for the two areas during Pacific times. A system of permanent villages in the Central Valley, along the major rivers and creeks, was one. Individuals and special task groups made forays from these settlements to procure particular resources in different areas, but the settlements were never empty. The foothill people of the other system maintained base camps in the lower foothill valleys. These camps housed the whole population during the winter half of the year. During the summer, both special task groups and family units left to hunt and gather in the higher mountains or to procure specific resources, but some people stayed behind in the lower camps. The Sierran pattern caused people to exploit systematically the high-elevation resources that had been used sparingly or not at all during the Archaic. The emergence of this pattern is seen in the appearance of the Martis Complex (Bennyhoff 1956; Elsasser 1960; Elston 1970, 1971; Elston et al. 1977; Fitzwater 1962, 1968; Rasson 1966).

A similar pattern of site distributions developed by Late Pacific times in northwestern California. The first settlers there, the Point St. George I occupations of Late Archaic times, followed a seasonally migratory way of life. By Late Pacific times, however, the development of effective salmon and oceanic fishing and the preservation, storage, and trade of foods permitted the growth of permanent settlements along the coast and on the lower Klamath River. Thereupon the sites in the surrounding mountains, which had been summer-season occupation sites for communities that wintered along the coast, became transformed into special-function sites for the exploitation of specific resources or for ritual activities.

Similar patterns emerged along the Santa Barbara coast and the Santa Monica Mountains. In Archaic times, communities made winter base camps along the coast and moved into the adjacent hills and inland valleys during the summer months to forage for seeds, acorns, and game animals. As Pacific cultures developed, the coastal settlements came to be occupied the year around, and only special task groups traveled into the mountains to procure specific resources. The withdrawal of populations to the coast created a vacant niche in the interior mountains and valleys that was filled by people who, for lack of rich enough focal resource bases, had to follow a more nearly Archaic way of life in spite of adapting to Pacific strategies generally. They maintained major base camps in the interior valleys and used the mountains seasonally. They traded with the coastal people, however, and also sent special task groups to collect food, raw materials, and export commodities.

Even in the arid interior deserts the Pacific settlement pattern developed, although the scarcity of water and food prevented populations from becoming very large or dense. Permanent villages were maintained at low elevations where water supplies permitted. The villages housed several kin groups each, and included a number of kinds of structures ranging from a communal sweathouse, a ceremonial house, a distinctive headman's house, and other substantial structures to simple sunshades, or *ramadas*, and storage granaries. The Cahuilla, of the region around Palm Springs, did not practice Archaic-style migration, but sent special task groups into other habitats to acquire specific resources (see Heizer 1978a: 575–79).

Perhaps the only significant exception to this general pattern was found in northeastern California, where the Surprise Valley Paiute practiced a more migratory way of life (O'Connell 1975). In Late Archaic times the people of this area had been able to maintain permanent settlements around a remnant Pleistocene lake. Subsequently the lake dried up, and mountain sheep, bison, and other big game that had been drawn to it retreated to more favorable refuges. The Pacific people in Surprise Valley were therefore forced to become more mobile rather than less in order to survive. This example illustrates the importance of environment to adaptation in Native California and indicates an effective limit of the Pacific method of adaptation.

In general, the developed Pacific site distribution pattern favored low elevations, where large numbers of people congregated for sedentary occupation or for special functions that required large numbers, such as fish processing or collective rituals. Sites at higher elevations based smaller groups and specialized purposes: art, rituals, astronomy, quarrying, food acquisition, or craft-material collection. As a rule, the highland sites also present more diversity in site types.

Technology

The key technological advances of the Pacific Period have already been noted: oceangoing canoes, fish dams, deep-sea fishing nets, and the bow and arrow. The Pacific Period was not characterized by rapid technological change, and most of the differences between Pacific and Archaic artifacts were nonutilitarian in nature: the introduction of new styles of beads, pendants, and other ornaments; changes in the popularity of particular notch positions on projectile point bases (notch position in general has no functional significance); shapes of stone bowls and milling tools; the development of elaborate ceremonial costumes; or the appearance of enormous obsidian bifacial "blades." Even strictly utilitarian objects, such as pestles, underwent stylistic rather than functional changes (see Appendix B).

Even so, the far greater productivity of Pacific economies over Archaic economies was due to social rather than technological factors. One feature of Pacific Period life that stimulated such developments was craft specialization.

In *craft specialization* one's productive energies are concentrated in the production of a single product or service rather than in the production of the entire array of goods and services needed in daily life. The specialist produces a surplus of a single product, and exchanges this surplus for other needed goods and services. Specialists enjoy the productive efficiency that comes from concentrating on a single product, as well as the high skill level that comes from specialized training and the prolonged, intense involvement with an item's production. They often put more hours of work per day into the production of their surplus than they might have put into the provision of their daily needs as generalists. Archaic householders were generalists; they produced all their own needs, with rare exceptions, and only as much of any good as they needed. Their mobile way of life and the need to transport their goods while migrating served to keep them from producing surpluses. Craft specialization develops only where sedentism develops, where surpluses can be stored for exchange. It also arises only where there is enough surplus food to release some people from the tasks of day-to-day subsistence activities.

Craft specialization began to emerge in Pacific times, although it was never highly organized and remained generally at the level of cottage industry. Individual artisans produced a wide range of luxury and utilitarian goods on a part-time or full-time basis. We saw some hints of this practice in the Late Archaic with the emergence of such part-time crafts as stone carving. This practice grew throughout the Pacific Period to produce the many kinds of specialist artisans: basketmakers, shell workers, canoe builders, navigators, net weavers, projectile-point makers, quarry workers, bow makers, and steatite carvers, for example. Specialization was most elaborate in the largest and richest societies, but some degree of specialization was attained throughout the state, helping to make Pacific cultures even richer than they might otherwise have been.

The technological changes that occurred during Pacific times nevertheless carried considerable economic impact, mainly because they were innovations in the organization of labor, offering craft specializations or cooperative labor groups. These developments enhanced the ability of Pacific peoples to focus on particular resources. For example, the development of the seagoing dugout canoe in northern California and the sewn-plank canoe in southern California allowed people for the first time to fish offshore systematically. The development of large nets for deep-sea fishing is related to this development. The technological developments enhanced the exploitation of high-abundance seasonal resources (in this case, schooling fish) and the use of cooperative labor crews (boat crews) and craft specialists (boat builders, boat captains, navigators, and boat owners).

Another example is the fish dam, best known from Kroeber's description of the Kepel structure (Kroeber 1925; Kroeber & Barrett 1960). The fish dam was a log structure built entirely across a river. Anadromous fish trapped behind the dam during their spawning run could be harvested in much vaster quantities than with traps, nets, or spears. The per-capita yield of a group of fishermen using dams greatly exceeded the yield of the same number of individual fishermen using any kind of one-man equipment. Like the canoe, this technological development makes the best use of a high-abundance seasonal resource (anadromous fish, in this case) and cooperative labor crews led by administrative specialists.

We emphasize cooperative labor to underline the significance of social organization in Pacific Period subsistence. Perhaps the only significant Pacific Period technological development that did not rely on social aggregates is the bow and arrow. The bow was certainly used in cooperative efforts, such as war and deer hunting, but none depended on this invention. Its spread can be understood in terms of the hunting advantages it offered in the brush and forests of the state.

Part of the continent-wide change, the bow began to replace the spear and the dart and spear-thrower during Pacific times by offering several advantages. It has greater range, more power, and potentially greater accuracy. It is less cumbersome to use in wooded habitats. Although Californians adopted the bow and arrow, they never became particularly renowned as bow makers, and their bows were never as powerful as those of many other prehistoric Americans (Kroeber 1925: 817–19). Perhaps as a consequence, Californians never developed the focal, cooperative deer-hunting expeditions characteristic of the eastern United States at that time. However, there was an increase in deer-hunting trips made from permanent villages during the Pacific. The bow improved overall hunting effectiveness, and thus may have contributed to the Pacific strategy. Since warfare was increasing as a group activity during Pacific times, the bow and arrow presumably aided cooperative enterprises in that endeavor as well.

Another aspect of the elaboration of Pacific life was demonstrated by its houses and villages. As noted earlier, Archaic people usually did not build substantial houses; nor did their settlements become complex. A typical Archaic settlement might include from one to a half-dozen or so simple brush huts, each generally circular in floor plan, with a packed-dirt floor and perhaps a fireplace in the middle. All the huts were about the same size and served the same function. There were no buildings intended for any special purpose. Pacific people, by contrast, built much more elaborate houses. They developed complex settlements of notable size, with several kinds of buildings serving various purposes other than housing.

A notable Pacific house type is the semi-subterranean pit house of central California. A pit house was built over a circular pit excavated 3–4 feet deep and 15–25 feet in diameter (roughly 1 m deep by 5–8 m in diameter). It had a fireplace in the center, beneath a smoke hole in the roof. Some groups built entrance ramps at ground level sloping down to the pit-house floor. In other cases, there was no formal doorway and entrance was by means of a ladder through the smoke hole. One or more heavy support timbers were set into the floor to hold up a framework of roof beams, which extended from the support posts out to the rim of the pit. They were then covered with brush or matting, and often overlaid by a final thick coat of tamped earth. In this

Fig. 67. This reconstructed Coast Miwok pit house, made at Point Reyes National Seashore by the Miwok Archaeological Preserve of Marin, features a single vertical post and radiating roof beams covered with wickerwork. The post is set into a pit dug 3 feet deep and 20 feet across (about 1 by 6 meters). The roof is pierced by a smoke hole, and the packed-earth floor has a hearth near the center post. Entrance is by a ground-level ramp covered with a brush roof. Compare this design with the floor plan of the house shown in Fig. 52.

Fig. 68. One of several styles of silos or granaries used by Pacific Period cultures, this structure served to store food surpluses through the winter. Typically, acorns would be kept here in the shell until needed. Each household would have its own granary, and a larger one might also be built next to the headman's house for civic purposes, such as hosting festivals or trading parties. Other styles of granaries are shown in Figs. 40 and 69. This example is a reconstruction made by the Miwok Archaeological Preserve of Marin at Point Reyes National Seashore.

way a domed, weatherproof house was created, which provided insulation against summer heat or winter cold and turned off the rain (see Fig. 67).

Many variations were made on the pit-house design. For example, many people who lived in the Sierra foothills built houses with conical or tepee superstructures rather than domes. These were covered with slabs of bark overlapped like shingles. In northwestern California the pits were dug in a rectangular shape, and the superstructure was made of redwood or cedar planks. Along the coast, many cultures used the pit-house design for sweathouses rather than dwellings (see Fig. 63). These sweathouses were smaller and had lower roofs and entrance ramps than houses.

Pit houses often had adjacent structures used as silos (Fig. 68). Set above ground on posts, they were fully enclosed except for small ports near the bottom from which seeds, acorns, or nuts could be withdrawn. The use of pits in the ground for storage was relatively rare in California. Many pit houses had milling appliances set permanently into the floor (note Fig. 52). Larger houses often had more than one milling slab or mortar base, suggesting either that more than one adult woman lived in the house or that one woman had multiple milling tools for different milling functions.

Pacific people also built several other kinds of special-function structures. Apart from the small storage silos just mentioned, some settlements had larger communal granaries. Village headmen often had larger and more elaborate houses than other families. Some communities boasted dance houses, which were huge pit houses used on ceremonial occasions. Sweathouses were found in virtually every substantial community. In southern California, large, roofless enclosures were built and used as chambers for dances and other public ceremonial functions. Many communities built small, light structures referred to as menstrual huts. Young women were secluded there at the onset of puberty, for fasting, instruction, and preparation for coming-of-age ceremonies. In some communities older women secluded themselves in these huts during menstruation. Ramadas were made in many parts of the state. These open, flat-roofed sunshades on posts were typically built next to permanent houses to serve as summer work and sleeping areas (see Fig. 69). Some coastal people built simple boat shelters to protect their canoes. All these special structures helped make Pacific villages archaeologically distinct from Archaic sites.

The development of architecture in California is not as well researched as it might be, at least partly because many forms of archi-

Fig. 69. The ramada was used in several parts of California from the southern deserts to the North Coast Ranges. A wall-less sun shade on poles, this specialized structure served as a summer outdoor working and living space. Ramadas were frequently built next to houses. When working, cooking, craft work, and sleeping were moved outside, the house then served as a convenient storeroom. Ramadas leave fewer archaeological traces than do houses, owing to simpler form, fewer features, and less-intensive use. Their packed-earth floors usually contain scatterings of discarded tools and waste flakes, however, along with concentrations of ash around the fireplace and the remains of the support posts at the periphery of the rectangular floor; thus, when they are recognized archaeologically, they can be readily distinguished from the floors of houses. This example is located in Point Reyes National Seashore, where the Miwok Archaeological Preserve of Marin has reconstructed a Coast Miwok village. Note the wickerwork granary structure to the left of the ramada and compare its form to those of the granaries shown in Figs. 40 and 68.

tecture have left few archaeological traces. This is true even for the Final Pacific. Many coastal people in central and southern California, for example, built their houses entirely above ground using simple frames of saplings tied into cones, domes, or arches and covered with bundles of thatch, mats of plaited reeds, slabs of bark, or layers of brush. Such materials are rarely preserved archaeologically (see Fig. 70). The remaining evidence for the house, such as the fireplace and packed earth floor, often cannot be told from an outdoor living surface in the absence of a defining pit. In such cases the only definite clue to the existence of a house may be a circular scatter of artifacts

around the fireplace, indicating that the artifact dispersal was confined by walls (see Fig. 71).

On the other hand, even when house patterns are distinct, excavation might not have been undertaken for a variety of reasons. California archaeologists have traditionally excavated initial test pits and
trenches to expose the profiles of the deep parts of sites to interpret
their chronological development; more recently, sampling programs
are favored. These approaches tended to preclude focusing on household and community organization through the excavation of houses
as units. (There are, of course, exceptions. See Miller's work at 4-
Butte-1 in Chartkoff & Chartkoff 1980; Treganza, Heickson & Woolfenden 1969.)

This trend is especially unfortunate because many Pacific Period
sites are excellent laboratories for the study of household and community organization. Houses in northwestern California from the Pacific
Period were rectangular, made of heavy planks, and built over rectangular pits somewhat smaller than the house itself. The roofs were

Fig. 70. This reconstructed house at Point Reyes National Seashore is typical
of houses made in coastal central and southern California. A frame of poles
lashed into a beehive shape supports the covering of bundled reeds. An uncovered frame can be seen behind the house. These houses were typically
made at ground level rather than over an excavated pit. Though less substantial than the earth-covered pit houses, reed-covered houses provided a surprising amount of insulation and protection from rain.

Fig. 71. Rock features are ubiquitous in California archaeological sites and often defy interpretation. Closer inspection can reveal important details in some cases, however. This rock assembly lies on the floor of the Late Pacific Period house shown in Fig. 52; it is the concentration in the lower left, seen here from the opposite direction. This concentration was clustered around a house post near the side of the floor. The elongated rocks are pestles of various grades of coarseness. A squat stone maul is near the back end of the scale/arrow. The fractured rocks may be cooking stones. The feature constitutes a set of kitchen tools found on the house floor, out of foot traffic but convenient to the hearth and built-in mortar.

made of plank or bark-slab shingles. Circular doors were located at one end, and the dirt became particularly compressed on either side of the door from foot traffic. The subterranean pits, 3–4 feet deep (about a meter), provided shelves or benches that ran around the house inside the walls. These benches served as sleeping platforms and storage areas, so they received different degrees of packing than did the floors. They also became areas of artifact accumulation. These structures are easily defined archaeologically, but few have ever been excavated.

The large size and complexity of Pacific settlements frequently resulted in the formation of miniature "neighborhoods," in which houses were grouped together on the basis of kinship ties between heads of households. Archaeologists have been able to recognize this fact by studying the patterns of house distributions. Complexity in sites can also be detected by the location of special-purpose structures within the site. From them, and also from distribution patterns of different kinds of artifacts, special-function areas can be determined. A headman's house, for example, frequently was located in the settlement's center; the menstrual hut and the sweathouse often marked the opposing edges of the settlement. In many settlements particular areas were designated as cemeteries, often outside of the house cluster itself. Some communities had special dormitories or other distinctive houses for bachelors. Artifacts found in such dwellings show that they were not ordinary family residences. Artifact distributions reveal where special work areas were located—areas where such communal tasks as fish smoking or acorn processing were undertaken or where toolmakers worked. This degree of patterning is a particular characteristic of Pacific settlements.

Subsistence and Economy

Earlier we noted the factors that characterized the Pacific focal economy and allowed it to develop. How did these factors work to produce the particular characteristics of Pacific archaeological traditions? We'll look at the most important of these factors: the focal concentration of key resources, the collection and storage of surpluses, and the development of trade and a money system. The role played by changes in social organization will be discussed later.

Focal Concentration on Key Resources. California's environment favored the hunter-gatherers, owing to its great ecological diversity and wide range of usable resources. It was unique in providing a combination of key seasonal resources that could be collected in vast quantities given the appropriate technology and organization. As noted earlier, the most important of these resources were acorns, hard seeds from grasses and chaparral plants, anadromous fish, and offshore schooling fish.

These resources combine high nutrient value with great seasonal abundance. Because acorns and hard seeds provide complete protein, they are both excellent dietary staples. Both occur in great quantity. A valley oak, for example, may yield 200–500 pounds of acorns annually (75–187 kg); a black oak or blue oak may yield 100–300 pounds (37–113 kg). One tree can provide up to a pound of food a day for one person for an entire year.

Fish, too, form exceptionally rich resources. The silver salmon weighs an average of 8–10 pounds (3–3.8 kg), the king salmon 20–25 pounds (7.5–9.3 kg), and the steelhead trout 3–4 pounds (1.1–1.5 kg). Three-fourths of the carcass is edible. The larger rivers carried tens to hundreds of thousands of fish each fall, providing millions of pounds of meat. Similar quantities of meat were available periodically from schools of deep-sea fish that frequented parts of the coast.

Pacific peoples learned to harness these resources. Their cultures rose to the highest levels—their populations were more dense, their social structures more complex, and their technologies more elaborate—when two or more of these resources could be exploited by the same group. These few especially productive resources were supplemented by the hundreds of other species found in various parts of the state, including shellfish, sea mammals, tule elk, rabbits, deer, buckeyes, wild iris bulbs, and manzanita berries.

Storage. The full potential of the key seasonal resources could not be realized, however, without storage. By storage, we mean the practice of stockpiling surplus foods past the time of harvest so that they will be available during seasons of scarcity. The practice is an extremely important Pacific Period development because it allowed communities to reduce the impact of seasonal food shortages.

Many of California's most important plant resources can be stored without any special processing or technology. Because of the arid environment in which these plants grow, they have evolved coverings that are resistant to drying and to many pest infestations. Acorns, nuts, pine nuts, buckeyes, manzanita berries, grass seeds, and chaparral seeds are examples. These plant products can be stored effectively for long periods in simple containers. Pacific people used granaries built near their houses to store such foods (see Figs. 40 and 68). They also kept storage baskets in their houses, and sometimes dug storage pits to hold some resources (see Fig. 72). The California climate is dry enough in most areas to have promoted preservation, so

Fig. 72. A fragment of burned basketry from the Finch Site, CA-But-12, a Final Pacific Period village on the Sacramento River. The whole fragment, found during excavation sticking out of a pit sidewall, was less than 4 inches across (10 cm), but when microphotographed in place the fragment's structure could be preserved. The basket had been lying on a house floor when the house burned and its roof caved in. The earth that fell with the roof beams smothered the fire. The basket was only partially carbonized and therefore survived for the archaeologist.

the development of storage did not require a special technological breakthrough. Rather, it required changes in the ways people behaved. They had to collect larger amounts of food than they would consume in the near future; they had to make storage facilities to keep their surpluses; and they had to have a permanent, stationary, protected place in which to locate these storage facilities.

The reason Archaic peoples did not practice storage arose from the way they gathered food, rather than from any mechanical or technological problem. During the Archaic, small family groups moved from camp to camp, except in the winter. Their need to move frequently precluded the collection of big surpluses. Archaic groups could have collected surpluses because the food was available in season, but if they had, they certainly could not have carried the stores with them from camp to camp. The collecting and processing of surpluses depended on the existence of a well-developed cooperative la-

Fig. 73. Site CA-Mrn-10, a Pacific Period shell midden in Marin County near San Francisco Bay; this view is 50 years old. The shell mound was built up over 3,000 years as the debris from food, fire hearths, and toolmaking accumulated around the village. An artificial mound, or kitchen midden, nearly 20 feet deep (6 meters) developed over the centuries, preserving evidence of the development of prehistoric life along the bay's shore. San Francisco Bay was ringed by over five hundred of these mounds; only a handful survive. (Courtesy of the Lowie Museum of Anthropology, University of California, Berkeley)

bor force, one that included many individual families. It also depended on the existence of a permanent place to bring and keep the food—one not too far from the point of collection (see Fig. 73). The development of storage therefore had to coincide with the rise of sedentism, the reduction or abandonment of the Archaic-style annual migration pattern, and the development of more complex forms of social organization.

The development of plant-food storage stimulated the storage of other resources. Anadromous fish were available in large numbers mainly during seasonal spawning runs in the larger rivers. By employing organized communal labor, huge amounts were harvested. The surplus was processed by smoking, drying, and pounding to produce dried fish sides or fish meal, which resisted spoilage.

Perhaps the single most important consequence arising from the development of storage was that food became available during the late winter and early spring. As a consequence, the death rate from late-winter starvation declined. Lifting this severe limiting factor allowed populations to grow much larger than they had during the Archaic; in turn, the growing populations produced more cultural change.

Trade. Archaic people, as we noted, were involved in trade to some degree. Archaic trade, however, was small in scope and relatively unimportant economically. In Pacific times, by contrast, the institutions and mechanisms of trade flourished, and trade grew to be a major element of the economy. By the end of the Pacific Period, Native Californians had also developed a form of money system, which enabled trade to be even more productive than it had been when it relied solely on barter (Chagnon 1970; C. King 1976, 1978).

The scope of Pacific Period trade was extensive. At one Sacramento Valley site, for example, analysis identified nine types of stone that had come from sources more than 50 miles from the site (80 km); in one case the source was more than 250 miles away (400 km), another more than 200 miles (320 km) in an opposite direction. Of the six species of seashell found there (among the several thousands of beads and other shell ornaments), the nearest possible sources ranged from 90 to over 200 miles away (145–320 km). Sources for these materials lay in all different directions, indicating the existence of a complex, widespread trade network (Chartkoff & Chartkoff 1980).

California seashells were traded as far east as New Mexico. Obsidian from the Mono Lake region crossed the Great Basin to Utah. Dentalium shells from Puget Sound were traded south to the Klamath River along overland trails. Catalina steatite, brought to the mainland by canoe, was traded far into the Great Basin (see J. Davis 1961; Erickson 1977).

Local trading was less spectacular but redistributed much larger volumes of goods. Village-to-village or partner-to-partner trading networks were developed on the coast, in the Central Valley, along the major rivers, and across the desert. Traders and middlemen grew wealthy through this enterprise. As their control over valued resources and surplus food increased, they gained a political, economic, and social power that had never before existed in California.

Many types of raw materials and manufactured goods were traded. Obsidian was exported from more than two dozen sources, chief among them the "glass mountains" near Clear Lake, Mono Lake, and Little Medicine Lake. In some cases, goods were shipped in several stages of completion, as well as the raw materials in bulk and as preforms. Steatite was exported from several sources in the state, but the most important was Santa Catalina Island, from which both raw steatite and finished pieces were shipped.

Lumps of natural tar, or asphaltum, used as a glue and as a caulking or waterproofing material for baskets, canoes, and other objects requiring sealing, were collected along the southern California beaches for trade inland, and at some inland oil seeps in northern California for export. The Northeast Pomo Indians of Sonoma County developed an important export industry based on the salt found in a natural deposit in their territory.

Localized sources of suitable lithic material for toolmaking, besides obsidian, figured importantly in regional trade. Some of these materials were Grimes Canyon fused shale from the western Santa Monica Mountains, Monterey banded chert from the South Coast Ranges, Franciscan chert from the North Coast Ranges, chalcedony from the northern Sierra, and Point St. George chert from northern coastal California. Coastal people exported shells as raw materials, as finished ornaments, and as manufactured shell money. Yew wood was exported from the Sierra, Cascades, Coast Ranges, and Klamath Mountains as a raw material for the manufacture of bows. Yew-wood bows were themselves a desired trade item. The scalps of red-headed woodpeckers and yellow flickers, desirable for ornamental and ritual purposes, were among some of the widely traded animal products. This partial list suggests the magnitude of Pacific Period trade, much of the nature of which can be reconstructed by tracing raw materials back to their sources (J. Davis 1961; Heizer 1978c).

Food also played an important role in Pacific Period trade. Food surpluses were traded, directly in some cases, for surpluses of other food or for other goods. Surpluses were also presented as gifts at trading occasions. Both practices had the effect of moving resources from one environment to another and from areas of plenty to areas of scarcity. The practice alleviated temporary, local food shortages and spread resources more evenly around the state. Because people could draw on the resources of a larger area, the carrying capacity was raised, in effect, allowing groups to become larger and population densities greater.

Food surpluses were also used during the community gatherings that accompanied trading. Feast giving and the distribution of food by headmen or wealthy individuals and groups regularly occurred at these gatherings. It served as a means of rewarding supporters, of repaying those who had contributed to the stockpile of goods to be traded, and of redistributing surplus food within the community.

One mechanism that enhanced trade greatly, especially late in Pacific times, was the development of a money system (Chagnon 1970) based on shell beads. Beads had been manufactured since the Archaic. By Late Archaic times, shell beads, valued as ornaments and burial offerings, were being traded inland. These uses persisted throughout the Pacific Period, but an additional use had emerged by the Late Pacific. Strings of beads began to be used as a medium of exchange.

Only certain types of beads were used this way. Their forms were generally distinct from those used as ornaments—an important fact in recognizing bead functions archaeologically. In northwestern California, the common form of money was the dentalium (*Dentalium*) shell, imported from Puget Sound. These horn-shaped shells were strung on cords about 30 inches long (76 cm). Only shells of the same size were strung together. The strings of shells were valued according to the size of the shells: a string of large shells was worth many times more than the same-length string of smaller shells. Individual beads of baked magnesite were valued even more highly. Purses of carved elk antler were made to store bead money. In central California, disk beads of clamshell (*Saxidomus* and *Tresus*), strung in standard lengths, served as the common form of money, although beads made from cut and whole olivella shell (*Olivella biplicata*) and beads of steatite and baked magnesite also served as money. In southern California, strings of shell disk beads used for money were made of mussel (*Mytilus*), clam (*Tivela*), abalone (*Haliotis*), and olivella (*Olivella*), along with tubular beads of olivella and *Mitrella* (= *Columbella*) (C. King 1978: 58–59).

Shell-bead money took on several characteristics of "real" money, in the modern sense. Strings of beads had mutually agreed-upon values and could be used to purchase goods and services, repay debts and obligations, and demonstrate wealth and status. Since shell money was made from raw materials having limited distribution, its source was controlled, usually by the people living along the coast. The practice of placing beads in burials in amounts proportional to the social importance of the deceased tended to control inflation, since it restricted the number of beads in circulation at any time (Chagnon 1970).

The bead money system was an important tool in the Pacific Period focal economy. Money could be used to purchase food during local shortages, or when seasonal resources were unavailable, from other communities in the trade network. For example, if a Central Valley group needed acorns and none were available locally, they could use beads to purchase surplus acorns from a group in the mountains. This group might use the beads later to purchase surplus salmon after the autumn fish run in the Valley was finished. In this way, shell money promoted trade by storing value, freeing the participants from the limitations of barter.

Society

The growth of the material wealth of Pacific cultures was paralleled by the growth of increasingly complex forms of society. Archaeological expressions of this growth included the development of larger settlements, a greater variety of houses and other structures within settlements, a clustering of houses within settlements to reflect neighborhood or kin groupings, rapidly growing amounts of "luxury" or nonutilitarian artifacts, growing differences in the amount of luxury artifacts owned by different households, the subdivision of cemeteries into areas dependent on social status, and the growing differences in the amounts of luxury goods buried with individuals of each area.

Many of the ideas archaeologists have about Pacific Period society are based on ethnographic accounts. Since survivors of more or less intact California cultures—at least in the more remote parts of the state—were still alive throughout the nineteenth and early twentieth centuries, the state has a particularly rich literature covering these traditional cultures. Archaeologists have used these writings to model late prehistoric cultures. Ethnographic ideas have also influenced our thinking about Archaic and Paleo-Indian cultures, but the immediacy and amount of literature that deals with the final stages of prehistory are so much greater that its influence on archaeological thought has been correspondingly greater. This ethnographic model has not yet been found to be in serious conflict with archaeological evidence, but a great deal of work still needs to be done to confirm and refine it, especially for the earlier stages of the Pacific Period.

As we have seen, Pacific Period societies supported large populations by means of their focal economies, augmented by trading, the accumulation of surplus food and goods, and the avoidance of wholesale seasonal migration. Just how large the populations of that time became is still debated, but authorities think that around A.D. 1770 California held about 310,000 people (plus or minus 30,000), which, we might note, is six times the size of the Spanish capital of Madrid on the eve of Cortés's conquest of Mexico (Cook 1976a: 42–44; 1978: 91). It is harder to make good population estimates for earlier periods, but some figures can be suggested that show the consequences of economic change for California populations.

At the end of the Pleistocene 12,000 years ago (10,000 B.C.), there may have been no more than 1,000–2,000 people in the whole state. During the Archaic that figure may have grown slowly to several times the Paleo-Indian population, but the actual numbers were still small. We feel that around 7,000 years ago (5000 B.C.) the state may have held no more than about 10,000–15,000 people. By the end of the Archaic, about 4,000 years ago (2000 B.C.), the population may have risen to 25,000–30,000. During the next 3,000 years, the increased productivity of Pacific Period economies may have allowed populations a three- to six-times growth, to 100,000–150,000. The stage was set for a final, rapid spurt in population growth, starting sometime after A.D. 1200 (800 years ago), because of the development of efficient deep-sea fishing, anadromous fishing, surplus collection, storage, trade, and money.

Cook's figures show that the population peaked at the moment of Spanish settlement, around 1770. It can be argued, however, that the ethnographically recorded societies of that era may have already passed their peak numbers, and that Cook's figure of 310,000 may actually represent a decline. This tentative inference fits more or less within Cook's 9–10 percent variance in his population estimate. It is based on as-yet-unsystematic observations that the size of cemeteries, the wealth in burials, and the variety of wealth items in burials may have been richer around 1700 than at the time of Spanish settlement 70 years later. If so, the peak in California population may actually have been reached by about 1700, and it may have been about 340,000–350,000 people.

If that level actually had been reached by 1700, what might have caused its decline to the lower figure cited by Cook? It could have been caused by the Pacific system's reaching its natural limit and thereafter undergoing population fluctuation. But some historical evidence suggests a different cause. Spanish sailors periodically abandoned ship in California before the time of permanent settlement (Lavender 1972: 64–69). Such contacts might have caused early epidemics to sweep through the nonresistant Indian populations, as they did after 1770. Diseases might also have been spread by contacts with the Southwest, where Spaniards had begun to settle as early as 1580. Regardless, the final answer awaits future research.

Although population growth was obviously stimulated by economic improvements, it in turn affected the economy. As populations grew, they placed more demands on the economy for food, products, and services, and greater stress on the social fabric of communities. Population size and the economy should be seen as interrelated factors rather than as causes or results (see Flannery 1968).

For example, one result of population growth in prehistoric California was the development of territoriality. Prehistoric groups probably always had some sense of territoriality, since free access by a group to the resources it needed was necessary for its survival and unrestricted competition with other groups for the same resources would have worked against survival. During Archaic times, however, groups were small and spread far apart, and people from one group could wander temporarily into the range of another group with little chance of contact or retaliation. Pacific Period populations were much denser, however, which meant that more people were packed into the same space. As the land became more fully populated, the distance between settlements decreased, pressures on resources increased, border violations were more likely to occur, and competition between groups increased.

A predictable result would have been that borders were formalized somewhat and guarded more jealously. In particular, the key food and trade resources in each territory were most likely defended strenuously. We would also expect that armed conflict in Late and Final Pacific times would have been greater than ever before, and in fact the number of burials showing signs of violent death rises sharply during the Pacific Period. Evidence shows that the Pacific was the time when the ethnographically known groups became established in their historically recognized territories. Ethnographic accounts describe warfare for every group, and reprisals for territorial violations were a frequent cause of war (Kroeber 1925; McCorkle 1978).

Besides the rising importance of territoriality, the development of more complex societies, discussed earlier, accompanied population growth. More settlements occurred in each region than earlier. In general there were more people in the average settlement, and greater differences in size between large and small communities (L. Bean 1978). And because the kinds of informal, democratic relationships that had governed Archaic communities were less effective in these larger, more complex communities, new degrees of internal division developed.

The headman of a large Pacific community had more formal authority, more economic power, and consequently greater social status than his Archaic counterpart. Other bases for social status were also beginning to emerge, including social rank, wealth, and rights to certain rituals and equipment. These rights and privileges were largely inherited through families, so that social position began to take on some characteristics of a class system.

Some of the individuals and families enjoying higher status were the special task leaders mentioned earlier. In a large community, comparatively few people could hold such leadership positions. As a result they gained disproportionately large shares of the community's resources. Wealthy families or individuals often owned important food sources, such as groves of oak trees or favored fishing places, or important pieces of capital equipment, such as canoes. In many cultures the owners of such resources allowed others to use them on request for a fee (normally a share of the yield), which gave the system some of the features of capital investment. In this manner, the sharing ethic of earlier times began to give way to a system of personal acquisition in keeping with the Pacific strategy of surplus storage and trade. Trade opportunities also created means for individuals or families to become wealthier than their neighbors. Wealthy people could put their wealth to use to gain greater prestige and power within their communities.

Cemetery remains provide one line of evidence for the rise in social stratification. In contrast to Archaic practices, Pacific burials displayed greater and greater differentiation as time went on. Most people were buried modestly, but a few individuals were buried with lavish offerings. Large cemeteries often had distinct areas for family or kin groups, and within each kin area were often a small number of clearly prestigious, or "elite," burials. These possessed not only a much larger number of burial offerings than those of other individuals, but also many more exotic and elaborate offerings.

The Northwestern California Archaeological Society participated in emergency excavations in the mid-1960's of the site CA-Mrn-27 at Tiburon (T. King 1971). (Many archaeological sites are known by place name or are named for landowners; others are known only by site number. In every county, sites are numbered consecutively in their order of discovery. This site, for example, was the twenty-seventh recorded for Marin County, California.) Among the remains destroyed by a construction project were the burials of 41 Early Pacific people. One thing the archaeological salvagers were able to learn was the distribution of shell beads among the burials. They recovered about 2,000 beads, most made from disks of olivella shell. They found that only 11 of the 41 buried individuals possessed any beads. In fact, two individuals possessed 1,400 of the 2,000 beads, and a third possessed an additional 255 beads. Not only were most individuals without beads, most had few if any grave goods of any sort. Furthermore, the distribution of burials within the cemetery showed that the individuals with the most beads were buried in a central area of the cemetery. They had been treated differently in another respect, as well: they alone had been cremated. King used this evidence to argue that the cemetery reflected marked status differentiation in this Early Pacific society.

A more dramatic instance of differential burial practice is seen at the Final Pacific site of Mescalitan Island, near Santa Barbara. Mescalitan Island, actually a knoll in the middle of the Goleta Slough, was destroyed by freeway construction in the 1950's, but the Santa Barbara Museum of Natural History had an opportunity to conduct excavations beforehand. The excavations revealed a cemetery of more than 200 individuals. Among them was the grave of an adult female accompanied by more than 20,000 shell beads, along with several dozen finely made steatite bowls, several of which were inlaid with abalone-shell ornaments. This burial, of the "Queen of Mescalitan Island," proved to be unique. Other individuals in the cemetery were accompanied by no more than a few dozen to a few hundred shell beads, and proportionately fewer grave goods of other sorts, indicating the high status of this woman in her community (Orr 1943).

At the Medea cemetery, now beneath a shopping center near Thousand Oaks, the UCLA Archaeological Survey was able to recover more than 400 burials before construction destroyed this Late/Final Pacific burial ground. In the cemetery, over 70 percent of the grave goods were interred with fewer than 10 percent of the burials. One adult male had a necklace of seven steatite tube beads. Each bead measured about 6 inches long and 2 inches in diameter (15 by 5 cm), with a hole drilled through it lengthwise; its surface was either polished or encrusted with abalone-shell inlays. The entire necklace weighed over 10 pounds (almost 4 kg). No other individual in the cemetery possessed more than one such bead. Although the Medea cemetery lacked the highly concentrated wealth found at Mescalitan Island and the unique burial treatment of elites, it too was divided into distinct areas or zones of burial that appear to have represented different kin groups, and clear differences in wealth were associated with the burials within each zone. Medea may, in fact, represent a more fully stratified society than the earlier Mrn-27 cemetery, in that it reflects a range of statuses rather than a single wealthy family or individual (L. King 1969).

A cemetery in the Livermore Valley area recently uncovered by freeway construction contained a Late Pacific burial with over 38,000 clamshell disk beads. Of the several thousand prehistoric burials excavated in California, there may not be another dozen with as rich a concentration of shell beads (Miley Holman, pers. comm. 1980).

Anthropologists think such differences in burial remains reflect the differences in status held by people in these cultures during their lives (C. King 1978, 1980; L. King 1969; T. King 1971, 1974; Stickel 1968).

Earlier we noted that one feature of social development during the Pacific Period was the appearance of special task groups to perform economic activities through cooperative labor. In earlier times, the nuclear family was not just the basic work unit, but substantially the only work unit. The family continued to be an important work force in Pacific society, but other organizations were developed as well. They increased economic productivity by performing tasks beyond the scope of the nuclear family. Offshore net fishing, for example, was accomplished by boat crews that were not nuclear family units. Their members were drawn from the whole community, and might or might not have been members of the same larger kin group. Trade expeditions might include dozens of men, each representing a different nuclear family. Some kinds of tasks, such as antelope drives or the construction of fish dams, might draw the cooperative labor of several neighboring communities. Some of these special task groups were organized along lines of kinship, but others were organized according to residence or skill. This distinction depended more on the circumstances of the moment than on the task at hand. The leaders of such tasks enjoyed extra power and prestige while performing their leadership functions. Their leadership helped to organize work and make it more productive and efficient. Both the productivity of special task groups and the fact that they were able to accomplish tasks beyond the abilities of individual families helped to enrich Pacific Period economies.

Accompanying the rise of cooperative labor organizations was the development of individual specialists, who acquired skills beyond the level expected of ordinary householders. Those with expert abilities enriched group life and earned social and economic rewards. Craft specialists, discussed earlier, worked in this way through the production of craft goods on a part-time or full-time basis. There were other kinds of specialists as well during the Pacific Period. Their contributions lay in the provision of services rather than products.

The headman is perhaps the most dramatic example of a service specialist. He provided organization, planning, and decision-making skills to make the work of others more productive. Leaders of special task groups provided similar services, though in more restricted circumstances. Other specialists included singers, storytellers, and herb doctors, who received payment for providing their particular skills.

Bean and Vane (1978) note that senior leaders in many religious societies also served as teachers for craft and service professions; teaching itself was a specialty.

Pacific societies had several kinds of religious specialists, including
healing spiritualists or doctors, leaders of public rituals, diviners,
"white" or beneficial magicians, were-doctors (shamans with the reputed ability to take animal form), and sorcerers. They indicate the
variety and complexity of Pacific society, and the significance of religious institutions in the operation of these societies.

The recognition of the individual skills of such specialists in Pacific
society counterbalanced the tendency toward a social class system
based on the inherited control of wealth and political power. Pacific
cultures maintained a great deal of flexibility by allowing considerable
latitude for individual abilities. For example, although the headman
position was generally inherited, it was maintained only if the individual displayed the necessary leadership ability. Otherwise, a headman might be removed by his constituency and replaced by a more
able individual. Skilled young craftsmen could hope to rise to positions of prominence even if they came from poor backgrounds (for an
illustration, see T. Kroeber 1959: 196). Among the Yurok of northwestern California, a wealthy man often adopted an able but relatively poor young male relative as his heir, giving him the training,
skills, social standing, and access to wealth necessary to validate a
high position in society (Theodoratus, Chartkoff & Chartkoff 1979).
Religious specialists might also draw their apprentices from the community at large, depending on an individual's ability and proclivities.

One of the most dramatic features of California's ethnographically
known cultures is the occurrence of great public ceremonies featuring
elaborate costumes, music, rituals, and choreography. Although most
information about these ceremonies comes from ethnographic sources
(e.g., Bean & Vane 1978), corroboration is provided by some archaeological manifestations, such as the ritual sites of northwestern California, the great dance houses of central California, and the brush-
ringed dance floors of southern California.

Few California ritual structures have been excavated (for an exception, see Miller's excavation of House 1 at the Patrick Site, in Chartkoff
& Chartkoff 1980), so this subject may become an important future
research topic, particularly if Native Californians make more use of
archaeology to learn more about their own past. Because of the lack of
research, it is not possible to trace California's ritual traditions back
into prehistory very successfully. Bean and Vane (1978) feel that these
traditions developed out of earlier shamanistic traditions. As noted

previously, shamanism seems to have arisen in Archaic times. No excavated examples of great ceremonial houses date from before the Late Pacific, so it may be that the public ritual traditions did not arise until after about 1,500 years ago (A.D. 500). Alternatively, it may simply be that inadequate archaeological research has left us no accurate knowledge of the appearance of these traditions. In this case, our understanding is based on ethnographic sources alone.

Four great regional patterns or traditional systems of religious movements arose in California during the Pacific Period: the World Renewal movement in northwestern California, the Kuksu Cult of the Sacramento Valley and North Coast Ranges, the Chingichgich movement of coastal southern California, and the Toloache Cult, which was widespread in the region south of the Delta. Though the details of these movements varied considerably, they also shared certain features: their ceremonies were conducted by religious societies that existed within communities; membership was usually restricted to those adult males who passed initiation tests; and shamans played important roles in these societies.

A man's ability to be admitted to a religious society, and to achieve high rank within it, generally depended on his wealth and social standing in the community at large, as well as on his personal skills. Religious societies often served important political roles, drawing together communities of different sizes and degrees of wealth or economic rivalry. They were also important economically, often serving as the intermediaries in trade. They also controlled some of the skilled crafts, provided for the specialized training for craft apprentices, and oversaw the distribution of goods within communities. All this was done in accordance with prescribed rituals to sanctify and legitimize the proceedings. Ritual systems thus provided the more complex Pacific societies with much of the organization that kinship alone was able to provide in Archaic societies (L. Bean 1978; Bean & King 1974; Bean & Vane 1978).

In historical times, two other ritual movements appeared in California as outgrowths of "ghost dance" movements that swept through the American West in the 1870's and 1890's. These movements, which sought to eliminate Europeans and restore pre-contact life through spiritual and magical means, bore many ceremonial similarities to the more traditional religious movements. Some of the largest central California dance houses were built during the "ghost dance" development (DuBois 1939). In addition, some denominations of more widespread Christian churches have developed distinctively Native American forms among some Native Californian communities. These religious institutions are still in existence but have not been the subjects of archaeological study.

Besides the rise of complex mechanisms to organize and control the people living within communities, Pacific times also saw the rise of mechanisms that controlled the relationship between communities. Kinship, trade, and religion provided some of these ties, but during the Late and Final Pacific there arose a new form of political organization that united communities into a more complex form, the tribelet.

Some writers have likened this organization to that of a true chiefdom, ruled by a powerful, authoritarian leader (e.g., T. King 1971), but most anthropologists do not believe that California tribelets were that centralized or were ruled by authoritarian leaders who could compel their subjects to obey their decisions. The leader of the tribelet did seem to control more resources and power than the headman of any other settlement in the tribelet, a fact that was reflected in Pacific burial practices.

The members of a family in one settlement within a tribelet might have kin in several other communities. In this way, kinship ties crosscut community organization and helped to hold the tribelet together. The value of the tribelet to Pacific Period society lay in just this ability to tie together into cooperative organizations, with political, religious, social, and economic links, communities that otherwise might be rivals. Through cooperation, communities were better able to fulfill their needs in the Pacific strategy.

Just how much more complex and sophisticated Native Californian cultures might have become and what directions they might have taken will never be known. With the arrival of the Europeans came an end to the autonomous Native Californian way of life. Starting with occasional contacts by land and sea in 1539–40, and then with permanent settlement in 1769, the foreigners brought with them new technology, new diseases, new religions, new economies, and the physical destruction of the old order. These changes are traced in the following chapter on the Historical Period.

CHAPTER FIVE

The Historical Period

Because of the great cultural variety in California during the Historical Period, no single scenario can express much of it. We have therefore chosen three brief vignettes, each showing a distinct way of life and each illustrating some dimension of Indian-White relationship in California at that time. Even so, a great many aspects of the Historical Period are still neglected.

1

A typical Spanish settlement might be located along the coast of southern California at the head of a shallow bay. There is no wharf; the occasional ship that visits the community anchors in the bay, and its crew reaches shore by rowboat. Several small boats and skiffs are pulled up onto the sand near a shed. The shed holds cattle hides, tanned, tied into bales, and waiting for shipment to Mexico and Spain. The shed is near one end of a tiny pueblo, which consists of a few dozen adobe structures. During the heat of the day a few dogs and pigs can be seen, resting in the shade of trees or buildings, while chickens scratch for seeds and insects between the houses and under the bushes. In some doorways, or on verandas and beneath ramadas, a few townspeople of Spanish or Mexican origin rest and visit. The few mercantile establishments are closed during the traditional mid-day siesta. The houses and stores straggle along the ill-defined, dusty streets leading up from the shore toward a larger, more imposing building at the opposite end of the community. The Spanish flag flying before this structure identifies it as the headquarters of the alcalde, the pueblo's civil administrator.

At the edge of town, not far from the alcalde's building, stands the presidio. This military garrison for the pueblo displays some of the precision of design lacking in the town. Its adobe buildings form a large square. Their windowless exterior walls are pierced only by a large gate that faces the sea and by a single sally port on the opposite side. The buildings open onto the central parade ground. Broad verandas shade the building fronts around the entire square. The commander's headquarters and chapel face the gate. Flanking these two buildings are officers' quarters and offices. Barracks, stores, and stables line the other sides. At midday a modest guard keeps watch while the company of fewer than a hundred soldiers rests from its regular duties of protecting the pueblo and the nearby mission.

Outside the town, on top of a low hill that overlooks the harbor and town, rises the adobe mission. Its half-completed sanctuary and belltower dominate the rectangular compound that houses the priests, offices, storerooms, and classrooms. Adjacent are the barracks where 2,000 Indian neophyte converts are held. Unmarried men are kept in separate barracks from unmarried women. Families are provided tiny apartments in another building. Indians provide virtually all the labor force for the mission's construction. After the siesta, Indian men will resume making adobe bricks under the direction of priest supervisors and some of the troops from the presidio. The women and older girls are learning to weave the coarse cloth that will be made into pants, shirts, and dresses for the neophytes. Tomorrow the troops will lead an Indian work force out into the fields, which need hoeing and irrigating. The crops are raised to feed the mission's population, since missions have to be self-sufficient. The padres will exempt the pregnant women from such work in an effort to get the neophyte population to replace itself. So far, the number of children raised has been far too few to sustain the neophytes' numbers.

The Indians themselves are often silent and demoralized. Many have lost contact with their families, or have seen members of their families die. The death rate at the mission is appallingly high and already the cemetery nearby is crowded. Many Indians find they cannot communicate with each other, since their languages differ; others have come from groups mutually hostile to each other. The mission padres are teaching the Indians Christianity, various industries and crafts, and the Spanish language. They encourage the Indians to marry in the church and to raise families in the separate huts and special barracks provided for this purpose. Some do marry, but few children are born, and many of the babies die soon after birth.

Sometimes Indians succeed in running away from the mission, but they are pursued by the troops and are usually recaptured and brought back. Recaptured runaways are usually beaten or put in stocks to discourage them from a second attempt. Because the Indian population at the mission keeps falling, the troops must regularly raid distant villages to bring in replacements.

2

*A typical rancho of the Mexican period is situated in a coastal valley. Oaks dot
the valley floor, shading a small winding creek. Chaparral blankets most of the
hillsides. Sheep and cattle graze on the grass and leafy brush of the valley floor
and the slopes. In the valley's center is a hacienda, an adobe house shaded by
oaks, that serves as headquarters for this land-grant rancho. A Mexican officer
holds the grant of eleven leagues of land—payment from the government for
his services in the frontier military force. He has retired from the army to become a rancher, to raise cattle, horses, and sheep, and the crops needed to feed
his stock and workers. He maintains a large house in town, where his wife and
daughters prefer to stay, but he brings them for part of each year to the ranch
so he can supervise his staff, and has built a residence in his headquarters compound for his family.*

*On his land had been a large Indian village occupied by several hundred
people. Not long after the rancher arrived on this land, however, a smallpox
epidemic swept through the village, killing all but a dozen or so people in the
space of a few weeks. The survivors left abruptly to take refuge with relatives
in more distant villages. The village now stands empty, its houses collapsed,
and shrubs and grass are beginning to reclaim it. Indians who had once
worked at the missions have drifted into the area looking for work. It was these
Indians who have built most of the ranch buildings: the adobe ranch house
with its low shed roof and sweeping veranda, the barracks for the vaqueros,
the barns, the storerooms, and the kitchen house.*

*Now the rancher can sit in the shade of his veranda and look out upon his
stables and gardens, where virtually his every material need is produced.
Ships from Mexico arrive infrequently, but the more aggressive Yankee and
English traders call at least once or twice a year, bringing the few manufactured goods he needs, such as iron tools and guns, and the luxury goods
longed for by his family—fine cloth, Parisian hats, porcelain dishes, gold
jewelry, and books. But where home crafts will suffice, the rancher has his
Mexican and Indian ranch hands and domestic staff produce workable substitutes for the imports.*

*The Indians working on the ranch perform most of the heavy labor. The
rancher in turn protects them from marauders, feeds them, provides medicine
for the ill, and sees to it that the young people receive some training in crafts.
The rancher's wife directs a small staff of Indian household servants. One Indian girl takes lessons with the rancher's daughters in reading and writing.
The rancher arranges to have a priest visit the ranch at least once every two
months to say mass, hear confession, and conduct any marriages and bap-
tisms that might be required.*

*This ranchero is reckoned by his fellow Californianos to be a wealthy, suc-
cessful man. He can boast of prime land for many varas, many head of livestock, a fast horse, eleven sons and daughters, a fine home in the town and*

another on his ranch, and great respect in the community. He takes his turn throwing lavish parties for the several dozen other Hispanic families of the region, the people of a distant pueblo, and the officers of the garrison. If his life is rude by European standards, it is nonetheless rewarding, and he reckons himself among the favored of God.

3

It is the 1870's, and a small group of Indians has managed to survive in the foothills of the Sierra. Their home is a cave, almost entirely concealed from the outside by heavy brush. Behind the brush, the cave's sandy floor extends for several hundred square feet, providing space for a group of a dozen Indians who sit about two small fires. They are the survivors of a village that once numbered more than a hundred people. Starvation, murder, and disease crippled the village, and, when some of the men stole cattle from a nearby ranch, the rancher and his hands tracked the stolen cattle to the village and killed almost everyone they found there. The survivors fled to this mountain cave to hide from further reprisals.

Most of the survivors belong to a single family, which was returning to the village from the hills when the massacre took place. They cannot catch salmon because they have been driven from their old fishing grounds along the river. Their last stores of seeds and acorns, gathered for the winter, were lost when the rancher burned their village. It is now late fall, and there are few seeds, acorns, or pine nuts left to be gathered at this time of year. Some deer can still be found, but the need for secrecy makes hunting difficult. The people fear that the ranchers may yet track them to this cave, and the greatest care must be taken to prevent discovery. Even providing for such basic needs as water and firewood has become a problem for the group, for if the same route is used frequently, a path may be worn from the creek to the cave, which might betray their presence.

When the village was burned, all the tools and equipment needed to carry on the activities of living were lost with it. The men must replace their stone tools and make new knives and milling tools for the women. The women must make new baskets at a time of year when few basketry materials are available. More is needed than can be quickly made.

The group is surviving on a day-to-day basis. People know nothing of what may happen to them or of what may have happened to the other Indian communities that lived near them on the river. Almost every aspect of their lives has been destroyed. The village shaman is dead, so there is no one who knows how to conduct all the rituals necessary for the proper conduct of their lives. The woman who knew more than anyone else about herbal medicines and healing magic was killed in the massacre, so there is no one to heal the sick properly. The best hunters in the community were killed. The group has no stored food, trade, or access to its accustomed hunting and gathering lands, so mem-

bers must spend every day in an unceasing hunt for food. Even if they are successful, people wonder what future is possible for them. There is a boy in the group who is almost old enough to marry, but there are no unmarried girls. Unless they can make contact with another group, the boy will remain unmarried and the people will see no future generations. White settlers continue to move into the countryside, and the people wonder when the newcomers will begin to move into the area near the cave. These grim thoughts are on the people's minds as they join together for their evening meal.

Native Californians had occupied California for more than 14,000 years, settling in every region, learning about its environments, and developing ever more effective ways of life. Within the last several centuries they were unusually successful for people who made their living exclusively through hunting and gathering.

Then a new sort of settler arrived, and the resulting clash of cultures brought most Native Californian societies to collapse. The cultures that managed to survive were severely altered, and Native Californians were reduced to the status of marginal citizens in a land once under their dominion. We know much more about the actual events of this part of California's archaeological record because, besides being more recent in time, the intruders brought with them the written word. This chapter of California's past is therefore documented in a way no earlier chapter could have been. No longer part of prehistory, it is the Historical Period.

THEMES OF THE HISTORICAL PERIOD

The Historical Period is that part of the past that lies within the scope of the written historical record. The first known event in California's recorded history was a Spanish exploratory trip to the Colorado River in 1539. This date could be used to mark the start of the Historical Period, but to do so presents a problem. The time of first contact between Native Californians and Europeans varied from group to group by more than three hundred years. There is no single date marking the end of prehistory and the beginning of recorded history for the whole state. Furthermore, early contacts with Europeans, fairly sporadic and transitory in nature, had only limited effect on Indian cultures. Yet some boundary must be adopted. We chose the year 1769 to mark the end of the Pacific Period because that year saw the beginning of permanent European settlement in California, with ensuing large-scale disruption of the Native California cultures. So, although history technically began to be recorded in California some

230 years earlier, we have allowed this time span to overlap the two periods.

The closing date for the Historical Period is the present. The current definition of antiquities, using National Historic Preservation Council guidelines, requires things to be at least a hundred years old, but archaeologists find value in studying things as recent as the present. An example can be found at the University of Arizona, where archaeologists have been studying the formation of the present-day Tucson municipal dump. There it is possible to learn about contemporary society from the garbage it discards—an inquiry with important implications for prehistoric archaeology (Rathje 1979). Archaeologists working on historical sites have an advantage over those who study the prehistoric period, in that archaeology and history benefit each other reciprocally. Historical documentation increases tremendously the kinds of information available to archaeologists, while providing controls that allow them to evaluate methods and assumptions. At the same time, archaeology also expands our knowledge of many historical events and periods, providing a perspective not often preserved in the written record (Deetz 1977; South 1977).

Just as with the prehistoric periods, we can point to some key themes of the Historical Period as seen from an archaeological perspective: the breakdown of Pacific Period focal adaptations, which also involved the breakdown of Native Californian cultures as a whole; the reemergence of pioneer settlement, this time among the various groups entering California for the first time; and the subsequent rise of urbanism and evolution of a multiethnic society.

The Breakdown of Pacific Period Focal Adaptations

The settlement of California by Europeans eventually led to the collapse of traditional Native Californian cultures. In the process, California Indian populations declined by at least 95 percent between 1770 and 1900. Central to this collapse was the destruction of the highly integrated, focal economies that had evolved during the Pacific Period. Missionization played a major part in this destruction, although its most direct influence was confined to the coast. Disease also played a major role. Yet, if all else had been equal, Native Californian populations might have been able to rebound from these losses, or at least to have stabilized at something approaching Archaic levels. After all, even after the Gold Rush, a good deal of the state was not heavily colonized until the late nineteenth or early twentieth centuries.

But all else was not equal. The root of the collapse of Pacific Period societies lay in the breakdown of regional interactions and the loss of access to regional resources that were vital to Pacific peoples. This phenomenon was progressive. It evolved throughout the various stages of European settlement until, during the period of Anglo-American settlement, it culminated in the appropriation of the state and its resources for extensive farming, ranching, mining, lumbering, commercial fishing, and rising urbanism. No provision was made in this progression for the California Indians, who could not even return to an Archaic way of life successfully because the habitats most important to the Archaic lifeway had been taken from them. The breakdown of focal economies was an inevitable consequence of European settlement, and the collapse of Indian populations followed as a further consequence. The survivors were forced to follow a more diffuse adaptation, one capable at best of supporting only a fraction of the Pacific Period population.

The Emergence of New Pioneer Settlements

The perspectives we used to view prehistoric cultures can also be used to view cultures of the Historical Period. California's earliest European settlers can be likened to the Paleo-Indians in the sense that both were pioneer settlers. The way of life created by the Spaniards and Mexicans in California revolved about a focal economy which, although it involved agriculture, produced only a fraction of the variety of crops grown in Spain or Mexico at the time. The staples of existence focused on a few primary crops: cattle, sheep, and cereal grains (principally wheat and maize). The Spaniards and Mexicans brought with them a previous way of life, but not in all its variety. This simplified version relied on those features that could be made to work in both their former home and their new one. It was a generalized way of life, in the same sense that the Paleo-Indian lifeway was generalized, and it did not immediately take advantage of California's unique and potentially valuable resources. As time went on, however, an accommodation was increasingly forged, in which Spanish and Mexican colonial cultures took on a distinctively California quality, an accommodation that incorporated certain aspects of Native Californian cultures. Like the Paleo-Indians earlier, they had begun to cease being pioneers.

The Rise of Urbanism and the Evolution of a Multiethnic Society

Urbanization is the development of cities or urban centers: highly structured settlements characterized by dense populations, formal administration, high degrees of labor specialization, and marked distinctions in wealth and status. Cities are linked to a support base of food-producing, exurban or suburban, market-oriented farms and ranches. They are tied to higher-level governments and to a national economy.

California today, with 24 million inhabitants, is highly urbanized, but it began evolving toward urbanism in the mid-nineteenth century. At that time, its population was not much larger than it had been just prior to Spanish settlement a century earlier. In tracing the course of urbanism in California, we can see that it involved the reorganization of both settlement and society, and not just a simple growth in population.

The trend toward urbanism was fostered by economic and political factors. California's economic growth after 1850 was based on its production of agricultural and ranch products, timber, and mineral resources, stimulated by a tremendous influx of people because of the Gold Rush. Networks of cities and towns arose to serve the primary producers, to channel imported goods to them, and to export the state's products. The location of San Francisco at one of the hemisphere's best deep-water harbors also made California a gateway linking America with the nations around the Pacific Ocean. At the same time, California's takeover by the United States and its accession to statehood imposed a highly structured system of government on the state. The establishment of federal, state, county, and municipal offices of government further reflected the centralization of the state's population in urban communities. A result of this trend was the creation of a new type of settlement—one with a distinctive archaeological form—the urban center.

At the same time that urbanization was emerging in California, the state witnessed a separate (but sometimes interrelated) phenomenon: the development of a multiethnic society. One interesting characteristic of California's Historical Period has been the continued immigration of people from different ethnic backgrounds. As a result, California has become one of the ethnically most complex regions of the nation. Formerly dominant groups were succeeded periodically by others. Since 1850 the dominant Anglo-American population has been augmented by new influxes of other ethnic groups. The many groups have interacted to greater or lesser degrees, yet they have also tended to maintain their identities in spite of the predominant popular image of America as a melting pot. Many of these peoples are completely unstudied archaeologically, but the potential is there, and such studies could reveal a great deal about the processes of ethnic interaction and persistence.

STAGES OF THE HISTORICAL PERIOD

The Historical Period passed through several distinct stages. Because of the existence of a historical record, a structure is automatically imposed on the historical era, a structure that focuses on specific individuals and events. Since the same is not true for the prehistoric era, it is hard to treat both periods within the same framework. The term "tradition," used to describe cultural reconstructions based on the archaeological remains of prehistory, is not really appropriate for historical cultures, since the actual names and much of the content of such cultures are known. Recognizing this problem, we have tried to organize the Historical Period into divisions that are as comparable as possible to the units used for the prehistoric periods. Rather than describe a series of archaeological traditions, we have divided the period into a series of successive historical stages. Each stage reflects a discrete period of time, a particular kind of cultural development, and a different dominant ethnic group.

Historical-period archaeology is still a new field in California. It has not yet provided enough data to allow us to characterize these stages from a basically archaeological point of view. We therefore rely heavily on historical documents to determine and describe each of these stages. Nevertheless, archaeology has already contributed some interesting information about these periods, and we will draw upon these contributions as much as possible in our discussions. Our divisions, which emphasize changes in the nature of the interaction between Indian and European cultures and the progressive development of the immigrant cultures, are the Exploration Stage (1539–1769), the Hispanic Stage (1769–1822), the Mexican Stage (1822–46), and the Anglo-American Stage (1846 to the present).

The Exploration Stage (1539-1769)

For nearly 250 years, starting in 1539, California was briefly visited by Spanish, British, and Russian explorers, traders, and trappers. This contact came sometimes from the Southwest, where Spain maintained colonies, but mostly from naval expeditions sent to explore the Pacific coastline (see Map 44).

The date 1539 marks the first of these contacts, when a detachment of Coronado's expedition from northern Mexico reached the Colorado River. Although the expedition did not penetrate the state, these Spanish explorers were apparently the first non-Indians to even reach the area. We say "apparently" because Asians may have sailed across

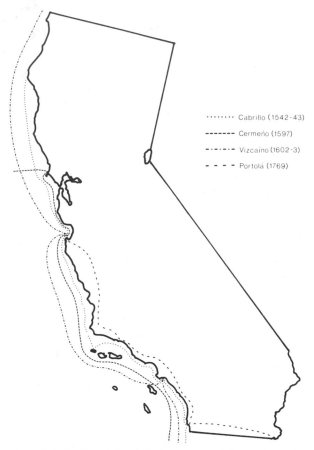

Map 44. Routes of early Spanish exploration in California, showing dates of contact. Spanish awareness of California's existence began with its sighting by a detachment of Coronado's expedition in 1539. Most other contacts made during the subsequent 230 years took place along the coast, the result of deliberate exploration or unplanned landfalls made by international trading vessels. Prior to 1769, when San Diego was founded, such contacts were brief, and their impact on native cultures was modest and localized.

the Pacific and accidentally or deliberately reached the coast of California earlier. The evidence for this is ambiguous at best, and if any such visits took place they made no impact on native cultures (Hutchinson 1969: 46–52).

Then, during 1542–43, a Portuguese navigator named João Rodrigues Cabrilho (Cabrillo in Spanish), leading a Spanish expedition, sailed along much of California's coast and became the first European to discover the bay at San Diego. Then, sailing north to the Los Angeles area, he called the region the "Bay of Smokes" from the many Indian campfires he saw. He passed the Santa Barbara area, noting its many large Chumash villages. He sailed at least as far north as Cape Mendocino, and may have been the first to discover Monterey Bay. Cabrillo died of an injury received on the trip, and was buried on San Miguel Island. Even though his journey was completed successfully by his second-in-command, Cabrillo's discoveries were little noted or remembered. He and his mate compiled many important ethnographic and geographical observations in the ship's log, however, which survived the voyage.

During the next two centuries, Spaniards visited California only occasionally. Spanish exploration waxed and waned according to the fortunes of the Mexican colonial administration, the politics in Europe, the threat of foreign competition on the colonial frontier, and the Manila trade. Miguel López de Lagazpi had conquered the Philippines for Spain in 1565–71, only a little later than Cabrillo's exploration of the California coast. Manila, the Spanish colonial capital in the Philippines, soon became an important trading center for such Asian goods as tea, spices, silk, furniture, and porcelain; these were exchanged for Mexican silver, and trading fleets brought goods from Manila to Mexico for transfer to the Atlantic coast and eventual shipment to Spain. The profits from the Manila trade were immense, but Spanish merchants soon persuaded the king that Mexican colonial merchants and their ships were taking too large a share. The king responded by reducing the Manila fleet to a single galleon yearly, with profits limited to the Spanish crown and certain Spanish merchants (although Mexican merchants were able to use bribery to buy space aboard the ship; Lavender 1972: 26–27).

When the galleon left Manila for Mexico, it sailed north to catch the favorable winds and currents. As a result, it struck North America far to the north of Mexico's Pacific port at Acapulco. Usually landfall was made along the California coast. The eastward passage was long and arduous. Crews were usually emaciated and scurvy-ridden before they reached land, and the ship was especially vulnerable to storms and pirates. This made the yearly galleon voyage a risky undertaking, and led Spain to think of building a naval base in California to receive the galleon and provide escort to Acapulco. In the end, however, the government decided that the maintenance of a distant base was too risky and expensive, and that the galleons would have to get to port on their own.

Then, in 1579, the British navigator Sir Francis Drake reached California. Circumnavigating the globe, Drake had rounded the tip of South America. He made his way north along the Pacific coast, looting several Spanish settlements along the way. Finding the coast above Mexico to be inhabited only by Indians, he sailed as far north as the Point Reyes area, where he stopped for five weeks to careen and repair his vessel, the *Golden Hind*. The exact site of this landing is a matter of hot debate; it could have been any of several sites from what is currently called Drake's Bay to Tiburon. Kroeber (1925: 275) reports that while Drake was ashore, he interacted with the local Indians. A number of European trade items have been found in archaeological sites of the area and some might be evidence of Drake's visit (see Fig. 74). A brass plate, purportedly inscribed by Drake to commemorate his discovery of California and his claim of "New Albion" for the British crown, was found in the area in the 1930's. Recent research has cast doubt on its authenticity, however (Heizer 1972).

The British did not follow up Drake's voyage of discovery with a colonizing effort, so they had no further impact on California or its native cultures (Forbes 1969: 23–24; Hutchinson 1969: 52–54). The Spaniards, however, were seriously alarmed by Drake's incursion and the threat it posed to their Pacific colonies and the newly developing Manila trade. They reconsidered the problem of establishing a presence in California. Sebastián Rodriguez Cermeño, captain of the Manila galleon *San Agustín* in 1593–95, was ordered to reconnoiter the coast on his return voyage in search of a favorable harbor for estab-

Fig. 74. This 6d. silver English coin, minted in 1567, was discovered at the Marin County site CA-Mrn-193, a Final Pacific Period coastal shell midden. It might be a relic of Drake's visit in 1579, but could also have come from a Spanish ship such as Cermeño's, since coins circulated internationally. Note the hole in the perimeter of the coin: California Indians often sewed pierced coins on their costumes as ornaments. The coin thus was substituted for a shell ornament in an Indian value system, an example of the limits of the impact of contact with Europeans on Indian cultures at that period. (Courtesy of the Lowie Museum of Anthropology, University of California, Berkeley)

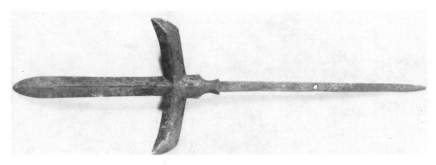

Fig. 75. This Japanese iron spearhead of the Magari Yari class was excavated at the Final Pacific Period site CA-Mrn-207 in Marin County. It represents the variety of Asian goods that made their way into coastal shell mounds. Since the goods tend to be concentrated on the Marin County coast, the most likely explanation for their occurrence is that they came from one or two shipwrecked Manila galleons, such as Cermeño's *San Agustín*, which was wrecked off Drake's Bay in 1595. (Courtesy of the Lowie Museum of Anthropology, University of California, Berkeley)

lishing a settlement. But his vessel foundered while at anchor in Drake's Bay, and the crew returned to Mexico only after a harrowing voyage in a small open boat. The shipwreck scattered a fortune in Asian trade goods along the beaches (see Figs. 75 and 76), and many objects found their way into archaeological sites around Point Reyes (Heizer 1941; Meighan 1950; Meighan & Heizer 1952).

The Mexican Viceroy, the Count of Monterrey, then sent Sebastián Vizcaíno on a similar mission in 1602–3. He explored the coast in three light ships thought more suitable for the treacherous waters of California. Vizcaíno apparently sailed as far north as Oregon, but, like Cermeño, failed to discover San Francisco Bay. He did discover the bay at Monterey, however, which he named in honor of the Viceroy in hopes of being appointed captain of the next Manila galleon. Unfortunately for Vizcaíno, the Count was soon ousted from power, and both Vizcaíno's dreams and the plans for colonizing California were abandoned.

During the next 150 years California was largely neglected by Spain. Trading ships from Asia occasionally foundered on the coast, or stopped for repairs, water, or provisions. Spanish artifacts and Chinese porcelains were acquired in small numbers by coastal Indians. A few surviving sailors from wrecked ships, or escapees from ships laying over, may have reached shore, either to be killed or to join Indian communities.

Hostilities occurred occasionally between the Europeans and In-

Fig. 76. This sherd of decorated Chinese porcelain was found during the excavation of CA-Mrn-232, a Marin County shell midden at Point Reyes National Seashore (fragment about 3 × 7 cm). A number of such sherds have
been found along this stretch of coast, perhaps all from the cargo of the *San
Agustín.* Whether the dishes were used or kept by the Indians as rare objects
is not clear, in contrast to the coin shown in Fig. 74. (Courtesy of the Lowie
Museum of Anthropology, University of California, Berkeley)

dians, sometimes arising from the kidnapping of Indian women by
sailors. Spanish genes may have been added to the Indian genetic
stock because of rape or marriage. And episodes of disease were
probably introduced by the Europeans to the nonresistant Native Californian populations. Although archaeological research has shown
that the Native Californian population declined after the end of the
Final Pacific (Cook 1976a, 1978), it may be that the population peaked
before the end of the Final Pacific, and that diseases introduced *before* permanent Spanish settlement affected the Indian populations.
Whatever the timing and the causes of the decline, it was apparently
confined largely to Indians living along the coast, and had comparatively less impact on inland groups. By and large, the contacts
were brief and had relatively little effect on Native Californian culture
as a whole. All in all, Indian-European relations were relatively amicable at this time, marked perhaps as much by mutual curiosity as
anything else.

The Spanish government's attitude toward California's colonization
began to shift again around the end of the seventeenth century. A
pearl fishery was developed in the Gulf of California. To make it more
secure, the Spanish launched an effort in cooperation with the Jesuits

to establish a chain of missions and military outposts among the Indians of Baja California. In 1702, Padre Kino, the founder of 26 missions in the American Southwest, reached the Colorado River. He realized that California was not an island, as had been previously believed, and that outposts in both Baja California and Alta California could be provisioned by land rather than by the more hazardous sea route. Kino died in 1711 without the inert colonial government in Mexico City acting on his idea, but it remained in circulation among Mexican intellectuals for the next half century.

Then, in 1747, the Russians discovered the Bering Strait and began to develop their own colonial empire in Alaska, expanding slowly down the coast. In 1756, the British wrested Canada from the French, and began to explore its western regions for possible commercial exploitation. Spain at last perceived the threat to its northern colonial frontier and moved to secure it. José de Gálvez was sent by the king to Mexico City as Visitador-General to take over the colonial government and revitalize it. Gaspar de Portolá, then governor in Baja California, was given administrative authority to colonize and govern Alta California, and was directed to lead a combined land-sea expedition to begin settlement before the end of the 1760's (Lavender 1972: 34–38). The era devoted solely to exploration had come to a close. Spain was about to embark on a wholly new enterprise in California. Of course, most parts of California were still largely unknown to the outside world, and exploration by Europeans would continue for many years.

The period had relatively little impact on California's archaeological record. Foreign visitors left few material remains to mark their visits, and Indian cultures were not significantly disrupted by these contacts. One of the most important contributions of these visits was the diaries and journals kept by some explorers describing these trips and the lands and peoples they encountered. Made by untrained and sometimes barely literate men, these earliest historical accounts provide a few shadowy glimpses of Native Californian cultures at the peak of their development. Even though, for the most part, these men could hardly be considered "unbiased observers," they have provided valuable information about such things as the appearance of the Native Californians they met and the locations of their settlements. Archaeologists and historians have found these documents to be of great value in reconstructing ethnographically known societies (Forbes 1969; Heizer 1978a; Heizer & Almquist 1971; Heizer & Whipple 1971; Hutchinson 1969; Lavender 1972; Schuyler 1978).

The Hispanic Stage (1769-1822)

European culture, as opposed to individual Europeans, reached California in the spring of 1769 when Gaspar de Portolá's expedition landed at San Diego. Gálvez's program for securing Mexico's northwestern frontier called for a few hundred priests, soldiers, and settlers to conquer and occupy a region nearly as large as Spain itself, a region already occupied by over 300,000 Indians. As improbable as the plan seems, it was based on Spain's largely successful experiences in northern Mexico, the Southwest, and Baja California, where indigenous societies were poorly equipped to resist the Spaniards' weapons and military skills.

Gálvez's program called for the establishment of three kinds of institutions: military garrisons (*presidios*), religious agrarian institutions (*misiones*), and civilian settlements and ranches (*pueblos* and *ranchos*). The program aimed to develop a gentry consisting of independent farmers, ranchers, and merchants and administered by local officials under the ultimate authority of the Viceroy and the King. The gentry was to serve as a militia to support the army in resisting Russian and British expansion. The system was to raise all its own food, to produce raw materials for export to the mother country, and to provide a market for manufactured goods exported from Spain and her more developed colonies. The new colony was to be prevented from having commerce with other European powers so as to ensure Spain's advantage (W. Bean 1977; Fages 1937).

The Spanish government would have liked to settle its frontiers with loyal citizen colonists who could have created an instant bulwark on the empire's borders, but it had learned through prior experience that few Spaniards could be lured to such remote regions. Failing that, the goal became the creation of a population of peasants and tradesmen from the native peoples who already occupied the region. For this reason, religious missions were made the center of the colonizing effort. Missionary fathers converted the natives to Christianity and taught them the arts and crafts of civilized life, transforming them in the process from scarcely human savages (in the Spanish view) to intelligent beings—*gente de razón*. If the Indians proved incapable of receiving instruction owing to their inability to appreciate the superiority of Spanish culture, experience in Mexico had shown that the presence of soldiers would lead to the creation of a new generation of mixed-blood peasants (mestizos) whose loyalty would be to Spain rather than to the traditional cultures of their Indian mothers.

Spain had had earlier experience with missionary programs. The

Jesuit Order had built missions in northern Mexico, the Southwest, and Baja California. The government intended to keep its missions operating only as long as it took to civilize the Indians—an estimated ten years. Afterward, each mission would be converted to the status of a parish church, its converts assuming civilized status as new farmers and ranchers. The mission lands would be given over to the converts, and the mission flocks and herds would be dispersed to stock the new enterprises. In time, the Spanish Crown grew suspicious of the loyalty of the largely non-Spanish Jesuits, and in 1767 removed them from the mission system and brought in the Franciscan Order to replace them. Thus, when Gálvez directed Portolá to mount a colonizing expedition for Alta California, it was the Franciscan fathers, under the leadership of Padre Junipero Serra, rather than the Jesuits, who were called on to establish the mission system.

Portolá led the first expedition of colonists from Mexico along the route suggested by Padre Kino nearly a century before: overland across the Sonoran and Colorado deserts—stopping first at San Diego to be resupplied by ship—and then north to Vizcaíno's anchorage at Monterey (Brandes 1969; see also Map 45). Over the next 52 years, 21 missions were founded by Padre Serra along the coast between San Diego and Sonoma, as well as a number of modest chapels and *asistencias*, or administrative branches of the missions. Two formal pueblos were chartered and built within the first ten years of settlement, at San Jose and Los Angeles; and military presidios were established at San Diego, Santa Barbara, Monterey, and San Francisco (see Figs. 77–79).

The Spaniards concentrated their settlements along the coast for several reasons. Indian populations were dense there. The coast could be defended and resupplied by sea with comparative ease and speed. Interior settlements would have presented greater logistical difficulties and heavier reliance on the extremely slow overland route from Sonora. And the coastal Indians already enjoyed to a considerable measure a settled village life, meaning that civilizing them, in Spanish terms, would be less challenging than the civilizing of, say, the more nomadic desert peoples. Development of the California colonies proceeded steadily, and by 1822 the non-Indian population in California had risen to 3,750 people (Hutchinson 1969: 64; Lavender 1972: 74–79).

As each mission was founded, a population of Indians was brought to it from the native villages of the vicinity, usually by force. The imprisoned native populations were used as slave laborers to build the missions, outbuildings, waterworks, and other facilities. In return,

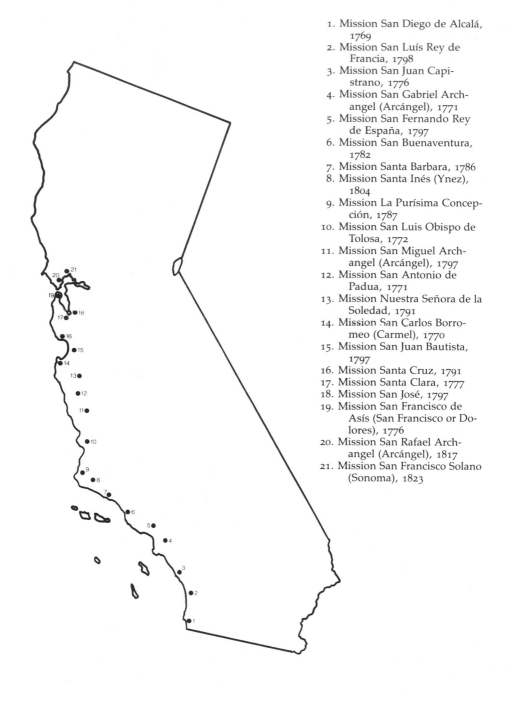

1. Mission San Diego de Alcalá, 1769
2. Mission San Luís Rey de Francia, 1798
3. Mission San Juan Capistrano, 1776
4. Mission San Gabriel Archangel (Arcángel), 1771
5. Mission San Fernando Rey de España, 1797
6. Mission San Buenaventura, 1782
7. Mission Santa Barbara, 1786
8. Mission Santa Inés (Ynez), 1804
9. Mission La Purísima Concepción, 1787
10. Mission San Luis Obispo de Tolosa, 1772
11. Mission San Miguel Archangel (Arcángel), 1797
12. Mission San Antonio de Padua, 1771
13. Mission Nuestra Señora de la Soledad, 1791
14. Mission San Carlos Borromeo (Carmel), 1770
15. Mission San Juan Bautista, 1797
16. Mission Santa Cruz, 1791
17. Mission Santa Clara, 1777
18. Mission San José, 1797
19. Mission San Francisco de Asís (San Francisco or Dolores), 1776
20. Mission San Rafael Archangel (Arcángel), 1817
21. Mission San Francisco Solano (Sonoma), 1823

they were taught the skills of brickmaking, ceramic-tile manufacture, weaving, pottery making, woodworking with metal tools, baking, cultivation, and ranching, among others. Conversion to Christianity was often accomplished by trickery, bribery, or force. A few Indians became literate, and some used the European painting techniques they had been taught to produce pieces for altar decoration. Some assisted the Spanish soldiers. Most, however, led existences of unrelieved misery and toil under close confinement (Heizer & Almquist 1971: 6–11).

These so-called "Mission Indians" were taken from a dozen or more Native Californian cultures (Shipek 1978). At the height of mission development, an estimated 55,000 Indians lived at the 21 missions, out of a total state population of between 260,000 and 270,000 (Cook 1976a). The numbers at the missions were raised to that level only by repeated raids by soldiers on "wild Indian" settlements, for population losses at the missions were consistently high. High death rates owing to disease, malnutrition, abuse, and culture shock horrified many of the padres, but the mission fathers were committed to their program and could do nothing to stem the loss of life (Heizer 1974a). Mission marriage and baptismal records show that the marriages and births among the Indian neophytes were far too few to replace the losses from death. Many Indian women regularly practiced abortion to prevent births, and many mothers who bore children of Spanish soldiers killed their babies (Lavender 1972: 82–90).

Mission losses were furthered by the escape of neophytes. Spanish troops pursued bands of escapees as far as the Central Valley, and recaptured Indians were routinely flogged, imprisoned, or placed in

Map 45 (facing page). Locations of Spanish missions in California and their founding dates. Spain hoped to secure the northwestern flank of its American colonial empire against Russian expansion through a settlement-and-pacification program. The plan included military garrisons, civilian towns, and religious missions. Of these elements, the missions were most crucial, because in them the Spanish hoped to organize Indians to provide the program's labor force and the population for a future peasantry loyal to the crown. The plan was developed from Spain's earlier experience in colonizing Baja California and the American Southwest. In these earlier efforts, the Jesuit Order had directed the mission programs, but the Jesuits fell out of favor with the Spanish government just before the launching of the California program. The Franciscans therefore established California's mission chain, starting with the first settlement in 1769 at San Diego and continuing until the Mexican Revolution of 1822 ended Spain's colonial programs in North America. The 21 missions established in that period were all located near the coast, since the only practical means of provisioning them was by sea.

Fig. 77. Mission Santa Barbara. This 1938 photograph shows the restored chapel with the front of the galleried compound to the left. The church structure typically formed a side of the mission compound. Dormitories for priests, neophytes' barracks, offices, kitchens, classrooms, storerooms, and workshops all formed part of the compound. Stables, barns, more workshops, and other outbuildings were built nearby. The mission compound formed a self-sufficient community for two thousand or more people. (U.S. Forest Service Photo)

Fig. 78. Mission San Luís Rey de Francia, built in 1798 (twelve years after the Santa Barbara mission), shows a slightly more Moorish flavor in its embellishments, though its compound design is similar. The mission cemetery, to the right of the church, has some graves dating back to the mission period. Some cemeteries were combined with formal gardens, partly for aesthetics and partly for practical reasons. The combination thus conserved space close to the mission and allowed the fathers to grow a number of European plants close at hand: fig trees, grapevines, and seasoning herbs, for example.

Fig. 79. Mission San Francisco Solano, built at Sonoma in 1823, is unusual in several ways. The last of the California missions, it is the simplest in architecture, although it employs the basic compound form. It is among the smallest, it is the farthest north, and it is the only one built under Mexican rule. Plans for the mission were developed by the Franciscans while Spain still ruled, but the Mexican Revolution occurred before construction began. The Franciscans were under suspicion after the Revolution because most were Spanish and had no particular loyalty to the new government. This mission was their last major project in California. Its simple style reflects both the straitened finances of the mission system and the growing influence of the "Monterey" style of colonial architecture: broad verandas supported by posts rather than the colonnaded arched walkways favored by the Spanish; low, pitched, tiled, overhanging roofs; simple post-and-lintel doorway construction; thick walls pierced by deep window recesses. Of all the missions, this is perhaps the most truly Californian.

stocks (Stickel & Cooper 1969). Escape was made even more risky because the Spaniards gradually eliminated the surrounding native villages, so that escapees had nowhere to go (see Map 46). Demoralized, cut off from access to family and food, and physically debilitated, the escapees had little hope of survival in their former homeland. Some escapees became raiders on the missions, trying to help others escape or stealing horses and goods from mission lands (W. Bean 1977; Heizer 1974a; Shipek 1978).

Although Spain did succeed in settling coastal California, the mission program failed to create a population of farmers, ranchers, and merchants from the neophytes. After 1810, the mission populations declined faster than they could be replenished, and most of the missions suffered from greatly reduced populations by 1820. Then, in 1821–22, Mexican revolutionaries joined with compatriots in many other parts of Latin America to overthrow their Spanish colonial governors. An independent Mexican nation was created. California had not been directly involved in the revolution, but Mexico's independence brought it control of the former colony. Spanish civil and military authority was replaced by Mexican, and the Hispanic era in Alta California was brought to a close.

Early European intrusion and settlement in California had different consequences than elsewhere. The fur trade dominated many of the early contacts elsewhere between Indians and Europeans, and often the fur trade was itself disruptive to traditional cultures. But in some areas (such as the Pacific Northwest, New York, New England, the Rockies, and the Great Lakes) it also led to temporary prosperity as Indians became participants in larger, cash-oriented economic systems. Even on the Great Plains, European intervention resulted in the spread of the horse, which led in turn to a focal emphasis on bison hunting.

Spanish colonization had a different result in California. No California group developed an economic partnership with the Spanish; in fact, the mission economies were less productive than the Indian economies they replaced. Although the Spaniards were technologically more sophisticated than the Indians in several respects, their economic institutions in the mission system were less complex and integrated than the traditional systems had been. The mission program disrupted the focal economies of California. Even the groups that were not missionized felt this adverse impact. Spanish settlement barred many of the remaining California Indians from traditionally important resources, such as clamshell beads, abalone shells, Catalina steatite, shellfish, and asphaltum. Vitally important trade relationships between the coast and the interior were severed. The inevitable result was an economic decline even for peoples who had never seen a European. Even had the Spanish been more careful in their missionization, they probably would never have been able to enter into economic partnership with non-mission Indians. The Spaniards had come for souls and land, not just furs or minerals.

Events showed that, from the Spanish perspective, colonization was begun none too soon. The feared Russian presence materialized in the early 1800's. Russia had been developing an Alaska colony for a half century, and had begun to explore southward in search of furs. Unlike the Spaniards, the Russians were interested in acquiring raw materials rather than settling the land. Their main target was the California sea otter, whose fur could be sold in China at great profit. In

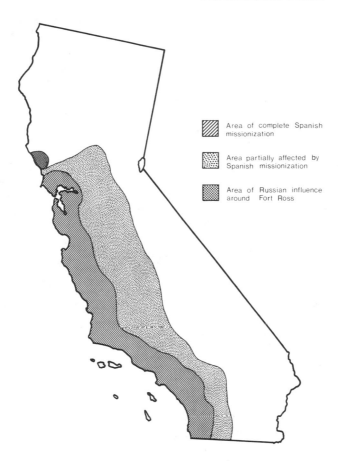

Map 46. Areas of Spanish and Russian influence in California, 1769–1822. The coastal hills and valleys from San Francisco Bay southward were effectively dominated by Spain, but the influence of Spanish presence was felt by California Indian communities as far east as the Sierra Nevada and the Colorado River. The Russian presence, though much more localized and limited in purpose, effectively limited the northward expansion of Spanish colonies. Russian influence was felt far to the south of Fort Ross, since sea otters were hunted as far south as Morro Bay and slaves were taken from as far south as San Nicolas Island.

1811 a Russian post was established at Bodega Bay, north of San Francisco. The next year it was moved to a more secure setting at Fort Ross, where it was maintained until 1841.

Russian relationships with California Indians were quite different from those of the Spaniards. The Russians did some of their own trapping, aided by the Aleut Indians they brought with them to California, but they also traded for furs with local Pomo Indians. The Russians and Aleuts were guilty of several atrocities committed against Native Californians, such as the San Nicolas Island massacre in 1830, in which all but twenty of the island's population were killed (Heizer & Elsasser 1963). In general, however, Russian relations with Indians were more amicable. A number of cases of Russian-Pomo bilingualism are known, for instance, and formal marriages between Russian men and Pomo women have been recorded. Although the Russians were not necessarily more humane than the Spaniards, their desire for furs, their disinterest in colonial settlement and land acquisition, and their desire for amicable trade relations all served to foster a better atmosphere between them and the Indians (Johnston 1962: 103; Kroeber 1925: 633–35). These conditions also meant that the Russians had far less impact on Native Californian cultures than the Spaniards had—and the Russian efforts are correspondingly less visible archaeologically.

Spanish settlement caused dramatic changes in California's archaeological record (Moriarty 1971). European styles of architecture and technology were introduced (Brandes 1969 and Moriarty & Weyland 1971; see Figs. 77–79). Metal came into use for the first time and spread to many Indian communities. Pottery had been rare prehistorically except in the southeastern deserts, where the manufacture of a plain, brown pottery ware known as Tizon Brownware appeared around A.D. 1000 (Evans 1969); but the Spaniards developed extensive ceramic industries in order to make containers and roof and floor tiles, and introduced the making of adobe building bricks. Domestic animals were imported to provide food, raw materials, plow labor, and transportation. By 1820, most of the missions had between 10,000 and 20,000 head of sheep and cattle and hundreds of horses in their pastures, and pigs and chickens were kept in the mission compounds. Studies of animal bones found at mission sites show that the neophytes, who did the bulk of the work at the missions, were taught Spanish styles of animal butchering and usually abandoned their traditional styles even when butchering game for their own use (Hoover 1979). Wheeled vehicles were introduced, particularly the ox-drawn *carreta*, a simple cargo wagon with two solid wooden wheels that turned on a log axle (Fig. 80). Even a few finer carriages were imported by colonial administrators and military commanders (Moriarty 1973). Although the padres frequently rode mules, horses were ridden by military, government, and civilian personnel, including some Indian neophytes trained as vaqueros to herd cattle from horseback.

Fig. 80. The carreta was the basic cargo vehicle under Spanish and Mexican rule in California. Drawn by a pair of yoked oxen, the cart provided slow but efficient transport in a land of few roads. Its simple design meant that it could be made by semiskilled carpenters using the simplest hand tools and local raw materials. It could be repaired easily, but was so solid that it did not often break down. And it did not require expensive metal fittings or highly crafted wood components that had to be imported from Europe. Consequently, it was perfectly adapted to the needs of a small colony on the remote fringe of the empire.

Many of the material remains from these activities have made their way into the archaeological sites that mark the missions, ranchos, pueblos, and remaining Indian settlements of this era.

Systematic agriculture, introduced into California by the Spaniards, had a profound effect on the native California resources and landscape. Several missions developed extensive waterworks to supply their buildings and fields. European crops were introduced: wheat, oats, barley, and other grains, grapevines, fruit and nut trees, vegetables, flowers, herbs, medicinal plants, and textile fibers. California's Mediterranean climate proved to be an especially hospitable setting for many species. In addition to the deliberate introductions, seeds from European grasses were carried inadvertently into the state in the wool of Spanish sheep. These hardy European grasses proved far more vigorous than the native perennial bunchgrasses, and within a few generations the state was blanketed with wild oats, mustard, star thistle, and other exotic species while the original grasses became nearly extinct. A century later, even many California Indians no longer realized that wild oat was not an original feature of the environment (see, for example, Goldschmidt 1951).

The adjustment by Europeans to colonial life is reflected in the artifacts they left behind. The immigrants tried, insofar as possible, to lead lives with which they were familiar. They imported some material goods, including weapons, iron tools, glass, and fine fabrics. But it was not possible to import everything they needed, since costs were high and shipping time-consuming and unreliable. Metal, in particular, was comparatively hard to obtain and therefore relatively rare and valuable. As a result, craftsmen, both Hispanic and Indian, produced a variety of European-style goods made of local California materials.

Virtually all local craft production was done in the missions, since there was only a tiny Hispanic military and civilian population, and the missions were the center of the Spanish attempt to concentrate the indigenous population. The padres introduced a variety of European crafts and skills, such as adobe manufacture and construction, tile making, pottery, hide tanning, weaving, blacksmithing, candle and soap production, baking, leatherworking, carpentry, farming, winemaking, and herding. These they taught to the captive mission Indians who, in turn, provided almost all the labor for these crafts. For the Indians who were missionized, much of their traditional culture and technology was replaced by Hispanic craft activities and technologies.

The loss of traditional technology was most complete in those areas in which Indian activities were in conflict with mission activities. This was particularly true for objects associated with men, whose traditional activities, such as hunting, fishing, warfare, and ritual, were almost totally prohibited by the padres. In other cases, certain kinds of activities practiced by Indians were not regarded as conflicting with Spanish goals and were allowed to persist. For example, at missions where married couples were provided family housing, women were allowed to practice their own domestic activities. These women continued to make and use such traditional items as baskets and milling tools. In still other cases, mission crafts involved skills with which Indians were already familiar, such as processing animal hides; in these cases both Indian and Spanish tools were used. The distinctive archaeological assemblage of mission and traditional artifacts reflects the emergence of a social order based, no matter how one-sided it may have been, on an interaction between these two cultures to produce a synthesized adaptation to California.

Another element was added to this era's archaeological remains by Mexican mestizos. Many of the farmers, ranchers, merchants, and infantry soldiers brought to California were Mexican rather than Spanish by birth, and in most cases of mixed Spanish and Mexican-Indian descent. These immigrants brought with them a mestizo culture that combined Spanish and Mexican elements into its own hybrid creations. The cultivation of corn, beans, chiles, and squash, the milling of grain on four-legged, well-shaped metates, the use of adobe rather than the Spanish plastered stone masonry for architecture, the wearing of poncho-style serapes and huge-brimmed sombreros, and a diet based on tortillas and frijoles were all mestizo contributions rather than Iberian. Although mestizos never constituted a large part of the population in California during the Hispanic period, some became individual landowners and rose to positions of growing importance as the Spanish plan to have Indian neophytes assume much of this role failed to materialize. Excavations at the Sanchez adobe near Pacifica, which was a farm that grew wheat to help feed Mission Dolores in San Francisco, reveals the characteristically mestizo nature of such holdings (Drake 1952; Miley Holman, pers. comm. 1980).

Eventually, missionization all but extinguished the traditional cultures of the coastal Indians in the 600 miles (965 km) between Tomales Bay and San Diego (see Map 46). In the area of the missions, Indian populations (apart from those confined to the missions themselves) were reduced by 90 percent or more, or even completely wiped out, and mission populations were maintained only by drawing from the surviving surrounding populations. Some Indians fled inland to areas held by other groups, where much of their own language and culture was submerged (Stickel & Cooper 1969). Individuals attached themselves in some cases to farms and ranches as peons or serfs, in order to survive after their own communities were destroyed. Montgomery's (1968) fictional account of the fate of Chief Marin, finding himself bereft of family and community upon release from the prison at Mission San Rafael, evokes this condition. From these few, and from the most resilient of the neophytes, a few representatives of some of the coastal cultures survived, and their descendants managed to bring some knowledge of their traditional cultures into the twentieth century.

As noted earlier, Hispanic colonization even affected Native Californian groups that were not in direct contact with the missions. In addition to the breakdown of the trade system and the lack of access to coastal resources, such important resource areas for people in the Coast Ranges as the grasslands in the river valleys and the groves or oaks were gradually preempted by Europeans for grazing lands. Pursuing Spanish troops periodically raided the Central Valley, leading to further hostilities. The permanent Hispanic population on the coast became a source for disease, to which the Indians had no resistance. By the nineteenth century, epidemics swept through the interior Indian populations as well as through the mission peoples. Thus the impact of Spanish settlement was felt far from its center, almost invariably to the disadvantage of the Indians.

The Mexican Stage (1822-46)

Inspired by the United States and French revolutions, liberal fervor swept through much of Latin America during the first two decades of the nineteenth century, and Spain soon lost almost all her New World colonies. Mexico, after winning her freedom in 1822, established a republic under a constitution modeled after that of the United States. In becoming independent, she assumed control of the colony of Alta California (Map 47). Spanish civil and military authorities were replaced by Mexicans under the new governor, José María Echeandía. This did not lead to wholesale cultural change in California's European population, but several important changes did occur.

The first change concerned relations between California and other nations. Spain had closed her colonies to ships of other European powers in order to preserve her trade monopolies. Visits by foreign ships to California ports were notable mainly for their rarity. Mexico, however, relaxed this practice. First England, and then the United States, began to send trading ships to California ports. California's major export items of the time were cattle by-products: hides for leather and tallow for candles and soap. At the time of the Mexican Revolution most of California's cattle were in mission hands, and the mission fathers turned to hide and tallow production as a source of badly needed income. Indian neophytes were put to work driving cattle down to the shore to be slaughtered. Hides were baled and stored in sheds along with the tallow rendered from the carcasses. When a Spanish ship landed along the coast, the mission would entertain the captain, strike a bargain, and row the cargo in small boats out to the anchored ship. With secularization, this trade passed into the hands of the rancheros. Chace (1969) points out how dependent the ranchero economy was on the cattle trade described so vividly by Richard Henry Dana in his *Two Years Before the Mast*.

Map 47. Areas of Mexican influence, 1822–46. The Mexican Revolution, completed in 1822, ended Spain's occupation of California. The new Mexican republic took over the Spanish colonies, gradually transforming California to a nearly independent, self-sufficient state whose economy was based on cattle ranching and foreign trade. Because expanding pastoralism took Mexican settlement much farther inland than Spanish settlement had gone, the number of California Indian communities directly affected by foreign colonization was much larger than it had been under Spain.

Mexico fostered this foreign trade partly to stimulate the colony's economy and partly because it provided the only large source of income available with which to finance its colonial administration. California's internal economy at this time operated principally on the barter system. Little cash was in circulation, in contrast with the economy during the Final Pacific Period. The Mexican government lacked the resources to support troops and civil servants in distant colonies, so it raised the needed funds by opening its ports and imposing duties on all foreign imports. Visiting ships were supposed to call at Monterey, where customs inspectors levied the import tax (W. Bean 1977; Beardsley 1946). Furthermore, the growing Mexican population in Alta California created a market for manufactured goods, and U.S. and British shippers responded vigorously to supply this demand. As a result, Yankee and English goods appear in archaeological sites of this era, mixed with Mexican, Spanish, and Indian artifacts.

This growing trade began to bring commercial agents to the colony. When California was first opened to foreign trade, sales and orders were made by each ship's officers when vessels called along the coast. A captain would have to seek markets for his imported cargo, and then purchase a cargo of hides and tallow from whatever rancheros he could deal with. By having permanent representatives in the substantial communities at San Diego, Los Angeles, Santa Barbara, and Monterey, however, shippers could arrive to find their imported cargos already sold, distribution arranged for, warehouses of hides awaiting loading, and orders already taken for the next voyage. By 1845, more than 700 U.S. businessmen and their families had joined the 7,000 Mexican Californianos living in the colony. These agents began to provide the colony's first commercial banking services. Since few financial resources were available locally, the Yankee agents began to provide funds and lines of credit to the Mexican rancheros, which strengthened the growing U.S. influence in the region.

Further U.S. influence resulted from visits by American fur trappers. With the opening of California's borders by Mexico, American trappers came overland to explore and exploit the interior. Jedediah Smith, who traveled up the Sacramento River, crossed the Klamath Mountains, and reached the sea in 1826, was the first of this breed. Although the fur trappers generally did not settle in California, they represented the first direct contact with foreigners for many interior Indian groups. These contacts very likely were responsible for the spread of diseases deadly to the native population. The great smallpox epidemic of 1830–33 in the Sacramento Valley, which may have killed as many as 60,000 Indians, was apparently started by a party of fur trappers traveling up the Sacramento River and on to Oregon in the fall of 1830 (Cook 1978: 92). So, in a fashion, the Americans had already become a forceful influence on Indian and Mexican cultures in California even before the War of 1846 ended Mexico's rule.

But by far the biggest change that the Mexicans made in California was the secularization of the missions. Some of the missions had been in operation for more than 60 years, far longer than Spain had originally intended, and the Spanish government had actually begun to develop plans for terminating the missions when the Mexican Revolution ended its rule. Although the Mexican takeover did not bring about an immediate end to the missions, it did accelerate the process. For one thing, the new Mexican constitution granted full citizenship, at least in theory, to all persons born within the republic's boundaries and regardless of race—including the Indians. For another, the new governor, Echeandía, had been a revolutionary soldier and was an ardent civil libertarian. He began to develop plans for ending the role of the missions and bringing freedom to the Indians soon after he arrived in California in 1822. Agitation for the end of the missions grew in both Mexico and California during the following decade. It was accompanied by plans to bring more colonists to the area north of San Francisco in order to create a stronger bulwark against the Russians and British. Liberal Mexicans hoped to bring Indians into the colonial communities to create the kind of integrated society they saw developing in some parts of Mexico. Commercial advantage was also seen to follow from the development of a larger civilized population.

Three factors above all others complicated the issue of mission secularization for all concerned: politics in Mexico, the role of the Franciscan fathers, and the readiness of the Indians to become full-fledged citizens in Mexican terms (W. Bean 1977; Lavender 1972). Back in Mexico, bitter factional disputes broke out between liberals and conservatives, and the mission-secularization issue became entangled in this conflict. Communication between Mexico and California was so intermittent, and the strength of the Mexican government so reduced, that between 1828 and 1832 the province of Alta California became almost a *de facto* independent nation. Although the Mexican Californians shared all the differences raging at home, they found common ground in preferring their autonomy, which made any administrative plans from Mexico difficult to carry out. Nevertheless, the idea of secularization received considerable support, perhaps mainly because the Californianos longed to appropriate the vast mission lands and herds for their own.

The Franciscans also were a problem because most of the padres were of Spanish birth and showed little loyalty to the new Mexican government; the padres were also the only group to provide genuine support for the Indians. Although Mexican liberals were committed to the ideal of full citizenship for all Mexicans, the dominating principle of self-interest precluded their making any real provisions for the protection of Indian rights in the event that the missions were finally closed.

The Indians themselves were scarcely prepared to leave the missions. After a half century of mission life, much of their original culture had been stripped away and the missions provided their only means of survival. Some individuals had attached themselves to Mexican communities as laborers, and among this group, poverty, disease, and alcoholism were rampant. Others had fled from the missions, joining groups of relatively undisturbed Indians. They were completely unwilling to return to any close association with the Spanish and Mexicans, and in some cases they raided isolated ranchos and mission herds. Altogether, the situation was not auspicious for the creation of a new, integrated society.

Nevertheless, the drive for secularization continued. On August 17, 1833, the Congress in Mexico City passed an act that called for the immediate transformation of the California missions into civil parishes (Lavender 1972: 102). José Figueroa, California's governor at the time, developed programs for the change. In theory, half of all mission lands, herds, seed stores, and farm machinery were to be turned over to the Indians in an enormous land reform that was to have created a population of indigenous peasant farmers and ranchers. The other half was to be managed by civil administrators for the benefit of the new towns that Mexico had planned to act as buffers against the Russian presence at Fort Ross and the British expansion in western Canada.

In reality, the Indians ended up with almost nothing, the new pueblos were not developed, and the programs to bring additional colonists from Mexico were thwarted. Instead, small numbers of the original Mexican Californianos managed to seize almost all the rich mission lands and form huge ranchos. Private land grants had been rare until then: Spain and Mexico combined had made only 51 grants to individual citizens between 1769 and the completion of secularization in 1834. In the next six years, over 300 grants were confirmed by the Mexican government, and even more were awarded between 1840 and 1846 (Hutchinson 1969: 66–69; Lavender 1972: 105–7). In a remarkably brief period almost all the productive farm- and ranchland in the colony was handed over to a handful of Mexican families, together with vast herds of cattle, sheep, and horses. Secularization ushered in "the period of 'pastoral Arcadia,' which gave California the gauzy and nostalgic heritage of dashing *caballeros*, beautiful *señoritas*, and the 'cattle on a thousand hills.' In all truth, this was one of the largest non-nomadic pastoral societies the world has ever known." (Hutchinson 1969: 68; see Fig. 81.)

If the Californiano era was bucolic for the privileged few, for the mission Indians it was an even more devastating time than the mis-

Fig. 81. A typical ranch house of the Mexican Stage, the Diego Sepulveda Adobe was originally built to shelter cattle workers from Mission San Juan Capistrano during the Hispanic Stage. Its form, size, and construction are similar to the José Sepulveda Adobe described later. Its Monterey Colonial architecture (see Fig. 79) features a low peaked roof whose broad overhangs form verandas, thick walls of mission-brick adobe, and deep window recesses. The original roof was of tules sealed with tar. The structure was built between 1817 and 1823 on the south bluff overlooking the Santa Ana River in present-day Costa Mesa. Don Diego Sepulveda, a former alcalde of Los Angeles, took over the building in the 1830's and made it his home and the headquarters of the Sepulveda Estancia. Today it is preserved as a city park.

sion period had been. Robbed of their promised legacy, denied the support of the missions, and unable to return to their pre-Hispanic life, they suffered severe crises. The numbers of mission Indians plummeted from 30,000 to 10,000 in the first decade after secularization. Most survivors ended up as virtual serfs on the feudal-style haciendas of the Californianos. The mission fathers may have captured them and forced them into submission, but at least some measure of food, shelter, and clothing had been provided, a new religion had been offered to replace that which had been taken from them, and some provision had been made to prepare them for a new way of life. The rancheros simply took advantage of what little was left. A lively traffic arose in selling Indian children to become household servants (Cook 1978; Heizer & Almquist 1971). Even the majority of missions themselves fell into ruins and were stripped of their artwork and building materials.

The system of ranchos that arose after secularization spread into

Fig. 82. Like the missions earlier, Sutter's Fort had to be a self-sustaining community for its residents. For the decade before the Gold Rush it was the only source of help and supplies for European and American travelers in the Sierra and Central Valley. It has been reconstructed on its original site, and archaeology contributed extensively to the accuracy of the reconstruction. Shown here is one of the corner bastions with a sally port at mid-wall to the right, largely hidden by brush. The walls enclosed a complex of buildings housing workshops, storerooms, living quarters, and even a primitive jail.

the Central Valley. It marked the first European settlement of that region and deprived the Indians of another critical resource zone. Land grants were awarded to non-Hispanics for the first time. In 1839 John Sutter received 11 leagues (roughly 1,000 square miles, or 3,000 km²) where Sacramento now stands (see Fig. 82). John Marsh purchased another 11 leagues between the site of Stockton and Mt. Diablo in 1836. John Bidwell acquired an equivalent tract between Chico and the Sacramento River in 1842 (W. Bean 1977; Lavender 1972).

Indians who lived in the Central Valley had either to accept the disruption of their lives and loss of life-supporting resources or to retreat into the Sierra and southern Cascades, which already were occupied by other Indian groups. The developing ranchos began to deprive Indians of access to the best fishing grounds, to the valley oaks and grasses, and to the migratory waterfowl, tule elk, and antelope. Surviving trade networks were disrupted. The well-integrated Pacific Period economies could no longer be maintained, nor could the large populations they supported. By 1845, California's Indian population fell to about 150,000 (Cook 1976a: 44). The Pacific Period way of life, which started to break down when Spanish settlement began, finally died at this point.

This did not mean the end of *every* form of traditional culture, or the death of all Native Californians. Rather, under the weight of severe population losses and the factors that had produced those losses, the structure of Pacific society collapsed. Even those cultures still outside the sphere of direct Spanish and Mexican influence were forced increasingly into a less focal, more diffuse economy. Reversion to a true Archaic economy was not possible, however. A true Archaic economy could not be restored because the movement of Indian groups was now severely restricted: Archaic-style seasonal migrations from the valleys to different environments in the high mountains could not be followed; and access to many critical resources was cut off. The remaining Indian groups were forced instead to diversify their diets, basing them on the resources available in their immediate territories. That strategy supplied less food than Archaic-style seasonal rounds, and populations fell accordingly.

The falling population levels themselves affected other aspects of surviving Native Californian culture, so that the distinctive social features characteristic of the Pacific Period largely or wholly disappeared during the Historical Period. Much of these cultures' social complexity rested on an economic base: trade and profit had helped to create social and economic distinctions within communities, and when trade was disrupted everyone was reduced to egalitarian penury. Many aspects of traditional life disappeared as specialists died without training their successors. And as the size and numbers of Native Californian settlements declined, the need for administrative specialists also declined. Village leaders, task group leaders, and craft specialists became unnecessary. Knowledge and skills disappeared with the people who knew and used them. Eventually even the very faith in the remaining order waned. New cults arose from desperation, promising to restore the old order through magic and ritual (DuBois 1939; Meighan & Riddell 1972).

The population decline traditionally has been blamed on the Native Americans' lack of resistance to European diseases. Equally important, but seldom mentioned, is the fact that many groups had already been severely weakened by malnutrition following economic collapse, which heightened their susceptibility to disease. Even if European diseases had never been a major factor, the collapse of Pacific focal economies alone would have caused a substantial population decline.

This weakening was carried into California's interior by the spread of the rancho system. Designed to produce a cash crop, the rancho was actually incapable of supporting more than a relatively few people on a very large amount of land. In this respect it was in direct conflict with the Indians, who needed the same land to support relatively large numbers of people in a very different form of economy and society. In this conflict the Indians, who had been decimated by disease, armed conflict, and the breakdown of their whole cultural world, were no match for the determined, ever-growing onslaught from the outside world. The growing number of settlers entering California, the entry of trappers into many parts of the state, and the spread of actual settlement from the coast into the interior meant that this stage had more profound effects on Native Californian populations than ever before. Even Indians living in relatively out-of-the-way areas, such as the foothills of the Sierra, were affected by disease and the loss of access to coastal and valley resources. Interior southern California was similarly affected. Only in far-northern California could Indian society persist in a relatively unaffected way, because this rugged, remote area still lay beyond the reach of European interests. But events in Texas 1,500 miles to the east (2,400 km) were soon to have important consequences for California as a whole.

The Anglo-American Stage (1846 to the Present)

Mexico might have taken a firmer hand in California's development during the crucial period of secularization except that its energies were absorbed by the closer and bloodier Texas revolution. Tension along the Texas-Mexico border remained high for the decade after Texas independence in 1836, distracting the Mexican government from events farther west. The United States annexed Texas in 1845, precipitating a war between the United States and Mexico. California's 7,000 Mexicans, isolated from Mexico City, unable to receive serious support, and burdened by factionalism and the presence of nearly 1,000 restive Anglo-Americans (Americans of English descent), could scarcely defend their enormous province. The approach of war in 1846 triggered a rebellion, fomented by Lt. John Charles Frémont, among the Anglo-American dissidents, during which they soon wrested control of central California from the Mexican officials and set up the Bear Flag Republic. A number of Mexicans supported this venture. But only three weeks later, the U.S. military, led by General Stephen Watts Kearny and Commodore John Drake Sloat, seized California, disbanded the Bear Flag Republic, and declared California an American territory.

The next two years were times of unrest and confusion. The Americans took over the reins of local government and transferred California from a Mexican province to an American territory. Anglo-Americans moved into central California in growing numbers, soon equaling the Californiano population in the south. The American military officers who had seized California were uncertain whether to maintain Mexican law until directed to do otherwise or to impose U.S. law. As Anglos and Californianos attempted to work out an accommodation to their new political reality, gold was discovered in the Sierra (W. Bean 1977).

John Marshall, an itinerant carpenter hired by John Sutter to build a sawmill at Coloma, east of Sacramento, made the discovery in January 1848. Sutter, realizing his vulnerability as a Swiss citizen with a Mexican land grant in a U.S. territory, tried to keep the discovery a secret, but word leaked out and within a few months thousands of Californians swarmed into the foothills of the Sierra. In December a speech to Congress by President Polk spread the news in the east. Over 150,000 miners and adventurers poured into California in the next two years. This Gold Rush sealed the fate of the remaining Native Californian cultures and pushed even the Californianos into a subservient position (for the archaeology of Sutter's Fort, see Olsen 1961; Payen 1961).

The 1849 Gold Rush was an anomaly in the history of the American West, transforming what might have been a gradual evolution into sudden, dramatic, and revolutionary change, and introducing elements into California that otherwise might never have developed. Although most of the massive influx of people came from the eastern United States, people from dozens of other nations were also represented. San Francisco was transformed overnight from a small pueblo into an international city. Sacramento and Stockton grew up overnight where previously there had been no communities at all. Enormous tent cities at first, they were supply centers and points of embarkation for the goldfields. Hundreds of mining camps sprang up in the goldfields, including many that were made up of particular racial or ethnic groups: Chinese, Italians, Mexicans, Blacks, Hawaiians, Portuguese, French, and Native Californians are examples. Few camps have been explored archaeologically. Suddenly, California had be-

Fig. 83. This ground-stone crushing wheel, known to have been made by miners from Chile and photographed in 1942 in Sequoia National Forest, represents a low-energy method of ore crushing. The 1849 Gold Rush brought argonauts from many nations, many of whom had previous mining experience and brought the technology of their backgrounds with them. Many of them shipped to Panama from the Atlantic states and then crossed the Isthmus. Ships in this service, which had of course to circumnavigate the tip of South America, stopped at ports along the coast of Chile, Peru, and Ecuador before picking up the argonauts in Panama. Along the way, South American miners boarded the ships, and thus constituted a fair percentage of the passengers reaching San Francisco. By the mid-1850's most of these low-energy mining efforts had been replaced by technologically more advanced methods, as the rich ores were played out and more efficiency in refining was needed to extract gold profitably. (U.S. Forest Service Photo)

come extremely diverse ethnically, but this diversity had not yet been fused into an integrated society (see Figs. 83 and 84).

Life in the goldfields was often violent and lawless. Many argonauts were rootless, ill adjusted, and uneducated. Others were fleeing from eastern urban poverty, from discrimination, or from the law. Still others were law-abiding, middle-class young men seeking wealth and adventure. The preponderantly male influx lacked the tempering influences of wives and children. Unlike the Anglo-American settlement of the Midwest and Great Plains, the '49ers did not bring with them the institutions of the community: civil government, schools, and churches. The goldfield camps and the cities servicing them sprang up largely lacking institutions of order and stability. They were characterized by large numbers of disaffected young males and

Fig. 84. Chinese wine jug from a Plumas County mining campsite. Before the Gold Rush the Oriental artifacts that made their way to California were mostly luxury or exotic items destined for foreign trade (e.g., Figs. 75 and 76). But when Chinese miners joined the Gold Rush, they were mostly men of poor families whose goods were simple and utilitarian. This ceramic jug, found in 1912 by I. W. Follett, measures 5⅓ inches (14 cm) in diameter. An authority on California fish and a scientist at the California Academy of Sciences, Follett has contributed to dozens of archaeological studies by identifying the species of fish whose remains were found in sites. (Courtesy of the Lowie Museum of Anthropology, University of California, Berkeley)

an extraordinary mixture of races and cultures. In the absence of organized government, vigilance committees sprang up. The dispensing of vigilante justice periodically became an excuse for committing atrocities against the outnumbered and powerless ethnic minorities, especially the Orientals and Indians. Such an unstable situation could not long endure. Most of the mining camps failed when gold discoveries declined, and were abandoned as quickly as they had arisen. But California's Gold Rush differed from those in the Klondike and elsewhere. Of the masses of people who came to California, many stayed, even after the prospect of sudden wealth began to fade. This population formed much of the basis for the development of urban centers in the state. Though barely studied archaeologically and still not fully documented historically, the Gold Rush represents an unusual and fleeting but still pivotal moment in the history of urban civilization.

The stimulus of the Gold Rush precipitated California into statehood in 1850, only four years after its seizure from Mexico. The territory's growing population, its strategic location, and the desire to protect and control the goldfields all helped promote the statehood movement. Statehood in turn brought an involvement in a national political and economic system and an imposition on the state of a complex governmental structure previously unknown in California. Under Mexican rule, California had a colonial capital at Monterey, but each population center retained a fair degree of autonomy. The missions and military, although formally structured, also usually exercised only local control. Pueblos were governed by an alcalde, a sort of appointed mayor, and territorial government was hardly more complicated.

After statehood, however, a state government was created, the state was divided into counties (eventually 58) with their own governments, and within each county one or more municipalities were incorporated. Each level of government had multiple branches. In addition, the federal government and various agencies, such as the army and navy, maintained branches in the new state. Land titles were registered for the state, and comprehensive tax rolls were begun. Although the vote was generally restricted to White males, voter registration was widespread, and elections at all levels of government drew much of the voting population into the governing process. For that matter, a significant percentage of the literate White males in the state held office at some level of government. The imposition of this system brought an unprecedented degree of structure and organization to the state.

The state's non-Indian population rose from about 15,000 in 1848 to nearly 225,000 in 1852 (Lavender 1972: 165). At the same time, the state's Indian population had fallen below 100,000 and was approaching 50,000 (Cook 1978: 91–93). Thus, in 1852, although the total number of people in California was not much greater than it had been a century earlier, its organization and makeup were vastly different. The imposition of a formal, statewide government was one aspect of this organizational difference. Another was the rise of urbanism.

In Mexican colonial times, Monterey was the sole official gateway to California. All incoming ships were supposed to stop there to be inspected for tax purposes. Monterey achieved a degree of urbanism due to the presence of the colonial administration and the representatives of foreign trade interests. Fledgling ports, which would later become centers of urban development, developed at San Diego, Los Angeles, and San Francisco. The Gold Rush greatly accelerated urbanization. Urban development was stimulated also by the subsequent effects of statehood and, finally, by industrialization. These stages in the progressive development of urbanism in California are marked by physical remains that have a great deal of largely unrealized potential for archaeological research.

The first stage of urban development, centered in central and northern California, resulted from the short-lived Gold Rush and was built on the establishment of a three-level hierarchy of communities. The bottom level consisted of hundreds of small camps scattered throughout the gold-bearing ranges to serve the needs of the miners. Volcano, near Jackson, was typical; it included a few stores, a hotel, a restaurant, and 37 saloons.

These towns were served in turn by small regional cities that arose to funnel miners and supplies into the goldfields. Prior to 1849, there were no towns in interior California. Cities were quickly established along the major rivers of the Central Valley. They connected the foothill towns with the port of San Francisco, using the Sacramento and San Joaquin rivers as their highways. These regional centers were located at points near the edges of the Sierra foothills where they could conveniently supply the mining camps. At the same time, boats coming up the rivers could bring supplies and travelers in quantity from San Francisco. Sacramento, on the Sacramento River at the mouth of the American River, is a good example. In 1848 it was part of Sutter's farmlands and no town existed. By 1850 it housed 10,000 people and burgeoned with docks, warehouses, wholesalers, retailers, laundries, restaurants, hotels, newspapers, saloons, and bordellos.

At the top of the hierarchy was San Francisco—the largest popula-

Fig. 85. Hydraulic water monitor. As the easily recovered placer gold was collected, miners turned to more and more intensive mining methods to recover the poorer and poorer ores. In 1849 most mining was done by individuals, but in the early 1850's mining companies were organized to use methods requiring cooperative labor, such as long sluice boxes. By the mid-1850's even more ambitious techniques were applied. When this instrument, a water monitor or cannon, was used to wash down entire hillsides, gold separated from the lighter matrix of earth and rock. Mining companies dammed streams higher in the hills and built water flumes to carry the stream downhill to the monitors. The tremendous pressure of the falling water, aided by the gradually constricting monitor tube, created a high-pressure water cannon that could dissolve or break up entire mountains.

Fig. 86. This century-old photograph of the La Grange Placer Mine, taken in what is now the Shasta-Trinity National Forest, shows hydraulic monitors at work washing down a mountainside, so that the rubble can be sluiced for gold. The monitor shown in Fig. 85 is the type used here. Hydraulic mining caused vast quantities of rubble to be washed downstream, raising river levels in the valleys, drowning towns, and ruining farmlands. By the late 1850's the number of miners had decreased and the number of farmers and ranchers had risen enough that the agricultural lobby was able to overcome the mining lobby in the state legislature and force an end to hydraulic mining. Thereafter, California's gold-mining industry was limited largely to tunnels and dredging. (U.S. Forest Service Photo)

tion center, the port of entry for supplies and miners arriving in California, and the single most important contact point between California and the rest of the world. The advantages that San Francisco enjoyed as a result of its harbor and proximity to the goldfields ensured its early and continued urbanization.

During the 1850's, the search for gold became more industrialized as placer deposits were played out or consolidated into larger holdings and machinery began to replace human labor (see Figs. 85–89). As miners began to leave the goldfields in the 1850's and 1860's, many mining camps were abandoned. At the same time, and in line with the developing urbanization, the emergence of state government and the development of farming, ranching, logging, and transportation industries led to the second stage in the organization and distribution of cities and towns (see Figs. 90–96). As agriculture began to spread into the valleys and foothills of almost every part of the state, hundreds of small communities arose to serve the towns and ranches. These communities replaced mining camps at the bottom level of the urban hierarchy, serving local farmers and ranchers as the mining camps had served the miners. Some of these towns became county seats, centers of administrative and commercial services. In this respect they differed from the mining camps. They also differed in that ranch and farm life was family-oriented, in contrast to the single-male character of mining communities, so that the services provided in the farm towns differed from those of the mining camps.

Cities, such as Sacramento and Stockton, retained their function as regional centers or middle-level distribution points by shifting their emphases from supplying mining camps to providing goods and services to the new agricultural communities, and by acting as collection points for the shipment of farm and ranch products to San Francisco and eventually to the world market. As agriculture spread, similar centers emerged in other parts of the state. The rise of other industries led to the development of a greater complexity in the existing middle-level cities and to the creation of new base-level and middle-level communities in areas where none had previously existed. For example, the launching of the redwood logging industry on the northern California coast gave rise to Eureka as a mill town, port, and regional center.

Starting in the 1850's, transportation systems were developed to tie these communities together. The initial lack of overland transport in central California tied the development of middle-level cities to the coast and major river systems because water transport afforded the only means of moving large volumes of freight. Steam packet boats

Fig. 87. Ruins of the Atwell Mill, Sequoia National Park, south of Yosemite. The industrialization of gold mining led to the construction of mills to crush gold-bearing ores and extract the gold and other valuable by-products. Most of the mills were abandoned when local ores were exhausted, since the cost of dismantling and transporting them was greater than the cost of building newer, more modern facilities elsewhere. The abandoned mills thus became part of the archaeological record. Prey to fire and decay, the organic components of the mills deteriorated faster than the metal parts. Archaeologists combine their excavation skills with archival research to help reconstruct these enterprises. (U.S. Forest Service Photo)

Fig. 88. The search for gold spread over most of the state. Fair quantities of gold were found in the Klamath Mountains, and a little turned up in the Penninsular Range. This hopper served a mill in northern San Diego County. Forest fires have destroyed many of these wooden structures, but traces of them often endure in the form of earthen water channels and foundation remnants. Many of the mills were developed by small-scale entrepreneurs who kept few written records. Such enterprises often vanished as quickly as they arose, and in many cases archaeology offers the only means of studying them. Archaeologists have begun to map the occurrence of water channels and foundations to preserve evidence of their existence before the last traces vanish. (U.S. Forest Service Photo)

appeared by mid-decade to link Sacramento, Stockton, Marysville, and other river towns with San Francisco. Huge "rafts" of logs were brought down the coast to San Francisco, and coastal steamer-schooners navigated the crude harbors of middle-level port towns (Hutchinson 1969: 157–69).

The middle-level centers were tied in turn to the many communities they served by road networks, over which stagecoach and freight wagon lines operated. The state was provided with the first rapid communication connection to the eastern United States in April 1860, when the Pony Express was inaugurated, with Sacramento as its western terminus. Then, in October 1861, when the transcontinental telegraph was completed, it replaced the Pony Express, not only providing communication with the rest of the nation, but also linking communities throughout the state. A transcontinental rail connection was begun from Sacramento east across the Sierra in 1865. Completed when it joined the Union Pacific in 1869 near Promontory Point, Utah, it provided a practical, rapid, low-cost way to move people and goods from coast to coast. A statewide rail network was developed over the next 50 years to link farm and ranch communities with the national rail system and with national and foreign markets. Over time, railroads replaced most boat and wagon transportation. Railroads caused the founding of certain towns, such as Amboy, Fenner, and Goffs, which were built as water stops in the Mojave Desert between Barstow and Needles. More-specialized railroads were built into the Sierra to serve the logging industry (see Fig. 91).

San Francisco, which had developed as a major urban center because of the Gold Rush, might have been expected to decline as the gold boom waned. But the growth of the state's agricultural economy helped the city to keep its importance as the gateway for import and export transportation. Completion of the transcontinental railroad reduced the need for ship transportation to bring the state's produce to the U.S. and European markets, but the city kept its position as the nation's major Pacific port and the link between Pacific nations and the rest of the United States. This fact ensured San Francisco's place as the West Coast's population and economic center for nearly a century.

Completion of other transcontinental rail lines to southern California (the Southern Pacific and the Santa Fe railroads) led directly to the rise of cities at the ports of Los Angeles and San Diego, and fostered development of southern California's agricultural industry. San Diego, for example, had a population of only about 2,000 in 1872. Its growth and economic development became possible only after a rail connection linked it to East Coast markets. Archaeologists have be-

Fig. 89. Many miners' camps began as tent towns, but as time wore on and winter weather closed in, more-substantial buildings were built. Isolated miners built thousands of small cabins, making as much use as possible of materials at hand. In later years, whenever hard times caused urban unemployment to rise, some men would return to the mountains to pan for gold, hoping to eke out enough to pay for their supplies. Some built new cabins; others refurbished abandoned ones. This ruin, in El Dorado National Forest, shows by the milled wood framing its door that it was resurrected (or built) in the twentieth century. These solitary sites add details that are rarely found in the historical records and that differ in many ways from the remains found in mining towns. (U.S. Forest Service Photo)

come particularly interested in studying the archaeology of the state's railroads for a number of reasons: their historical importance is unquestionable, their distinctive physical structure makes them readily studied, and their effects on the state's development are easily measured.

The third major stage in urban development was the emergence of industrial cities surrounded by suburban residential communities. This development came late in California, where large-scale industrialization did not become significant until the Second World War. The state's early industrial development, including the Olema lime kilns (Treganza 1951) and the Zinn brickyards of Sacramento (Treganza 1968), reflected important changes from the Mexican era, but the small-scale industries had developed to serve local markets. Large-scale industries serving a national and world market are a much more recent phenomenon, and as yet there has been no archaeological study of them in the state.

Apart from creating new kinds of settlements, urbanization brought other archaeologically recognizable changes. Some reflect the evolution of technology, such as the introduction of railroads, electricity, or mechanized farming. Others reflect evolving cultural values. For example, the Hispanic preference for adobe architecture was not shared by Anglo-Americans, who preferred to build with wood, which required sawmills. In the mother-lode country the Anglo-Americans made extensive use of fieldstone to construct buildings, which required the establishment of cement works for making mortar. In the lowlands, fired clay bricks were used, stimulating the establishment of brickyards as early as 1847 (Treganza 1968). These architectural preferences reflect not only differences in cultural values, but also a greater reliance on industrialization and socioeconomic complexity to achieve the same architectural ends.

In these urban centers, much of the state's ethnic diversity, discussed earlier, began to become integrated into a functioning society. This process, still far from complete, is only beginning to be studied archaeologically (see, for example, Deetz 1980).

As the predominantly Anglo-American society developed, the state's earlier inhabitants, the Mexican Californianos, lost much of their position of prominence (Jordan 1973). After 1846, the Spanish and Mexican land grants gradually passed into Anglo hands through a variety of means. Much of what had been grazing land was turned into more intensively worked farms and ranches, and most of the Mexican Californiano population joined the state's growing urban population. Eventually their distinct culture became largely submerged within the much larger numbers of more recently arrived immigrants from Mexico.

One of California's largest ethnic groups, the Chinese, began to arrive during the Gold Rush (Evans 1980). Recruited by labor contractors to work in the mines, men came to California with the intention of saving their earnings and returning home to their families in China. By the early 1850's there were over 30,000 Chinese workers in California; over 20,000 landed in San Francisco in the one year 1852. Many worked for Anglo-American miners; others formed mining ventures of their own; and still others settled in cities and towns to provide service to other Chinese and to the general community as importers, merchants, and doctors, for example (Greenwood 1980). Cities such as San Francisco and Sacramento and mining camps such as

Fig. 90. Because most of the early buildings of the Anglo-American Stage were made of wood, the demand for lumber swelled with the Gold Rush. By the mid-1850's logging was established in the Sierra Nevada and on the western edges of the North Coast Ranges, where water allowed the transport of logs to mills and markets. This century-old photograph from the Hume Logging Company shows a mill crew resting from the dismemberment of a giant bole. (Courtesy of the Michigan State University Archives and Historical Collections)

Fig. 91. Starting in the 1860's the lumber industry in California began to use narrow-gauge trains to haul logs out of the mountains to the mills. As the rail lines snaked through the forests, companies were able to expand their operations away from the rivers that first supplied their transportation. Here the Hume Company's Shay locomotive No. 1 poses on a trestle near present-day Kings Canyon National Park. In the foreground lie the portable buildings of a temporary logging camp. The ruins of these camps differ markedly from those of mining camps of the same age because the two industries used such different equipment and the workers led different ways of life. Even though the wooden structures have burned or decayed and the rails and iron machinery were salvaged for scrap, the scatters of debris and prepared roadbeds left by logging railroads and camps preserve their existence archaeologically. (Courtesy of the Michigan State University Archives and Historical Collections)

Fig. 92. An alternative to logging railroads was the water flume, a wooden trough on a trestle that tapped mountain streams and carried logs down the trough on the water to a mill at the terminus. The Sierra Nevada, with its great elevations and plentiful supplies of water and timber, made flumes technically feasible. The flumes wove around mountainsides to descend at steady gradients, often requiring spidery trestles to be built to span deep defiles. As this Hume Company trestle shows, the flumes had several problems of their own: forest fires destroyed great sections, leaving the charred remnants lining the canyons; and sometimes the planks of the flumes gave way, sending hundreds of logs cascading through the breach. Since flumes left far fewer archaeological traces than railroads, archaeologists are only beginning to study them. (Courtesy of the Michigan State University Archives and Historical Collections)

Fig. 93. The flume shown in Fig. 92 ended at Hume Lake, where the Hume-Bennett Company lumber mill was located. The flume is the curved structure in the lower left. At the millpond, the logs were loaded onto a conveyor (trestle in upper right) to be carried to the saw in the mill building. (Courtesy of the Michigan State University Archives and Historical Collections)

Fig. 94. Hume-Bennett lumber mill. This 1911 photograph is a posed publicity shot taken by a professional photographer for the firm to use in its promotions. It shows the company's two Shay locomotives at the upper left, while the mill complex looms over a network of flumes, trestles, and conveyors. Sheds and stacks of drying lumber are at the right. Though the mill and the

Weaverville and Oroville soon featured Chinese quarters, often with distinctive architecture (Hall 1958; Hansen 1970). The Chinese are noteworthy among California's ethnic groups for having brought with them a significant portion of their culture, including architecture, religion, dress, diet, housewares, and medicine (Etter 1980). Many artifacts associated with Chinese culture have found their way into archaeological deposits, forming a distinctive component still little studied (for an exception, see Langenwalter 1980).

As the yield from the mines declined, many Chinese returned home; but others remained, working in cities or on ranches and farms. Dozens of miles of stone fences in Butte County, for example, are reputed to have been built by Chinese workers (see Figs. 97 and 98).

During the late 1860's and 1870's, the need for workers for railroad construction spurred new waves of Chinese immigration. Outbreaks of anti-Chinese violence at the time (during the Panic of 1873, for example) testify to the difficult relations between Anglo-Americans and Chinese, a situation that has improved gradually over the following century. Many families arrived to join the men already in the state. The resulting family settlement in cities and small towns created an enduring Chinese component in California society, one that has main-

wooden structures are long gone, cement foundations, roadbeds, the mill-pond dam, and other remains survive to provide archaeological evidence of the industry. The site is now protected in the Sierra National Forest. (Courtesy of Michigan State University Archives and Historical Collections)

tained its ethnic identity while becoming increasingly integrated into the economic, social, and political fabric of the society as a whole (W. Bean 1977; Chinn, Lai & Choy 1969; Ng 1972).

Other ethnic groups have been studied even less archaeologically than have the Chinese. For example, more than 2,000 Blacks came to California from the eastern United States during the first few years of the Gold Rush (Lapp 1977). Some joined the White, Chinese, and other miners; some worked in all-Black mines and lived in all-Black settlements; and still others moved into the newly developing cities. Hawaiians, or Kanaka, also came to the mines in some numbers, and there was at least one Portuguese mining camp. The town of Sonora was founded by miners from the State of Sonora in Mexico. Later waves of immigration brought the Irish in the 1870's in some numbers, as well as smaller numbers of Welsh, Scots, and Cornishmen. Japanese and Filipino immigrants began to arrive in the 1900's. Each of these groups (and many others) brought distinctive cultural backgrounds that may be reflected in the archaeological record, and excavations may reveal new facets of their histories of settlement, adaptation, and integration into California society.

Apart from the fates of immigrant groups, the destinies of Native Californians were changing at this time. When the United States took

Fig. 95. Explosion and fire at Hume-Bennett Mill. Shortly after the photograph in Fig. 94 was taken, a boiler-room explosion caused a disastrous fire at the Hume-Bennett Mill; some of the wreckage is seen here. The golden age of the California lumber industry was drawing to a close. As the virgin forests were logged over, the cost of timber recovery rose. A national environmental-protection effort in the early part of the century led to the founding of the National Forest Service, among other things, which for the first time imposed restrictions on the lumber industry. Although fires had occurred earlier, once the cost of rebuilding became greater than the chance for economic return, the rebuilding of mills tapered off, and the mill ruins entered the archaeological record. (Courtesy of the Michigan State University Archives and Historical Collections)

Fig. 96. Officials of the Hume-Bennett Company walk amid the ruins of the company's mill (see Fig. 95). The vast quantity of steel from the mill was salvaged for the war effort during the First World War, but a great deal of perishable and imperishable waste was left behind to help form the site's archaeological record. Records such as these photographs are valuable aids to the archaeologist, who uses details in them to identify features in the site. At the same time, archaeological study brings to light many details about such sites that at the time were thought not worth recording, but which now help make the past more interesting and understandable. (Courtesy of the Michigan State University Archives and Historical Collections)

Fig. 97. "Chinese" wall near Chico, Butte County. The contributions of Chinese workers to the building of California's cities and railroads is as well known as their role in the Gold Rush, but they made other contributions as well. Many farms and ranches benefited from Chinese help. Miles of these stone walls, assembled in the process of clearing fields in the mid-nineteenth century, served to define boundaries and keep in livestock. Some county residents still term these structures "Chinese" walls because many were built by Chinese workers.

Fig. 98. The network of century-old stone walls that cross several California counties form a megalithic archaeological monument marking an important nineteenth-century transition: the rise of ranching in the Anglo-American Stage. These structures, some still in use, can be seen even in satellite photographs.

over California in 1846, about 150,000 Native Californians still survived (Cook 1976a: 44). The missions had been disbanded fifteen years before, and the surviving neophytes dispersed, principally into the coastal region of southern California, the South Coast Ranges, the Transverse Range, and adjacent parts of the Central Valley and deserts. Survivors of the missions made up only a small part of this total, however, since of the 72,000 Indians who had been brought into the mission system over the previous 65 years, only 18,000 remained at the 21 missions at the time of abandonment (Cook 1978: 92). The rest of the Indian population was composed of people who lived outside the areas of heaviest European settlement. These areas were the hills and valleys of the Sierra, the southern Cascades, the Klamath Mountains, the North Coast Ranges, the northern California coast, the northeastern California basin and range country, the interior deserts and ranges, and (prior to 1840) the Central Valley.

These people were still trying to maintain a more or less traditional way of life. By 1850, however, the number of California Indians had fallen to about 100,000; by 1855, to 50,000; and by 1900, to 20,000 (Cook 1976a: 44, 70; Cook used the federal-government standard of a minimum of one-sixteenth Indian ancestry for his figures). By 1900 Indian communities living completely outside the sphere of Anglo-American society no longer existed. Many factors produced these changes, including the Gold Rush and the extensive peopling of the state by diverse immigrants; the replacement of the existing rural agrarian Mexican society by an industrial, urban society; the impact of various government laws and policies; and the relationship of Native Californian peoples and their cultures to the now-dominant Anglo-American society (for fuller treatment, see especially L. Bean 1974, 1978; Bean & Blackburn 1976; Bean & King 1974; Bean & Vane 1978; Castillo 1978a,b; Cook 1976a,b, 1978; Heizer 1974a,b; Heizer & Almquist 1971; Shipek 1978; Stewart 1978).

The decade from 1845 to 1855 was the single most disastrous period in the history of the California Indians. Their population fell by two-thirds in ten years, from 150,000 to 50,000 (Cook 1978: 93). That this decline coincides with the Gold Rush is no coincidence. Already suffering from serious population decline, disease, economic collapse, culture shock, and military conflicts with the Spaniards and Mexicans, the surviving Indian communities suffered sudden and devastating new dislocations from the Gold Rush. Miners flooded the Sierra, southern Cascades, and Klamath ranges, while farmers, ranchers, and settlers quickly spread out across the Central Valley and other valleys and foothills. Surviving Indian communities were dispossessed of most of their remaining resource bases, often through violence. Although fighting was the direct cause of only a small proportion of the total population decline, in some cases it was responsible for most of the losses suffered by particular groups (e.g., J. Johnson 1978).

Even after the immediate impact of the Gold Rush, Indian populations continued to decline. Between 1855 and 1900, the estimated total Indian population for the whole state fell to about 20,000 people (Cook 1978: 93). This final, and almost complete, decline was caused partly by the factors just noted, but there were also other factors, and additional consequences.

Some groups suffered complete extermination. Although it was possible for a few Indian communities to survive after 1855 by retreating from the areas settled by Anglo-Americans, eventually the new settlers began to fill every part of the state. In competition for land, the Indians, with fewer resources, fewer numbers, and less-advanced technology, could not compete. Disease, starvation, and military conflict led to the extinction of the Chimariko, Halchidhoma, Wappo, Yahi, and other groups. Massacres by Anglo-Americans also played a prominent role in these extinctions. Newspapers of the period recount many incidents of random violence against Indians: of casual murder and of massive reprisals for petty offenses (see, for example, Heizer 1974a,b; Heizer & Almquist 1971). These atrocities were not limited to these four groups by any means, but other, usually larger, groups had at least a few survivors. In some Indian communities, virtually every child in the settlement was kidnapped and sold into slavery in another part of the state (Cook 1976b), depriving that community of its next generation and further accelerating the population decline. The story of Ishi (T. Kroeber 1959), a Yahi found starving and alone in the foothills near Oroville in 1911, relates the story of the last American Indian to have lived almost completely outside the sphere of Anglo-American society. But this portrait is also symbolically important because the fate of Ishi, the last living member of the Yahi, mirrors the fate of traditional Native American culture in California.

Many of those who survived actual extinction were confined to reservations. The U.S. government had developed a reservation policy to deal with Native Americans elsewhere, so it was not surprising that this policy was extended to California when it became a state. Although often justified in humanitarian terms, the actual function of the reservation system was to eliminate competition between Whites and Indians for land by confining the Indians to isolated, remote tracts of land that Whites did not want. In principle the land was held by the government in trust for the Indians. The government promised to provide support and services to the Indians who agreed to cede their rights to their traditional homes and accept reservation confinement. Shortly after California's statehood, U.S. commissioners secured marks from Indians on eighteen treaties, never ratified by the Senate, that yielded most of the state to the U.S. government. Some evidence indicates that the treaties did not represent informed or authorized decisions on the part of the Indian signers (see, for instance, Heizer 1978e).

Eventually the federal government established a reservation system in California, under the administration of the Bureau of Indian Affairs. As in the rest of the United States, the reality of the reservation experience fell far short of the ideal. Promises of food, supplies, housing, health care and education frequently were not kept. The effects of dislocation and culture shock on the Indians were pervasive. The reservations were usually in remote areas and lacked resources that would have allowed Indians to make some sort of living. Different, incompatible groups were often placed on the same reservation. The resulting privation was located far enough from public view to allow it to be largely ignored.

Other surviving Indians lived on rancherias, which differed from reservations (Castillo 1978a; Hill 1978). These small, peripheral, remnant Indian communities had managed to survive long enough to be granted legal recognition. The federal government assumed trust status for rancherias as well, and problems similar to those of the reservations were common. By 1900, however, a significant portion of the state's surviving Indians lived on either reservations or rancherias.

Indians living under these conditions suffered not only population decline, but considerable loss to their remaining cultures as well. Only in some very remote corners of the state, where interaction with Anglo-American society was still moderate, did traditional culture survive to any greater degree. The Klamath River, the Pit River, and northern parts of the North Coast Ranges (see Figs. 99–102) offered some of these refuges.

At the same time programs were being established to acculturate some Indians. It was assumed that, since Indian culture could not survive, the best salve was to prepare Indians for assimilation into modern society. The Sherman School in Los Angeles typified such an effort. Children from many different Indian communities were sent by government mandate to be educated at this boarding school, far from any contact with their families, communities, or cultures. English was the only language of instruction, and the only cultural values and information taught were Anglo-American. Although such programs succeeded in breaking down the cultural identities and family ties of many children, causing severe psychological and social problems, they were unsuccessful in preparing the Indians to enter the mainstream of society.

As the century wore on, however, a growing percentage of Indians did become involved with the now-dominant Anglo-American society to one degree or another. In the nineteenth century there was not yet a significant urban Indian population. Indians were denied many rights of citizenship, including the right to vote, to serve on juries, to testify at trials, to own property in the same way as Whites, and to purchase alcoholic beverages. The legal status of Indians under U.S. law bore many resemblances to that of children, criminals, and the mentally incompetent. They were denied equal access to employment, financial institutions, and education. It is not surprising that there were few Indians successfully involved in urban, industrial society at this time. Most Indians approached Anglo-American society by living in rural areas or on the edges of towns. They lived in poverty, on lands that Whites did not want, exchanging labor for cash, and supplementing their wages with varying amounts of traditional hunting, fishing, and plant collecting. This was the condition of most of the 20,000 remaining Indians in California in 1900.

The state's Indian population stopped declining around 1900 and by 1910 had begun to rise (Cook 1976a: 70). This was not due to any significant changes in the Anglo-American treatment of Indians. Instead, it meant that Indian numbers had been so reduced that Whites no longer viewed Indians as direct competition for land and resources. Military hostilities against Indians had declined a generation earlier, and the practice of kidnapping had been virtually eliminated. With the relaxation of these pressures, it was possible for small numbers of Indians to survive, albeit at a poverty level.

Today, Indians in California number about 100,000 (Cook 1978). The figure probably includes 15 percent or more Indians who have migrated from other states, as part of the general migration that has been the main source of urban growth in California for the last 40 years. The 1960 census showed only about 40,000 Indians living in the state (Cook 1976a: 74–77), so most of the growth has occurred in the last 20 years. Employment, education, and social and health services for Indians have improved somewhat each decade, although Native Californians still remain the poorest segment of contemporary California society.

The survival and management of reservations and rancherias in the state has been promoted by government programs and periodic reform movements, but other, more numerous programs and laws have served to withdraw support and services from the reservations and rancherias and to close them down. These contrary directions in fed-

Fig. 99. After the Gold Rush, surviving Indians were able to follow traditional subsistence activities only where permanent Anglo-American settlement did not preempt the land. In this nineteenth-century photograph, taken in the high Sierra, a Miwok conical burden basket containing some basketry winnowing trays leans against a temporary shelter. The iron bar (lower left) was used to weigh down the base of the shelter. (U.S. Forest Service Photo)

Fig. 100. A Diegueño temporary shelter near Palomar Mountain in northern San Diego County. As the Forest Service uniform indicates, the photograph was taken a half century ago, but the shelter was old even then. A temporary campsite made by a single family to exploit oak and chaparral resources in Cleveland National Forest atop the Penninsular Range, it reflects the return to a small-scale, more diffuse, Archaic-like existence by the survivors of the fall of the missions. (U.S. Forest Service Photo)

Fig. 101. This photograph, probably taken about 1920, shows four Miwok women in the Sierra National Forest. The bark-slab house behind them, more substantial than the temporary shelters shown in Figs. 99 and 100, was built over a pole frame and has a roofed doorway passage (right rear). A cooking basket in the foreground is flanked by two pots—notable introductions. A traditional burden basket is in the foreground on the left, and two traditional winnowing trays rest on a shelf on the side of the house. The camp was located in an area that had been logged over; thus, growth was not as mature as today. In some cases the reduction of mature habitats favored plant gathering, since many seed-bearing plants flourish in disturbed habitats. Many prehistoric peoples capitalized on this pattern by periodically burning off mature forest and chaparral habitats. One consequence of Anglo-American land management was the reduced ability of the Indians to stimulate the production of wild-food resources in this way. (U.S. Forest Service Photo)

Fig. 102. This 1929 photograph, probably taken near Owens Valley, shows a Shoshonean brush shelter at a pine-nut gathering station. Two conical burden baskets lean against it. The prepared-earth base of the house suggests more substance than a temporary shelter would require, indicating that the camp is more comparable to a seasonal occupation site. The camp is another instance of the resumption of Archaic-like seasonal gathering in areas where Anglo-American settlement did not preempt the land and its resources. (U.S. Forest Service Photo)

eral policy have made it impossible for Indians to adapt to any consistent program. One net result of these programs is that most of the lands Native Californians owned or controlled in 1900 have now been taken from them (Castillo 1978a,b; Shipek 1978; Stewart 1978). This process has forced much of the state's Indian population to migrate into cities and towns, where they generally live outside the framework of traditional community, kin, and family relationships.

In spite of these difficulties, California Indians have managed to survive as a distinct biological group, and aspects of the traditional cultures of many Native Californian societies have endured. This can be seen in two different respects. On the one hand, Native Californians have adapted and adjusted themselves and their ways of life to existence in Anglo-American-dominated society, modifying their traditional cultures to make them more appropriate to contemporary life

Fig. 103. Stoney Creek Rancheria was established in the nineteenth century in the foothills of western Glenn County as a remnant settlement of the Nomlaki people, the central division of the Wintun language group. The semi-subterranean dance house is similar in design to a pit house but much larger. Dance houses appeared in the second half of the nineteenth century as part of a religious movement that began in response to the collapse of the traditional way of life under the impact of Anglo-American settlement. A number of Native American communities in northern California still maintain dance houses for religious observances. (U.S. Forest Service Photo)

Fig. 104. Guard-tower ruin. This collapsed structure, high in the Klamath Mountains, reflects an age not yet studied archaeologically: the Second World War. The cabin was built to shelter an observer watching for enemy aircraft, and is one of a number of such outposts established in wilderness areas along the coast. In northwestern California some of these stations were occupied by Native Americans, and some by Anglo-Americans. The cultural differences between the two groups may be reflected in the archaeological remains at the cabin sites. These sites as a group should be distinct from miners' cabins, Forest Service guard stations, and other twentieth-century occupation sites in these mountains.

and incorporating features of the dominant culture into their own. The result is a distinctive ethnic tradition, which by 1900 differed from what it had been in 1850, and differs today from what it was in 1900.

On the other hand, some aspects of traditional culture have survived, with little significant change since the Gold Rush, within the body of contemporary Indian culture (see Fig. 103). It should be pointed out that there has been almost no archaeological research at reservations, rancherias, or other settings that might shed some light on the nature and processes of this rather remarkable survival, so our knowledge of it derives primarily from ethnographic studies (for a study combining ethnographic and archaeological data of this period, see Theodoratus, Chartkoff & Chartkoff 1979). In general, basketry and certain other crafts, the construction of sweathouses and dance houses, and the making of ritual costumes have survived to varying degrees, along with the knowledge of traditional subsistence techniques like acorn leaching and salmon fishing. In addition, traditional religious activities have endured to varying degrees in many parts of the state (usually remote areas), as have such social features as patterns of social relationship, travel to visit kin, and burial rites.

Many Native Californian communities foster the teaching of their traditional language and culture to their children. The political and legal sophistication of many Indians today allows them to deal with some success with the growing, changing maze of agencies that confront them and impinge on their cultural continuity. Thus, although wholly traditional life has ended for California's Indians, they may be able to preserve distinct ethnic identities, so that their cultures, descended from thousands of years of development and adapted to more than two centuries of enforced contact with other cultures, will endure (see Fig. 104).

ARCHAEOLOGY OF THE HISTORICAL PERIOD

Until environmental impact studies made them more common, archaeological studies of historical sites were fairly infrequent. The influence of A. L. Kroeber (see Appendix A), the relatively recent nature of California's historical remains, and the anthropological—rather than historical—orientation of most California archaeologists caused most archaeological research in the state to be devoted to prehistoric cultures. Some archaeologists have been interested in excavating historical sites for a long time, however, and historical archaeology has become an important field within archaeology (Deetz 1977; South 1977). In order to indicate the variety of archaeological remains dating to the Historical Period in California, and the kinds of things archaeologists can say about them, we will describe seven of the most important projects that have been undertaken in the state (see Map 48; space precludes discussing a number of other important

Map 48 (facing page). Excavated sites of the Historical Period. Relatively few non-Indian sites were excavated by California archaeologists until the last few years. This map indicates the locations of non-Indian sites for which excavation reports have been published. The number of such sites should be considerably greater in another decade. These sites, which by definition fall within the historical period, have been grouped by ethnic group. Many of them also have evidence of California Indian presence. In addition, it should be mentioned that many Final Pacific Period Indian sites also were occupied into the historical era and reveal information about the impact of contact with foreigners on indigenous culture.

1. Fort Humboldt
2. William B. Ide Adobe
3. Fort Ross
4. Drake's Bay
5. Petaluma Adobe
6. Old Sacramento
7. Sutter's Fort
8. Somersville
9. Mission San Juan Bautista
10. White Ranch
11. Mission Nuestra Señora
    de la Soledad
12. Mission San Antonio
    de Padua
13. Mission San Luis Obispo
    de Tolosa
14. Mission La Purísima
    Concepción
15. Royal Presidio of
    Santa Barbara
16. Mission San Buenaventura
17. Hugo Reid Adobe
18. Los Cerritos Adobe
19. Sepulveda Rancho
20. Mission San Luís Rey
    de Francia
21. Mission San Diego de
    Alcalá
22. Royal Presidio of
    San Diego

Spanish sites (1769–1822)

Mission San Juan Bautista (9)
Mission Nuestra Señora de la Soledad (11)
Mission San Antonio de Padua (12)
Mission San Luis Obispo de Tolosa (13)
Mission La Purísima Concepción (14)
Royal Presidio of Santa Barbara (15)
Mission San Buenaventura (16)
Mission San Luís Rey de Francia (20)
Mission San Diego de Alcalá (21)
Royal Presidio of San Diego (22)

Mexican sites (1822–1846)

Petaluma Adobe (5)
Hugo Reid Adobe (17)
Los Cerritos Adobe (18)
Sepulveda Adobe (19)

Anglo-American sites (1846–1929)

Fort Humboldt (1)
William B. Ide Adobe (2)
Old Sacramento (6)
Somersville (8)
White Ranch (10)

Others

Fort Ross (Russian) (3)
Drake's Bay (Spanish or possibly British) (4)
Sutter's Fort (Swiss) (7)

studies). All the sites discussed are located on protected, public lands. They are either already open to public visits or should be soon. It is because of public protection and accessibility that we are drawing attention to these sites instead of a number of others that could be equally informative (see also Appendix G).

Shell Mounds at Drake's Bay

During the 1940's, Robert Heizer and Clement Meighan, then working for the University of California at Berkeley, excavated several shell-midden sites around Drake's Bay, now part of the Point Reyes National Seashore (Heizer 1941; Meighan 1950; Meighan & Heizer 1952). There they found a group of sites that had been occupied by Final Pacific peoples (subsequently the ethnographically known Pomo Indians) who were living around the bay when Sebastián Rodriguez Cermeño's ship, the *San Agustín*, foundered off the coast of Point Reyes in 1595. These settlements therefore represent the exploration stage of California's Historical Period. Some of Cermeño's crew made it to shore and were assisted by the Indians, and much of the cargo that the 200-ton *San Agustín* had brought back from Manila eventually washed up on shore. This episode allows us to view the results of even a brief, isolated contact between Europeans and Native Californians.

Some of the goods from the *San Agustín* made their way into Indian technology. Chinese porcelains were used as dishes, and sherds of bottle glass were turned into projectile points (see Fig. 76). Metal artifacts were used as long as they lasted. But even though some of Cermeño's crew may well have stayed with the Pomo, the Spaniards did not teach the Pomo to do things in a different way. It was the Spaniards who adopted Indian culture when they remained with the Pomo, not the reverse. The Pomo were not led to begin making glass or pottery, or to smelt metal ores. They did not take up European-style farming, they did not start to build churches or adobe houses, and they did not take up other forms of Spanish culture.

Why didn't the Spaniards have a stronger impact on the Pomo? Put simply, because Indian life was already highly successful there. The brief visits by European explorers were too infrequent and irregular to cause more than the most minor changes in traditional life. The only technological change of consequence was the use of materials from the shipwreck to substitute for local raw materials while the supply lasted. The methods used to make the final products did not change, however, nor did the kinds of items made. In this case Spanish trade goods were somewhat like whale carcasses washed up on the beach—a windfall to take advantage of, but not something to depend on or use as the basis for a new way of life.

This situation provides an important lesson about the workings of well-functioning cultures and the impact of individual disruptive events on them. The process of changing a culture is not simple. Because the components of a culture interact with each other to form integrated systems, they cannot be easily replaced without affecting other parts of the system. It is noteworthy that the material the Drake's Bay people chose for toolmaking was glass, the culturally produced equivalent of the natural glass, obsidian, that they already used to make their tools. No new technology was needed. The glass could be used while it lasted without disrupting the rest of the system, and when the glass was gone the system could continue to function as it had before. This one example of a cultural system suggests why many archaeologists are skeptical about claims that cultures were changed by visits from outsiders when the visits were so limited.

Mission La Purísima Concepción

The first major project to investigate the archaeology of California's Historical Period was begun at Mission La Purísima Concepción near Lompoc in the 1930's. Mark R. Harrington led a crew of Civilian Conservation Corps excavators on the project. Work was continued over the next 30 years by James Deetz, Norman Gabel, and Richard Humphrey. The mission itself was founded in 1787 in what is now downtown Lompoc. A massive earthquake in 1812 destroyed the mission buildings, and it was relocated at its present site. Excavations at the relocated mission demonstrate the impact of European settlement on Indian cultures (in this case the Chumash) during the Hispanic Stage.

The most substantial excavation done at the mission site was of the Indian barracks, which Harrington and Gabel had partially exposed and Deetz completely cleared (1963). These barracks, which had lined the side of the mission quadrangle opposite the church, smithy, and padres' quarters, consisted of two-room apartments that had been occupied by married Indian couples. In studying the artifacts found in these apartments, Deetz found that traditional female-related items, such as milling tools and stone bowls, were common, whereas traditional male-related artifacts—those involved in such tasks as hunting, religious rituals, and war—were rare. This was apparently because most male activities were regulated by the mission fathers, and European activities in this regard had replaced traditional Indian ones.

Married women, by contrast, were allowed to keep their own households and to prepare their family's meals in order to promote Christian marriage and maternity.

Deetz also found that, over time, the proportion of Spanish artifacts in the barracks gradually increased relative to Indian artifacts. He compared this finding with data from the Alamo Pintada Site, an inland Chumash settlement that was contemporary with the early phases of the mission but far enough away that it lay beyond the sphere of mission dominance. He found almost no Spanish influence among the artifacts at Alamo Pintada, and concluded that the replacement of Indian artifacts by Spanish ones was directly related to the Indians' engagement in European-style activities (Deetz 1963: 173–75).

Deetz gained further insight into the processes of change through excavation of the mission's hide-soaking vats used in tanning. He found that neophytes used traditional flaked-stone tools and bone scrapers instead of European tools to scrape cattle hides, but that the bone tools were made of cattle bone rather than the traditional deer bone. Deetz reasoned that hide preparation had been a traditional male Indian activity. When the mission fathers introduced tanning, Indian men were able to—and allowed to—adapt their own techniques to the task, producing a unique combination of practices that combined Indian and European elements (Deetz 1963: 170–72). His study shows that the replacement of Indian with Spanish culture and technology was not absolute or uniform at the different missions. The loss of traditional Indian technology was related to the kinds of crafts introduced by the Spanish, and to the parts of Indian technology that were adaptable to Spanish crafts and mission life, or at least not in conflict with it.

Matters of ideology, however, were extremely important to the padres, and these aspects of culture were forcibly changed, completely and summarily. This fact is reflected in Richard Humphrey's (1965) excavation of 50 burials in the neophyte cemetery at the mission. Burial practices were closely regulated by the fathers because of their religious significance. Humphrey found that the European burial style—in extended, supine position (on the back)—almost completely replaced the traditional Chumash burial practices (cremation or flexed burial). Furthermore, the neophyte graves were almost totally lacking in grave goods, in keeping with European practice but contrary to traditional Chumash practice.

In religious matters, then, the Spanish effort at directed cultural change was relatively immediate and complete for the captive mission Indians. In other areas of culture, where Indian practices could be made to serve desired ends or where at least they did not conflict with the missions' programs, Indian technology managed to survive to varying extents. In some cases Indian and European cultures even merged to produce new combinations of practices particularly adapted to the California environment of the time (Deetz 1963; Gabel 1952; Harrington 1940; Humphrey 1965; Schuyler 1978).

Fort Ross

Fort Ross, now a state park near Point Arena, was the only permanent non-Spanish installation built in California before the 1830's. In 1809 the Russian American Fur Company tried to establish a post near Bodega Bay to exploit the sea otter and to start a farming community. The settlement never developed satisfactorily, and was relocated to its present site in 1812, where it remained for 29 years. Russian trappers and traders brought with them Aleut Indians from Alaska to hunt sea otters, and hired local Pomo Indians to build the fort and work on the farms. The Russians got along comparatively well with the Pomo, even occasionally entering into marriage and certain kinds of cultural exchange. By 1841 the local sea-otter population had been seriously depleted, and the farms had failed to prosper. The Russians withdrew from the fort, taking their Aleut allies with them. The fort was purchased from them by John Sutter in perhaps his least prudent investment. This venture bankrupted him, and the fort was abandoned soon after and left to fall into ruins.

Adan Treganza began excavations at the fort in the early 1950's. Research has continued periodically since then under the auspices of the State Department of Parks and Recreation (1954).

Fort Ross is important in part as the state's only non-Hispanic early historical site, and also as a source of information about the interaction between Indians and a non-European culture—an interaction of a different sort than the Spaniards provided. Most excavations at Fort Ross were aimed at discovering the fort's actual structure and the placement of installations within it. For example, Treganza was able to show that the walls of the original chapel were 8–12 inches (20–30 cm) away from the place where they were presumed to have been on the basis of historical records. He also demonstrated that the fort's well had enough water and a high enough water table to provide water during the driest part of the year.

Study of the fort's artifacts showed that neither the Aleuts nor the Pomo lived within the stockade. The Aleut settlement has never been found. Six Pomo villages near the fort have been test excavated, establishing their contemporaneity with the fort.

The Pomo had considerable contact with the Russians and Aleuts, but did not give up their cultural autonomy. During more than a generation of continuous interaction, the Pomo acquired large numbers of European goods, many of which were reworked into Pomo forms. Glass and porcelain beads and pendants were used in Pomo ornamentation, for example, and projectile points and scrapers were made of glass sherds. Although the Pomo served as laborers and farmers for the Russians, they did not live in the Russian colony, returning to their own villages daily to continue their regular lives. As a result, the impact of Russian culture on the Pomo was limited, so limited that there is no evidence of the loss of Pomo craft skills. The Pomo farmed for the Russians but did not use this knowledge for their own subsistence. When the Russians left, the Pomo abandoned farming.

The striking contrast between the Russian and Spanish impacts on Indian culture arose from the very different purposes for which the two settlements were established. The Spaniards established a master-dependent relationship with the Indians, leading to cultural destruction and, as a largely unforeseen result, depopulation. The Russians established a relationship of comparative mutual interaction, which apparently benefited both sides and did not lead to cultural collapse (William H. Olsen, pers. comm. 1980; Francis Riddell, pers. comm. 1980; Schumacher 1971, 1972; Schuyler 1978; Treganza 1954).

The Sepulveda Adobe

In 1836–37, during the Mexican Stage of the Historical Period, a Californiano named José Sepulveda acquired a grant from the government that included lands once belonging to Mission San Juan Capistrano. There he established Rancho Cerrito de las Ranas (later named Rancho San Joaquin), which extended from Newport Bay eastward to the Santa Ana Mountains. Taking over a small adobe building that the mission had built near Newport Bay in 1819 to shelter cattle herders, he established a home and headquarters that he and his family occupied until 1864 (see Fig. 81). In 1968, Paul Chace conducted excavations at this site for the Irvine Company, in conjunction with the Charles Bowers Memorial Museum and the Pacific Coast Archaeological Society (Chace 1969). His research reveals something of the interaction of Mexicans and Indians in the post-secularization period and the involvement of Mexican rancheros in foreign commerce.

The Sepulveda Adobe was a three-room structure with thick adobe walls and a flat roof covered with a layer of asphaltum. It was of a style called "Monterey colonial" (Evans 1969), typical of the Mexican Stage. The census of 1836 showed no occupants at the ranch since Sepulveda did not bring his family there from Los Angeles until 1837.

By the 1844 census the ranch housed Sepulveda, his wife, ten children, and one male Mexican servant, but no Indians. The 1850 census (the first made under the U.S. administration of California), however, showed that Sepulveda and his family had five Indians living on the ranch as staff (Chace 1969: 51–52). Despite this fact, excavation at the site found no trace of artifacts that could be attributed to Indian manufacture at that time, except for a kind of pottery, Tizon Brownware, that was originally developed in the southern California desert. This utilitarian ware was made by local Indians, and constituted 7 percent of the pottery found at the rancho site.

William Evans (1969) has studied the occurrence of Indian pottery in southern California at this and other Mexican Stage sites. He finds that the occurrence of Indian wares actually increased at that time. His explanation is that there was a lack of domestic sources of Mexican household pottery, that is, that there were no manufacturers of Mexican-style pottery in southern California at that time. Indians coming to work at the ranchos after secularization met some of the demand for utilitarian pottery by producing a form of Indian pottery that originally had been made only in southern California desert cultures. How this actually occurred is not yet known, but it seems to represent an interesting instance in which Mexican and Indian cultures fused to produce a new, uniquely Californian, adaptation.

The ceramic studies provide another interesting glimpse into rancho life. Of more than 1,000 sherds found at the ranch, nearly 70 percent could be traced to the country of origin: England (50 percent), Mexico (4), China (3), the United States (2), France (2), and Scotland (1), in addition to local Indian (7). The imported pottery was mainly luxury ware rather than utilitarian, and the contrast of the tiny dirt-floor cabin crowded with children and a cabinet filled with imported ceramics is striking. Chace notes the extreme dependence of rancho life on international trade in cattle by-products, rather than as a life of pastoral self-sufficiency (Gothold 1969). In fact, he notes an observation made by a French traveler of the day that any luxury good sold in Boston or London could be bought in California, even if the actual amount of such goods was not great (Chace 1969: 53). The relative importance of English and U.S. ceramics is also striking. Data from this and other sites show that the Mexican occupation of California was heavily involved in, and dependent on, foreign trade.

The William B. Ide Adobe

William B. Ide migrated to California in 1845, worked with John Frémont in the rebellion against Mexican rule, and was the only president of the short-lived Republic of California. After the U.S. takeover, he built a rancho overlooking the Sacramento River near present-day Red Bluff. His adobe ranch house, now a state park, was excavated by Adan Treganza (1958b, 1968) in the late 1950's. Ide's ranch is somewhat similar to the ranchos of the Mexican Stage, but archaeological research indicates important differences between them.

Ide built his adobe around 1853 or 1854 to be the headquarters of a cattle ranch. The house had only three small rooms. Ide used adobe bricks for the walls, but otherwise departed from the typical "Monterey" style. His house had a pitched roof covered with heavy shake shingles, low overhanging eaves, and sub-roof beams to support the roof. It also had a formal chimney of fired clay bricks. One of Treganza's goals was to determine whether the fireplace had been built as an integral part of the house, since it seemed an anomaly among the traditional adobes built during the Mexican Stage. He showed through excavation that the fireplace had indeed been built with the rest of the house. He characterized Ide's house as representing an American "mountain man" style, rather than a true Californiano adobe, of a simplified architectural style brought from the east and adapted to the new landscape in a manner somewhat reflective of a pioneer settlement (Treganza 1968: 3–5). The fireplace bricks had no maker's marks, but Treganza found that the Anglo-American settlers of California, preferring their own building styles to existing ones, had begun to build brickyards in Sacramento as early as 1847, and that Ide's bricks may well have been shipped upriver from there.

Treganza was struck by the fact that he found no Indian artifacts at the adobe, in spite of the fact that a village site lay only a few hundred yards away and that a number of other sites occur in the vicinity (Treganza 1968: 12–15). Robert Schuyler made a similar comment about the excavation of the White Ranch, which was built in 1852 in the southern Sierra, where Buchanan Reservoir now is (Mannion 1969: 248–58; Schuyler 1978: 78). A local Indian village only 2.5 miles (4 km) from the ranch could have provided labor for construction; the rancher, however, imported Chinese laborers for the job. In fact, notes Schuyler, the early Anglo-American settlers in California tended to avoid routine interaction with the Indians altogether.

Old Sacramento

During the Gold Rush the city of Sacramento sprang up along the edge of the Sacramento River near Sutter's Fort. A tent city in 1849, its population swelled to 10,000 by 1850, and temporary shelters were soon replaced by more permanent wood and brick buildings. The Sacramento River served to link the city with San Francisco, first by sailboat and then by steamboat. When stage and freight service was developed, Sacramento became the major embarkation point for the northern goldfields. During the decade after its founding, Sacramento became (in 1854) the capital of the new state. It has continued to grow since then and is the state's fourth largest metropolitan area (Hall 1958: Lavender 1972).

Excavation was undertaken in Sacramento in the 1960's when proposed freeway construction along the city's waterfront threatened to destroy the city's original quarter. Because there had been little urban archaeology in California, this project is a major contribution. The University of California at Davis began excavations in 1966 under the direction of Jay W. Ruby. Work has proceeded steadily since then under a number of directors from several area colleges and universities. The State Department of Parks and Recreation has used much information from this research in the restoration of Old Sacramento State Historic Park.

Excavations have uncovered the foundations of a number of buildings that date to the original construction of the city. Building styles, building materials (especially fired clay brick in the downtown area), and even the city plan are typical of the eastern United States rather than adaptations of Spanish or Mexican styles already in use in the region. Old Sacramento was in many ways very like a midwestern American city transplanted to the west. One interesting discovery was that the original street level of the city was 10 feet (3 m) lower than today. After repeated flooding of the Sacramento River convinced officials to raise the city, buildings were sealed at the ground floor and the surrounding streets were filled in to the depth of the second floor. Doors and windows were cut into the new first floors, and the former first floors became basements (see Fig. 105).

Most of the buildings held commercial enterprises: a variety of stores, restaurants, business and professional offices, saloons, and apparently a bordello, all of which reveal the mining orientation of the city and the international origins of its inhabitants. Sacramento is one of the earliest sites to reveal substantial amounts of Chinese artifacts. Ruby was able to identify tentatively a laundry and a Chinese tenement in the blocks of buildings he excavated (pers. comm. 1966).

As with the Ide Adobe and the White Ranch, any evidence of Native Californian culture was wholly absent from the early city in spite of the fact that Sutter, whose fort lay only a mile away, had made extensive use of Indian help in his own enterprises. Apparently during the Anglo-American Stage the Chinese largely adopted the role formerly played by Indians in Hispanic and Mexican times, that of

Fig. 105. A block of buildings in Old Sacramento is currently under excavation by archaeologists. The present street level is indicated by the line of cars and the buildings beyond. The mid-nineteenth-century occupation level is exposed in the foreground. The original streets and ground floors were buried when the city's streets were raised a level to avoid flooding. The Old Sacramento district, located along the waterfront of present-day Sacramento, has yielded thousands of relics dating from the city's first two decades.

providing labor and services for the dominant ethnic group. The negative evidence from Sacramento shows that Indian culture and settlement had been displaced from at least the immediate vicinity of Sacramento in rather short order. There is no evidence to show that the Anglo-Americans made any place for Indians in their development of this or any other urban center.

Somersville

In the 1850's coal was discovered at Mt. Diablo in eastern Contra Costa County, where the East Bay Regional Park Commission has now established the Black Diamond Reserve. Mining was begun in the late 1850's to provide fuel for San Francisco, and a series of towns arose in the area to house miners. Somersville was one such community. It reached its heyday in the 1870's and 1880's, when the town's population stood at more than 500 and more than a dozen businesses flourished to serve the miners and their families. The mines began to close down in the 1890's when newer strikes in Washington State provided coal to San Francisco at lower cost than the mines at Mt. Diablo could meet. By 1905 Somersville had been abandoned. During World War I the town was razed to salvage iron for the war effort, and by the 1960's almost every visible trace of Somersville had disappeared (Deetz 1980 and pers. comm. 1980).

James Deetz of the University of California at Berkeley began excavations at Somersville in 1979 (see Fig. 106). The town was known locally as a Welsh community because mining families from Wales lived there, but Deetz found it was home to at least a half-dozen ethnic groups, including the Cornish, Irish, Italians, Mexicans, Chinese, and perhaps several others unidentified, as well as the Welsh (Howard 1980).

With so many different ethnic groups sharing one small community, what happened to their ethnic identities over time? Did Somersville become a melting pot in the face of shared employment and

Fig. 106. Excavation at Somersville, which flourished in the 1870's and 1880's on the north slope of Mt. Diablo, in Contra Costa County, only to be abandoned by 1905. Here, excavators are studying the remains of a residential district, looking for evidence of debris scattered around the houses in hopes of discovering the degree to which ethnic differences among households are reflected in material remains. Since houses at Somersville were separated by vacant lots, the trash from one household is separate from that of others. And because historical records from the town identify the location of each house and its occupants, such things as ethnic background can be identified independently of the archaeological data. (Courtesy of the Lowie Museum of Anthropology, University of California, Berkeley)

Fig. 107. Because Somersville lacked a water source, all the town's water was hauled daily by train in tank cars from the ship channel 6 miles (10 km) north. One of the hotels in Somersville built a cistern to trap rainwater, but it was abandoned for a larger, brick-lined one in the late nineteenth century and allowed to silt up, trapping trash that had made its way into the pit. When the hotel was finally abandoned around 1905, the new cistern was deliberately filled, and a number of large artifacts were tossed into the cistern to reduce the amount of dirt that had to be shoveled in. Among these artifacts were some train wheels and this cast-iron stove from the hotel. The process of deposition in this case bears some similarities to the filling in of some Pacific Period pit houses. (Courtesy of the Lowie Museum of Anthropology, University of California, Berkeley)

continuous interaction, or did each group retain its own separate identity? The short life span of the town and the fact that it was abandoned rather than being overlaid by successive occupations make Somersville an excellent place to study the nature of early multiethnic communities in California. Deetz notes, "There may be no place in the country that combines such an ethnically diverse population with such an undisturbed condition" (Howard 1980: 3).

As research at Somersville proceeds, Deetz will continue to look for clues, in the form of artifacts and features, that can be associated with the ethnic identity of its inhabitants. Most mining families built and furnished their own houses, for instance, and ethnic differences may be expected there. Italian families of the period were known to have baked their bread in backyard ovens, whereas others baked in the kitchen. Ethnicity is also displayed by various dietary habits and by such practices as the way animals were butchered. Some groups typically butchered animals by separating bones at the joints, while others chopped through the bones themselves. Some groups cut carcasses into large segments, others into small pieces. Some groups ate primarily off plates; others ate mostly from bowls. Groups who typically cut up meat on the plate would have left plates bearing many knife scratches, whereas groups that cut up meat before serving would not. These kinds of clues shed light on ethnic survival and integration at Somersville.

To its advantage, the Somersville project has access to many documents and photographs from the town's past. There are even some surviving former residents to be interviewed. Deetz points out, however, that the details of peoples' ordinary lives and the nature of their activities are not very fully or even accurately reflected in historical documents, and that study of their archaeological remains can greatly enlarge and illuminate our understanding of their lives. Archaeology in this way gives us a picture based on what people actually did, as well as on what they chose to record in their writings. The Somersville project promises to add a great deal to our knowledge about life in California before the turn of the century (Deetz 1980; see also Fig. 107).

PERSPECTIVES ON THE HISTORICAL PERIOD

Yurok Indians say that when the first sailing ships came up the Klamath River in the nineteenth century, the people fled into the forest and hid for days, fearing that the end of the world had come (Milton Marks and James Stevens, pers. comm. 1978). And in many respects it had. The coming of the Europeans to California brought an end to the world that California Indians had known, although a new world emerged to replace it. The archaeological study of these worlds amplifies and enriches our understandings of them, beyond what may be learned from historical records alone.

A comparison of the relationship between Native Californians and different groups of immigrants, from Europe and elsewhere, and the differing attitudes of the immigrants toward the land and its resources are themes already mentioned. The Spaniards came to California with a program for settlement that included Indians as important components. The Spanish plan for deliberately directed cultural change sought to transform indigenous cultures into Hispanic ones. This policy, though aimed at the destruction of traditional cultures, was not derived from inherent antipathy toward native peoples and their cultures, nor was it intended to destroy the native population itself. Native Californians had a specific place in the Spanish scheme of things, in both practical and ideological terms. Furthermore, the Spanish concept of colonial land tenure was oriented more toward the use of the land and its resources on behalf of imperial policy than toward the title of land for ownership in and of itself. In this view, a landholder had the right of use of all that lay within his domain, including its people. Use rights, granted by a divinely empowered monarch, superseded human and civil rights.

It is not too much to say that the Spaniards viewed the people on the land *as* resources. Although they valued their Indian populations for their labor, they also saw promise for the Indians as *gente de razón*, potential converts harboring souls worthy of salvation. As Cook (1976b) points out, though the Spanish did not think of Indians as quite equal to themselves, the natives were still important as potential citizens and as potential parents for future Hispanic generations. The Spaniards advocated the creation of a mestizo population and did not view with the same horror as Anglo-Saxons and Anglo-Americans the intermarriage of people from different races and ethnic backgrounds. Indians and mestizos were to become peons for the most part, but this end was not regarded as necessarily a bad thing. The Spanish viewed the system of peonage as a benign social system in its ideal form, providing for the needs of subjects while serving God and empire. This can be seen archaeologically at La Purísima and other sites, where the institutions of marriage and the family were promoted (if ineffectively) through provisions for special housing and domestic privileges, and where spiritual needs, as the Spanish defined them, were scrupulously served in burial.

The Russians, on the other hand, did not come to California to establish colonies. They came for a specific resource. Their only goal for the land was to establish a post and conduct whatever building and farming seemed necessary to support it. There was no ideological basis for their effort, so they were unconcerned about the persistence of Indian culture and they did not attempt to replace Pomo skills with their own. As excavation data from Fort Ross show, the Pomo had no real cultural impact on the Russians, and though Russian goods reached the Pomo there was little or no permanent impact of the relationship.

With the Mexican Revolution and subsequent secularization of the missions, cultural change was no longer directed, and events were left to follow their own course. The Mexican colonial government did not try, as Spain had, to replace the cultures it was taking away with alternatives. Yet Indians still had a place in the system, even if that place was at the bottom of the social order. Mexicans preserved the Spanish attitudes toward landholding, which permitted the rise of Indian peonage, thereby leaving participating Indians with some sort of social and economic role to fulfill. In keeping with the constitutional separation of church and state in Mexico itself, Mexico's colonial policies lacked any ideology to be taught to the Indians. Policies were guided by a pragmatism that took advantage of the Indians as an available labor supply.

The coming of the Anglo-Americans, however, produced a situation in which Indians had no functional role to play at all. In contrast to the Spaniards and Russians, the Anglo-Americans came not just to extract resources or to use the land, but to possess it. Anglo-Americans regarded California's Indians as part of the *natural* environment, not the *social* environment. Indians were regarded as things, to be exploited or ignored as the occasion directed. If Indians got in the way of the possession of the land, either as impediments or as rivals, they were removed either by confinement to reservations or by extermination. There was no ideological motive to save souls, and the Anglo-Americans rejected the Spanish goal of creating a mestizo population to people the frontier and supply a labor force (Cook 1976b).

This chapter's themes have included the breakdown of traditional society in California, the pioneer settlement of other cultures, and the development of an urbanized, multiethnic society. That California's Indian population fell by 150,000 under 77 years of occupation by a few thousand Europeans and Mexicans, and dropped an additional 140,000 (to about 6 percent of the original figure) under 54 years of Anglo-American domination, represents an extraordinary human tragedy. It also marks a historical episode that can be understood as the consequence of the social, political, economic, and cultural processes that produced and governed it. It is from an understanding of these processes that any insights into the future may be gained. This topic will be considered in the next chapter, but at this point we want to consider what archaeology has contributed to our knowledge of what happened in California during this period.

In contrast to the preceding chapters, much of the reconstruction presented in this chapter has come from historical sources, to which archaeology has contributed comparatively little. In large part this is because California has an immense wealth of historical documents and comparatively little Historical Period archaeology to date. It is also because the archaeologists who have studied Historical Period sites have not yet contributed anthropological perspectives to our knowledge of California's history.

In Chapter 1 we drew attention to some fundamental distinctions between the approaches to the past taken by historians and by anthropologically oriented archaeologists. It is in the study of periods like California's recent history that these distinctions become clearest.

The historical approach rests on the study of written records, which, as we noted before, provide vast amounts of information and tend to focus on specific individuals, events, things, times, and places. They also tend to have certain biases, in that they overrepresent the White, the well-to-do, the male, the adult, and (by definition) the literate. They also reflect what the writer wished to record, which may or may not be a faithful account, and in any event presents only the perspective of the individual.

The anthropological approach emphasizes the idea that people participate in life within a cultural context, which provides them with rules and models for behavior and strategies for living. It stresses the patterns in the daily life of the people in a community, rather than the unusual or unique examples of behavior that might be more attractive to the historical record. The anthropological approach aims to discover the processes that govern behavior and thereby shape the formation of the archaeological record (South 1977: 5–11; 1979: 235). Archaeology complements history by providing information about material remains that suggest what people actually did, rather than what they chose to write of their actions. Historical archaeology, however, can also provide alternative insights into how and why particular events occurred. It obviously cannot change the basic facts of the past, any more than historical research can (apart from the correction of errors of fact), but archaeology can shed new light on our ideas about the character of an era and the forces that shaped it.

The historical archaeology done in California has made such contributions. Deetz's excavations at La Purísima, for example, brought to light the fact that certain kinds of Indian technology persisted during missionization, and that this survival varied according to sex and to the role of the activity in the mission's activities. Chace's excavations at the Sepulveda Adobe showed that Indians were given a functional place in the Mexican rancho system and that certain aspects of Indian technology were even fostered under that system. At the same time they suggested the importance of British, as opposed to American, participation in the cattle trade of that era, a possibility that conflicts with current interpretations and may provoke new research. Treganza's work at the Ide Adobe, in contrast with the Sepulveda Adobe, showed the non-interaction of Anglo-Americans and Indians at nearly the same time, an apparently culturally based difference that was also evident at the White Ranch and Old Sacramento.

The Old Sacramento project illuminated what Schuyler (1978: 79) has called the immediate and wholesale importation of an industrialized society by the Gold Rush. The historical record stresses the rough, unorganized nature of the argonauts' lives, but the archaeological record at Old Sacramento emphasizes the immediate establishment of brickyards, lumber mills, lime works, printing presses, glassworks, and the whole array of commercial services that arose to provision and sustain the miners. Neither history texts nor archaeological reports provide much detail about the true scope of the state's ethnic diversity after 1849, or the consequences of the prolonged interaction of these groups, but Deetz's research at Somersville may shed new light on the subject. Archaeology, then, has already contributed to our understanding of the historical era as well as that of the prehistoric.

Yet as valuable as these contributions have been, what impresses us about historical archaeology in California is its potential for the future. We have only outlined some of the major trends in the state's history, and all of them are either almost or wholly unstudied archaeologically. To cite a few examples, we still know very little about how the state's Indian peoples survived the holocausts of the nineteenth century and what differences there were between those who survived and those who perished. Written records provide us with very little data about life on reservations and rancherias. We know much too little about daily life and community makeup in the mining camps, in logging camps, and in the hosts of small farming and ranching communities that arose and often perished after a few decades. We have few detailed records about life and culture in the early fishing, railroad, and oil camps, about Indian and White Civilian Conservation Corps camps during the Great Depression, about twentieth-century placer mining and its relationship to hard times in the cities, about the Second World War Japanese internment camps, prisoner-of-war camps, or conscientious-objector camps, or the similarities and differences among them. As the archaeology of the Historical Period develops, our understanding of California's history will become richer and more accurate, and whatever information may be learned from it will be better lessons as a result (Schuyler 1979, 1980; South 1979).

CHAPTER SIX

Conclusions

California's archaeology records 15,000 years or more of human history. Immense changes took place in that time. What began as an initial settlement by a few tiny groups of Paleo-Indians developed into an enormous concentration of elaborate Native American cultures. The course of their history was truncated by European conquest, leading to the formation of an even more complex archaeological record as successive waves of non-Indian immigrants settled in the state in coexistence with the surviving Native Californians. Within this rich and diverse record can be found clear patterns of adaptation and historical development.

PATTERNS AND PROCESSES IN CALIFORNIA'S PAST

Cultural development in California, as we see it, has been characterized by long epochs of slow growth and development, in which the social patterns on which economies were based could evolve to their fullest levels of development. The long archaeological record, the generous environment, and the relative degree of isolation afforded California by its coast, mountains, and deserts gave cultures the time, the means, and the opportunity to evolve. In their freedom from intervention, California societies developed remarkable ways of life, with dense settlements and elaborate achievements in art, architecture, religion, technology, economy, and social structure. California cultures are all the more fascinating to social scientists because they were developed without dependence on agriculture. California Indians may have evolved the most sophisticated hunting-and-gathering economies in the world. Their achievements in mastering the subtle intricacies of complex environments and their exploitation without serious abuse to the resource base can scarcely be overstated.

Prehistoric California cultures grew to be not only complex and sophisticated, but stable and enduring, capable of sustaining themselves for centuries or millennia. The importance of understanding why some cultures endure and others break down is another reason the study of California's past is so important to anthropologists. Particularly for the last several thousand years, a record of growth like that in California is rarely found in the archaeological or ethnographic record. Its study allows scientists to determine the nature and limits of such systems, the forces that promote stability or promote change, and the courses that change takes.

In spite of this stability and gradual growth, the state's cultural development was not one of simple, straight-line progression to ever more complex cultures. Although there are few signs of revolutionary changes or watersheds in the state's prehistory, certain fundamental reorientations did occur. These reorientations derived from adaptations whose origins far predate their periods of prominence. They are seen to have gained importance as existing patterns reached their maximum levels of development and began to be constrained by growth-limiting factors. What had been only minor strategies then became increasingly important as they proved sufficient to overcome the limits. As came to be relied on more and more, they tended to emerge as the characteristic adaptations of their eras, until they too reached their maximum levels of development and began themselves to be constrained by growth-limiting factors. The cycle repeated; hitherto minor elements of adaptation proved in turn to be more successful at relieving these newly limiting pressures, and economies began to develop in still newer directions.

This overtly evolutionary interpretation of California's prehistoric cultural development is suggested by the course of the archaeological record. The absence of abrupt changes there has made California's archaeology difficult to understand, but it also makes California an exceptional place to study evolutionary processes at work. In the gradual but significant shifts that took place, it is possible to indicate those forces that worked to promote change and those elements of culture that did or did not respond.

The first major shift was from Paleo-Indian to Archaic subsistence strategies, which we characterized in Cleland's terms as a change from focal to diffuse adaptation. The change was a response to a gradually changing environment, a gradually vanishing suite of Pleistocene food resources, and an achievement by the Paleo-Indians of the maximum carrying capacity for their population in their way of life. With the combination of growing demands on resources and shrinking supplies, a series of changes began. One was a habitat shift, initially to a habitat not too different from the one previously occupied, and eventually into more and more different habitats. This shift was accompanied by a resource transfer, from a heavily carnivorous diet to one predominantly herbivorous. This transfer allowed a drop to a lower trophic energy level, which made more energy available and relaxed the limits on population growth. This factor alone would have caused Archaic population levels to rise well beyond Paleo-Indian levels. The energy-source transfer also increased the diversity of species used, and in this diversity Archaic peoples found some relief from another limiting factor—fluctuations in the natural abundance of specific resources.

The Archaic pattern also depended on the elaboration of technology and the development of specialized tools that allowed certain practices enhancing adaptation to be conducted on a large scale for the first time. This diversification can be seen to derive from the penetration of new ecological niches by Archaic settlers. The typical pattern was the settlement of a new habitat in which resource use was limited and tended to be similar to patterns followed by earlier cultures. Gradually more and more resources in the new environment were brought into use, with tools developed in the process to make the use of the resources more productive. Only after long periods of development did the exploitation of the habitat begin to approach its potential.

Why did the process take so long? There is no simple or obvious answer. One factor may be the necessity to accumulate knowledge about a new habitat. Pioneer settlers like the Paleo-Indians would often have found new habitats a wholly new experience, and whenever Archaic settlers moved into new niches they too acted as pioneer settlers for a while. The newness can have lasted only so long, however, even for Paleo-Indians. Hunters and gatherers must be good natural scientists to be successful, and even the Paleo-Indians were superbly successful in their adaptations. To argue that they did not learn enough about their environment in the course of thousands of years is not very persuasive.

Population pressure may have had something to do with fostering change, but as an explanation for change it leaves a lot to be desired.

Societies, even very small ones, can indeed suffer from population pressure, since any way of life has limits to the number of people it can reliably support. Yet there are many solutions to population pressure, and adaptive change is not an inevitable response; starvation, disease, conflict, and emigration all can reduce local population pressure.

Systems and evolutionary theory offer some possible explanations. One systems concept, sometimes called Romer's Rule, holds that groups faced with change continue to act as much like they used to as possible and change as little as they can while still surviving. Evolutionary theory suggests that the rule is so because in conservatism lies security. Old ways are already worked out and predictable; new ways, even if promising, pose risks and unknowns. Geneticists know that most mutations do not manage as well as established traits, which have already been preserved because of their proven advantages. The more substantial the mutation, the more likely it is not to succeed and the more serious its problems are likely to be. For cultures, the challenge is survival in an uncertain world, and the issue of reliability is of genuine adaptational significance.

In this view, the slow and piecemeal change in Archaic cultures becomes understandable. Changes occurred only when survival pressures made change advantageous. Even then, people modified their lifeways as little as possible. Over broad regions and long time spans, many groups tried many experiments in adaptation. Some efforts worked well, some poorly, and some not at all. Over time, the more effective strategies were repeated. Because the level of interaction among groups was low, it took a long time for the efforts of different people to become combined into various permutations, some of which proved even more fruitful in combination than individually, and others of which did not. The slow maturing rate of Archaic cultures was as much a problem of information flow as anything else.

The Archaic strategy eventually proved to be far more fruitful than the Paleo-Indian approach from which it had sprung. The growth in subsistence and migrational complexity of Archaic cultures was fundamentally additive: one resource did not replace another, but was added to the existing group of exploited species to make larger totals and more reliable supplies. Although the actual total of resources recovered varied from environment to environment, we see the strategy as being the same whether one looks at the deserts, the valleys, or the coast.

In the shift to the Archaic strategy, the fundamental unit of labor remained the same. In Paleo-Indian times the basic labor units were the individual and the family, and this pattern held true in Archaic times. Archaic cultures did not raise their productivity by creating new labor units; rather, they increased productivity by intensifying the scheduling of the existing units of labor. The scheduling of seasonal rounds was keyed to the ripening patterns of desired plant and animal resources. This intensification gave much larger yields to Archaic populations, but the scheduling approach bore its own limits: a family could visit only one resource at one time; and it could make only so many moves and travel only so many miles in a season. At some point, for every group, further intensification reached a point of diminishing returns. That point marked the carrying capacity of that environment for the Archaic way of life.

These maximums were being reached by roughly 4,000 years ago in several parts of California. The pressures on populations that stemmed from reaching the maximums helped induce another fundamental shift in survival strategies. We have identified it as the Pacific Period adaptation, and have characterized it, in Cleland's terms, as a trend toward a focal economy. This shift was fundamentally different from the Paleo-Indian focal strategy, however, both in its traits and in the character of its starting point.

The Pacific strategy began with the highly diffuse Archaic mode of adaptation and intensified the exploitation of certain resources until they became staples. In order to achieve this intensification it was necessary for Pacific cultures to depart from several Archaic patterns. Pacific cultures took several practices that existed in Archaic times and made them far more important than ever before. Trade, surplus collection, redistribution, and storage were all intensified. The food resources that drew Pacific Period focus were all types that occurred in huge seasonal abundance. Archaic people had used the resources, but only as foods during the season of availability. Pacific peoples developed the collection of surpluses over and above what was needed for immediate use. They saved the surpluses to use during subsequent periods of scarcity, and they developed storage and redistribution mechanisms to bring the surpluses from times of plenty to times of scarcity and from households of plenty to households of scarcity. Shell money was developed to make the system work even more effectively, since it stored the value of the resources and could be converted into food resources (among other things).

These practices had a dramatic impact on the carrying capacity of the environment. But the increase in carrying capacity was also stimulated by fundamental changes in the organization of labor. The Pacific cultures created newer and more complex units of labor to add to those of earlier times. These larger aggregates accomplished things that their members could not have accomplished individually, and recovered more calories as collectives doing certain tasks than the same number of people could have recovered operating as individuals or families. The Yurok fish dam at Kepel, the fishing crews of the Chumash, and the rabbit drives of the Owens Valley Paiute are all examples. Some of these aggregates were organized along lines of kinship, others on the basis of residence in the same community, and still others on aggregations of communities. In most cases the aggregations were task-specific; once the task was completed, the organization dissolved.

In the organization of Pacific society, leadership figures emerged. The institution of the headman may have had its roots in ancient Archaic cultures, but it flourished in Pacific times. Other forms of leadership arose after the Pacific Period had begun. The big- or rich-man pattern of northwestern California is one example; the rabbit-boss tradition of the desert is another. These leaders affected the carrying capacity of the environment by coordinating activities and people to make collective activities more productive. In many cases they operated systems of surplus collection and redistribution. Both headmen and big men acted as intercommunity trade negotiators—the headman as a representative of his community, the big man as a wealthy individual who traded to earn more wealth and supported his community and followers by distributing rewards, sponsoring feasts and religious observances, and helping his poorer relatives.

California cultures were able to gain the benefits of raised carrying capacity without developing complex political organizations. In other parts of the continent, communities of similar size were organized into more complex forms of political organization, such as tribes, chiefdoms, or kingdoms. California cultures interest anthropologists in part because of their ability to achieve large size and considerable wealth with less political complexity, with less emphasis on formal authority, and with less emphasis on militarism. The development of social complexity based on trade and labor organization is especially interesting in prehistoric California because it can be viewed apart from the complexity based on the more usual factors of conquest or agriculture.

As in the Archaic, these developments did not appear suddenly or as whole complexes. They appeared piecemeal, developed slowly through different combinations in different communities, and proceeded until effective strategies were worked out in each part of the state. The resulting adaptations proved far more productive than the

Archaic approach and were accompanied by the growth of much larger communities and denser populations. The pressures on resources caused by population growth helped fuel continued economic development.

The surplus and wealth orientations of Pacific Period cultures also stimulated the growth of artisanry. The craftsmanship and design of Native Californian artists is still poorly known and deserves much wider recognition. The final developments of California Indian culture by the eve of the European invasion were outstanding in terms of art, architecture, religious ideology, ceremonialism, and technology, not to mention a sophisticated economy and complex social forms. California Indian costumes were as impressive as those of the Great Plains tribes. California ceremonial lodges expressed architectural achievements comparable to the great kivas of the Southwest. California basketry was unsurpassed in technical quality and design, and, it should be noted, a good California basket represented many times more handwork than a fine pottery vessel from the Southwest. California stone carving was as excellent as any on the continent. Woodworking from northwestern California compares favorably with that of the Northwest coast. The sewn-plank canoe of southern California is perhaps the most complex technological creation in watercraft of the whole New World, and the curved shell fishhook is a masterpiece of beauty and functional efficiency.

The development of Pacific Period cultures was halted by European invasion and settlement. The coming of the Europeans brought a third shift in the orientations of cultural development. Here a true watershed was crossed. It is easy to regard European immigration as a fundamental break that closed down the old order and ushered in a new set of rules. But even though the change was sudden and dramatic, the processes at work can be seen to have been similar to those that operated earlier in prehistory.

For California's Indians, the arrival of the Europeans ended the trend toward focal economies and brought a shift back toward diffuse adaptations. European settlement led to a breakdown of the intercommunity infrastructure that had evolved in Pacific times. The result was the survival of only the simplest units of production in the traditional economic system: the individual and the family. Though each surviving individual performed as much labor as ever before, each community suffered from the loss of the subsistence produced by the other levels in the more complex organization. Aboriginal communities could not generate the same number of calories per capita as before, and carrying capacity and population level declined. We would see a similar result today if suddenly the freeways or the railroads were to stop operating; our communities would suffer equally drastic reductions in the quality of life and in social complexity.

The European immigrants, on the other hand, entered California as pioneering settlers, comparable in that sense to the Paleo-Indian pioneer settlers. The Europeans developed in California what was essentially a focal economy, though it was generalized compared to that in the homeland. Whereas diffuse Indian cultures had exploited hundreds of species of plants and dozens of animal species, the Europeans made use of few, and mainly those brought from Europe and capable of being raised in many different habitats. The Spanish and Anglo-American colonial economies were much simpler than those of their parent cultures, with fewer elements and of a relatively unspecialized nature. The colonial economies were both pioneering and focal in the same sense as were the Paleo-Indian economies. Even with the benefits of farming, herding, machinery, shipping, money, and foreign trade, the Hispanic population remained very small as long as the economy remained focal, and populations remained thinly distributed in a narrow range of environments. When the United States took over the area, there followed a trend toward more diffuse adaptations, with settlement in more environments. This trend, though severely skewed by the Gold Rush, was not fundamentally altered. The peak of diffuse adaptation for the newcomers seems to have been reached in the early part of this century, from which point an evolution toward a newer form of focal economy developed as key industries evolved into major foci. Agriculture, lumbering, mining, manufacturing, and transportation became specializations that grew out of more modest nineteenth-century bases.

The makeup of historical California cultures differs obviously from that of prehistoric cultures, but the processes that govern their growth and development are the same. These processes may be seen at work more easily by looking at the prehistoric cultures because fewer distracting variables interfere.

A brief example may illustrate one of the more fundamental of these processes: the impact of environmental limits on populations and economies. No culture grows unchecked. All populations are resource-dependent, and some resources essential to growth are scarcer than others. The scarcest essential resource exerts the most pressure against growth; it functions accordingly as the most important limiting factor. The limiting factor differs from culture to culture, but when the limits of one factor are overcome, another is soon revealed to assert new limits. For prehistoric cultures, food and water tended to be the most severe limiting factors. People used cultural developments to help overcome various limits in the food supply, but in the deserts, where water came to be in short supply as the Pleistocene lakes dried up, water limits became even more severe than food limits and people had to pattern their movements to maximize their access to water.

Today food and water are still important limiting factors, but their impact has been reduced much more than in prehistoric times by the application of cultural developments. Early in this century metropolitan centers such as San Francisco and Los Angeles were able to overcome the inherent limits of local water sources and food-producing resources through transportation technology. The Hetch Hetchy Reservoir, the Owens Valley Aqueduct, and the Colorado River Project carry water from areas of surplus to areas of deficit, allowing the deficit areas to raise the ceilings on growth imposed by their limited resources and permitting population levels to rise above the limits supportable by local resources alone. Similar limits in local food supplies were relaxed when railroads and highways were developed. Food surpluses could be produced economically in areas of low population density because the means to move the surpluses to areas of higher density had been developed. These methods of relaxing limits are comparable to those taken by the Pacific Period cultures, who used surpluses, storage, trade, money, and redistribution to achieve similar results.

The carrying capacity of the environment for Pacific Period cultures was determined by the continuation of these strategies. As we noted, when European invasion made it impossible for the practices to continue, carrying capacity fell. We can see that, for the Pacific Period cultures, there was an inverse relationship between complexity and stability. Although their complex interactions raised the carrying capacity over Archaic levels, the security of the increased populations was reduced, because more-complex systems can go wrong in more places, and a breakdown anywhere in the system will affect the system as a whole.

Although the details of the modern subsistence system in the state obviously differ from those of the Pacific cultures, the dynamics are comparable. Today's populations are vastly greater, but the subsistence system is vastly more complex and therefore greatly more vulnerable to breakdown. Any breakdown in the transportation system for food and water would have serious implications. Local supplies of food and water for today's cities would last only a few weeks at best. Any permanent reduction in the ability to transport either food or water to these centers would bring about a radical drop in carrying capacity. The declines in population levels, social complexity, and economic productivity that occurred at the end of the Pacific Period could be expected in the future under those circumstances. The effects would not be precisely the same, since California today is tied to the nation and, to a lesser extent, to the trading world (which prehistoric cultures were not), but comparable kinds of breakdown could be expected.

More-positive relationships can also be seen. Prehistoric cultures devised fairly successful means to cope with ethnic and linguistic differences and to produce functioning economies that grew and developed not just in spite of the differences but also by using them to advantage. California today may be the most ethnically complex region in the world, and a good understanding of the processes by which such complexity was used to advantage in the past may provide important lessons for the future.

OLD QUESTIONS AND NEW DIRECTIONS IN RESEARCH

What, then, should archaeology be doing to increase its understanding of these processes, its store of data? Hundreds of sites have been excavated in California, and it might be wondered what is left to be learned. In fact, a great many basic questions remain unanswered. Research attacks old puzzles—we now have some understanding of the general course of California prehistory—but also leads to newer puzzles that could not even have been perceived until knowledge had advanced to a certain point. Archaeologists have a good deal of fun debating what the hot issues and major questions are likely to be a few years down the road. This speculation is not just idle exercise, however, since it shapes the direction of future research, for scholars generally choose what they hope will be important problems to pursue. Here are some of the questions and topics that look important today.

Kroeber initiated archaeological research at the University of California more than 80 years ago, and one of the first questions he asked was when California was first settled. We cannot answer his question with much more security today than then. The question itself is exciting but not as important as it seems. What is important is that the study of California's first settlers, the Paleo-Indians, is only now becoming accepted as a legitimate field of scientific research. In ten years we should know much more about the distribution of Paleo-Indian groups around California, about their persistence over time, and about differences among cultures within the Paleo-Indian Period. Much basic research remains to be done about Paleo-Indian subsistence, settlement, technology, and society. To date, no single substantial excavation of a California Paleo-Indian site has been described in print.

Cultures of the Early and Middle Archaic are almost as unknown. Whole areas of the state still are virtual blanks for those periods. Even those areas for which traditions are known are not well studied as a rule, since few sites have been excavated and most of those few have been small-scale projects rather than studies of whole settlements. We do not know how incomplete our knowledge is for these periods, or how accurately the information that has already been collected reflects what is actually in the archaeological record.

These gaps in knowledge involve not just time periods but whole areas of the state. Most parts of California still have undergone little or no systematic archaeological research. We not only do not know much about their archaeology, but we know equally little about the relationships between those areas and the better-excavated parts of the state. This is particularly true of the forested, the mountainous, and the desert parts of California. Although the recent growth of cultural-resource management has caused a marked rise in the number of surveys conducted around California, there has been an actual decrease in the number of substantial excavations of the sort that reveal the internal structures of sites and provide large, reliable samples of artifacts to study (see Appendix A).

Many other interesting questions arise from the great variety of, and distribution patterns of, languages in the Final Pacific Period. Archaeologists are attracted to the potential of linguistics for suggesting reconstructions of the histories of ethnographic groups, even if the migration-oriented explanations offered by linguists are not always accepted. Were the ancestors of Hokan-speaking peoples the original Archaic populations of California? Did ancestral Penutian speakers colonize the Central Valley early in the Late Archaic? Did they displace Hokan speakers or did they occupy a vacant ecological niche? Were the Yukian speakers the descendants of the original Borax Lake settlers, or were they recent immigrants? Were the Modoc (Kutenai speakers) the original Nightfire Island and Surprise Valley people, later displaced from the Great Basin by drought or by ancestral Shoshonean speakers?

Was there an occupational hiatus in the deserts of southern California? Did the ancestors of Shoshonean speakers really occupy the desert region as far west as the coast only 1,500 years ago? If so, did they move into an abandoned environment or did they displace a resident population? If they displaced another people, what was that group, and to whom were they related? What happened to them, and what gave the ancestral Shoshoneans a competitive advantage over them?

Did the Athapaskans and Algonkians of northwestern California move into an unoccupied ecological niche in the coastal-riverine environment, bringing a new form of adaptation, or did they push out some ancestral Hokan speakers already living there? How did such diverse language groups come to share virtually identical cultures in only a few hundred years? How can the tremendous linguistic diversity of the Final Pacific Period be explained in general, and what relationship to the archaeological record does the diversity bear? Such questions intrigue archaeologists throughout the state. Some progress has been made in recent years in the association of particular archaeological remains with specific language groups (see, for example, Aikens 1978; Elsasser 1978a; C. King 1978; True 1968; Warren & True 1961), but much remains to be learned.

Beyond the many unanswered questions about *what* happened in California's past, there are equally important and unanswered questions about *how* and *why* things did or did not happen. For example, we know that the Channel Islands of southern California were being settled as early as the start of the Middle Archaic, but we have no real idea of how this was done, or what drew people to the islands so early. Nor do we understand why, if they could reach the islands, they made so little use of the sea's resources for so long. Or why the central and northern coastal regions were settled so much later than the southern California coast.

Prehistoric methods of subsistence are generally understood, but comparatively little is known about their development. Why did hard-seed use appear so much earlier than nut or acorn use, for example? It has been argued that ancient Californians had to learn how to leach acorns before they could begin to take advantage of that valuable resource, but that explains nothing about the apparent failure to use digger-pine nuts, sugar-pine nuts, or pinyon nuts until later.

We noted earlier that Pacific Period cultures achieved their high levels of development without relying on food cultivation. Why they did not make use of farming is a question that is still not answered, but one that should draw continuing interest (see, for example, Heizer 1964, 1978b). In general, we need to learn the importance of farming to the rise of complex cultures, since except for the cultures of North

America's Pacific Coast there has been an intimate relationship world-wide between the appearance of farming and the rise of complex societies.

But although we might agree that farming is not crucial to the rise of complex cultures, we cannot explain why Pacific Period cultures did not take it up. It was not because they did not know how—all California groups planted tobacco in prepared plots and saved the seeds for the next year. It was not because they had no access to food crops—southern California groups in particular made trading expeditions to the Colorado River and the Southwest, where the farming of corn, beans, squash, pumpkins, and cotton was practiced. Nor was it that winter rains and summer drought prevented the growing of such crops—simple dry farming of many crops is possible in the state. In the deserts of southern Arizona the prehistoric Hohokam peoples used irrigation canals to help in growing crops. The ancient Californians traded with the Hohokam and could have established farming on the Pacific Coast with less effort than the desert people spent maintaining their own crops.

Some writers have tried to solve the problem by defining it away. Henry T. Lewis (1973), for example, has argued persuasively that many California groups practiced quasi-agricultural techniques. The Mono Indians, for example, stimulated the growth of certain stream-side grasses by building small rock dams across arroyos to slow runoff, trap fertile silts, and increase the soil's water absorption. Many groups regularly burned off hillside shrubbery to stimulate the growth of desired plants that appeared soon after fires.

Lewis has done a valuable service by showing just how ecologically sophisticated many Pacific Period groups were in their subsistence practices. He begs the question about farming, however, because Pacific Period groups did not grow domesticated food crops or raise domesticated food animals. They obviously did very well without domesticated foods, but why they opted to stay away from food production remains a mystery.

An equally interesting puzzle is why ancient Californians did not make use of ceramic technology to become potters. The problem is similar to that of the absence of farming in the sense that the ancient Californians had knowledge of the technology from direct contact with peoples who employed it—as with farming, there was no environmental reason why pottery could not have been made and used. Actually, within the Late and Final Pacific Period some desert groups began to make and use pottery vessels. The mystery is why the larger, richer, more settled groups of the coast and Central Valley did not take up the practice.

Other important research problems are suggested by the recently developed field of historical archaeology. We need to learn much more about the nature of the interactions between Indians and foreigners during the period of exploration, and what the consequences of those contacts were for both cultures. The aspects of Indian culture that were able to survive missionization, those that were lost, and those that evolved through interaction with Hispanic culture into new forms are still not well understood.

The nature and role of mestizo culture in Spanish California, and the relations between mestizos and Indians, have not yet been seriously studied. There has been little investigation of the responses of interior Indian cultures to the loss of contacts with coastal peoples that resulted from missionization, nor do we yet know very much about the spread of European cultural elements into indigenous cultures before the settlement of the interior by non-Indians. The desertion of mission life by escaped neophytes brought both mission culture and coastal Indian culture to inland groups that sheltered the escapees, and we haven't yet found the archaeological record of the social and cultural consequences of such situations.

The spread of pueblos and ranches before and after the secularization of the missions has not yet received much archaeological study. The role played by Indians in this movement needs a great deal of clarification.

The period of statehood also offers significant research questions. In Chapter 5 we noted that there were research opportunities for the study of California's urbanization, the rise of industries, and the rise and fall of small towns. To that list we might add the opportunity to study the phenomenon of boom-and-bust towns as a cultural form. California has hundreds of small ghost towns of many sorts that offer fine laboratories for such research. Studies have not yet begun of sites created by such isolated individuals as fire guards, wartime airplane spotters, hard-luck miners from the Great Depression, or hobos. Such sites could reveal things about changing styles over time, differences in cultural background, and relationships between socially isolated individuals and the general society.

On a different theme, the persistence of traditional Indian religious activities warrants a major research effort. Archaeology is one way to document the continuation of such activities from prehistoric times to the present. The documentation of both the practices and the physical remains associated with them are legally critical when rural land-development projects are planned by the federal government.

One factor leading to new and exciting research questions has been the contact of archaeology and anthropology with other disciplines. The collaboration of scholars from different disciplines within universities and the personal interests of specialists in other areas who have become involved in archaeology have led to the infusion of new ideas, research methods, and data into traditional archaeological research. Fields as varied as sociology, geology, botany, and chemistry have been brought into the archaeological enterprise, leading to new insights and causing archaeologists to ask questions and collect data that had not concerned them before. For example, once geochemists showed that it is possible to determine from which lava flow a particular obsidian artifact came, archaeologists began to search for the locations of all the obsidian sources in the state (which not even geologists knew) and began to use obsidian-source data to ask questions about the direction, size, and mechanisms of prehistoric trade in the material. And as suggested by the next section, the development of scientific technology in many fields is expanding archaeological horizons in more and more directions at an ever-growing pace.

TECHNOLOGY AND NEW DIRECTIONS IN RESEARCH

Archaeological research is directed by questions, but certain questions can be asked only because technological developments have allowed archaeologists to use new kinds of data or previously known data in new ways. California archaeology has been at the forefront of a number of technological revolutions, and its leadership should continue if funding permits. Innovations range from data processing to dating methods, from satellite photography to the microscopic study of stone tools. Many approaches are still in their infancy, and major developments can be expected in the next ten to twenty years.

Data processing, for example, is beginning to make possible many kinds of research that could not have been attempted before. Computers have been with us for some time, and archaeologists are increasingly using them to analyze artifact collections statistically, to study the distributions of artifacts in sites and the kinds of sites found in a given region. The recent development of microcomputers has allowed archaeologists to take their computers to the excavation, and thus to obtain the results of analyses quickly enough to change their excavation tactics literally from one day to the next.

Software developments also have expanded computer use. In the past few years some researchers have begun to develop computerized simulation models of past cultures, models that combine archaeological, ethnographic, and ecological data to determine past economies, subsistence practices, and settlement patterns. Archaeologists using these models have begun to be able to predict the kinds of archaeological resources to be found in different environments. As such models are tested and refined, more of the archaeological record will be predictable, and the kinds of surveys and excavations needed to gather new data will be more specifically foreseen. One expected development of this approach will be the use of models to predict the contents and internal structure of types of sites, a practice that could reduce the need for many kinds of excavation.

The study of plant remains in archaeological sites should increase in the next several years. California archaeologists have made a great deal of use of the animal remains found in sites, but the study of plant remains has lagged because of problems in recovering and identifying them. Many plant remains have perished, but some kinds, such as carbonized seeds and charcoal, survive in many sites. The recently developed technique of flotation, a method of separating plant remains from the soil of archaeological sites, allows archaeologists to recover these macrofossils, so that specialists can identify the species. The study of plant pollens, or microfossils, has also been hindered by the inability of archaeologists to recover them, but recent developments have improved the recovery techniques in this area also. With this evidence archaeologists can learn more about the kinds of plant resources that occurred near sites, the resources that past peoples used, and the climate of the time.

Radiocarbon dating has been an important technique in California archaeology for over 30 years. Researchers in the state have been making important advances in recent years in the reliability and scope of this method. A major advance of the 1970's was the use of tree-ring dates from the ancient bristlecone pine to improve the accuracy of the age determinations given by radiocarbon dating. It was found that carbon-14 dates tend not to be as old as the true dates. The Suess correction coefficient, developed from the bristlecone pine studies, has allowed the recalibration of existing dates to give a more accurate picture of the past. Breakthroughs predicted for the coming decade include developing ways to date materials older than the current maximum for C-14, about 50,000–70,000 years, and applying these methods to date materials that so far have not proved reliable for C-14 dating, such as sea-mammal bone and bone collagen. Current developments allow accurate determinations from smaller and smaller samples, which makes the method useful in more cases than ever before. The cost of C-14 dating, which is not dropping, is probably the single biggest handicap to its use.

Another dating technique that should become important is thermoluminescent dating, which works on pottery and other materials that have been subjected to high temperatures. Much of the pioneering work on this technique has been done in California. Ten years ago the approach was not particularly reliable, but great progress has been made, and the technique can realistically be expected to become applicable to California sites in the coming decade or so. Although prehistoric pottery tends to be found only in the southern California deserts, baked clay figurines and cooking balls are more widespread, and fire ovens and hearths are found even more widespread. Since thermoluminescent dating should work on these items, the technique is expected to become important.

Another dating technique developed primarily in California is obsidian-hydration dating. Introduced a quarter of a century ago, this method allows the direct dating of artifacts made of obsidian. The method measures the amount of hydration rind that has developed below the artifact's surface as a result of the chemical action of atmospheric moisture on the artifact. Research has been aimed at understanding the factors that affect the rate at which hydration rinds form. This work has been combined with the analysis of trace elements in obsidian by using neutron activation analysis or x-ray fluorescence. These computer-aided analyses allow the source from which an obsidian artifact originated to be identified. There are more than two dozen obsidian sources in California, and each has different combinations of trace elements. These differences help produce variations in hydration rates. Advances along these lines of research have helped make obsidian hydration a valuable and low-cost dating method. More work is needed on determining obsidian sources, on determining the causes of hydration-rate variation, and on using C-14 dates from sites that yield associated obsidian artifacts to cross-check obsidian hydration rates under different conditions. The widespread use of obsidian in California prehistory and the low cost of measuring hydration should stimulate continued research on the method in the coming decade.

FUTURE RESEARCH TOPICS

Some researchers identify their interests by problem or question. Others associate themselves with particular methods and techniques. Still others orient their work around areas of topical interest. Several topics appear to be emerging as important foci for research in the next decade or so.

The field of paleoenvironmental studies is a young, rapidly expanding area of archaeology, first advanced in California by Clement Meighan (1959b). In recent years archaeologists have been able to draw increasingly on research from other fields to help reconstruct past environments and to understand the relationship between small-scale climatic change and cultural change. Recent studies in the southern Sierra (Moratto, King & Woolfenden 1978) and around San Francisco Bay (Bickel 1978a,b) have shown that microenvironmental changes were significant factors in shaping local adaptations. Because prehistoric occupation sites are excellent places to recover many kinds of environmental data, further growth and collaboration in this field can be expected.

Paleo-Indian studies have lurked around the fringes of anthropological archaeology in the state, but in the next decade they should move into the mainstream. The impetus, perhaps, has been a marked growth in desert archaeology in the last several years because the major landowner there—the federal government—has begun to fund environmental-impact studies. The desert is where much of the state's Paleo-Indian remains occur, and with systematic surveys being done for the first time in many parts of the desert, archaeologists now have access to Paleo-Indian data in some quantity. Equally important, this work is being done by archaeologists who also study all the rest of the archaeological record, rather than by a small group of dedicated specialists as in the past; accordingly, Paleo-Indian studies are becoming a mainstream research activity, and Paleo-Indian data are being described along with other kinds of archaeological remains in mainstream reports. If these studies lead to the recognition of some unique types of technologies more ancient than the Folsom and Clovis materials, it may become possible, within a few years, to define more than one Paleo-Indian tradition. Another nascent avenue of research is the comparative study of California Paleo-Indian materials with Upper Paleolithic data from eastern Asia. This line of study may lead to new insights into the settlement of the New World. But even if it serves only to ensure an increase in systematic Paleo-Indian studies, that alone will answer many currently unanswerable questions, while leading to new ones.

The field of historical archaeology, at the other end of the time spectrum, can also be expected to expand markedly in the next decade or two. More and more archaeologists are becoming attracted to the research potential of historical-period sites to answer many of the kinds of questions about culture and cultural processes that previously had been studied only on prehistoric data. The rich written records of the historical period give the archaeologist many kinds of data not available to the prehistorian, and the existence of the calendar provides very sensitive measures of time.

Two other factors are causing the growth of historical archaeology. The first is the body of federal, state, and local laws that protect Paleo-Indian and other prehistoric archaeological remains. Environmental-impact studies done under those laws include historical archaeology. The second is the growing resistance of Native Americans to the archaeological study of many prehistoric sites. With this in mind, a number of archaeologists have turned to pursuing their research at historical sites, where no one objects. Not only are these factors causing growth in historical archaeology, they are shedding light on the backgrounds of many other ethnic groups that have contributed to California's growth but have not been given prominent places in historical or archaeological literature.

Settlement archaeology, which explores the distribution of a culture's sites in the environment, started to rise in importance in the past fifteen years and will continue to grow in the 1980's. Settlement archaeologists study the types, distributions, and numbers of sites in different environments, and the aspects of past economies and environments that determined site distribution patterns. Because many parts of the state are only now being surveyed thoroughly enough to allow settlement patterns to be revealed, this field should see continued growth.

Another recently developed field that should remain important is the study of past forms of society or social organization. This "paleo-sociology," as Jennings (1974: 359) calls it, reflects efforts in the 1960's to make archaeology more of a social science by using archaeological data to reveal social relationships within and between communities. California has seen some important research in this area (see, for example, L. King 1969; T. King 1974; Stickel 1968). Much of this work has concentrated on the study of Indian cemeteries, under the assumption that people bury their dead in some reflection of the person's status in life. Because Native Californians have grown increasingly resistant to such research on grounds of desecration, it will not be surprising to see cemetery studies decline in the future while archaeologists find other kinds of data on which to base these studies. The analysis of prehistoric houses offers one possible line of research in this area.

California is also seeing growth in the study of lithic technology, the manufacture and use of stone tools. Since prehistoric California cultures used stone as their major industrial raw material, the study of the ways stone tools were made and used is important if we are to understand past cultures better. Some very promising approaches developed in the past few years should find increasing use in the next decade or so. Some studies have involved the experimental reproduction of prehistoric tools using traditional methods of toolmaking. In others, researchers have experimented with the use of stone tools to understand better their possible functions. In still others, microscopes have been used to study the minute patterns of wear on tool edges. These microwear studies have also included the manufacture of modern, replica stone tools, which were used under controlled conditions on various raw materials that prehistoric peoples might have used. When the modern replicas are studied under the microscope, wear patterns on them can be compared to wear patterns found on prehistoric tools to shed light on the uses to which the ancient tools might have been put. All these approaches reflect the use of laboratory experiments to study the past, certainly among the most exciting and innovative directions in current research.

PROBLEMS AND POTENTIALS

Vigorous research fields grow and change, and change brings problems as well as benefits. Theoretical, social, and economic issues confronting California archaeology in the coming years will affect the ability of the public to benefit from the discipline, and much of the future health of the discipline will depend on how California archaeologists respond to these problems in the next decade.

The practice of archaeology in California has grown rapidly in the last decade because of cultural-resource management (see Appendix A). A good deal of effort has been channeled in this direction at the expense of more traditional activities, which have consequently declined. For example, ten or fifteen years ago a dozen or more summer field schools trained college students in archaeology. In recent years only one or two have been held each summer, and the access of the public to high-quality training in archaeology has thus been greatly reduced (see Appendix E). The growth of cultural-resource management also means that few if any projects are now launched purely for research. This fact has affected the growth of knowledge in many areas and means that a great deal of the archaeological fieldwork that gets done under cultural-resource management actually adds little to our body of knowledge about the past.

Cultural-resource management projects require the writing of reports, but the reports for the most part end up in the filing cabinets of the sponsoring agencies and do not reach other scholars or the general public. Much data remains unpublished. Most of the journals that published reports on California archaeology a generation ago are defunct and others have not risen to replace them. Archaeologists who find themselves increasingly occupied with working for funding agencies write little for their colleagues or the public. The vast majority of environmental-impact studies prepared by archaeologists are superficial surveys that tell something about the resources to be found in a region but very little about what is in any site. Thus, although there is much more fieldwork being done today than a decade ago, most archaeologists know less about what their colleagues are doing.

At the same time, cultural-resource management has severely reduced the number of substantial excavations done in the state, and many kinds of questions about the past can be studied only through the intensive excavation of individual sites.

Such pressures also affect large-scale excavations. Native Americans are calling increasingly for a voice in the fate of the archaeological remains left by their cultures, which has made it less possible for archaeologists to conduct major excavations. In addition, the cost of major excavations has risen enormously in recent years, riding along with inflation. As university budgets shrink relative to their position fifteen to twenty years ago, the ability of archaeologists to mount major excavations has also declined.

At this writing, the nation's economy is in a recession, and the federal government, the current mainstay of archaeological research in California through its cultural-resource-management programs, is reducing its commitment. Since other support for archaeology has already declined, federal cutbacks can be expected to lead to an absolute decline in the archaeology done across the nation.

We have shown that there is a great deal of value to be gained from California archaeology, but will the value be realized? Will there be sites for people to visit, museums for education, books for the public, journals for scholars? Will there be university programs for training new scholars? Will there be resources to inform and educate the public? Will research be able to add to the existing body of knowledge, to ask and answer new questions? The discipline is at an important crossroads, and two things will determine its future. The first is the ability of archaeologists to retrench in an era of limits, to make better use of fewer resources, to better serve the public and their profession.

The other is the interest of the public in securing its heritage by seeing to it that sites are studied and protected, and that knowledge is gained for the benefit of all. Today's and tomorrow's Californians are the stewards of their cultural heritage. In the end, it is they who will choose to exercise or default their stewardship, to claim or ignore the enrichment of their heritage.

If we can draw a lesson from some of the explanations given earlier for past changes, it can be suggested that there is promise for new progress in California archaeology. In the past, environmental change has led to cultural response, and there is no reason to suspect that the same will not continue to happen. In straitened times, archaeology will not continue to be practiced as before. It could just wither away as a nonessential luxury, but certain signs suggest otherwise.

One thing the past has shown is that in times of stress people try a lot of different modifications of their behavior to try to maintain their previous way of life as much as possible. Invariably a way of life would be changed, and often the modifications led to new opportunities, which in turn produced further changes and new growth.

Archaeology in California will not continue as it has been, and some aspects of it will likely decline, but there is a good chance that growth will take place in new directions. University resources are shrinking (see Appendix D), but other sectors of society have shown new interest in archaeology (see Appendix F). A California excavation, at Somersville, was featured on the national television series *Odyssey*, for example. Scholarly journals in California archaeology are struggling at the moment, but more-popular magazines are starting to carry stories about California archaeology that reach much broader audiences than the journals ever did. The Yuha Desert Burial Site, for example, was featured in the January 1982 issue of *Science Digest*, where the story was read by many more people than ever saw the original report (Childers 1974).

Such shifts and changes do not just represent one element of society picking up the slack caused by shrinkage of another element. Different sources of support for archaeology produce different results in the way archaeology is conducted and perceived. The fact that archaeological reportage is now being carried by public media is creating a degree of popular interest and widespread notice that active reportage within scientific circles did not. (For films about California archaeology, see Appendix G.) Broader public interest can be converted in turn to support for archaeological projects within communities (see Appendix C). A recent example of such local support is the George Page Museum at the La Brea Tar Pits in Los Angeles. The Page

Museum, though primarily a paleontological museum for the study of animal and plant specimens recovered from the tar pits, also contains archaeological remains. One of the most modern and beautiful museums of its kind in the nation, it was built and operated with a large amount of private funding from a great number of donors in the Los Angeles area. It also reflects a new and fruitful combination of private and municipal financing to achieve results that neither element could achieve alone. Also important is the fact that it has achieved a dramatic level of public visibility of, and interest in, ongoing research at the tar pits, something the university-based research programs never achieved on their own.

The organization of California archaeology will surely be different in ten years than it is today. Changes in available support will certainly place new demands and challenges before archaeologists in their efforts to reveal, understand, and interpret the past. Yet the innovations suggested above indicate that many efforts may prove even more fruitful than any being made today, and that Californians' interest in, understanding of, and appreciation for their state's past may be richer than ever before. And in the end, what better use can California archaeology have?

APPENDIXES

THE HISTORY OF ARCHAEOLOGY
IN CALIFORNIA

Systematic archaeology began in California more than a century ago. Since then, study in this field has taken several turns in direction. It is easier to understand the explorations and writings of California archaeologists if something is known of the historical development of their field.

Several writers have reviewed the history of California archaeology. The articles by Heizer (1978b) and Warren (1973) are especially valuable, but they, like all the sources, are limited in scope. Heizer's survey, which emphasizes the development of archaeology at the University of California, Berkeley, does not cover many developments elsewhere. Warren's paper is intended more to summarize cultural sequences in California than to present the history of research; thus it, too, does not treat some important developments.

This survey will not detail the lives and accomplishments of every researcher. It spotlights, instead, major themes that guided much research and places them in a wider context. Those interested in a broader history of American archaeology might see Willey & Sabloff (1974). Here we follow seven major interests that have motivated research within the state: museum collection, regional chronology, the reconstruction of cultural history, the "new archaeology," historical archaeology, public archaeology, and amateur archaeology.

MUSEUM COLLECTION

The first scientific archaeology in the state was organized by museums from Europe and the eastern United States for the collection of artifacts to display. Three expeditions of the 1870's exemplify this interest. In 1875 Paul Schumacher, an agent of the U.S. Coast Survey, was dispatched to the Santa Barbara area to collect antiquities. In a few weeks he gathered 15 tons of artifacts from coastal middens on the mainland and Channel Islands. He used the notes he compiled on his excavations to write a report, published by the

Smithsonian Institution, that helped to found the tradition of scholarly writing about California antiquities. Soon thereafter, the Smithsonian's Bureau of American Ethnology persuaded the U.S. Geographical Survey West of the 100th Meridian, led by Lt. G. M. Walker, to make further collections along the coast for the Bureau. A third collecting effort, led by the French nobleman Alphonse Pinart, dispatched Léon de Cessac to Santa Barbara in 1877 to make archaeological collections for France. De Cessac was able to ship back a good deal of material before his financing collapsed, which prevented him from publishing his own reports.

Museum sponsorship of collecting expeditions was not aimed solely at the recovery of specimens for display, although the desire to gain prestige through displaying exotic artifacts was a powerful motivation. Artifact collections were also regarded as a means of learning about and understanding other cultures. Zoos and natural-history museums arose at the same time through much the same motivation. This goal, the collection of representative antiquities from around the globe, took expeditions to many regions, and gathering artifacts became simply one facet of the effort to gather systematically, identify, classify, and describe all sorts of natural phenomena from uncharted corners of the world. Although these early collectors were not trained in archaeological methods and had little interest in the people and cultures that made the artifacts, they belonged to an honorable scholarly tradition of natural history. They worked systematically, made careful notes and records, published their findings, catalogued their collections, and founded many important museum collections.

Museum expeditions continued to be important well into the present century. The Southwest Museum, the Los Angeles County Museum of Natural History, the San Diego Museum of Man, the Santa Barbara Museum of Natural History, and the University of California's Museum of Anthropology were responsible for many of the first systematic excavations throughout the state. Over time, museums hired more fully trained researchers, and the quality of work progressed as research directions evolved. Many museums throughout the state still support archaeological research, but in the last half century other institutions, particularly universities and colleges, came to predominate in research leadership. Today, museum archaeologists share a smaller but still vital part in the rich and varied traditions of research in California archaeology.

THE INTEREST IN REGIONAL CHRONOLOGY

The most important challenge in archaeology has always been to understand the similarities and differences among remains. Change over time became a way to explain such variation, but early archaeological collectors recognized only the different forms of artifacts. Determining the ages of sites and their artifacts thus became the first truly archaeological problem to occupy researchers. Today's battery of dating methods stems from this need to be able to tell how old things are.

The development of research into chronology is tied in large part to the development of the archaeology program at the University of California, Berkeley. The first anthropology chairman there, Frederick Ward Putnam (Fig. A.1), also directed the Bureau of American Ethnology in Washington, D.C., and was interested in the historical roots of the American Indians. Since the Indians were nonliterate and left no written histories, Putnam saw archaeol-

Fig. A.1. Frederick Ward Putnam, Director of the Bureau of American Ethnology at the Smithsonian Institution, Washington, D.C., was appointed first chairman of the Anthropology Department at Berkeley. Though an absentee chairman, Putnam, seen here speculating about the authenticity of a reputedly Ice Age skull, was responsible for bringing A. L. Kroeber to Berkeley. (Courtesy of the Lowie Museum of Anthropology, University of California, Berkeley)

Fig. A.2. Alfred L. Kroeber helped found the Department of Anthropology at the University of California, Berkeley. Among anthropology departments, only the one at Columbia University is older. Kroeber was a prodigious scholar, who published over five hundred books, monographs, and journal articles covering the whole range of anthropology: ethnology, archaeology, linguistics, and physical anthropology. He is best known for his research on California Indians, although he never conducted any archaeological excavations in California (he did make important excavations in Peru and the American Southwest). He helped set the anthropological orientation of archaeology in California, however, by training most of the subsequent two generations of California anthropologists and by sending many of his students and colleagues to excavate sites around the state. This portrait was taken in New York in 1947, when Kroeber was nearing retirement. He died in 1960 while attending an anthropological conference in Austria. (Courtesy of the Lowie Museum of Anthropology, University of California, Berkeley)

Fig. A.3. Franz Boas, a German immigrant, was America's first anthropologist. He trained the holder of the first Ph.D. in anthropology while at Clark University, founded the first department of anthropology (at Columbia University), was Kroeber's professor (see Fig. A.2), and shaped Kroeber's approach to anthropology, which was subsequently developed in California. (Courtesy of the Lowie Museum of Anthropology, University of California, Berkeley)

Fig. A.4. Phoebe A. Hearst, wife of newspaper tycoon William Randolph Hearst, was an important early benefactor to the Anthropology Museum and Department at Berkeley. Her support helped launch the university's program of archaeological excavations throughout California. She is shown here at an early commencement exercise. (Courtesy of the Lowie Museum of Anthropology, University of California, Berkeley)

Fig. A.5. Nels C. Nelson, the Swedish archaeologist, is shown here bathing while on expedition in Mongolia. Nelson, one of the earliest excavators of San Francisco Bay shell mounds, brought to Berkeley from Europe some of the most advanced archaeological methods of the time, and helped establish California as a leading American center in innovative field methods. (Courtesy of the Lowie Museum of Anthropology, University of California, Berkeley)

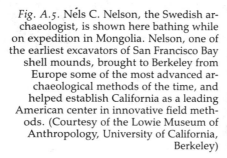

ogy as a way to reveal the prehistoric Indian past. Berkeley's first full-time anthropologist, A. L. Kroeber (Fig. A.2), was most interested in the cultures of California's surviving Indian peoples, but he saw archaeology as a way of tracing the historical stages of development of those cultures, the course leading to their final forms. In this regard he followed the thinking of his own professor, Franz Boas (Fig. A.3), America's first anthropologist and the trainer of most of the first generation of anthropologists in the nation. Boas established the "American Historical" school of anthropology. According to this line of thought, a present-day culture owes its form to its history of development, and the description of a culture's history is therefore necessary to the explanation of the culture's nature. Boas's first important student was Kroeber, who joined the faculty at Berkeley when patron Phoebe Apperson Hearst (Fig. A.4) endowed the university's Museum of Anthropology. He founded the nation's second department of anthropology (Boas had founded the first, at Columbia University), and added an archaeology program to the university.

Nels C. Nelson and Max Uhle came to Berkeley in the 1900's (Fig. A.5). Although each later developed a research career elsewhere, the two launched the excavations of several shell mounds around San Francisco Bay. The sites chosen were large and deep in hopes that they would prove to be built up of visible layers, which would allow the identification of groups of artifacts from different ages. The hope proved in vain; the Bay Area's shell mounds turned out to lack visible layering in spite of their depth. In response, Nelson developed a technique of dividing the sites into artificial levels and separating the remains of different ages from each other. The very difficulty of determining the ages of California sites has stimulated archaeologists to develop new methods of site dating, and the state remains a center of innovation in such techniques today.

The goal of discovering the chronology of each part of California was primary to archaeological investigation for the first half of the twentieth century. Among other important researchers, Malcolm Rogers (1929, 1945) developed the basic sequences for the southern California deserts and the San Diego County coast. David Banks Rogers (1929) and Ronald Olson (1930) established the first sequence for the coast around Santa Barbara. Lillard, Heizer, and Fenenga (1939) established the first sequence for central California. Through the 1960's, much of the state's archaeological literature was aimed at describing specific local assemblage types and determining their places in the area's sequence of prehistoric cultures, and much of the effort devoted to the analysis of artifacts attempted to refine local sequences and discover the usefulness of particular types of artifacts for dating sites.

Archaeologists had to learn what made up the archaeological record and how different forms of artifacts and assemblages were related to each other over time before they could begin to deal with questions that went beyond chronology to ask why the archaeological record took the form it did. As knowledge of the state's archaeological record began to accumulate, it became possible to turn attention to such questions. Gradually the effort to elaborate the state's regional sequences came to be seen as a means to an end rather than as an end in itself. But because there still remain some parts of the state for which the basic sequences are not yet known, the goal of developing local chronologies still motivates a good deal of research.

Revealing local chronologies dominated much archaeological research of the time not only in California, but throughout the nation. In most states, however, these chronologies were gradually integrated into much broader frameworks embracing whole states or larger regions. As we noted in Chapter 1, California remained (and remains) unique in that real statewide chronological frameworks have never been defined, much less joined to those of the rest of the continent. For a variety of reasons, the emphasis on chronology did not lend itself to generalization or integration, and few California archaeologists have shown much interest in developing more general schemes.

THE RECONSTRUCTION OF CULTURAL HISTORY

A "pure" chronologist would be interested only in describing the kinds of remains found in sites and assigning them to their proper time periods. By contrast, someone interested in the reconstruction of cultural history would also be interested in reconstructing the kinds of cultures that created the various assemblages of the past. Cultural-historical reconstruction may be regarded as the anthropology of extinct societies, describing the lifeways and activities practiced by ancient peoples who cannot be studied by observing or interviewing them.

The reconstruction of cultural history stems from the influence of cultural anthropology on archaeology. California was one area where this focus was strongly expressed. In few other places in the nation had Indian cultures survived so long as in California. Cultural anthropologists were able to record those cultures by interviewing people who had lived in them. Cultural anthropologists saw archaeology as a way to study the history of these nonliterate cultures, whereas archaeologists saw the cultural record as a way to interpret the behavior that produced their archaeological remains. Although Kroeber felt too overwhelmed by the task of recording the knowledge of California's surviving Indians to take up archaeology himself (see Fig. A.6), he saw to it that archaeological research was undertaken by his department. The combination of a very late prehistory, a rich ethnographic literature, and anthropologists who wanted to use archaeology and ethnography together caused California archaeologists to make an early start in the reconstruction of past cultures.

The tracing of ethnographic cultures to archaeological remains of late prehistory, known as the "direct historical approach" in archaeology, shows the use of ethnography to interpret the archaeological record (Heizer 1978b). Such cultural reconstructions were being attempted as early as 1918. L. L. Loud, for example, used the cultural record of the Wiyot Indians to help reconstruct the cultures that produced the archaeological sites around Humboldt Bay (Loud 1918; see also Fig. A.7).

Early attempts at cultural-historical reconstruction focused primarily on aspects of culture dealing with subsistence and technology. D. B. Rogers (1929), for example, used tool and food remains to reconstruct the basic diets of a succession of prehistoric cultures around Santa Barbara. This emphasis reflected the kinds of remains that were most common in California sites: stone and bone tools, the waste of toolmaking, and bone and shell from food waste. It also reflected the fact that the interpretation of dietary and technological practices was fairly direct and required few inferences. The chain of reasoning needed to interpret such aspects of culture as social relationships and ideology is considerably more complicated.

Fig. A.6. Alfred L. Kroeber at a site in the Sacramento Valley, in the early 1930's, the only known photograph of Kroeber at a California excavation. Although he conducted his own excavations outside of California (see Fig. A.2), Kroeber looked to archaeology to reveal the roots and prehistoric development of the California Indian cultures he studied. Many of Kroeber's students received field training in archaeological methods at excavations such as this one in the Sacramento Valley directed by Jeremiah B. Lillard. (Courtesy of the Lowie Museum of Anthropology, University of California, Berkeley)

As a result, the development of cultural-historical reconstruction has been uneven. Interest in economies and technologies developed early and matured by the 1950's with such studies as Meighan's reconstruction of the prehistoric cultural ecology on Catalina Island (1959b). This interest has continued to dominate the reconstruction of past cultures, but by the 1950's some beginnings had been made toward the reconstruction of other aspects of culture. Treganza (1958a), for example, studied the organization of households in the area of Trinity Reservoir (now Clair Engle Lake). Within the next decade

Fig. A.7. Llewellen L. Loud was a custodian at the Anthropology Museum in Berkeley when Kroeber sent him off to collect specimens from around the state. Loud's excavations at Humboldt Bay provided an epochal study in the archaeology of northwestern California. This photograph, taken in 1917, shows Loud modeling an aboriginal bird-skin cape from the Museum's collection. (Courtesy of the Lowie Museum of Anthropology, University of California, Berkeley)

some researchers were using burial data to reconstruct social relationships in communities (L. King 1969), and by the 1970's a few scholars had begun to reconstruct patterns of prehistoric religious practices from archaeological data (see, for example, Hudson, Lee & Hedges 1979).

Although archaeologists still lag behind cultural anthropologists in their ability to describe cultures from data, they do a much richer job today than ever before. They also have the advantage of being able to study cultures over long time periods, to observe and analyze changes over time in ways that elude cultural anthropologists. Thus, the reconstruction of cultural history continues to be an important focus in California archaeology as the most important research goal.

THE "NEW ARCHAEOLOGY"

Starting in the 1960's, archaeology throughout the nation, including California, was convulsed by an intellectual upheaval that called itself the "new archaeology" (Willey & Sabloff 1974). Not so much a unified philosophical movement as a collection of vaguely related new directions, the "new archaeology" movement changed the language and practice of archaeology in California (as elsewhere). As a self-conscious movement it is no longer active, or even coherent, but its impact is still evident.

The "new archaeology" was pursued along several avenues. One was a self-directed effort to improve the scientific rigor of archaeological research by emphasizing research designs, the formation and testing of hypotheses, the overt explanation of observed patterns in the archaeological record, and the development of lawlike principles of human behavior from archaeological evidence. Another was a recognition of statistics and quantitative classification as powerful tools for archaeology. In this vein many archaeologists developed expertise in computers, programming, and the principles of taxonomy. A third thrust of the movement improved sampling methods, prediction, and simulation modeling. A fourth area was concerned with going beyond "normative," or idealized, reconstructions of culture to recognize ranges of variation in cultural practices. In an attempt to discover the processes by which the archaeological record was formed, a fifth avenue studied the natural processes of deposition and the cultural practices regarding the use and discarding of material objects.

These varied interests made for some fragile alliances among archaeologists with competing interests, and the movement could not be sustained. Yet it dramatically changed how archaeology is done and what archaeologists must know. Today's archaeologists must be able to develop research designs, use computers in their analyses, and employ sophisticated sampling methods. Whether or not these changes have led to better archaeology is unclear, but they have unquestionably led to different archaeology.

HISTORICAL ARCHAEOLOGY

Among archaeologists, those who specialize in the excavation of sites of the historical era have identified themselves as historical archaeologists. Loosely speaking, most archaeologists could fall in this group, since a great many sites have levels in them dating to the period of written history. But in the more specific sense, and as James Deetz (1977) defines it, historical archaeology deals with the spread of European cultures around the world in the past five hundred years.

Historical archaeology as a discipline stands somewhat apart from the kind of prehistoric archaeology predominant in California. Whereas prehistoric archaeology stems mainly from anthropology, historical archaeology also has important roots in history and archival science. Many historical archaeologists see their work as confirming and elaborating the details of written history; to others, the studies of human history of this field are of a different sort from those of anthropological archaeologists because the historical record lets them study particular individuals and events.

In America the major developments of historical archaeology have been centered mostly in the east, but California has seen some important developments in this field because of great public interest in the Spanish missions and mission-period culture along with the drama of the 1849 Gold Rush. Archaeological research at mission sites was under way by the 1930's (see Harrington 1940, for example). Beardsley's research at Monterey (1946) is an important early step in the study of the Mexican period through archaeology, and Treganza's excavation at the Olema limeworks (1951) helped launch the study of California's early industrial development by archaeologists. By the 1950's a number of projects were in full swing at Fort Ross, Sutter's Fort, the Marshall gold-discovery site, several missions, and other historical-period sites. But perhaps the first archaeologist to identify himself as a historical archaeologist in California was James Deetz, whose research at Mission La Purísima Concepción set a new high standard for historical-period site research in the state (Deetz 1963).

Historical archaeology has continued to grow in importance in California archaeology. Two things in particular have helped spur this interest beyond scholarly curiosity. One was the passage of the National Historic Preservation Act of 1966 (P.L. 89-665), which gave historical sites equal status under the law with prehistoric and aboriginal antiquities. The other has been the growing resistance of Native Americans to the excavation of aboriginal sites without their consent. Efforts by Indians to have more say in the fate of sites that belong to their own cultural heritage have led many archaeologists to shift their focus to sites belonging to other cultures.

PUBLIC ARCHAEOLOGY

To this point, we have looked at intellectual movements that directed the research efforts of archaeologists. The archaeologists themselves remained the same group of scholars with the same sorts of jobs, mainly in museums and colleges. The public-archaeology movement represents something different: archaeological research conducted for new and non-research-oriented reasons and funded by new sponsors.

Public archaeology developed from its roots in the Depression to maturity in the 1960's. Today it provides most of the financial support for archaeology throughout the nation. Although a great deal of research is conducted through public archaeology, the goal of this movement is not the study of the past as such. Rather, the goal is to preserve information and physical remains from the past in order to conserve the nation's cultural patrimony.

The main source of support in this effort is the federal government, with state and some local governments providing additional support. Justification for government involvement is based on the idea that archaeological sites represent a valued and nonrenewable cultural resource of the nation which, left unprotected, would be destroyed and lost to posterity. Government action to protect antiquities can be traced to 1906, when the first Antiquities Act was passed, making it a crime to molest antiquities on federal lands. Mesa Verde National Park was created at the same time, marking the first time the government established a preserve for archaeological sites.

Government involvement expanded in the 1930's with the construction of the Tennessee Valley system of reservoirs. As part of that project, funding was provided to salvage some of the contents of the hundreds of Indian village sites slated for destruction by reservoir construction. The government of that era also seized upon archaeology as a useful way to create jobs for unemployed workers during the Depression. Though this make-work program ended during the Second World War, government involvement with archaeology continued. After the war, when more reservoirs, highways, and gas pipelines were built, funding was provided to study threatened sites. Important pieces of federal legislation—the National Defense Highways Act of 1956, the National Historic Preservation Act of 1966, the Reservoir Salvage

Act of 1960 and its Amendment of 1974 (the Moss-Bennett Act), the National Environmental Policy Act of 1969, the Antiquities Act of 1980, and others— have added more specific responsibilities for the protection of antiquities to federal agencies and federally regulated institutions. These laws also led to the allocation of funds for implementation, and to the development of comparable programs in many state and some local governments.

These laws and programs have led to the emergence of a new profession within archaeology: *cultural-resource management*. Some of these archaeologists determine the impact proposed land-use projects would have on the archaeological resources of an area. Others are employed by government agencies to administer public-archaeology programs. Because much of the actual work is done on a contract basis, often by private firms, a significant number of archaeologists are employed in the private sector for the first time. Their goals include studying the impact of development proposals, preserving data that would otherwise be lost, lessening the impact of development at particular sites, and making profits for their firms. These interests are all fairly new for archaeologists, and the discipline has been undergoing some interesting growing pains as a result.

The public-archaeology movement has been stronger in California than anywhere else. California now has more practicing archaeologists than any other state, and most make their living partly or wholly from public archaeology. California has pioneered in the passage of state and local laws protecting antiquities. The vast majority of field research done in California today is done as public archaeology, so much so that research and training excavations have almost ceased to exist.

Many researchers see the growth of public archaeology as a mixed blessing, a tail wagging the dog. Although public archaeology supports a great volume of field investigation, much of the work contributes little to growth in knowledge, consisting instead of site-discovery surveys. Substantial excavations that reveal the past in generous detail are rarely if ever conducted through public archaeology, and the results of the fieldwork are not often described in scholarly literature; findings are described in reports submitted to the funding agencies rather than circulated among scholars. The agencies, in turn, provide little or no support for the preparation and publication of research results. Even more regrettably, the agencies tend to give even less support for the care of the artifact collections that result. At present, the hard-pressed federal government is decreasing its support of public archaeology, so the movement may be on the wane. Some researchers see this trend as a betrayal of public trust; others welcome the chance to change the direction of the remaining programs in public archaeology to a more scholarly course.

AMATEUR ARCHAEOLOGY

Archaeology is unique in that amateurs have long played a major role in conducting the primary research. Amateur, or avocational, archaeologists are not dabblers; they are skilled researchers who contribute to knowledge about the past purely through interest rather than as a way to earn a living. The best amateur archaeologists enjoy as much respect among professional scholars as do their highly skilled professional colleagues (see Appendix C).

California has more amateur archaeologists and more amateur societies than any other state. The amateur movement became developed in the 1930's,

Fig. A.8. 1930's excavation crew at site CA-SJo-68, Sacramento Valley. Jeremiah B. Lillard's amateur archaeology club at Sacramento Junior College pioneered Central Valley archaeology. Though an amateur, Lillard helped train many prominent archaeologists. *Bottom row:* Arnold R. Pilling, Robert F. Heizer, M. Pilorz, L. Langford; *top row:* Robert Greengo, James Bennyhoff, J. Miller, Clement Meighan, and R. Adams. (Courtesy of the Lowie Museum of Anthropology, University of California, Berkeley)

particularly under the leadership of Dr. Jeremiah B. Lillard, then president of Sacramento Junior College, who organized an archaeology club at the college and sponsored the excavations that established the sequence of prehistoric cultures for central California (see Lillard, Heizer & Fenenga 1939; see also Fig. A.8). Since then, more than two dozen amateur archaeological societies have arisen throughout the state. Such groups typically conduct their own surveys and excavations, hold conferences to share knowledge, publish reports on their research, support museums that display and interpret findings and artifacts from excavations, and work closely with colleges, universities, and government agencies to develop and care for the archaeological resources of their communities. Through the Society for California Archaeology, amateurs join with professionals to promote the state's archaeological heritage as a whole. The amateur movement is more vigorous today than ever before and should continue to be an important force in the development of California archaeology.

CALIFORNIA PREHISTORIC ARCHAEOLOGICAL DATA AND TECHNOLOGY

This appendix defines a number of terms used in the book and in archaeological literature. Many terms used by archaeologists to describe remains in the past, such as artifact, feature, and site, have common English meanings but are used in archaeology with somewhat different meanings as technical terms.

The basic unit of archaeological data is the *artifact*. In the broadest sense an artifact is anything of human creation. A poem or philosophy is as much a human artifact as a spear point. Archaeologists use the term more narrowly to refer to something material that is preserved archaeologically, such as a stone or bone tool or a potsherd. An artifact may be the deliberately made tool or the waste product of the toolmaking process. The term also tends to be restricted to objects that are portable and that consist of one or a few parts. A house or fireplace, for example, is a human artifact, but such complex, large, and nonportable constructions are typically called *features*.

Artifacts and features are normally found in *sites*. An abandoned village is a common type of site, but there are many other kinds, such as cemeteries, fortifications, butchering camps, quarries, religious centers, and harvesting stations. The location of a single artifact is termed a *find-spot* among California archaeologists, because the word *site* is reserved for locations at which a variety of archaeological remains occur together. The term site conveys the idea that past activities have been concentrated enough to produce clusters of discarded objects, allowing it to be distinguished from the surrounding, nonhuman environment.

The production of most kinds of sites includes the creation of an *anthrosol*, technically a soil altered by human activity. Discarded food, human wastes, ash, charcoal, and other humanly produced additives change the chemical and physical structure of an anthrosol, often giving it a distinctive color and texture. Archaeologists commonly use the term *midden* to refer to an anthrosol. Although strictly speaking the term means "refuse heap" or "accumulation of refuse," archaeologists find that in most sites refuse is mixed into the soil rather than deposited in distinct piles on top of the soil.

In addition to features and artifacts, middens contain ecofacts and manuports. An *ecofact* is a natural object that has been used or modified by humans though not manufactured in the technical sense. Bones and shells left over from cooking, for example, are ecofacts; fireplace ashes and rocks fractured from the heat of fires are ecofacts. *Manuports* are unmodified objects that have been moved to sites from their areas of natural occurrence. Because this transporting reflects patterns of cultural activities, manuports interest archaeologists even though the objects themselves are not artifacts.

Middens contain objects and distinct patterns of chemicals, and both the relationships among the objects and the proportions among the chemicals form valuable archaeological data. Objects occur in different quantities and in different patterns of distribution within sites; archaeologists excavate in such a way that both the different numbers of things and the different distribution patterns can be preserved or recorded. These essentially quantitative or statistical patterns contribute to the archaeological record just as the objects themselves do, and provide valuable clues to past activities that the objects alone do not reveal. Different proportions and areas of concentration of chemicals also provide important data about the kinds and locations of activities carried out at sites.

All remains are not found within sites. Artifacts or features found apart from recognized sites are termed *isolates*. The kinds, numbers, and distributions of isolates in a region can provide important clues to the ways past people used their environment outside the limits of sites. Often the sites themselves cannot provide this information. Archaeologists thus study sites in the context of the larger environment. The distribution of sites within an environment forms a *settlement pattern*. Archaeologists reconstruct settlement patterns to help understand a past *settlement system*, the more general concept that includes the behavior patterns of people living in an environment, the resources in the environment they used, and the distribution of their activities within the environment.

The remains of one culture that occur within a site are called an *assemblage*. Most prehistoric sites have only one assemblage, but some larger, richer sites may have two or more. The term *component* is sometimes used to mean the same thing as assemblage.

In their attempt to describe the archaeological record, archaeologists might describe every artifact at a site individually, but the effort would be wasteful for two reasons. First, the descriptions would be mostly repetitive, since artifacts tend to share many traits. Second, it would ignore the patterns among artifacts within assemblages, and patterns themselves form important cultural traits. Instead, archaeologists describe archaeological remains in terms of types: sets of remains for which the shared traits are more important than the differences between individual specimens. Much archaeological writing is devoted to defining what types of remains occur within sites and to comparing the types among assemblages. The names given to types form the basic vocabulary of archaeology.

Archaeologists determine the types present in an assemblage, the frequency or percentage of each type, and the patterns of distribution or location of the members of each type within the site. Archaeological traditions are defined (see Chapter 2) when similar assemblages of similar ages are found in an area. The test for similarity uses the classifications that divide the assemblages into a series of finer and finer categories, the finest being a set of types.

An archaeologist begins dividing an assemblage at a very general level into artifacts, ecofacts, features, and unmodified raw materials. The greatest attention is given to artifacts, but the logic followed in analyzing the other categories is similar. At the second level of division, the assemblage is separated into *industries*, groups of artifacts made of the same raw material and with the same techniques of manufacture. At this level, a ceramic or pottery industry would be separated from a bone industry, and a chipped-stone industry would be separated from a ground-stone industry.

The next level of division is based on the form of artifacts. Archaeologists study *formal attributes* (the traits of form) of artifacts, and define types as groups of artifacts that share a number of formal traits.

It should be remembered that many objects made by past peoples do not survive archaeologically. Objects of leather or basketry, for example, are not often preserved in California sites; consequently, they do not figure much in the archaeological literature.

CERAMIC INDUSTRY

Although ceramics did not play much part in the prehistoric technologies of California, in contrast to most parts of North America, the technology was used by a number of Pacific Period groups. Three kinds of ceramics were made: pottery "cooking stones," clay figurines, and pottery vessels.

Pottery "cooking stones" are small balls of clay that have been baked or fired (see Fig. 53cc). As with all pottery, the clay has some temper mixed with it to prevent its cracking when being baked. These cooking stones were used prehistorically in the Delta area as cooking stones for stone boiling. The local environment, an alluvial floodplain, lacked stream cobbles that were used for the purpose elsewhere.

Figurines of fired and sun-dried clay were made by Pacific Period cultures of the Central Valley and adjacent Sierra (see Fig. 54). Some figures were human-like, some were animal-like, and some had more abstract features. Occasional examples have been found in the Bay Area, in the Los Angeles area, and in the southern California deserts. Similar figurine traditions are known from the Great Basin and the Southwest. It is generally thought that these figurines served a role in ritual or medicine, but the functions of these prehistoric objects have not been established.

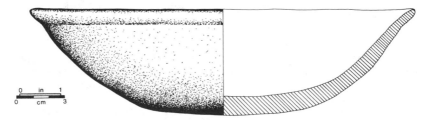

Fig. B.1. Undecorated brown pottery bowl from southeastern California; the type, Tizon Brownware (or Desert Brownware), dates to the Late and Final Pacific periods.

Pottery vessels were made only in the last thousand years of prehistory by groups in the southern California deserts (Fig. B.1). This pottery was an unpainted, undecorated brown ware generally called *Tizon Brownware* or *Desert Brownware*. A limited variety of vessel forms was made, among which storage jars, water bottles, and shallow dishes were most important. A small number of *sherds* or pieces of painted pottery from the Southwest have been found in middens along the southern California coast.

SHELL INDUSTRY

Although coastal people obviously had the greatest access to shells, shells were traded throughout California, and almost every group from the Archaic onward made shell artifacts. In Gifford's exhaustive discussion of the varieties of California shell artifacts (1947), he showed that the most important use of shell was for the production of *beads* and *pendants*. Many bead types served as forms of money as well as ornaments (see Chagnon 1970; C. King 1978).

Shell was worked by breaking or hammering into fragments of the desired general size and shape. Finishing the shape was done by grinding or abrading against a coarse rock. Beads and pendants were usually drilled for stringing; the drills were sticks with stone tips or hand-held chipped-stone drills. *Disk beads* were often drilled and strung before their outer edges were finished by grinding; the whole string of beads was then ground on the string at one time to save labor and produce a more uniform size and shape. Californians did not etch or acid-engrave shells, but Late and Final Pacific groups in some areas did incise lines on some shell ornaments.

The bead was the most commonly produced shell artifact form in prehistoric California. Disk beads, usually of clamshell or olivella, were a standard money form when strung. *Clamshell disk beads* tended to be smaller in later periods (Figs. 53k,q,r). Olivella beads were squares cut from the side of the shell (*square-cut olivella beads*; Figs. 33n, 44j, 46i) or whole shells whose pointed ends were ground off to provide holes for stringing (*spire-lopped olivella beads*; Figs. 33m, 44f, 46g, 47h, 49e,f, 53h). Horn-shaped *dentalium beads*, imported from Puget Sound, were also spire-lopped and strung; northwestern California groups used them as money (Fig. 56i). The burned surfaces of many beads do not result from manufacturing, but from the beads being thrown into funeral bonfires or abandoned in houses that burned down.

A variety of shell pendants was made, especially by Late and Final Pacific groups of central California. Most pendants were simple plummet-shaped forms (Fig. 49p), but a number of elaborate forms appeared in the Delta and Bay areas, embellished by incised lines in many cases. Some examples had two, three, or more holes drilled for stringing. The preferred shell for pendant-making was the abalone (*Haliotis*), several species of which occur off the southern and central California coasts. Abalone is thick and dense, sturdy enough to be worked easily, and it has a glossy, mother-of-pearl interior surface that was highly prized (Figs. 33r,s, 44p, 46l, 49m,s,t).

An important tool form from coastal southern California was the *shell fishhook* (Figs. 49n,o). It was made from a disk of clamshell 25–50 mm across. The disk was drilled, and the hole in the center of the disk was reamed out with a tapered sandstone tool to create a ring. The ring was cut through at one point;

one end of the gap was sharpened and the other was notched to attach a fish-line. Such hooks were amazingly effective.

Whole abalone shells were used by coastal groups as dishes and storage containers. The natural shell has a series of holes across its surface, through which the shellfish respires. Indians plugged the holes, usually with tar or pitch, to create sturdy, watertight containers. The Canaliño Tradition (see Chapter 4) also used abalone shells in burials, particularly to hold the bones or ashes of small children.

Larger California rivers held river mussels, and saltwater mussels thrived along many stretches of rocky coast. Many groups used whole mussel shells as spoons.

A number of coastal and central California peoples used shell beads or frag-ments as decorations or inlays. Some baskets were decorated with shell span-gles, and many ground-stone artifacts such as *bowls*, *pipes*, and *charmstones* (see below) were decorated with inlays cemented in place with pitch or tar. Shell ornaments also were attached to ceremonial costumes, but examples are hardly ever found archaeologically.

BONE INDUSTRY

Mammal and bird bone, and horns and antlers, were important raw materi-als for prehistoric toolmaking. Gifford (1940) provides the most complete discussion of California bone technology. Bone is commonly preserved in prehistoric California sites. Most specimens are unworked food remains, but Californians made a number of important tool forms of bone, horn, and antler.

Bone was broken into usable forms by hammering, splitting, and incising. Fragments were finished by grinding and polishing. The surfaces of bone ar-tifacts were sometimes decorated by incising shallow lines with stone tools. Some forms, such as needles and pendants, were pierced with stone drills to make eyes or stringing holes.

Bone awls (Figs. 29e, 44t, 56m) and needles (Figs. 33x, 44w, 49bb, 56n) were among the most common and important bone tool types. They were impor-tant in basketmaking and for making some kinds of clothing and costumes. Some needles had eyes; others did not. Some blunted awls served as punches.

Some groups made barbed harpoon points, especially in northwestern Cali-fornia (Figs. 53t, 56q). Most riverine fishing groups made leisters (three-pointed fish spears) using bone barbs. Bone fishhooks were rare (Figs. 49v, 56l), but many groups fashioned toggles of bone, pointed at each end and tied by the middle, that were used as hooks (Figs. 33w, 44v, 56p). Early pre-historic cultures, such as the Paleo-Indians, used bone to make spear fore-shafts. Bone daggers were never common in California.

Bone was also used to make decorative and socially significant artifact types (Figs. 33u, 44u, 49w). Some forms of beads and pendants were ground from bone, usually in forms similar to shell beads and pendants (Figs. 33v, 44y, 56k,o). Hollow tubes made from bird leg or wing bones were used as whistles (Figs. 44x, 53u), mouthpieces for stone pipe bowls (Fig. 53w), or ear-rings for pierced ears (Fig. 53v). Bone pieces, often highly polished and some-times decorated with incised designs, were used as pieces in gambling games. Long, curved bone implements, often called strigels, were apparently used to scrape the body during sweat baths (Fig. 56y).

Tines from deer antlers were widely used as tools for the pressure-flaking of chipped stone. Well-used antler-tine tips acquire a distinctive abrasion pattern that identifies them. Groups in several parts in the state used elk antler to make wedges for splitting logs (Figs. 56s,z). An antler wedge is made from a tine and has one end beveled to fit into a crack in a log. The other end is cut square, so that it can be driven by a stone hammer. In northwestern California, dentalium-shell money was kept in purse-like containers carved from elk antler.

GROUND-STONE INDUSTRY

The industrial tools and ornaments in this group were made by grinding, abrading, pecking, pounding, and polishing, rather than by chipping or flaking.

Among the most common and important industrial ground-stone tools were those used to grind seeds and to pound nuts and acorns. These *milling tools* include *manos* (Figs. 29c, 30i, 33h, 46m) and *milling stones* (Figs. 29a,b, 30h, 33g, 46n), used to grind seeds, and *mortars* (Figs. 31g, 33i, 43n, 49ee, 53dd) and *pestles* (Figs. 31f, 33j, 43m, 44bb, 49cc), used for pounding. Milling stones and manos were made of sandstone, granite, or other coarse-grained stone. Milling stones were flattish slabs, and manos were smaller, loaf-shaped stones moved against the milling slabs in a rotary motion. Well-used milling stones developed oval depressions, and manos developed flattened sides from this action. Mortars were stone basins within which the cylindrical pestles were pounded. Some mortars were thick-walled stone bowls, and others were flat slabs onto which bottomless baskets were attached to create hopper mortars. Pounding with pestles on these slabs left different wear patterns from grinding on milling slabs.

Particularly in the Pacific Period, some mortars and milling slabs were made on exposed bedrock surfaces rather than on portable blocks or slabs of stone. These *bedrock mortars* and *grinding slicks* apparently were functionally equivalent to the more portable tools (Fig. 41).

Soft sandstone, steatite, and similar rocks were used to make *stone bowls* and pots in a variety of shapes (Figs. 49ff, 56u). Stone bowls had thinner walls than mortars since they were not made for pounding in. Such vessels were used for cooking and storage, and as water containers and funeral urns for cremation ashes. Some were decorated with shell inlays, but carved decorations are rare. Some groups used flat slabs of steatite to make frying griddles, or *comals* (Fig. 49gg).

Cupule rocks, or *rain rocks*, occur in several parts of the state and apparently date from the Pacific Period (Fig. 53ee). These rocks are bedrock boulders on whose surfaces up to several hundred small, shallow holes or cupules have been chipped and ground. In some cases these pecked boulders have been associated ethnographically with rain-making ceremonies, but in most cases their functions are unknown. Many sites have yielded small, fist-size cobbles with similar holes in them; again, their functions are unknown.

California sites yield a variety of notched and grooved cobbles. One group includes fist-sized cobbles across the face of which one groove has been worn. These tools are commonly called *arrow-shaft straighteners* because they presumably were used to get the kinks and bends out of arrow shafts (Fig. 53z). Their grooves have varied shapes: those with U-shaped grooves may well have been used to straighten shafts; those with V-shaped grooves may have been used for sharpening bone awls and needles. Another group of notched cobbles includes flattish pebbles on opposite sides of which are pecked notches, and rounder pebbles around which are cut grooves. These tools are called *net weights* and were used in hunting and fishing (Figs. 56*w*,*x*).

Stone balls are also common (Fig. 47*m*). Some may be naturally round pebbles used for stone boiling or other tasks; others may have had their shapes improved by grinding. *Polishing stones* are oval pebbles with striations on one or both faces from polishing other materials (Fig. 46*o*). *Pecking stones* are more elongated rocks with intense battering at one end (Fig. 46*p*). One function of these tools was the production of roughened surfaces on milling slabs. *Abrading stones* are coarse, cylindrical tools used like files or sandpaper to smooth other materials, as in the making of shell fishhooks (Fig. 46*q*).

The techniques of this industry were also used to make a variety of ornamental and ritual objects. *Stone beads*, both disk and tube, were made as early as the late Archaic Period (Figs. 44*n*, 49*x*,*y*,*z*, 53*l*,*m*,*o*). *Stone pendants*, *plummets*, and *charmstones* appeared nearly as early (Figs. 29*g*, 30*f*,*g*, 33*l*, 35*o*, 43*i*,*l*, 44*q*,*s*,*aa*, 48*f*, 49*aa*, 53*y*). An important Pacific Period artifact was the *stone pipe*: it had a tapered stone bowl, a straight body, and usually a bird-bone bit or mouthpiece fixed to the stone with tar or pitch (Figs. 33*k*, 49*dd*, 53*bb*, 56*r*). Californians also made a small number of incised pebble *effigies* or figurines.

Hammerstones are included among ground-stone tools because their edges are modified by the battering they do. Some hammerstones are cobbles used solely for battering. Others are exhausted chipped-stone cores (see below) subsequently used as hammers, which created a hybrid category: *core hammerstones* (Fig. 29*p*). Still other variants include chipped-stone chopping tools, used so much that most of their flake scars wore away. These examples show that the distinctions between industries sometimes become blurred because the criteria used to define tool types overlap.

CHIPPED-STONE INDUSTRY

Chipped-stone artifacts are made by the removal of chips or flakes to shape the piece. Chipped stone is the most common industry in most California sites.

California toolmakers used several chipping or flake-removal techniques. In *percussion flaking*, flakes were struck off with a hammer. A *hard hammer*, such as a hammerstone, removes a thick, robust flake; a *soft hammer*, such as a cylinder of wood or a long bone, produces a thinner, more delicate flake. In the *anvil technique*, the rock was struck against the hammer, rather than the hammer against the rock, as when a tool was smashed against a projection of bedrock. The anvil technique produces very rugged flakes and is used mainly to break apart large pieces of toolmaking rock. *Pressure flaking*, the most refined of all removal techniques, is accomplished by pressing a punch, usually the tip of a deer antler tine, against the edge of a tool to remove very small, thin, delicate flakes. All these techniques involve driving energy into the tool to cleave the rock along desired lines; different techniques give the toolmaker varying degrees of control over the removal process and achieve different results.

Ancient Californians were selective in their choice of rock for chipping.

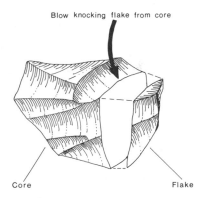

Fig. B.2. The basic products
of stone chipping.

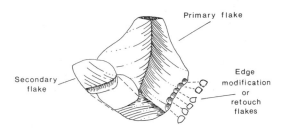

Though coarse-grained or soft rocks were used to make ground-stone tools, fine-grained hard rocks were used to chip. Chert, jasper, and chalcedony—all colloidal silicates or crypto-crystalline silicates—were the preferred rocks for making projectile points and other fine-quality tools. Obsidian, the natural volcanic glass, was also favored. Had flint been available, it would undoubtedly have been used as well. These rocks all could be flaked easily and with great control over the results, owing to their fine crystalline structure (or, in the case of obsidian, because it lacked a crystalline structure). More robust tools, such as choppers and scraper planes, were made of somewhat coarser rocks such as basalt and andesite. These rocks could not be flaked as delicately but were more robust and withstood pounding better without damage.

The flaking process produces three by-products: the *flake*, the *core*, and the *hammer*, all of which are modified by the process of toolmaking and therefore become artifacts (Fig. B.2). The flake is the chip driven off; the core is the block of stone from which the flake is removed; and the hammer separates the two. Both flakes and cores may be shaped into implements, becoming *flake tools* or *core tools*. In other cases, their shapes may lend themselves to use without further finishing, in which case they become *utilized flakes* or *utilized cores*. Still other flakes and cores may be discarded as waste without use, in which case they are *non-utilized flakes* or *non-utilized cores*. If a core has so

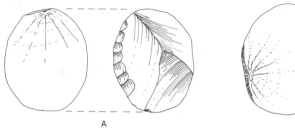 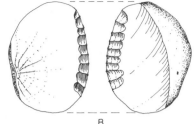

A   B

Fig. B.3. Alternative patterns of retouch on the edge of a flake or core: *a*, unifacial retouch; *b*, bifacial retouch.

many flakes removed from it that no more can be removed, it becomes an *exhausted core*.

California archaeologists distinguish between *primary flakes* and *secondary flakes*. A primary flake is a major removal from a core; a secondary flake is a small removal made either to shape a core or to shape a flake into a tool. Primary flakes are generally produced in the early stages of breaking apart or *reducing* a core. Some primary flakes are *decortication flakes*, flakes on whose back are some of the *cortex*, or weathered exterior, of the core. Decortication flakes are removed to take away the irregular surfaces of the rock and to get to the clean, regular, unoxidized interior of the rock. Greater control may be had over the results when such fresh rock is used. Other primary flakes are removed to reduce the core to a desired form or to serve as blanks on which flake tools are made.

The removal of secondary flakes, or *retouch*, is a subsequent stage of the core-reduction process. *Shaping flakes* produce the final form of the tool. *Edge-modification flakes*, usually very tiny, complete the preparation of a tool's cutting edge. *Rejuvenation flakes* remove irregularities from cores so that more flake removal can be done. *Spalls* are rejuvenation flakes with thick, usually rectangular, cross sections.

When retouch is done, it may be *unifacial* or *bifacial* (Fig. B.3). A unifacial tool is one on which flake removal has been done along an edge, so that all the flakes are removed in the same direction, and all the subsequent *flake scars* left on the tool are on the same side, or face, of the tool. In bifacial retouch, flakes are removed on both sides of the same edge, leaving flake scars on both surfaces of the tool.

Like the distinction between core tools and flake tools, the distinction between unifacial tools and bifacial tools is a general one. The two distinctions crosscut each other, creating four categories: unifacial core tools, bifacial core tools, unifacial flake tools, and bifacial flake tools. Specific artifact types are defined within these groups.

Unifacial core tools have a working edge made by retouching the edge in one direction. An example is the *scraper plane* or *plano-convex scraper*, a dome-shaped tool made by chipping an edge that intersects with a flat surface (Fig. 29*r*). The edge is generally steep. A rugged planing or scraping tool with a flat bottom results. *Choppers* are made on oval cobbles by chipping a unifacial edge along one side (Figs. 3*f*, 29*p*, 47*l*). This tool is used for chopping rather than scraping, for example, to break apart the joints of a carcass.

Bifacial core tools come in more forms than unifacial core tools in California. Many *knives* are made on bifacially chipped cores. Typically they have retouch over their surfaces as well as along the edges and have oval, regular outlines, with smooth, finely flaked cutting edges (Figs. 27*a,b*, 28*j*, 46*e*). *Bifaces* are similar in form but larger and more rugged, as a rule. Something called a biface would lack the distinctive, well-retouched cutting edge of the knife (Figs. 3*b*, 43*d*, 56*v*). The term "biface" is also used as a generic term by some archaeologists, however, to refer to any bifacially retouched piece. A distinctive form of biface is the *preform* (Fig. 66). Preforms are often associated with sites where chippable stone is quarried. In many cases some quarried stone is roughly worked into bifacial ovals, easily packed for shipment, and later easily reduced to tool forms. *Discoids*, another distinctive bifacial core form, have roughly circular outlines and are chipped on both sides from the edge inward. *Chopping tools* are choppers that have been retouched bifacially, rather than unifacially, along an edge (Figs. 3*f*, 29*o*). Unlike most bifacial core tools, their working tends to be confined to the tool's edge rather than the entire tool body.

Unifacial flake tools make up the largest variety of chipped-stone tools. Most of them are varieties of *scrapers* or scraping tools (Figs. 3*d,f*, 27*f,g*, 29*s*). Rather than having distinctive shapes, most of these tools are characterized by distinctive working edges. Some edges are made *straight*, some *concave* or indented, and some *convex*. A deeply concave edge with retouch inside the curve is called a *notched scraper* (Figs. 28*i*, 29*u*, 43*g*). An extremely convex edge with retouch around the curved protrusion is called a *nosed scraper* (Fig. 56*aa*). When several deep convex removals are made next to each other on a scraper's edge, the result is a serrate or sawtooth edge, making a *denticulate scraper* (Figs. 47*i*, 56*bb*). Some flakes are chipped to leave a sharp spur sticking out, creating a *graver* (Figs. 27*h*, 28*h*, 53*f*). California sites occasionally yield apparent *burins*, unifacially retouched flake tools used to carve bone or wood, and made by breaking or retouching the flake to leave a spur the thickness of the flake's cross section (Fig. 56*cc*). A somewhat more common form is the *teshoa flake*, a large and not too thick flake taken off a river cobble on the diagonal (Fig. 56*dd*). Some teshoa flakes are associated with the cleaning of fish. Apart from such distinctive forms, most unifacial flake tools are not easily typed, because their shapes and sizes are irregular and even their edges may crosscut categories, as when two kinds of edges occur on the same tool. Does a notched convex scraper go with the notches or with the convex scrapers?

Unifacial flake tools also are classified according to where the retouch occurs on the tool. A flake's geometry can be expressed according to the location of retouch compared to the place where the blow was struck that detached the flake from the core (Fig. B.4). The *striking platform* has a distinctive crushed mark and defines the *proximal end* of the flake. The side that came off the core, or *ventral face*, has on it the *bulb of percussion*, a distinctive knob formed when the force of the blow first entered the flake to detach it. The existing back of the flake was the outside of the core before the flake was detached and becomes the flake's *dorsal face*. The sides of the flake are its *lateral edges*. They usually are longer than the ends are wide, but some flakes are wider than long with reference to the striking platform. A scraping tool can

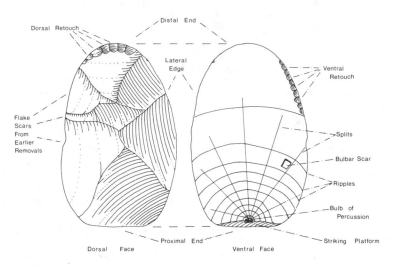

Fig. B.4. The geometry of a flake.

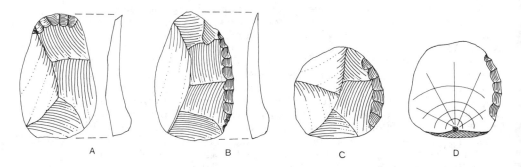

Fig. B.5. Positions of retouch on flake scrapers: *a*, end; *b*, side; *c*, dorsal face; *d*, ventral face.

be an *end scraper* (Figs. 29*t*, 35*j*) or a *side scraper* (Figs. 3*g*, 27*d,f*, 29*s*, 43*e*, 46*d*, 48*g*), depending on where the retouch is done (Fig. B.5). End scrapers can be proximal or *distal* (if worked at the opposite end). The retouch can be on the dorsal or ventral side of the edge. All these distinctions create categories into which the irregularly shaped unifacial flake tools can be put. Archaeologists find that different past cultures preferred different scraper forms. Sometimes the differences can be linked to economic activities, but in other cases the preferences seem to reflect purely stylistic choices.

Bifacial flake tools tend to have more regular forms because the more extensive chipping done to them alters their shapes more completely (Figs. 35*k*,*l*). *Projectile points* are the best-known bifacially flaked stone tools (Figs. 4, 28*a*–*f*, 29*i*–*n*, 30*a*–*d*, 31*c*, 33*a*–*f*, 35*a*–*g*, 43*a*,*b*,*c*, 44*a*–*d*, 46*a*,*b*,*c*, 47*a*,*b*,*c*, 48*a*,*b*,*c*, 49*a*–*d*, 53*a*–*d*, 56*a*–*e*); very rarely, a unifacially flaked point may be found. All are roughly triangular in shape, but they vary tremendously in specific shapes, sizes, and details of the form of the base where the point is hafted to a projectile shaft. The weight of the point varies with its size. The size, shape, weight, color, and preferred raw material all were subject to a great deal of stylistic choice among prehistoric peoples. Points therefore are fairly sensitive indicators of the age and cultural identity of a prehistoric group; archaeologists accordingly spend more attention analyzing projectile points than any other form of chipped-stone tool.

Stone knives form another group of bifacially chipped flake tools (Figs. 27*a*,*b*, 28*j*, 31*a*, 43*d*, 46*e*, 48*d*). Some stone knives are made from cores, but more are made from large and not particularly thick flakes. They tend to have elongated oval shapes, and their edges are finely retouched. *Stone drills* form another group. Drills have one or more long, narrow protrusions or drill tips (Figs. 3*e*, 31*d*, 35*i*, 43*h*, 46*f*, 48*e*, 53*e*, 56*f*). A tip typically has a roundish or triangular cross section and tapers to a blunt point. The bodies of the drills, where they are held or hafted, vary considerably.

BLADE INDUSTRY

A blade is a specialized form of chipped-stone flake, so unique in its shape and manufacture that it often is treated as a separate category by archaeologists (see Fig. B.6). Blades are best known from the European Upper Paleolithic (Old Stone Age, 35,000–12,000 B.C.). Some blade industries are known in the Americas, for example, in late prehistoric Mesoamerica and the Arctic Small-Tool Tradition.

A true blade is made on a distinctive cylindrical core called a prismatic core. The blade is a flake from this core form. It is long and narrow, with parallel sides; the striking platform and bulb of percussion are at one end, and the back (dorsal) face of the blade is marked by one or two ridges that run the length of the blade. They are the edges of flake scars from earlier removals from the core. The blade has a lens-shaped (lenticular) cross section. In any

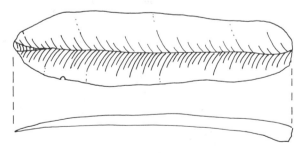

Fig. B.6. An idealized blade from a prismatic core.

large collection of flakes from a California site one is likely to find a few examples that tend to resemble blades. As far as is now known, however, no California culture had a true blade industry. (But see Figs. 47*i–l* for bladelike tools.)

OTHER INDUSTRIES

Prehistoric Californians worked in other materials besides bone, shell, and wood. They made extensive use of plant fibers, for example, to make baskets, nets, mats, and string (Figs. 29*v,w*). They undoubtedly made a number of kinds of wooden artifacts, such as bows, arrow shafts, and dishes. Leather must have been used for making such things as containers, costumes, and drum heads. These materials all are organic and are not often preserved archaeologically in California (see Fig. 72). So rare are they that our knowledge of them comes almost entirely from ethnographic rather than archaeological sources (see Heizer 1978a).

APPENDIX C

AMATEUR ARCHAEOLOGY IN CALIFORNIA

One unique feature of archaeology is its tradition of amateur, or volunteer, participation. Interested lay people take part in research and contribute to knowledge about the past. Sometimes they work alongside professional scholars, and sometimes independently in their own avocational organizations. Good work by amateur groups is often on a par with professional scholarship, so that in many cases the difference between amateur and professional archaeology is more a matter of employment than quality.

Archaeological research has so many dimensions and draws on so many skills that people of almost any age or skill level can find useful ways to contribute. The amateur-archaeology tradition offers a way for people to participate in research at their level of ability and to the extent they wish. Most groups have members ranging from teenagers to retired persons, and because California has more amateur archaeology societies than any other state, there are many opportunities for involvement.

AVOCATIONAL AND PUBLIC-PARTICIPATION ARCHAEOLOGICAL GROUPS

Amateur-archaeology societies perform many services. Most members join with little or no archaeological experience, and learn about archaeology by working with others who share their interests. All reputable amateur societies work with professional-quality standards of research and ethics, usually aided by advisors who are professional archaeologists. These groups offer support for the study and preservation of the state's archaeological resources, while contributing directly to the growth of knowledge about the state's past through survey and excavation. Many have their own publications in which members describe their research.

Amateur groups bring their interests to their communities. Many groups set up displays at fairs, schools, museums, and libraries, describing their area's archaeology and illustrating the nature and importance of research.

Many groups provide speakers and programs for schools, churches, and civic groups. Some societies have helped their communities make environmental-impact assessments of proposed developments. These studies are especially valuable to small communities that would experience difficulty paying to obtain the information. Amateurs have performed many rescue or salvage excavations to save information from sites threatened with destruction. They contribute labor and expertise to professional research, greatly enhancing the results and giving the taxpayers better value.

The following list includes 24 avocational archaeology societies and public-participation groups in California. Although most parts of the state are represented, the list does not include every avocational group in the state. There is no central listing of all such groups, although the Society for California Archaeology tries to keep in communication with all known groups. New groups form, old ones disband; addresses change. If this list does not include an organization in your area, contact your local college or museum to ask if a local group exists.

Society for California Archaeology, c/o Department of Anthropology, California State University, Fullerton, CA 92634. Area of interest: statewide in California.

Antelope Valley Archaeological Society, P.O. Box 1774, Lancaster, CA 93539. Area of interest: western Mojave Desert.

Archaeological Survey Association of Southern California, c/o Armacoast Library, University of Redlands, Redlands, CA 92373; *or* P.O. Box 516, La Verne, CA 91750. Area of interest: western Los Angeles County, eastern Riverside and San Bernardino counties.

Fort Guijarros Museum Foundation, 6217 University Avenue, San Diego, CA 92115. Area of interest: historic Fort Guijarros.

Fresno County Archaeological Society, 1944 North Winery Avenue, Fresno, CA 93703; *or* P.O. Box 11882, Fresno, CA 93775. Area of interest: San Joaquin Valley, southern Sierra.

Friends of Calico, c/o Margaret Herleman, Independence, CA 93526. Area of interest: the Calico Site and early desert occupations.

Imperial Valley College Museum Society, 422 Main Street, El Centro, CA 92243. Area of interest: Imperial County and Colorado Desert.

Kern County Archaeological Society, P.O. Box 6743, Bakersfield, CA 93306. Area of interest: southern San Joaquin Valley and adjacent mountains.

L.S.B. Leakey Foundation, Foundation Center 206-85, Pasadena, CA 91125. Area of interest: research support, especially for studies of early settlement in the New World.

Miwok Archaeological Preserve of Marin, Inc., 2255 Las Gallinas Avenue, San Rafael, CA 94903. Area of interest: Marin County.

Mojave-Sierra Archaeological Society, c/o Maturango Museum, P.O. Box 1776, Ridgecrest, CA 93555. Area of interest: Mojave Desert, east slope of Sierra, southern Sierra.

Pacific Coast Archaeological Society, P.O. Box 926, Costa Mesa, CA 92627. Area of interest: Orange County and coastal southern California.

Riverside Archaeological Society, P.O. Box 5072, Riverside, CA 92517. Area of interest: interior southern California.

Sacramento Anthropological Society, c/o Department of Anthropology, California State University, Sacramento, CA 95819. Area of interest: central California.

San Bernardino County Museum Association, 2024 Orange Tree Lane, Redlands, CA 92373. Area of interest: interior southern California.

San Diego County Archaeological Society, Box A-81106, San Diego, CA 92138. Area of interest: San Diego County and coastal southern California.

San Fernando Valley Archaeological Society, 17081 Devonshire Court, Northridge, CA 91324. Area of interest: Los Angeles County.

San Luis Obispo County Archaeological Society, P.O. Box 109, San Luis Obispo, CA 93401. Area of interest: central California coast and southern Coast Ranges.

Santa Barbara Archaeological Society (Lompoc Chapter), 200 South H Street, Lompoc, CA 93436. Area of interest: western Santa Barbara County.

Santa Barbara Trust for Historic Preservation, P.O. Box 388, Santa Barbara, CA 93102. Area of interest: City of Santa Barbara and vicinity.

Santa Clara County Archaeological Society, 396 West San Fernando, San Jose, CA 95110. Area of interest: Santa Clara County, southern San Francisco Bay area.

Santa Cruz Archaeological Society, Inc., c/o Santa Cruz City Museum, 1305 East Cliff Drive, Santa Cruz, CA 95062. Area of interest: Santa Cruz County.

UCLA Friends of Archaeology, c/o Institute of Archaeology, University of California, Los Angeles, CA 90024. Area of interest: archaeological research in general, including all of California.

Ventura County Archaeological Society, 60 Olsen Road, Thousand Oaks, CA 91360. Area of interest: Ventura County.

RELIC COLLECTING AND AMATEUR ARCHAEOLOGY

The collecting of archaeological artifacts as a hobby has a long history in our nation. Hobbyists regard their pastime as healthy and harmless, if not positively useful. Some are not concerned about the opinions of archaeologists, but many are genuinely puzzled to find that professionals and serious amateur archaeologists reject the legitimacy of relic collecting. The distinction between relic collection and amateur archaeology therefore needs to be made clear.

Relic collectors are interested in artifacts as objects. An artifact is regarded as something that is intrinsically interesting and valuable. Relic collecting shares some of the values of art collection but is also descended from the Renaissance *dilettanti* of Europe—those wealthy collectors who delighted in all objects of art and nature. Their collections, among other things, led eventually to the birth of natural history but were not yet scientific. Today's relic seekers share this passion for the search and acquisition of objects as ends in themselves.

Amateur archaeology, by contrast, is part of the same scholarly tradition as professional or academic archaeology. It is distinguished mainly by the fact that its followers do something else for a living and pursue archaeology purely out of interest. For them, an artifact is important because it is a piece of data that tells something about the past. Their goal is learning about the past, rather than acquiring objects from the past. Artifacts are correspondingly valued for what they do rather than for what they are.

Amateur archaeologists see artifacts not just as data, but as parts of sites. The position of an artifact in a site and its relationship to other artifacts in the site are regarded as data just as much as the artifacts themselves. In contrast, relic collectors gather objects without recording this information.

The recording of information leads to other differences, as well. Amateur archaeologists participate in research, meaning that they share the information they gain with other researchers, through published reports and lectures at archaeological conferences. They also make their data available by placing their collections and accompanying records in museums to which other archaeologists have access. Relic collectors generally gather artifacts to own them.

Archaeologists maintain the public nature of their work for two reasons. On a philosophical level, scientists have confidence in the accuracy of each other's work because conclusions can be confirmed independently. They obviously cannot reexcavate each other's sites, but they can reexamine each other's collections. Re-study of museum collections is done quite frequently, and it is possible only when scholars have access to each others' collections. Realistically, this cannot happen if excavators store their collections at home. Museums provide centralized storage with access available to researchers. Museums also provide safer storage with better protection against fire and theft than archaeologists could offer at home. Amateur archaeologists participate philosophically in a community of scholars, rather than acquiring for their own personal gain, and their values about collecting and ownership reflect this.

There also is a more practical reason for public access. Advances in science make it possible to gain more and more information from collections every year. It is usually possible to re-study old collections to learn things the original excavator could not have considered. Such progress is possible only if the collections are kept together. For example, until recently it was generally assumed that tools of the same shape were used for the same job, and many archaeologists interpreted their sites accordingly. But recent experiments in the microscopic study of stone-tool edges have shown that many tools of the same shape were actually used for different jobs. We can now tell not only what tools were used for different purposes, but in some cases even the specific purpose. Re-studying collections can lead to entirely different interpretations. Re-study is possible, however, only if the collections have been kept together and are accessible together with the excavation records. This is one reason, incidentally, why museums do not sell off their "extra" artifacts to relic collectors. For research, there are no "extra" artifacts. Each one may possess just as much important or even unique information as any other. Artifacts seem to be needless duplicates only to those who know little about them.

To collect artifacts is to destroy sites and the original relationships among artifacts within sites. This information can never be replaced; once lost, it is lost forever. Research archaeologists, including amateurs, cause destruction just as relic collectors do. The difference is that research archaeologists use the opportunity to record information and provide knowledge about the past, whereas relic collectors just destroy.

Joining an archaeological society, then, offers one of the most rewarding ways to pursue an interest in archaeology while contributing to the preservation of the state's archaeological heritage.

COLLEGE AND UNIVERSITY PROGRAMS IN CALIFORNIA ARCHAEOLOGY

Formal study of California's archaeology, which is rarely taught in high schools or adult education programs, generally requires enrollment in a college-level program. In some cases participation by nonstudents can be arranged through the institution, and most institutions offer a range of student statuses to accommodate interested people.

California has more than two hundred colleges, universities, and junior colleges, public and private. A great many offer some archaeology courses, but comparatively few offer regular courses on California archaeology. Equally uncommon are courses on the methods of archaeological fieldwork and laboratory study that use California archaeological remains. We list below a number of college programs in the state where courses, training, and progress toward degrees can be pursued.

ARCHAEOLOGICAL FIELD SCHOOLS

Archaeological field schools are training courses. Usually offered in the summer, they introduce students to methods of excavation and survey. Field schools are normally conducted at archaeological sites, so that students help excavate sites while they learn. The subject matter in these field schools frequently includes map making, artifact processing in the laboratory, methods of preservation, artifact typology, Indian cultures, and regional archaeology.

Ten or twenty years ago a dozen or more field schools were held in California each summer. Recently the number has dwindled. In the American Anthropological Association's annual guide to field schools for 1983, for example, only two were listed in California: the University of Santa Clara and California Polytechnic University, San Luis Obispo.

Many other colleges offer training opportunities in less-formal settings, however. Research excavations and some environmental-impact-mitigation projects are used partly as opportunities to train new students. Some sort of field training can usually be arranged at colleges that have ongoing programs in California archaeology. Others may establish field schools that are not listed in the American Anthropological Association's guide. Contact your local college or university to ask if a field school will be held in the coming summer, and if enrollment is possible for outsiders. Summer programs generally have extremely flexible enrollment policies. It may also be useful to ask whether other training opportunities exist.

The annual AAA Field School List, issued around the beginning of March each year, is available to the public from the American Anthropological Association, 1703 New Hampshire Avenue, NW, Washington, D.C. 20009. The 1983 price was $3, prepaid. The list covers the entire United States and several foreign countries.

ACADEMIC PROGRAMS

The colleges and universities in the list below have established formal programs in California archaeology and archaeological-methods training. Each offers a bachelor's degree in anthropology, and virtually all offer a program at the graduate level (at least a master's degree and in some cases a doctorate). It is not always necessary to be enrolled in a college on a full-time or regular basis in order to take course work there, but some people (such as teachers) may need a formal degree-granting program. A number of other colleges and universities also offer individual courses in California archaeology on a regular or periodic basis, so it is worthwhile to call colleges in your community. Although these programs can be expected to continue into the foreseeable future, the information about specific contact people may become outdated quickly.

OTHER PROGRAMS

College-based programs may offer other opportunities for experience in California archaeology. Several schools, for example, have museums of anthropology or archaeology that welcome volunteers. The University of California sponsors a research expedition program that frequently offers opportunities to participate in California excavations; it is open to nonstudents. Anthropology departments and museums at area colleges should be contacted to learn whether such programs are offered.

COLLEGES AND UNIVERSITIES WITH PROGRAMS IN
CALIFORNIA ARCHAEOLOGY

California State College at Stanislaus, Department of Anthropology and Geography, 800 Monte Vista, Turlock, CA 95380; (209) 633-2127. Highest degree: M.A., special major within Interdisciplinary Studies. Resource contact: Dr. Lewis K. Napton.

California State University at Chico, Department of Anthropology, Chico, CA 95929; (916) 895-6193. Highest degree: M.A. Resource contacts: Dr. Keith Johnson, Dr. Makoto Kowta.

California State University at Dominguez Hills, Department of Anthropology, Carson, CA 90747; (213) 515-3443. Highest degree: B.A., major in Anthropology. Resource contact: Dr. Edward Weil.

California State University at Fresno, Department of Anthropology, Fresno, CA 93740; (209) 487-1002. Highest degree: B.A., major in Anthropology. Resource contacts: Dr. Michael J. Moratto, Dr. Dudley M. Varner.

California State University at Hayward, Department of Anthropology, Hayward, CA 94542; (415) 881-3168. Highest degree: M.A. Resource contacts: Dr. Lowell J. Bean, Dr. George R. Miller.

California State University at Long Beach, Department of Anthropology, 1250 Bellflower Blvd., Long Beach, CA 90840; (213) 498-5171. Highest degree: M.A. Resource contacts: Dr. Keith Dixon, Mr. Franklin Fenenga, Dr. E. Jane Rosenthal.

California State University at Los Angeles, Department of Anthropology, Los Angeles, CA 90032; (213) 224-2571. Highest degree: M.A. Resource contact: Dr. Fred Reinman.

California State University at Northridge, Department of Anthropology, 18111 Nordhoff Street, Northridge, CA 91324; (213) 885-3331. Highest degree: M.A. Resource contact: Dr. Louis J. Tartaglia.

California State University at Sacramento, Department of Anthropology, 6000 J Street, Sacramento, CA 95819; (916) 454-6452. Highest degree: M.A. Resource contacts: Dr. William J. Beeson, Dr. Jerald J. Johnson, Dr. Dorothea Theodoratus.

California State University at San Diego, Department of Anthropology, San Diego, CA 92182; (619) 286-5527. Highest degree: M.A. Resource contacts: Dr. Larry L. Leach, Dr. Dan Whitney.

California State University at San Francisco, Department of Anthropology, 1600 Holloway, San Francisco, CA 94132; (415) 469-2046. Highest degree: M.A. Resource contacts: Mr. Miley Holman, Dr. Gary Pahl, Dr. Robin Wells.

California State University at San Jose, Department of Anthropology, San Jose, CA 95192; (408) 277-2533. Highest degree: B.A., major in Anthropology. Resource contacts: Dr. Joseph A. Hester, Dr. Thomas N. Layton.

California State University at Sonoma, Department of Anthropology, 1801 East Cotati Avenue, Rohnert Park, CA 94928; (707) 664-2312. Highest degree: M.A. Resource contacts: Dr. James A. Bennyhoff, Dr. David A. Frederickson.

University of California, Berkeley, Department of Anthropology, Berkeley, CA 94720; (415) 642-3391. Highest degree: Ph.D. Resource contacts: Dr. Polly Bickel, Dr. James J. F. Deetz; Archaeological Research Facility; Lowie Museum.

University of California, Davis, Department of Anthropology, Davis, CA 95616; (916) 752-0745. Highest degree: Ph.D. Resource contact: Dr. D. L. True; Center for Archaeological Research.

University of California, Los Angeles, Department of Anthropology, Los Angeles, CA 90024; (213) 825-2511. Highest degree: Ph.D. Resource contacts: Dr. Brian D. Dillon, Dr. Clement W. Meighan; Institute of Archaeology; Archaeological Survey.

University of California, Riverside, Department of Anthropology, Riverside, CA 92521; (714) 787-5524. Highest degree: Ph.D. Resource contacts: Dr. Sylvia Broadbent, Dr. R. E. Taylor, Dr. Philip J. Wilke; Archaeological Research Unit.

University of California, Santa Barbara, Department of Anthropology, Goleta, CA 93106; (805) 961-3331. Highest degree: Ph.D. Resource contacts: Dr. Michael Glassow, Dr. Pandora Snethkamp; Museum of Anthropology.

ARCHAEOLOGICAL MUSEUMS IN CALIFORNIA

More than a hundred museums in California display archaeological remains and graphic interpretations of the past. Almost every one of the state's 58 counties has some sort of historical museum, county museum, or municipal museum with a case or two of Indian, Chinese, or European artifacts. No one museum offers a truly substantial presentation of California's archaeology, but a number of them go beyond the dusty case of arrowheads to present more sophisticated interpretations of the archaeological record.

Charles W. Bowers Museum, Santa Ana

The Bowers Museum displays artifacts representing over 8,000 years of southern California prehistory, with a particular emphasis on the late prehistory of Orange County. The museum has an even richer display from the historical period, but few artifacts came from archaeological research.

2002 North Main Street, a few blocks south of Interstate 5. Open 9–5 Tuesday–Saturday, plus 7–10 Wednesday and Thursday and 1–5 Sunday; closed New Year's Day, July 4, Thanksgiving, and Christmas. Free.

California State Indian Museum, Sacramento

The State Indian Museum occupies the majority of a small adobe building on the grounds of Sutter's Fort. Its one room of displays concentrates on ethnographic artifacts from Indian peoples of central and northwestern California, but in the center of the room is a rare display of the central California archaeological sequence established by Lillard, Heizer, and Fenenga (1939). It illustrates the phases of the last four thousand years of central California prehistory with charts and representative artifacts. Impressive displays of ethnographic baskets and boats join other presentations of traditional Native California technology.

2618 K Street, a block west of Interstate 80. Open 10–5 daily except New Year's Day, Thanksgiving, and Christmas. Free.

California State University at Chico Anthropology Museum

The best anthropology display on a college campus in the state, the museum presents the ethnography and archaeology of the northern Central Valley and surrounding mountains. Its displays draw heavily on archaeological research sponsored by the college. Displays include historical remains from the nineteenth century, as well as prehistoric reconstructions and interpretations. The museum also serves as a training program in museum methods for the university's students.

Old Union building in the center of campus, on First Street south of Broadway. Open 10–5 Monday–Friday except holidays. Free.

Eastern California Museum, Independence

This is one of the few museums in eastern California with archaeology displays. Though small, the museum's holdings include some important prehistoric and ethnographic artifacts of Indian cultures from the Mojave Desert region and eastern Sierra slopes. Interpretations of late prehistoric cultures are important parts of their display.

Grant Street three blocks west of the county courthouse. Open 9–5 daily except New Year's Day, Thanksgiving, and Christmas. Donation requested.

Fresno Museum, Fresno

The museum displays cultural remains of the Yokuts Indians, whose traditional territory was the San Joaquin Valley and surrounding foothills. One impressive display features a traditional Yokuts summer house from the Sierra foothills with complete furnishings. The museum also presents some archaeological remains from the area, although they are secondary.

1944 North Winery Avenue. Open 10–5 daily except holidays. Free.

Los Angeles County Museum of Natural History, Los Angeles

The museum was an early sponsor of archaeological research and has displayed information about southern California's archaeology for many years. Chief features are interpretations of coastal prehistory and the archaeology of the Channel Islands. Elsewhere in the building are displays on the area's ecology and history.

900 Exposition Boulevard, in Exposition Park next to the University of Southern California campus and the Los Angeles County Memorial Coliseum, a block west of Harbor Freeway (California Highway 11). Open 10–5 Tuesday–Sunday except New Year's Day, Thanksgiving, and Christmas. $1 for adults, $.50 for children and students.

Robert Lowie Museum of Anthropology, Berkeley

The Lowie Museum has quite a different orientation from the Anthropology Museum at California State University, Chico. Rather than offering a permanent display that interprets the state's archaeology, ethnography, and history, the Lowie Museum has some permanent exhibits on specific subjects, such as the life of Ishi. It also hosts temporary and visiting exhibits. One exhibit, for example, featured the university's excavations at the nineteenth-century mining town of Somersville (see Chapter 5).

Kroeber Hall, on the University of California campus, facing the new art museum on Bancroft Way at the south edge of campus, near the intersection of Bancroft with College Avenue. Open 10–4 Monday–Friday, noon–4 weekends. $.50 for adults, $.25 for children.

Malki Museum, Banning

This small museum is particularly important because it is run by Native Californians and is affiliated with the Morongo Indian Reservation. It features displays on the cultures of Indian peoples of inland southern California, such as the Cahuilla and Serrano. It emphasizes ethnographic interpretations, but some of the artifacts on display are archaeologically significant. Malki Museum is an important sponsor for the publication of anthropological research on Native California cultures, and its book counter is a valuable resource.

11-795 Fields Road; Fields Road is an offramp for Interstate 10 just east of Banning, and the road to the museum is posted. Open 10–5 Tuesday–Sunday. Free.

Marin Miwok Museum, Novato

This community-sponsored museum is devoted to the interpretation of Miwok Indian culture and to the archaeology of the Marin County area. The permanent exhibits of this small museum illustrate methods of archaeological excavation, the technology used by the Miwok to make stone tools, beads, and basketry, and interpretations of area ethnography and archaeology. The museum also maintains a vigorous outreach program, bringing traveling exhibits to schools, churches, and community organizations throughout the county and much of the Bay Area.

2200 Novato Boulevard, about two miles west of U.S. 101. Open 10–4 Tuesday–Saturday, 12–4 Sunday. $.50 donation requested.

Oakland Museum, Oakland

Oakland's city museum is one of the most modern and beautiful multipurpose museums in the country. The exhibits in the natural-history wing are devoted to the traditional cultures of the central California Indians. The displays are mostly ethnographic, but they contain some archaeological materials. They make use of innovative methods of graphic presentation with the emphasis on visual information; explanation tends to be skimpy. The anthropological displays are next to excellent presentations of the various types of environment in California, which help to show the kinds of habitats within which California Indians lived.

10th and Oak streets in downtown Oakland, six blocks north of Highway 17. Open 10–5 Tuesday–Saturday, noon–7 Sunday. Free.

San Bernardino County Museum, Redlands

This major, modern museum in interior southern California houses anthropological displays featuring the prehistoric and ethnographic cultures of the inland deserts and mountains. Of particular interest are the museum's presentations of archaeological research into the early Archaic and Paleo-Indian cultures of the region.

Alongside Interstate 10 in Redlands; take the California Street offramp. Open 9–5 Tuesday–Saturday, 1–5 Sunday. Free.

San Diego Museum of Man, San Diego

The museum is housed in a group of buildings around the California Quadrangle in Balboa Park, San Diego. The complex offers displays on world prehistory and ethnography, but it emphasizes the Indian cultures of the Americas, and California is well represented. The Museum of Man has sponsored research in southern California anthropology for over a half century; important displays deal with interpretations of cultures from the Colorado Desert, the San Diego County coast, and the Channel Islands.

Balboa Park is crossed by Cabrillo Freeway (California 163), which passes just to the west of the Museum of Man; the San Diego Zoo lies just to the north. Open 10–4:30 daily except New Year's Day, Thanksgiving, and Christmas. $1 for adults, $.50 for students, $.25 for children 6–16.

Santa Barbara Museum of Natural History, Santa Barbara

Anthropological research in the county and on the northern Channel Islands, conducted under the museum's longtime sponsorship, provides the basis for displays that interpret the area's archaeology and ethnography. Cultures from the Archaic to historical times are interpreted. Included are many examples of the spectacular craftwork of the Chumash Indians and their predecessors.

2559 Puesta del Sol Road, not far to the north behind the Santa Barbara Mission. Summer hours: 9–5 Monday–Saturday, 10–5 Sunday and holidays; otherwise 9–5 Monday–Saturday, 1–5 Sunday and holidays. Closed New Year's Day, Thanksgiving, and Christmas. Free.

Southwest Museum, Highland Park

This institution is one of the earliest sponsors of archaeological research on California Indian cultures. Its displays treat a much wider range of American Indian peoples than most museums, but the southern California desert, coast, and islands are especially well represented. Important examples of prehistoric technology are offered. The museum has been a major publisher of archaeology and ethnology for southern California, and its bookstore offers many such publications.

234 Museum Drive, just north of Pasadena Freeway (California 11) and east of Golden State Freeway (Interstate 5). Open 1–4:45 Tuesday–Sunday; closed August 15–September 15 and holidays. Free.

Wattis Hall of Man, San Francisco

The hall was recently renovated and contains spectacular, life-size dioramas of ethnic groups from eight parts of the world. Among them, in the center of the hall, is a cut-open reconstruction of a Yurok Indian plank house from northwestern California, complete with authentic furnishings and mannequins in traditional dress. Unobtrusive legends on the guard rails supplement the interpretation and artifacts. Archaeological specimens from coastal sites enrich the display, although it is based mainly on ethnographic data.

The Wattis Hall of Man is part of the California Academy of Sciences building, which faces the de Young Memorial Museum in Golden Gate Park. The hall is in the same building as Steinhart Aquarium, in a wing behind the astronomy section. Open 10–5 daily and somewhat later in the summer. $1 for adults, $.50 for those 12–17 or over 65, $.25 for those 5–11; free to all on the first day of each month.

APPENDIX F

CALIFORNIA ARCHAEOLOGICAL SITES OPEN FOR VISITING

Visiting an archaeological site brings the archaeological record to life. There you can walk where the site's makers walked, see the horizons they saw, and visualize the environment in which they lived. In your mind's eye you can restore their houses and re-people their settlement. A visit to a site adds a dimension to the reconstructed past that usually is missing in books and museum displays. In some cases you can also see archaeologists at work, recovering even more information about the site's past.

California has more recorded archaeological sites than any other state, but most are not suitable or useful for visiting for a couple of reasons. First, unprotected sites that are made known to the public almost invariably are vandalized, ruining them for both scientific research and public education. For that reason, we do not want to draw attention to sites that are not under active protection.

In addition, few California sites have much about them that a visitor can readily understand unless some research has already been done there, leading to interpretive reports and interpretive displays. Fortunately, a number of sites have been excavated and are well protected, and some of these have been developed for public visiting.

Berkeley Bedrock Mortar Sites

Several rock outcrops containing bedrock mortars occur in public parks in the hilly part of north Berkeley. Bedrock mortars are not common in the Bay Area, and these mortars are perhaps the most accessible examples in this part of the state. The mortars are found in hillside habitats that used to be blanketed with native grasses and chaparral, intermixed with oak groves. Probably springs once provided water near the mortars. No excavations have been made near the mortars, and any archaeological deposits have long since been destroyed. The largest and most accessible group of mortars is found in a small park at the intersection of Indian Rock Drive and Park Avenue. The park is open continuously, with no admission fee.

Big and Little Petroglyph Canyons National Historic Landmark

Located in the Naval Weapons Center in the Mojave Desert (where Kern, Inyo, and San Bernardino counties meet), Big and Little Petroglyph Canyons contain the largest concentration of rock carvings (petroglyphs) open to the public in America, and perhaps in the world. More than 20,000 glyphs can be seen along 5 miles of canyon walls. Patterns range from abstract and geometric designs to naturalistic figures of animals. Archaeologists think the carvings were made over a long period of time. Some may predate the presumed immigration of Shoshonean-speaking people into the region around 1,500 years ago, and others are more recent.

The petroglyphs are difficult to reach; some areas are accessible only with four-wheel-drive vehicles. Visits can be made only on weekends, between 9 A.M. and midnight, and then only when the testing range is not in use. At least two vehicles authorized by the Weapons Center must make the trip together. The road into the complex, 44 miles long and only partially paved, is reached via the main gate at China Lake. No admission fee is charged. Visitors should call the Weapons Center well ahead of time, at (619) 939-9011, to find out if the petroglyphs can be visited on a particular weekend. The main gate at China Lake is reached via U.S. 395, 10 miles east of Inyokern, or 10 miles north on the Ridgecrest road (3 miles north of Ridgecrest).

NOTE: Here, as at all rock-art sites, the glyphs cannot be outlined in chalk or in any other way disturbed, under penalty of law.

Calico Mountains Archaeological Project

Located in the desert foothills east of Barstow in San Bernardino County, Calico is one of the most controversial, and possibly most ancient, sites in the nation. Excavation began here in 1964, directed by Dr. Ruth D. Simpson in collaboration with famed African archaeologist Louis S. B. Leakey. Excavators felt the site might contain traces of human settlement 50,000–100,000 years old, though other authorities question both the age of the site and the authenticity of many claimed human artifacts. Research continues there under the sponsorship of the San Bernardino County Museum and other agencies.

The site is open to the public. Interpretive materials are available, and at times visitors can watch excavations in progress. The site is open daily from dawn to dusk; no admission fee is charged. To reach it, travel east from Barstow on Interstate 15 for about 8 miles to the Minneola Overpass offramp, then north on a marked road about another 8 miles.

Chumash Painted Cave State Historic Park

Located north of the city of Santa Barbara, off Highway 154 near San Marcos Pass, this state park preserves the only example of multicolored (polychrome) cave paintings (pictographs) open to the public in California. It is one of the finest examples of Native American rock art in the nation. Recent ethnographic and archival research has shed a great deal of new light on Chumash rock art, showing much of it to be associated with a complex, sophisticated body of mythology and some with astronomy. These paintings are protected to prevent vandalism, but they may be viewed by visitors, and interpretive materials are available at the park's interpretive center. For more information, see Grant's *The Rock Paintings of the Chumash* (1965). The park is open daily from dawn to dusk, with no admission fee.

Coyote Hills Regional Park

Coyote Hills Regional Park, near Fremont on the southeastern shore of San Francisco Bay, contains three prehistoric shell-mound sites. One, the Patterson Mound Site (CA-Ala-328) has been excavated off and on for 25 years by area universities and is now available for public access. The mound originally stood about 10 feet high and 100 feet across. Half of it survives, surrounded by a high chain-link fence kept locked except during tours. The site was first occupied around 1500 B.C., and people lived there more or less continuously for the next 3,300 years until removed by the Spanish. In historical times the people living there belonged to one of the many tribelets of people in the Bay Area who spoke the Costanoan language.

The site can be visited only by guided tours, which are given each Saturday at 2 P.M. Visitors gather at a parking lot just inside the park's gate and are escorted along a half-mile trail by park naturalists. An informative lecture is given at the site, partly overlooking the old excavations and partly in an amphitheater built in the excavation area. During the lecture, the speakers bring out ancient artifacts and modern replicas to help illustrate prehistoric life. Also on the site is a reconstructed Costanoan settlement, with semi-subterranean ceremonial house and sweathouse, dwellings made of tule, storage silos, and ramadas.

More artifacts and interpretive materials are displayed at the park headquarters. One display features a replica of the Costanoan reed boat. Built by park staff and volunteers in 1979, it was paddled across San Francisco Bay. Trails and catwalks in the park lead visitors out over the tule marshes to the edges of the Bay's once-rich oyster beds, into the hills once covered with chaparral, and to oak groves where Patterson Mound's people collected food and resources. Although the mound can be visited only on Saturdays, the rest of the park is open daily from 8 A.M. to 10 P.M., with no admission fee. The park is reached from California Highway 17 via Patterson Ranch Road southbound 1.5 miles.

Diego Sepulveda Adobe Park

The Diego Sepulveda Adobe, built in 1823, served as a herder's cabin for Mission San Juan Capistrano until it became the home of the Diego Sepulveda family after secularization of the missions (see Chapter 5). Situated in Costa Mesa on the southern bluffs of the Santa Ana River, the adobe commands an impressive view of the surrounding area. The site was excavated by volunteers from the Pacific Coast Archaeological Society in the 1960's, and data from their research aided in the building's restoration and interpretation. The adobe is now part of a city park located in Costa Mesa on Adams at Mesa Verde West Drive. It is open Saturday and Sunday 1–5 P.M., with no admission fee.

Fort Ross State Historic Park

The state's only Russian site, Fort Ross offers a reconstruction of some of the original structures in the redoubt (see Chapter 5). Much of the 1930's restoration was destroyed by fire in 1970 and 1971. The stockade, chapel, and two blockhouses have since been further restored. Archaeological excavations in the 1950's and 1960's have contributed to this recent restoration as well as to the current interpretation of the fort's history. Some excavated remains can be seen.

California Highway 1 passes through the park. The fort can be reached by this highway by driving north of Jenner about 10 miles. The park is open daily 10–5; the fee is $2 per car.

William B. Ide Adobe State Historic Park

Located on the west bank of the Sacramento River near Red Bluff, the Ide Adobe preserves one of the earliest Anglo-American homes in northern California (see Chapter 5). The adobe is situated in a small park at the river's edge, together with several outbuildings of designs characteristic of the mid-nineteenth century. All the structures are reconstructions. Reconstruction of the Ide Adobe was aided greatly by archaeological excavations made in the 1950's by archaeologists from California State University at San Francisco. Some artifacts from the excavations are displayed within the house.

The park is reached from downtown Red Bluff rather than from Interstate 5. Travel north 2 miles on old California 99 to Adobe Road, then east on Adobe Road a mile to the park. The park is open 8–5 daily, with no admission fee.

Indian Grinding Rock State Historical Park (Tco'se)

Located in the Gold Rush country near Jackson, in Amador County, Tco'se (pronounced sha-tsee) is the site of a major village of the northern Sierra Miwok and their immediate prehistoric ancestors. The site's major archaeological features include an immense slab of limestone bedrock on which 363 rock carvings (petroglyphs) are still faintly visible, and among which are 1,185 bedrock mortar cups—the largest concentration of bedrock mortars open to the public in western North America. The bedrock exposure, measuring 173 by 82 feet, can be seen from raised wooden walkways. Nearby stand a number of recently reconstructed Miwok buildings, including a great ceremonial roundhouse, a semi-subterranean sweathouse, several dwellings, and some small storage structures. These buildings are used for gatherings and religious observances by area Miwok during the summer. A community center, still under construction, will house displays on traditional Miwok culture and history. Information and artifacts from excavations conducted by the State Department of Parks and Recreation also will be featured.

The park is open all year from dawn to dusk; the fee is $2 per car. The park lies 9 miles east of Jackson; from California 49 drive 9 miles east on California 88 to Pine Grove, then 1.5 miles north on a marked county road.

Maze Stone County Park

Located near Hemet, in western Riverside County, Maze Stone County Park preserves one of the few examples of rock carvings (petroglyphs) open to the public in southern California. The petroglyphs form a complex geometric design incised on a large boulder. Their age and function are unknown. The design, which is reminiscent of a maze, is unique in California rock art, leading some authorities to question whether it is an authentic Native American work of art. Whether or not the design is authentic, the method of manufacture is typical of California petroglyphs.

The park is reached from Hemet by proceeding west on California 74 nearly 5 miles, then turning right on a marked county road for another 3 miles. Hours are dawn to dusk, with no admission fee.

Mission La Purísima Concepción State Historic Park

Mission La Purísima Concepción has been studied archaeologically more than any other mission (see Chapter 5). Not surprisingly, then, archaeology has contributed more here than at the other missions. The mission dates from 1813 and was begun because the original mission was destroyed in the earthquake of 1812. Eight of the structures and the basic elements of the mission water system have been restored or reconstructed. Artifacts from the excavations are displayed in the mission museum. Artisans undertake mission-period crafts during the summer.

The mission lies on the northeastern side of Lompoc in western Santa Barbara County. Lompoc is reached via California Highway 1 or California Highway 246. The park's entrance is on Purísima Road at County Road S-20, about 3.5 miles northeast of downtown Lompoc. The park is open all year except New Year's Day, Thanksgiving, and Christmas. Between October 1 and May 31 the hours are 8–5; for the rest of the year, 9–6. The fee is $.50 for adults, free for those under 18.

Old Sacramento

Located on the east bank of the Sacramento River, Old Sacramento presents a reconstruction of the city's architecture in its first two decades (see Chapter 4). Contemporary shops and automobile traffic detract from the period feeling of the place, but the restorations are authentic. The State Department of Parks and Recreation is involved with the study, reconstruction, and administration of the district, but independent concessionaires operate the places of business within its boundaries.

Old Sacramento's reconstruction has been based heavily on archaeological studies. Excavations have been under way there since 1965. Excavation data have been combined with historical research to improve the authenticity of reconstructions and restorations. Since excavations are continuing, at times it is possible to watch archaeologists at work. The state's new railroad museum is located in the district, and as railroad archaeology develops in the next decade or two it should begin to be featured in the railroad museum.

Old Sacramento is reached via Interstate 80 or Interstate 5 to downtown Sacramento; proceed to the surface intersection of Second and H streets. There is no charge to enter the district, but most parking in the area is in pay lots. The district is open 24 hours daily throughout the year; individual businesses keep varied hours.

Old Town and Royal Presidio of San Diego

San Diego's Old Town presents reconstructions of buildings dating back to the first century after the city's founding in 1769. It reflects an earlier era and a different culture from Old Sacramento, but in their blend of authentic restorations and modern commerce the two developments are similar in feeling. Unlike Old Sacramento, San Diego's Old Town does not yet reflect much contribution from archaeology. Excavation has been going on there for more than a decade, however, and displays and reconstructions are being developed from this research. On some occasions excavators can be seen at work.

The Royal Presidio, located next to Old Town, also has been the scene of excavation in recent years. It is particularly noteworthy for being the only presidio in the state to have been excavated extensively and then prepared for public visit. Still under development, the presidio's restoration will be continued for the next decade or more.

The Old Town district is part of the city of San Diego, and is open 24 hours daily throughout the year. Individual buildings have varied restrictions and visiting hours, and some charge admission fees. Old Town lies south of Mission Bay, at the intersection of Rosecrans at Fort Stockton and Juan streets. Walking tours are led daily at 2 P.M.

Point Reyes National Seashore

Located on the coast north of San Francisco, Point Reyes is a locale of great prehistoric and historical significance (see Chapters 3 and 4). A major population center during the Pacific Period, it was the location of the shipwreck of Cermeño's Manila galleon in 1595. It is a possible candidate for the landing spot of the English buccaneer Sir Francis Drake in 1579.

Actual sites have not yet been developed for visiting at Point Reyes, but a regional archaeological society has reconstructed a Miwok village in the park in cooperation with the National Park Service. The reconstruction relies on knowledge gained through archaeological research in the region as well as on ethnographic accounts. The group responsible is the Miwok Archaeological Preserve of Marin (MAPOM), whose volunteers worked with Seashore personnel to build a replica of a coast Miwok settlement near the Bear Valley Visitor Center. Located a fourth of a mile from the visitor center via a marked trail, the village is a center of activities during the summer, when MAPOM members rebuild structures and carry on traditional Miwok crafts. Informative signs describe several aspects of traditional life. The village includes a large, semisubterranean ceremonial building, a sweathouse, several dwellings in various stages of construction, granaries, and ramadas.

The park is open at all hours throughout the year, with no admission fee. It is reached via California Highway 1; the turnoff is a quarter mile north of Olema.

Sutter's Fort

Sutter's Fort, located in downtown Sacramento, is a reconstruction of the 1839 headquarters compound of Sutter's New Helvetia colony (see Chapter 5). The fort is operated as a historical park by the State Department of Parks and Recreation, which also supports research on this historical site. Archaeological excavations, conducted mainly in the late 1950's and early 1960's, contributed to the accuracy of the fort's reconstruction and interpretation. Some of the materials excavated are on display. Self-guided tours and informative signs help interpret the site.

The fort lies in a small park, together with the State Indian Museum. It is reached via Interstate 80, which passes just to the east of the park. Exit west to the intersection of 28th and L streets. The fort is open 10–5 daily except New Year's Day, Thanksgiving, and Christmas. The fee is $.50 for adults, $.25 for those under 18.

Yosemite National Park Visitors' Center

Yosemite Valley was a major population center for Sierra Miwok people when Europeans first entered the area. A number of archaeological sites exist in the valley. Research over the years at Ah-Wah-Nee, a village site near the visitors' center in Yosemite Village, has yielded evidence of Pacific Period life prior to the arrival of Europeans. This data supplements records made through interviews with nineteenth- and twentieth-century Miwok people. The information was used in the reconstruction of several Miwok structures behind the visitors' center, and in displays in the visitors'-center museum. Miwok people of the vicinity are employed by the National Park Service to demonstrate traditional skills and crafts, such as the grinding and leaching of acorns and the making of baskets. These demonstrations are given daily in the reconstructed village. Original bedrock mortars are located within the village complex.

The Yosemite Visitors' Center is located in Yosemite Valley. The valley is reached from the south via California Highway 41, from the west via California 140, and from the northwest via California 120. Highway 120 also gives access from the eastern side of the Sierra during the warmer months when it is not blocked by snow. The entrance fee for the park is $3 per car. The park is open daily throughout the year, but the number of visitors to the Valley is controlled, which may result in delayed entrance, and bad winter weather may block access roads.

FILMS ON CALIFORNIA ARCHAEOLOGY
AND RELATED SUBJECTS

Films provide an excellent introduction to archaeology for the general public, and a number are available to groups and individuals interested in pursuing this subject. Fortunately, although there are only a few films dealing specifically with California archaeology, a relatively large number explore related subjects, topics that should enhance the viewer's understanding of California's archaeological record. These topics include the archaeology of North America in general, the theory and techniques of archaeological fieldwork, the ethnography of California Indians, and California history.

All of the films listed here are available for rent by responsible individuals or groups (many are also available for purchase, and interested parties should contact the distributors listed below). A little background about primary distributors and rental organizations may be helpful.

When producers handle the marketing of their own films, they are the "primary distributors." Potential customers must contact the producer of each film they are interested in renting; for this, they must know the producers of the various films and their addresses. Sometimes a film is available only through the primary distributor. When this is the case, we have indicated the name and address of the producer in the individual film's entry below.

Fortunately, for the majority of films there is a second level of film distribution. Producers often sell or lease the distribution rights for their films to college and university media centers. These centers ("secondary distributors") are excellent sources of films for the general public. Catalogues are available from virtually every media center, either free or for a small fee, listing the films offered for rent or purchase. Each catalogue also describes the procedures followed by that particular center in renting its films.

The single best source of educational films for people living in California is the University of California Extension Media Center, in Berkeley. The UCEMC catalogue lists over four thousand titles and is available upon request. The catalogue spells out in detail exactly how to go about ordering films. Since approximately two-thirds of the films listed below are available through UCEMC, we heartily recommend this resource. For further information, the reader should either acquire a copy of the Center's catalogue or contact the Center by mail or telephone (see below).

In compiling our list of films, we consulted not only the UCEMC catalogue, but also the catalogues of over two hundred other primary and secondary distributors. But the UCEMC, along with about four dozen other university media centers around the country, belongs to the Consortium of University Film Centers, and all of these centers list their holdings in a single combined catalogue, known as the "Bowker catalogue." This catalogue, which also lists the addresses and lending policies of its member institutions, is available for use at the UCEMC office, in the reference libraries of many universities and colleges, and through the educational-media service offices of many local school districts. The films listed here do not represent an exhaustive compilation of all the films that could conceivably bear on California archaeology. Though we did try to list all of the films that seemed most pertinent and readily available, many more are of potential interest, especially in such fields as California history. Anyone interested in locating additional films on this or any other topic is advised to consult the Bowker catalogue.

Educational Film Locator of the Consortium of University Film Centers and R. R. Bowker Company, 1st edition. 1978. New York and London: Bowker.

Three other catalogues are also helpful.

Bean, Lowell John, and Sylvia Brakke Vane. 1977. *California Indians: Primary Resources. A Guide to Manuscripts, Artifacts, Documents, Serials, Music and Illustrations.* Ramona, Calif.: Ballena.

Films for Anthropological Teaching. 6th edition. 1977. Prepared by Karl G. Heider. *Special Publication of the American Anthropological Association*, Number 9. Washington, D.C.

Index to 16-mm Educational Films, 6th edition. 1977. National Information Center for Educational Media (NICEM). Los Angeles: Univ. of Southern California.

Beyond the nearly two-thirds of the films available through the UCEMC, most of the remaining ones are available through one or more of the other Consortium members. Many of these institutions are located at a considerable distance from California, however, so that potential renters may be interested in pursuing a third, more local, source of films. Many of the films listed in this appendix, and others besides, may be rented or borrowed through one of the local public libraries, museums, or school districts that maintain film libraries. Often these institutions make their films available to local civic groups and nonprofit organizations free or for a small fee. An example of this sort of arrangement is the cooperative film service offered to the residents of Contra Costa County, California, by the county's public library system and the office of the superintendent of schools. The catalogue for this library of approximately four thousand films is available at the county's main and branch libraries and includes many titles on California history and Indians. The disadvantage of using such sources is that borrowers must themselves determine whether or not a film is locally available, and where film libraries are located. Often, too, holdings are small, dated, and less comprehensive than those of a university media center. In many cases these sources remain an excellent and convenient way of obtaining films, however, and the borrower may want to check locally before renting from a media center or producer.

A rental source is given for each of the films listed. When the film is available only through the producer, we have listed the producer's name and address with the film. When the rental source is a university media center, however, we have for the sake of convenience used a code to indicate the name, address, and telephone number of the center. Borrowers should call or write directly to the indicated institution or institutions (some films are available from more than one) for rental information.

UCEMC   The University of California Extension Media Center
2223 Fulton Street
Berkeley, CA 94720
(415) 642-0460
When a film listed below is available from UCEMC, we have included its catalogue number for ease of reference.

BOS U   Boston University
Krasker Memorial Film Library
765 Commonwealth Avenue, Boston, MA 02215
(617) 353-3272

IDA SU   Idaho State University
Audio Visual Services
Campus Box 8064, Pocatello, ID 83209
(208) 236-3212

IND U   Indiana University
Audio Visual Center
Bloomington, IN 47401
(812) 335-2853

KENT SU   Kent State University
Audio Visual Services
330 Library Building, Kent, OH 44242
(216) 672-3456

PENN SU   Pennsylvania State University
Audio Visual Services
Special Services Building, University Park, PA 16802
(814) 865-6314

PURD U   Purdue University
Audio Visual Center
Stewart Center, West Lafayette, IN 47907
(317) 494-2760

U ARIZ   University of Arizona
Bureau of Audio Visual Services
Tucson, AZ 85706
(602) 884-3282

UCEMC   See first entry

UCLA   University of California at Los Angeles
Instructional Media Library, Royce Hall 8
405 Hilgard Avenue, Los Angeles, CA 90024
(213) 825-0755

U COLO   University of Colorado
Educational Media Center
348 Stadium Building, Boulder, CO 80302
(303) 492-7341

U ILL   University of Illinois
Film Center
1325 South Oak Street, Champaign, IL 61820
(800) 367-3456

U IOWA   University of Iowa
Audio Visual Center
C-5 East Hall, Iowa City, IA 52242
(319) 353-5885

U MICH   University of Michigan
Audio Visual Education Center
416 Fourth Street, Ann Arbor, MI 48103
(313) 764-5360

U MINN   University of Minnesota
Audio Visual Library Services
3300 University Avenue, SE, Minneapolis, MN 55414
(612) 373-3810

U NEB   University of Nebraska at Lincoln
Instructional Media Center
Nebraska Hall 421, Lincoln, NE 68588
(402) 472-1911 or 472-1910

U NEV   University of Nevada at Reno
Audio Visual Center
106 College of Education, Reno, NV 89507
(702) 784-6083

US FLO   University of South Florida
Film Library
4202 Fowler Avenue, Tampa, FL 33620
(813) 974-2874

U TEX   University of Texas at Austin
General Libraries, Film Library
Box W, Austin, TX 78712
(512) 471-3572

U UTAH   University of Utah
Instructional Media Services
207 Milton Bennion Hall, Salt Lake City, UT 84112
(801) 581-6112

U WASH   University of Washington at Seattle
Instructional Media Services
23 Kane Hall DG-10, Seattle, WA 98195
(206) 543-9900 or 543-9909

U WIS/L   University of Wisconsin at LaCrosse
Film Rental Library
127 Wing Communications Center
1705 State Street, La Crosse, WI 54601
(608) 785-8040 or 785-8045

U WIS/M   University of Wisconsin at Madison
Bureau of Audio-Visual Instruction
1327 University Avenue, Madison, WI 53706
(608) 262-1644

U WYO   University of Wyoming
Audio Visual Services
Box 3273 University Station
Room 14 Knight Hall, Laramie, WY 82071
(307) 766-3184

WASH SU   Washington State University
Instructional Media Services
Pullman, WA 99164
(509) 335-4535

Films are listed according to topic. All films are 16 mm. Included in each entry are certain classes of information: the title, the date of production or release, the film's running time, whether it is in color or black and white, the rental source, and wherever possible, the rental price. Often, there is a short description of the film.

CALIFORNIA ARCHAEOLOGY

Archaeology—Pursuit of Man's Past   1967
Well-done film for beginning students. Demonstrates various archaeological techniques at a Chumash site in Ventura County, Calif. Shows how archaeological data is recovered and what it can tell us of prehistoric life. Junior high through lower-division college levels.
Color, 15 mins. Rental: UCEMC #9728. $20.

4-Butte-1: A Lesson in Archaeology   1968
Excellent film for beginning as well as advanced students. Rather than taking a "how-to" approach, this film emphasizes archaeology as anthropology, as it follows an archaeological field school at a Maidu site in the Sacramento Valley, Calif. Beautifully filmed; many awards.
Color, 33 mins. Rental: UCEMC #7175. $38.

Lost Mission   1976
The excavation of Mission San Buenaventura in Ventura, Calif. Shows the discovery and excavation of the mission. Film describes the destructiveness of pothunting and makes a strong plea for scientific excavation.
Color, 18 mins. Rental: UCEMC #9807. $26.

GENERAL NORTH AMERICAN ARCHAEOLOGY

Clues to Ancient Indian Life   1964
Prehistoric art and communication is reconstructed using ancient rock art. Discusses ways we know about the past; makes a plea for preservation of archaeological sites. English or Spanish sound track. Middle grades to adult.
Color, 10 mins. Rental: U ARIZ.

The Early Americans   1976
Excellent introduction to North American archaeology. Describes the early peopling of the New World and subsequent development over time. Stresses the relationship between man and his environment. Describes sev-

eral analytical techniques used in archaeology. Produced by the Shell Film Unit.

Color, 41 mins. Rental: Shell Film Library, 1433 Sadlier Circle W. Drive, Indianapolis , IN 46239.

Early Man in North America 1972

Emphasizes need for site protection and salvage (and shows scenes of California salvage archaeology). Describes the rise of American archaeology and shows several of the more spectacular sites. Visually appealing and good for general audiences, this film is an excerpt from *In Search of the Lost World*.

Color, 12 mins. Rental: Films, Incorporated, 144 Wilmette Avenue, Wilmette, IL 60091.

First Americans 1969

Good overall review of the peopling of the New World, using real sites and interviewing the excavators. Takes a conservative view of the antiquity of man in the New World, arguing for no sites older than 20,000 years ago. Produced for television.

Color, 53 mins. Rental: UCEMC #8567. $37.

History of Archaeology 1962

A lecture by Jesse Jennings, well-known American archaeologist. Surveys the development of archaeology as a discipline. Part of a television course, and intended for lower-division college students.

Black and white, 29 mins. Rental: U UTAH.

How Man Adapts to His Physical Environment 1970

Shows examples of people who have changed their environments to meet their needs. Presents the Pueblo and Navaho Indians and early Europeans.

Color, 20 mins. Rental: U ARIZ, U COLO, KENT SU, U ILL, IND U, U IOWA, U MINN, U WIS/L.

Indian Origins—The First 50,000 Years 1975

The entry of early man into the New World and his subsequent spread over the North American continent.

Color, 18 mins. Rental: KENT SU, U ILL, U WIS/L, U WYO, WASH SU.

In Search of the Lost World 1972

Simplified treatment, but well-done and entertaining presentation. Follows the development of Indian cultures in the New World from the original peopling to European contact. Film broken into shorter segments: *Who Discovered America?* and *Early Man in North America*. General to lower-division college audiences.

Color, 52 mins. Rental: UCEMC #9723. $41.

The Marmes Archaeological Dig 1972

Describes the excavation of an early-man site in southeastern Washington. Shows that many techniques are used to understand as much as possible about man's past.

Color, 18 mins. Rental: PENN SU, U WASH.

Mystery Murals of Baja California 1977

Well-filmed study of the rock art of Baja California, containing a great deal of factual information about the caves in which the pictographs were found. More an adventure film than a scientific one, it was filmed by an amateur archaeologist.

Color, 29 mins. Rental: UCEMC #9804. $35.

Prehistoric Man   1967
Focuses on the development of early man in North America, from entry into the New World to contact with Europeans. Emphasizes Colorado, and shows scenes of Mesa Verde.
Color, 17 mins. Rental: UCEMC #9786. $24.

Rock Paintings of Baja California (revised edition)   1975
Well done and entertaining, one of the better films on this subject. Includes a brief introduction to pictographs and petroglyphs around the world. Shows the paintings and how they were painted, their meaning, and their age.
Color, 17 mins. Rental: UCEMC #9180. $17.

Rock Paintings of Baja California   1968
A longer and earlier edition (see above), with more information about the expedition and the environment in which the art occurs and the culture that produced it.
Color, 25 mins. Rental: UCEMC #8840. $28.

Who Discovered America?   1972
An edited segment of *In Search of the Lost World*. Discusses the debate between scholars who believe that New World civilizations evolved independently and those who believe that they were influenced by contacts with Old World civilizations. General to lower-division college audiences.
Color, 14 mins. Rental: UCEMC #9724. $22.

ARCHAEOLOGICAL METHOD AND THEORY

Advance into the Past: Modern Archaeological Methods   ca. 1973
German film with English narration. Shows the various technical aids that have been developed to facilitate site location and to minimize the time and expense involved in excavation. Despite simplistic narrative, the film is useful for college-level students.
Color, 27 mins. Rental: Consulate General of the Federal Republic of Germany, 6th Floor, International Building, 601 California Street, San Francisco, CA 94103.

Archaeology in the Laboratory   1973
Excellent film about Henry de Lumley's excavation in Grotte du Lazaret, a Paleolithic cave site in France. Shows the contributions of many sciences to the reconstruction of the cave's environment and culture. College-student level.
Color, 27 mins. Rental: F.A.C.S.E.A., 972 Fifth Avenue, New York, NY 10021.

The Artifacts   1973
Third in the series including *The Survey* and *The Dig*. A "how-to" film that covers the field recording, laboratory analysis, and interpretation of artifacts from a site in Washington State.
Color, 20 mins. Rental: U NEV.

The Dig   1969
Second in the series including *The Survey* and *The Artifacts*. A "how-to" film that demonstrates excavation, measurement, and recording techniques at a shell-midden site in Washington State. Does not explain *why* the data is being collected.
Color, 20 mins. Rental: U ILL, WASH SU.

Digging into the Past—Archaeology   1976
Archaeologists and students in southwestern Illinois sort artifacts and perform chemical analyses and other laboratory work to reconstruct the past.
Color, 14 mins. Rental: U ILL.

Digging Up the Past   1965
Reenacts the discovery, and shows the techniques of excavation, of a variety of sites in Washington State. Shows the variability of sites, discourages pothunting. Good introduction to archaeology for high school students, but juvenile dialogue.
Color, 24 mins. Rental: PENN SU, US FLO, U WASH, WASH SU.

Five Foot Square   1968
Shows the field and laboratory techniques involved in excavating a site in Ontario, Canada. Also shows how bone tools were manufactured. Good introductory film for general audiences, but techniques shown are very traditional, with little cultural interpretation.
Color, 30 mins. Rental: UCEMC #9729. $31.

Gate Cliff: American Indian Rock Shelter   1974
Excavations by David H. Thomas in Utah show how modern archaeological method and theory have affected the way that field research is conducted. This is demonstrated at a stratigraphic excavation and a survey. Good for high school, college, and general audiences.
Color, 24 mins. Rental: UCEMC #9731. $28.

Graveyard of the Gulf   1975
A popular presentation of underwater archaeology, as conducted near Padre Island, Texas, on a Spanish silver fleet. Film does not make clear *why* work was undertaken, other than for salvage.
Color, 35 mins. Rental: U TEX.

Living Archaeology   1975
Shows how artifacts can be used to reconstruct prehistoric life. Shows the manufacture of an arrowhead.
Color, 10 mins. Rental: BOS U.

Mill Creek Village   1973
Informative, entertaining film about the excavation of a site in northwestern Iowa. Field techniques are explained and village life reconstructed. Good for general and advanced audiences.
Color, 27 mins. Rental: UCEMC #9734. $28.

Modern Methods of Archaeological Excavation   1967
French film with English narration. Shows the excavation methods used on a variety of French sites. Also shows the efforts of the French government to inform the general public through on-site museums.
Color, 19 mins. Rental: UCEMC #9839. $25.

Point of Pines   1955
Well-done film showing the various archaeological techniques used in the excavation of a site in Arizona by the University of Arizona Field School. Little cultural reconstruction.
Color, 22 mins. Rental: UCEMC #9730. $22.

Stop Ruining America's Past   1968
Strong plea for the preservation of America's archaeological sites. Shows the threat of land development to important mound sites in southern

Illinois. Shows salvage efforts and suggests how sites might be saved. Black and white, 27 mins. Rental: UCEMC #8052. $19.

The Survey 1972
First in the series including *The Dig* and *The Artifacts*. Shows the various techniques used in an archaeological survey in Washington State. Not well organized.
Color, 20 mins. Rental: WASH SU.

ARCHAEOLOGICAL DATING PROCEDURES

Archaeological Dating: Retracing Time 1976
Shows how techniques such as pottery seriation, the study of stratigraphy, tree-ring dating, archaeomagnetic dating, obsidian hydration, and radiocarbon dating can be used to date a site in New Mexico.
Color, 18 mins. Rental: UCEMC #9530. $23.

Atom and Archaeology 1973
Shows how atomic technology may be used to date archaeological artifacts. Experts in the field explain the use of carbon-14, thermoluminescence, etc.
Color, 25 mins. Rental: UCEMC #9763. $29.

Dating Game: How Old Are We? 1977
Describes the development, by Jeffrey Bada, of amino acid racemization as a dating technique. Explores the controversy in dating human remains raised by this technique.
Color, 29 mins. Rental: UCEMC #9769. $35.

How Old Is Old? 1971
Various methods of dating archaeological remains are explored, including thermoluminescence, dendrochronology, carbon-14, and potassium-argon.
Color, 30 mins. Rental: U ILL, U MINN, U NEB.

Nuclear Fingerprinting of Ancient Pottery 1970
Shows how chemical and nuclear analyses may be used to date ancient pottery. Produced by the Lawrence Laboratory at the University of California, Berkeley, this well-done film is an award winner.
Color, 20 mins. Rental: UCEMC #8278. $17.

REPLICATIVE EXPERIMENTS IN ARCHAEOLOGY

Alchemy of Time 1972
This film and *Ancient Projectile Points, Flint Worker,* and *Hunter's Edge* all feature Donald Crabtree, a master knapper and expert on prehistoric stone tools. All the films show what are felt to have been the original techniques to simulate the production of prehistoric stone tools. This film shows how heat treatment improves the flaking quality of some lithic materials, and how fluting was produced on Folsom and Clovis points. Except for *Flint Worker,* these films are intended for advanced audiences with previous knowledge.
Color, 26 mins. Rental: UCEMC #9716. $28.

Ancient Projectile Points 1972
See *Alchemy of Time,* above. This film shows the various techniques involved in pressure flaking. Unfluted types of American projectile points are reproduced.
Color, 28 mins. Rental: UCEMC #9715. $28.

Blades and Pressure Flaking   1969
  Very good film on stone knapping. François Bordes demonstrates how blades were produced. Donald Crabtree demonstrates pressure flaking. A well-presented, award-winning film.
  Color, 21 mins. Rental: UCEMC #7447. $30.

Flint Worker   1972
  See *Alchemy of Time*, above. This film explains the basic concepts of lithic technology and shows the processes of stone flaking. Best film of the four on this topic for beginning audiences.
  Color, 28 mins. Rental: UCEMC #9713. $27.

Hunter's Edge   1972
  See *Alchemy of Time*, above. This film shows how blades were manufactured at American and Japanese sites.
  Color, 28 mins. Rental: UCEMC #9714. $28.

The Shadow of Man   1969
  Good film on knapping for the advanced viewer, featuring Donald Crabtree. Although filmed at a prehistoric obsidian quarry in Oregon, not really about prehistoric quarrying. Not an introductory film.
  28 mins. Rental: IDA SU.

ETHNOGRAPHY OF THE CALIFORNIA INDIANS

Acorns: Staple Food of California Indians   1962
  Traditional acorn harvesting, processing and storing techniques are demonstrated by Pomo Indians. Suitable for all audiences.
  Color, 28 mins. Rental: UCEMC #5804. $35.

Alice Elliott   1977
  The story of one of the few remaining Pomo basketmakers. The film tells of her life, shows her baskets, and discusses traditional designs. Award-winning film.
  Color, 11 mins. Rental: UCEMC #10058. $23.

Basketry of the Pomo—Introduction   1962
  The first in a series of three, this film shows the gathering of raw materials for basketmaking and the methods of manufacture used by the Pomo, among the world's best basketmakers. The emphasis is on technology in all three films, and all feature a rather dry narrative style.
  Color, 30 mins. Rental: UCEMC #5801. $35.

Basketry of the Pomo—Forms and Ornamentation   1962
  The second in a series, this film shows the various shapes, sizes, and design elements used in Pomo basketmaking.
  Color, 21 mins. Rental: UCEMC #5803. $30.

Basketry of the Pomo—Techniques   1962
  The third in a series, this film shows in greater detail the various weaves used in Pomo basketmaking, and the use of feathers in the design.
  Color, 33 mins. Rental: UCEMC #5802. $38.

Beautiful Tree—Chishkale   1965
  This film shows the important role played by the acorn, focusing on the tan oak and the southwestern Pomo. Acorn processing and cooking techniques are detailed, and the cultural importance of the acorn described. Award-winning film.
  Color, 20 mins. Rental: UCEMC #6479. $29.

Bryan Beavers: A Moving Portrait   1969
Attractive and well-done film about a Maidu Indian, a man who has experienced two cultures. He reflects on his life and talks about the Maidu as the film follows his daily activities.
Color, 30 mins. Rental: UCEMC #8024. $24.

Buckeyes: Food of California Indians   1961
The harvesting and processing of buckeyes, an important food source, by the Nisenan Indians.
Color, 13 mins. Rental: UCEMC #5766. $25.

Dream Dances of the Kashia Pomo   1964
Essie Parrish, a Pomo shaman, is featured along with other Pomo women performing five dances of the Bole Maru religion. This film was made at the same time as, and is related to, *Kashia Men's Dances* and *Pomo Shaman*. Accurate films, but best shown to audiences with some prior knowledge.
Color, 30 mins. Rental: UCEMC #6461. $35.

Game of Staves   1962
Demonstrates and explains a Pomo gambling game.
Color, 10 mins. Rental: UCEMC #5805. $22.

Hupa Indian White-Deerskin Dance   1958
Shows a ten-day ceremony, including the rituals, dance, and costumes, that is still being held by the Hupa Indians.
Color, 11 mins. Rental: UCEMC #4990. $18.

Indian Family of the California Desert   1967
This film shows how the Cahuilla Indians adapted to a desert and mountain environment. Various aspects of their culture, including technology, hunting, and ceremonies, are presented.
Black and white, 16 mins. Rental: BOS U, U ARIZ, U COLO, U WIS/M.

Ishi in Two Worlds   1967
This is the moving story of Ishi, last of the Yahi Indians. Beautifully filmed, and based on the book by Theodora Kroeber, this film also tells the story of what happened to the California Indians. Winner of highest awards.
Color, 19 mins. Rental: UCEMC #7399. $24.

Kashia Men's Dances: Southwestern Pomo Indians   1963
See *Dream Dances of the Kashia Pomo*, above. This film presents four Pomo dances, along with costumes and brush enclosure.
Color, 40 mins. Rental: UCEMC #5904. $42.

Kiliwa: Hunters and Gatherers of Baja California   1975
This film has been included although it is not about a California group. Shows how the Kiliwa have adapted to their desert environment and to the effect of modern technology on their lives.
Color, 14 mins. Rental: UCEMC #9165. $25.

Obsidian Point-Making   1964
Features a Tolowa Indian making an obsidian arrow point. Also explains the uses of obsidian and the customs connected with it.
Color, 13 mins. Rental: UCEMC #6474. $25.

Pine Nuts   1961
The Paviotso and Paiute of the Great Basin are seen harvesting and preparing the piñon nut. The Washo Indians also relied on this staple food.
Color, 13 mins. Rental: UCEMC #5768. $25.

Pomo Shaman 1964
See *Dream Dances of the Kashia Pomo*, above. This film is a shortened version of *Sucking Doctor*. Essie Parrish, a Pomo shaman, performs a curing cere-mony. Shown without narration, this film is not really suited to beginning students or general audiences.
Black and white, 20 mins. Rental: UCEMC #6464. $24.

Sinew-Backed Bow and Its Arrows 1961
Shows a Yurok Indian making a sinew-backed bow and its arrows.
Color, 24 mins. Rental: UCEMC #5767. $32.

Sucking Doctor 1964
See *Pomo Shaman*, above. The complete film of the second night of a curing ceremony. Of the two, this is the better document, but should be shown to advanced audiences.
Black and white, 45 mins. Rental: UCEMC #6684. $37.

Washo, Parts I and II 1968
A very good film, relating the traditional Pine-Nut Dance and Girl's Pu-berty Dance to contemporary Washo culture. Written and directed by Ve-ronica Pataky, who spent ten years with the Washo.
Black and white, 56 mins. Rental: IND U, UCLA, U MINN, U WIS/M, WASH SU.

CALIFORNIA'S HISTORICAL PERIOD

California and Gold 1958
Tells the story of the Gold Rush and traces the subsequent development of California into a modern state. Uses old pictures and scenes where events occurred. May be viewed as Part III of *California's Dawn* series.
Color, 15 mins. Rental: UCEMC #3022. $19.

California's Dawn, Part I: Spanish Explorers 1963
Uses maps, diaries, books, and paintings to tell the story of the early explo-ration of California.
Color, 13 mins. Rental: UCEMC #6058. $18.

California's Dawn, Part II: Missions, Ranchos and Americans 1963
Concludes California's history before the Gold Rush, from the mission pe-riod to the American takeover. *California and Gold* may be viewed as Part III in this series.
Color, 15 mins. Rental: UCEMC #6059. $19.

California's Mother Lode 1955
Scenes of actual mother-lode sites are used to tell the story of the Gold Rush.
Color, 20 mins. Rental: UCEMC #2876. $24.

The Chinese-American—The Early Immigrants 1973
The role of the Chinese during the Gold Rush and the building of the trans-continental railroad. Describes the persecution the Chinese experienced.
Color, 20 mins. Rental: U ILL.

Faces of Chinatown 1963
The story of the Chinese immigrants in San Francisco from 1877 to 1911. Historical photographs are used to illustrate life in early Chinatown. Well-done, award-winning film.
Black and white, 27 mins. Rental: UCEMC #6467. $15.

Gold Dredge 1973
Shows how the huge gold dredges operated to remove gold from river gravels, focusing on the last of these dredges in operation on a riverbed in the Sacramento Valley.
Color, 17 mins. Rental: UCEMC #8447. $27.

The Gold Rush . . . and the 49ers 1976
Using live-action photography, old photographs, paintings, and graphics, this film tells the story of the Gold Rush and its consequences.
Color, 22 mins. Rental: IND U, U UTAH.

Goodbye God, I've Gone to Bodie 1974
The story of Bodie, a California gold-mining town. Filmed in the Bodie of today—a ghost town—its story is told by narration and song.
Color, 11 mins. Rental: UCEMC #8645. $23.

Hard-Rock Gold Mining 1974
Shows how, after the panning gave out, miners began to tunnel for gold. Shows the operations of the last surviving hardrock mine.
Color, 20 mins. Rental: UCEMC #8843. $29.

History of Southern California, Part I: From Prehistoric Times to the Founding of Los Angeles 1967
Uses original historical materials to follow the history of the area from prehistory through the founding of the Pueblo of Los Angeles.
Color, 16 mins. Rental: U ARIZ.

History of Southern California, Part II: Rise and Fall of the Spanish and Mexican Influences 1967
Relates the economic and cultural history of the area from 1776 to 1865. Focuses on missions, traders, ranchos, and the decline of the Indians and the Spanish.
Color, 18 mins. Rental: U ARIZ.

Hydraulic Gold Mining 1973
Uses historical photos and accounts, plus present-day scenes, to tell the story of hydraulic mining in California. Describes the conflict between the miners and the farmers.
Color, 17 mins. Rental: UCEMC #8495. $23.

Life in a California Mission: 1700 1976
Filmed at actual missions, this film shows many aspects of life in the Spanish missions.
Color, 15 mins. Rental: KENT SU, U ILL, U WIS/L.

Mission Life (second edition) 1966
Depicts life in a California mission at about 1776, including the role of the Indians.
Black and white, 20 mins. Rental: Arthur Barr Productions, 3490 E. Foothill Boulevard, Pasadena, CA 91107.

Placer Gold 1968
Shows the methods used in gold mining during the Gold Rush: the gold pan, rocker, long tom, and sluice box.
Color, 10 mins. Rental: U ARIZ, U ILL.

Rancho Life (second edition) 1964
Depicts life on the early ranchos, including work and festivities.
Color, 20 mins. Rental: U ARIZ, IND U, UCLA, U ILL.

Sacramento—A Place to Remember   1967
   The history of Sacramento, from its founding on. Shows the historic areas of the city and describes the restorations.
      Color, 28 mins. Rental: Vista Productions, Inc., 371 Fifth Street, San Francisco, CA 94107.

The Spanish Explorers   1963
   Depicts the history of California during its exploration and occupation by Spain.
      Color, 13 mins. Rental: U ARIZ, U ILL, U UTAH.

The Story of Old California   1964
   Tells the story of California's early history, focusing on the role played by many ethnic groups.
      Color, 14 mins. Rental: Le Mont Films, P.O. Box 63 or 17622 Willard Street, Northridge, CA 91324.

CONTEMPORARY ISSUES IN CALIFORNIA INDIAN LIFE

Dispossessed   1970
   Describes the conflict between the Pit River Indians and Pacific Gas and Electric Co. over lands formerly occupied by the Indians. Traces the history of the dispute and the effect it has had on the Indian way of life.
      Color, 33 mins. Rental: UCEMC #8015. $30.

Forty-Seven Cents   1973
   Like the film above, this documents the efforts of the Pit River Indians of northern California to recover their land. It records the history of the Indians' legal battles with the U.S. government and the current economic situation of the Indians. Winner of several awards, including the Emmy Award.
      Black and white, 25 mins. Rental: UCEMC #8616. $26.

Way of Our Fathers   1972
   Very good film, showing the efforts of several northern California Indian groups to preserve and revive their traditional cultures. Explores the contemporary Indian experience and how traditional values are being taught.
      Color, 33 mins. Rental: UCEMC #8176. $38.

MISCELLANEOUS

American Indian Influences on the United States   1972
   Shows the many practical and philosophical contributions that Native Americans have made to modern American life. Uses historical graphic material and re-creations of tribal dances.
      Color, 20 mins. Rental: UCEMC #9217. $27.

Have You Considered Archaeology?   1968
   A basic, light introduction to the field of archaeology, appropriate for high school or lower-division college audiences. Does not develop archaeology as anthropology, however, or make clear to the audiences exactly what archaeology and anthropology are.
      Color, 15 mins. Rental: Stuart Scott, Department of Anthropology, State University of New York at Buffalo, Buffalo, NY 14214.

Island of the Blue Dolphins   1965
   Taken from the Universal film based on Scott O'Dell's novel of the same

name. The story is very loosely based on a historical event of the early 1800's, in which a Chumash girl was marooned on an island off the coast of southern California. Neither the ethnographic elements nor the historical events portrayed should be taken literally. Not suitable for young children.

Color, 20 mins. Rental: UCEMC #7087. $21.

Ramona 1910

An excerpt from the D. W. Griffith film starring Mary Pickford; based on the book by Helen Hunt Jackson concerning the fate of the Indians of southern California at the hands of the whites.

Black and white, 12 mins. Rental: U MINN.

BIBLIOGRAPHY

BIBLIOGRAPHY

Adam, D. P. 1967. Late Pleistocene and Recent palynology in the central Sierra Nevada, California. *In* E. J. Cushing and H. E. Wright, Jr., eds., *Quaternary Paleoecology*, pp. 275–302. New Haven, Conn.: Yale Univ. Press.

Adovazio, J. M., J. D. Gunn, J. Donahue, and R. Stuckenrath. 1978. Meadowcroft Rockshelter, 1977: An overview. *American Antiquity* 43(4): 632–51.

Aikens, Melvin. 1978. The Far West. *In* Jennings 1978, pp. 131–81.

Alt, David D., and Donald W. Hyndman. 1975. *Roadside Geology of Northern California.* Missoula, Mont.: Mountain Press.

Antevs, Ernst. 1948. Climatic change and pre–White Man. *University of Utah Bulletin* 38: 168–91.

————. 1952. Climatic history and the antiquity of man in California. *University of California Archaeological Survey Reports*, No. 16, pp. 23–31. Berkeley.

Bada, Jeffrey L., and Patricia M. Helfman. 1975. Amino acid racemization dating of fossil bones. *World Archaeology* 7(2): 160–73.

Bada, Jeffrey L., Roy A. Schroeder, and George F. Carter. 1974. New evidence for the antiquity of man in America deduced from aspartic acid racemization. *Science* 184: 791–93.

Bailey, Edgar H., ed. 1966. Geology of northern California. *California Division of Mines and Geology Bulletin* No. 190. San Francisco.

Bakker, Elna S. 1971. *An Island Called California.* Berkeley: Univ. of California Press.

Balls, Edward K. 1965. *Early Uses of California Plants.* Berkeley: Univ. of California Press.

Baumhoff, Martin A. 1955. Excavations of Site Teh-1 (Kingsley Cave). *University of California Archaeological Survey Reports*, No. 33, pp. 40–72. Berkeley.

————. 1963. Ecological determinants of aboriginal California populations. *University of California Publications in American Archaeology and Ethnology*, Vol. 49(2), pp. 155–236. Berkeley.

————. 1978. Environmental background. *In* Heizer 1978a, pp. 16–24.

Baumhoff, Martin A., and J. S. Byrne. 1959. Desert side-notched points as a time marker in California. *University of California Archaeological Survey Reports*, No. 48, pp. 32–65. Berkeley.

Baumhoff, M. A., and D. L. Olmstead. 1964. Palaihnihan: Radiocarbon support for glottochronology. *American Anthropologist* 65(2): 278–84.

Bean, Lowell J. 1974. Social organization in native California. *In* Bean & King 1974, pp. 11–34.

———. 1978. Social organization. *In* Heizer 1978a, pp. 673–82.

Bean, Lowell J., and Thomas C. Blackburn, eds. 1976. *Native Californians: A Theoretical Retrospective*. Socorro, N.M.: Ballena Press.

Bean, Lowell J., and Thomas F. King, eds. 1974. 'Antap: California Indian political and economic organization. *Ballena Press Anthropological Papers*, No. 2. Socorro, N.M.

Bean, Lowell J., and Harry W. Lawton. 1973. Some explanations for the rise of cultural complexity in native California, with comments on proto-agriculture and agriculture. *In* Lewis 1973, pp. v–xi.

Bean, Lowell J., and Sylvia B. Vane. 1977. *California Indians: Preliminary Resources. A Guide to Manuscripts, Artifacts, Documents, Serials, Music and Illustrations*. Socorro, N.M.: Ballena Press.

———. 1978. Cults and their transformations. *In* Heizer 1978a, pp. 662–72.

Bean, Walter. 1977. *California: An Interpretive History*. 3rd ed. New York: McGraw-Hill.

Beardsley, Robert K. 1946. The Monterey custom house flagpole: Archaeological findings. *California Historical Society Quarterly* 25: 204–18.

———. 1948. Culture sequences in central California archaeology. *American Antiquity* 14(1): 1–29.

———. 1954. Temporal and areal relationships in central California archaeology. Parts I and II. *University of California Archaeological Survey Reports*, Nos. 24 and 25. Berkeley.

Bennyhoff, James A. 1956. An appraisal of the archaeological resources of Yosemite National Park. *University of California Archaeological Survey Reports*, No. 34. Berkeley.

Benson, Larry V. 1978. Fluctuations in the level of pluvial Lake Lahontan during the last 40,000 years. *Quaternary Research* 9: 300–318.

Benson, Lyman. 1969. *The Native Cacti of California*. Stanford, Calif.: Stanford Univ. Press.

Berger, Rainer. 1975. Advances and results in radiocarbon dating: Early man in America. *World Archaeology* 7(2): 174–84.

Berger, R., R. Protsch, R. Reynolds, C. Rozaire, and J. Sackett. 1971. New radiocarbon dates based on bone collagen of California Paleoindians. *University of California Archaeological Research Facility Contributions*, No. 12, pp. 43–49. Berkeley.

Bettinger, Robert L. 1977. Aboriginal human ecology in Owens Valley: Prehistoric change in the Great Basin. *American Antiquity* 42(1): 3–17.

Bettinger, Robert L., and R. E. Taylor. 1974. Suggested revisions in archaeological sequences of the Great Basin in interior southern California. *Nevada Archaeological Survey Research Papers*, No. 5, pp. 1–26. Reno.

Bickel, Polly. 1978a. Changing sea levels along the California coast: Anthropological implications. *Journal of California Anthropology* 5(1): 6–20.

———. 1978b. Correction to sea level article. *Journal of California Anthropology* 5(2): 296–97.

———. 1979. A study of cultural resources in Redwood National Park. Unpublished ms. on file, Redwood National Park, Crescent City, and Sonoma State College, Rohnert Park.

Bickel, Polly, and Sally S. Salzman. 1979. New developments in northwestern California anthropology: Studies in Redwood National Park. Paper read at Second Conference on Scientific Research in the National Parks, November 1979, San Francisco.

Bischoff, James L., W. Morlin Childers, and R. J. Schleman. 1978. Comments on the Pleistocene age assignment and associations of a human burial from the Yuha Desert, California: A rebuttal. *American Antiquity* 43(4): 747–49.

Bischoff, J. L., Richard Merriam, W. M. Childers, and Reiner Protsch. 1976. Antiquity of man in America indicated by radiometric dates on the Yuha burial site. *Nature* 261: 128–29.

Bischoff, James L., and Robert J. Rosenbauer. 1981. Uranium series dating of human skeletal remains from the Del Mar and Sunnyvale sites, California. *Science* 213: 1003–8.

Blackburn, Thomas. 1974. Ceremonial integration and social interaction in aboriginal California. *In* Bean & King 1974, pp. 93–110.

Bonnischen, Robson. 1979. Pleistocene bone technology in the Beringian refugium. *Archaeological Survey of Canada Papers*, No. 79. National Museum of Man, Mercury Series. Ottawa.

Borland, Hal. 1976. *The History of Wildlife in America*. Washington, D.C.: National Wildlife Federation.

Brandes, Raymond. 1969. Excavations at Mission San Diego. *Masterkey* 43(3): 124–37.

Brown, Vinson, and George Lawrence. 1965. *The Californian Wildlife Region*. 2nd ed. Happy Camp, Calif.: Naturegraph.

Brown, Vinson, and Robert Livezey. 1962. *The Sierra Nevada Wildlife Region*. Happy Camp, Calif.: Naturegraph.

Bryan, A. L. 1969. Early man in America and the Late Pleistocene chronology of western Canada and Alaska. *Current Anthropology* 10: 339–65.

Bryan, Bruce. 1970. Archaeological explorations on San Nicolas Island. *Southwest Museum Papers*, No. 22. Highland Park, Calif.

Buckley, J., and E. Willis. 1970. Point St. George I, California. *Radiocarbon* 12(1): 172–75.

Butzer, Karl J. 1971. *Environment and Archaeology: An Ecological Approach to Prehistory*. 2nd ed. Chicago: Aldine.

Campbell, Bernard M., ed. 1976. *Humankind Emerging*. Boston: Little, Brown.

Campbell, Elizabeth W. C., and William H. Campbell. 1935. The Pinto Basin site. *Southwest Museum Papers*, No. 9. Highland Park, Calif.

———. 1937. The Lake Mohave Site. *In* E. W. Campbell et al., eds., The archaeology of Pleistocene Lake Mohave: A symposium, *Southwest Museum Papers*, No. 11, pp. 9–24. Highland Park, Calif.

Canby, Thomas Y. 1979. The search for the first Americans. *National Geographic* 156(3): 330–64.

Carter, George F. 1957. *Pleistocene Man in San Diego*. Baltimore: Johns Hopkins Press.

———. 1980. *Earlier Than You Think*. College Station: Texas A & M Univ. Press.

Castillo, Edward. 1978a. The impact of Euro-American explorations and settlement. *In* Heizer 1978a, pp. 99–127.

———. 1978b. Twentieth-century secular movements. *In* Heizer 1978a, pp. 713–18.

Chace, Paul C. 1969. The archaeology of "Cienega," the oldest historical structure on the Irvine Ranch. *Pacific Coast Archaeological Society Quarterly* 5(3): 39–55.

Chagnon, Napoleon A. 1970. Ecological and adaptive aspects of California shell money. *Archaeological Survey Annual Report*, Vol. 12, pp. 1–26. Los Angeles: Univ. of California.

Chard, Chester. 1975. *Northeast Asia in Prehistory*. 2nd ed. Madison: Univ. of Wisconsin Press.

Chartkoff, Joseph L. 1978. Transect interval sampling in forests. *American Antiquity* 43(1): 46–53.

Chartkoff, Joseph L., and Kerry K. Chartkoff. 1968. 1967 excavations at the Finch Site: Research strategy and procedures. *Archaeological Survey Annual Report*, Vol. 10, pp. 315–70. Los Angeles: Univ. of California.

———. 1973. Test excavations at the May Site, Seiad Valley, Siskiyou County, California. Unpublished ms. on file, Michigan State Univ., East Lansing.

———. 1975. Late period settlement of the middle Klamath River of northwest California. *American Antiquity* 40(2): 172–79.

———. 1979. Archaeological resources of the Chimney Rock Section, Gasquet–Orleans (G–O) Road, Six Rivers National Forest, California. *In* Theodoratus, Chartkoff & Chartkoff 1979, pp. 187–760.

———. 1980. Archaeology of the Patrick Site, 4-But-1. *Robert E. Schenck Archives of California Archaeology*, No. 77. Society for California Archaeology, Treganza Museum of Anthropology, San Francisco State Univ.

Chartkoff, Joseph L., and Jeffrey Childress. 1974. An archaeological survey of the proposed Paskenta-Newville Reservoir in Glenn and Tehama counties, northern California. *Robert E. Schenck Archives of California Archaeology*, No. 24. Society for California Archaeology, Treganza Museum of Anthropology, San Francisco State Univ.

Chartkoff, J. L., K. R. Johnson, and D. S. Miller. 1976. Ground stone industries in the Sacramento Valley, California. *Robert E. Schenck Archives of California Archaeology*, No. 63. Society for California Archaeology, Treganza Museum of Anthropology, San Francisco State Univ.

Childers, W. Morlin. 1974. Preliminary report on the Yuha burial, California. *Anthropological Journal of Canada* 12: 2–9.

Chinn, Thomas W., Mark H. Lai, and Philip P. Choy, eds. 1969. *A History of the Chinese in America: A Syllabus*. San Francisco: Chinese Historical Society of America.

Clark, Donovan. 1961. The obsidian hydration dating method. *Current Anthropology* 2: 111–14.

———. 1964. Archaeological chronology in California and the obsidian hydration method. *Archaeological Survey Annual Report for 1963–1964*, Vol. 6, pp. 143–211. Los Angeles: Univ. of California.

Cleland, Charles E. 1976. The focal-diffuse model: An evolutionary perspective on the prehistoric cultural adaptations of the eastern United States. *Midcontinental Journal of Archaeology* 1: 59–76.

Clewlow, C. W., Jr., ed. 1977. Four rock art studies. *Ballena Press Publications on North American Rock Art*, Vol. 1. Socorro, N.M.

———. 1978. Prehistoric rock art. *In* Heizer 1978a, pp. 619–25.

Cook, Sherburne F. 1976a. *The Population of the California Indians 1769–1970*. Berkeley: Univ. of California Press.

————. 1976b. *The Conflict Between the California Indian and White Civilization.* Berkeley: Univ. of California Press.

————. 1978. Historical demography. *In* Heizer 1978a, pp. 91–98.

Crabtree, Robert, Claude N. Warren, and D. L. True. 1963. Archaeological investigations at Bataquitos Lagoon, San Diego County, California. *Archaeological Survey Annual Report for 1962–1963*, Vol. 5, pp. 319–70. Los Angeles: Univ. of California.

Cruxent, José M. 1962. Phosphorus content of the Texas Street "hearths." *American Antiquity* 28(1): 90–91.

Curry, R. R. 1971. Holocene climatic and glacial history of the central Sierra Nevada, California. *Geological Society of America Special Paper* 123. New York.

Curtis, Freddie. 1959. Arroyo Sequit: Archaeological investigations of a late coastal site in Los Angeles County, California. *Archaeological Survey Association of Southern California Papers*, No. 4. Los Angeles.

Davidson, Keay. 1981. Del Mar man is only 11,000 years old, 2 geochemists contend. *Los Angeles Times*, Aug. 30, 1981, Part IX, p. 8.

Davis, Emma Lou. 1963. The desert culture of the western Great Basin: A lifeway of seasonal transhumance. *American Antiquity* 29(2): 202–12.

————. 1974. Paleo-Indian land use patterns. *Pacific Coast Archaeological Society Quarterly* 10(2): 1–16.

————. 1975. The "exposed archaeology" of China Lake, California. *American Antiquity* 40(1): 39–53.

————. 1978a. The ancient Californians: Rancholabrean hunters of the Mojave Lake country. *Science Series*, Vol. 29. Los Angeles: Los Angeles County Museum of Natural History.

————. 1978b. Mammoths, models and muddles: A commentary on Mosimann and Martin's "Simulating overkill by Paleoindians." *Pacific Coast Archaeological Society Quarterly* 14(4): 22–26.

Davis, Emma Lou, Clark W. Brott, and David L. Weide. 1969. The western lithic co-tradition. *San Diego Museum Papers*, No. 16. San Diego.

Davis, Emma Lou, George Carter, Herbert Minshall, Morlin Childers, and Chris Hardaker. 1979. Macrolith industries of southern California. Unpublished ms. delivered at the 14th Pacific Science Congress, August 1979, Khabarousk, USSR.

Davis, Emma Lou, and Richard Shutler, Jr. 1969. Recent discoveries of fluted points in California and Nevada. *Nevada State Museum Anthropological Papers*, No. 14, pp. 154–78. Reno.

Davis, James T. 1960. The archaeology of the Fernandez Site, a San Francisco Bay region shellmound. *University of California Archaeological Survey Reports*, No. 49, pp. 11–52. Berkeley.

————. 1961. Trade routes and economic exchange among the Indians of California. *University of California Archaeological Survey Reports*, No. 54. Berkeley.

Davis, James, and Robert Elston. 1972. New stratigraphic evidence of late Quaternary climatic change in northwestern Nevada. *In* Don D. Fowler, ed., Great Basin cultural ecology: A symposium, pp. 43–56. *Desert Research Institute Publications in the Social Sciences*, No. 8. Reno.

Davis, James T., and Adan E. Treganza. 1959. The Patterson Mound: A comparative analysis of the archaeology of site Ala-328. *University of California Archaeological Survey Reports*, No. 47. Berkeley.

Decker, Dean. 1969. Early archaeology on Catalina Island: Problems and potential. *Archaeological Survey Annual Report*, Vol. 11, pp. 69–84. Los Angeles: Univ. of California.

Deetz, James. 1963. Archaeological investigations at La Purísima Mission. *Archaeological Survey Annual Report for 1962–1963*, Vol. 5, pp. 161–244. Los Angeles: Univ. of California.

———. 1977. *In Small Things Forgotten*. Garden City, N.Y.: Anchor Books.

———. 1980. What is historical archaeology? *Odyssey Magazine*, pp. 32–34. Boston: Public Broadcasting Associates.

Donnan, Christopher B. 1964. A suggested culture sequence for the Providence Mountains (eastern Mohave Desert). *Archaeological Survey Annual Report for 1963–1964*, Vol. 6, pp. 1–27. Los Angeles: Univ. of California.

Drake, R. J. 1952. Samplings in history at the Sanchez Adobe, San Mateo County, California. *El Palacio* 59: 19–29.

Driver, Philip. 1961. *Indians of North America*. Chicago: Univ. of Chicago Press.

Drover, C. E. 1975. Early ceramics from southern California. *Journal of California Anthropology* 2(1): 101–7.

———. 1978. Prehistoric ceramic objects from Catalina Island. *Journal of California Anthropology* 5(1): 78–83.

Drover, C. E., R. E. Taylor, T. Cairns, and J. E. Erickson. 1979. Thermoluminescence determinations on early ceramic materials from coastal southern California. *American Antiquity* 44(2): 285–95.

DuBois, Cora A. 1939. The 1870 Ghost Dance. *University of California Anthropological Records*, Vol. 3(1), pp. 1–151. Berkeley.

Elsasser, Albert B. 1960. The archaeology of the Sierra Nevada in California and Nevada. *University of California Archaeological Survey Reports*, No. 51, pp. 1–93. Berkeley.

———. 1978a. Development of regional prehistoric cultures. *In* Heizer 1978a, pp. 37–57.

———. 1978b. Two unusual artifacts from the Sierra Nevada of California. *Journal of California Anthropology* 5(1): 73–78.

Elsasser, Albert B., and Robert F. Heizer. 1966. Excavations of two northwestern California coastal sites. *University of California Archaeological Survey Reports*, No. 67(1), pp. 1–150. Berkeley.

Elston, Robert. 1970. A test excavation at the Dangberg Hot Spring Site (26-Do-1), Douglas County, Nevada. *Nevada Archaeological Survey Reports*, Vol. 4(4). Reno.

———. 1971. A contribution to Washo archaeology. *Nevada Archaeological Survey Research Papers*, No. 2. Reno.

Elston, R., J. O. Davis, A. Leventhal, and C. Covington. 1977. The archaeology of the Tahoe Range of the Truckee River. Unpublished ms. on file, Northern Division of the Nevada Archaeological Survey, University of Nevada, Reno.

Erickson, Jonathan E. 1975. New results in obsidian hydration dating. *World Archaeology* 7(2): 151–59.

———. 1977. Egalitarian exchange systems in California: A preliminary view. *In* T. K. Earle and J. E. Erickson, eds., *Exchange Systems in Prehistory*, pp. 109–26. New York: Academic Press.

Etter, Patricia. 1980. The West Coast Chinese and opium smoking. *In* Schuyler 1980, pp. 231–41.

Evans, William S., Jr. 1969. California Indian pottery: A native contribution to the culture of the ranchos. *Pacific Coast Archaeological Society Quarterly* 5(3): 71–81.

———. 1980. Food and fantasy: Material culture of the Chinese in California and the west, circa 1850–1900. *In* Schuyler 1980, pp. 243–56.

Evermann, B. W., and H. W. Clark. 1931. A distributional list of freshwater fishes known to occur in California. *California Fish and Game Commission Bulletin*, No. 35. Sacramento.

Fagan, Brian. 1977. *Elusive Treasure: The Story of Early Archaeology in the Americas*. New York: Scribner's.

Fages, Pedro. 1937. *A Historical, Political and Natural Description of California*. Translated by Herbert Priestly. Berkeley: Univ. of California Press.

Fenenga, Franklin. 1973. Archaeological work in the Hidden Valley Reservoir area, Madera County, California. Unpublished ms. on file, Arizona Archaeological Center, National Park Service, Tucson.

Ferlatte, William J. 1974. *A Flora of the Trinity Alps*. Berkeley: Univ. of California Press.

Fitting, James E., ed. 1973. *The Development of North American Archaeology*. Garden City, N.Y.: Anchor Books.

Fitzwater, Robert J. 1962. Final report on two seasons' excavations at El Portal, Mariposa County, California. *Archaeological Survey Annual Report for 1961–1962*, pp. 234–85. Los Angeles: Univ. of California.

———. 1968. Big Oak Flat: Two archaeological sites in Yosemite National Park. *Archaeological Survey Annual Report*, Vol. 10, pp. 275–314. Los Angeles: Univ. of California.

Fladmark, K. R. 1979. Routes: Alternate migration corridors for early man in North America. *American Antiquity* 44(1): 55–69.

Flannery, Kent V. 1968. Archaeological systems theory and early Mesoamerica. *In* Betty J. Meggers, ed., *Anthropological Archaeology in the Americas*, pp. 67–87. Washington, D.C.: Anthropological Society of Washington.

Flint, Richard F. 1957. *Glacial and Pleistocene Geology*. 3d ed. New York: Wiley.

Forbes, Jack D. 1969. *Native Americans of California and Nevada: A Handbook*. Happy Camp, Calif.: Naturegraph.

Frederickson, David A. 1968. Archaeological investigations at CCo-30 near Alamo, Contra Costa County, California. *Center for Archaeological Research at Davis Publications*, No. 1, pp. 1–187. Davis: Univ. of California.

———. 1974a. Cultural diversity in early central California: A view from the North Coast Ranges. *Journal of California Anthropology* 1(1): 41–53.

———. 1974b. Social change in prehistory: A central California example. *In* Bean & King 1974, pp. 55–74.

Freeman, John F. 1965. University anthropology: Early departments in the United States. *Kroeber Anthropological Society Papers*, Vol. 32, pp. 78–90. Berkeley.

Friedman, Irving, and William Long. 1976. Hydration rate of obsidian. *Science* 191: 347–52.

Friedman, Irving, and R. L. Smith. 1960. A new dating method using obsidian. Part I: The development of the technique. *American Antiquity* 25(4): 476–522.

Fritz, John, and Fred Plog. 1970. The nature of archaeological explanation. *American Antiquity* 35(3): 405–12.

Fryxell, Roald, et al. 1968. Human skeletal material and artifacts from sediments of Pinedale (Wisconsin) glacial age in southeastern Washington, United States. *Proceedings of the 8th International Congress of Anthropological and Ethnological Sciences, 1968, Ethnology and Archaeology*, Vol. III, pp. 176–81. Tokyo and Kyoto.

Gabel, Norman E. 1952. Report on archaeological research project at La Purísima Mission State Monument during June 25 to August 4, 1952. Unpublished ms. on file, California State Department of Parks and Recreation, Sacramento.

Galdikas, Biruté. 1968. The Mulholland Site (4-LAn-246), an occupation site in the Santa Monica Mountains. *Archaeological Survey Annual Report*, Vol. 10, pp. 162–76. Los Angeles: Univ. of California.

Galdikas-Brindamour, Biruté. 1970. Trade and subsistence at Mulholland: A site report on LAn-246. *Archaeological Survey Annual Report*, Vol. 12, pp. 107–48. Los Angeles: Univ. of California.

Garfinkel, Alan P. 1978. "Coso" style pictographs of the southern Sierra Nevada. *Journal of California Anthropology* 5(1): 95–101.

Gerow, Bert. 1974. Co-traditions and convergent trends in prehistoric California. *San Luis Obispo County Archaeology Society Occasional Papers*, No. 8. San Luis Obispo.

Gerow, Bert, and Roland W. Force. 1968. *An Analysis of the University Village Complex with a Reappraisal of Central California Archaeology*. Stanford, Calif.: Stanford Univ. Press.

Gifford, Edward W. 1940. California bone artifacts. *University of California Anthropological Records*, Vol. 3(2), pp. 153–237. Berkeley.

———. 1947. Californian shell artifacts. *University of California Anthropological Records*, Vol. 9(1), pp. 1–114. Berkeley.

Glassow, Michael A. 1965. The Conejo Rock Shelter: An inland Chumash site in Ventura County, California. *Archaeological Survey Annual Report*, Vol. 7, pp. 19–80. Los Angeles: Univ. of California.

———. 1977. An archaeological overview of the northern Channel Islands, California, including Santa Barbara Island. Unpublished ms. on file, Western Archaeological Center, National Park Service, Tucson.

Glennan, William S. 1971. Concave-based lanceolate fluted projectile points from California. *Masterkey* 45(1): 27–32.

———. 1976. The Mannix Lake lithic industry: Early lithic tradition or workshop refuse? *Journal of New World Archaeology* 1(7): 43–61.

Goldschmidt, Walter R. 1951. Nomlaki ethnography. *University of California Publications in American Archaeology and Ethnology*, Vol. 42(4), pp. 303–443. Berkeley.

Gothold, Jane. 1969. Observations on the recovered glass. *Pacific Coast Archaeological Society Quarterly* 5(3): 56–60.

Gould, Richard A. 1966. Archaeology of the Point St. George Site and Tolowa prehistory. *University of California Publications in Anthropology*, Vol. 4. Berkeley.

———. 1972. A radiocarbon date from the Point St. George Site, northwestern California. *University of California Archaeological Research Facility Contributions*, No. 14, pp. 41–44. Berkeley.

———. 1977. *Explorations in Ethno-Archaeology*. New York: Academic Press.

Grant, Campbell. 1965. *The Rock Paintings of the Chumash*. Berkeley: Univ. of California Press.

———. 1978. Chumash: Introduction. *In* Heizer 1978a, pp. 505–8.

Grant, Campbell, James W. Baird, and J. Kenneth Pringle. 1968. Rock drawings of the Coso Range, Inyo County, California. *Maturango Museum Publications*, No. 4. China Lake, Calif.

Grayson, D. K. 1976. The Nightfire Island avifauna and the Altithermal. *Nevada Archaeological Survey Research Papers*, No. 6, pp. 167–86. Reno.

Green, F. E. 1963. The Clovis blades: An important addition to the Llano Complex. *American Antiquity* 29(2): 145–65.

Greenwood, Roberta S. 1969. The Browne Site: Early milling stone horizon in southern California. *Memoirs of the Society for American Archaeology*, No. 23. Salt Lake City.

———. 1972. 9000 years of prehistory at Diablo Canyon, San Luis Obispo County, California. *San Luis Obispo County Archaeological Society Occasional Papers*, No. 7. San Luis Obispo.

———. 1978. Obispeño and Purisimeño Chumash. *In* Heizer 1978a, pp. 520–23.

———. 1980. The Chinese on Main Street. *In* Schuyler 1980, pp. 203–30.

Griffin, James B. 1979. The origin and dispersion of American Indians in North America. *In* Laughlin & Harper, 1979, pp. 43–55.

Haag, William G. 1962. The Bering Strait Land Bridge. *Scientific American* 206(1): 112–23.

Hall, Carroll D. 1958. Old Sacramento: A report on its significance to the city, state and nation, with recommendations for the preservation and use of its principal historical structures and sites, part 1. Unpublished ms. on file, California Department of Parks and Recreation, Sacramento.

Hansen, Gladys. 1970. *The Chinese in California: A Brief Bibliographic History*. Portland, Oreg.: Abel.

Harrington, Mark R. 1940. Temporary Indian barracks at Purísima Mission. Unpublished ms. on file, California Department of Parks and Recreation, La Purísima State Historical Monument, Lompoc, Calif.

———. 1948. An ancient site at Borax Lake, California. *Southwest Museum Papers*, No. 16. Highland Park, Calif.

———. 1957. A Pinto site at Little Lake, California. *Southwest Museum Papers*, No. 17. Highland Park, Calif.

Harris, Marvin. 1968. *The Rise of Anthropological Theory*. New York: Columbia Univ. Press.

Harrison, William A. 1965. Mikiw: A coastal Chumash village. *Archaeological Survey Annual Report*, Vol. 7, pp. 91–178. Los Angeles: Univ. of California.

Harrison, William A., and Edith S. Harrison. 1966. An archaeological sequence for the Hunting People of Santa Barbara, California. *Archaeological Survey Annual Report*, Vol. 8, pp. 1–89. Los Angeles: Univ. of California.

Hayes, Steve, and Paul V. Long, Jr. 1969. Stone artifacts from Ora-96. *Pacific Coast Archaeological Society Quarterly* 5(3): 63–70.

Haynes, C. Vance. 1964. Fluted projectile points: Their age and dispersion. *Science* 145: 1408–13.

———. 1969. The earliest Americans. *Science* 166: 709–15.

———. 1973. The Calico Site: Artifacts or geofacts? *Science* 181: 305–10.

Heizer, Robert F. 1941. *Archaeological Evidence of Sebastian Rodríguez Cermeño's California Visit in 1595*. San Francisco: California Historical Society.

———. 1947. Francis Drake and the California Indians, 1579. *University of California Publications in American Archaeology and Ethnology*, Vol. 42(3), pp. 251–302. Berkeley.

———. 1949. The archaeology of central California I: The Early Horizon. *University of California Anthropological Records*, Vol. 12(1), pp. 1–84. Berkeley.

———. 1951. A prehistoric Yurok ceremonial site (Hum-174). *University of California Archaeological Survey Reports*, No. 11, pp. 1–4. Berkeley.

———, ed. 1953. The archaeology of the Napa region. *University of California Anthropological Records*, Vol. 12(6), pp. 225–338.

———. 1964. The West Coast. *In* Jennings & Norbeck 1964, pp. 174–237.

———. 1972. *California's Oldest Historical Relic?* Berkeley: Robert H. Lowie Museum of Anthropology, Univ. of California.

———, ed. 1974a. *The Destruction of California Indians: A Collection of Documents from the Period 1847 to 1865 in which are Described Some of the Things that Happened to Some of the Indians of California.* Santa Barbara: Peregrine Smith.

———, ed. 1974b. *They Were Only Diggers.* Socorro, N.M.: Ballena Press.

———, ed. 1978a. *Handbook of North American Indians 8: California.* Washington, D.C.: Smithsonian Institution.

———. 1978b. History of research. *In* Heizer 1978a, pp. 6–15.

———. 1978c. Introduction. *In* Heizer 1978a, pp. 1–5.

———. 1978d. Trade and trails. *In* Heizer 1978a, pp. 690–93.

———. 1978e. Treaties. *In* Heizer 1978a, pp. 701–4.

Heizer, Robert F., and Alan F. Almquist. 1971. *The Other Californians: Prejudice and Discrimination Under Spain, Mexico and the United States to 1920.* Berkeley: Univ. of California Press.

Heizer, Robert F., and Martin A. Baumhoff. 1962. *Prehistoric Rock Art of Nevada and Eastern California.* Berkeley: Univ. of California Press.

Heizer, Robert F., and C. William Clewlow, Jr. 1973. *Prehistoric Rock Art of California.* 2 vols. Socorro, N.M.: Ballena Press.

Heizer, Robert F., and Albert B. Elsasser. 1953. Some archaeological sites and cultures of the central Sierra Nevada. *University of California Archaeological Survey Reports*, No. 21. Berkeley.

———. 1963. Original accounts of the Lone Woman of San Nicolas Island. *In* Robert F. Heizer and Albert B. Elsasser, eds., *Aboriginal California*, pp. 121–81. Berkeley: Univ. of California Archaeological Research Facility.

———. 1964. Archaeology of Hum-67, the Gunther Island Site in Humboldt Bay, California. *University of California Archaeological Survey Reports*, No. 62, pp. 5–122. Berkeley.

Heizer, Robert F., and John Mills. 1952. *The Four Ages of Tsurai.* Berkeley: Univ. of California Press.

Heizer, Robert F., and Adan E. Treganza. 1944. Mines and quarries of the Indians of California. *California Journal of Mines and Geology* 40(3): 291–359.

Heizer, Robert F., and M. A. Whipple, eds. 1971. *The California Indians: A Source Book.* 2nd ed. Berkeley: Univ. of California Press.

Helfin, E. 1966. The Pistol River Site of southwest Oregon. *University of California Archaeological Survey Reports*, No. 67(2), pp. 151–282. Berkeley.

Henn, Winfield G., Thomas L. Jackson, and Julius Schlocker. 1972. Buried human bones at the "BART" Site, San Francisco. *California Geology* 25: 208–9.

Hester, Thomas R. 1973. Chronological ordering of Great Basin prehistory. *University of California Archaeological Research Facility Contributions*, No. 17. Berkeley.

———. 1980. Early populations in prehistoric Texas. *Archaeology* 33(6): 26–33.

Heusser, L. E. 1977. Marine pollen in Santa Barbara, California: A 12,000-year record. *Geological Society of America Bulletin*, Vol. 89, pp. 673–78. New York.

Hickerson, Nancy P. 1980. *Linguistic Anthropology.* New York: Holt, Rinehart and Winston.

Hill, Dorothy. 1978. *The Indians of Chico Rancheria.* Sacramento: California Department of Parks and Recreation.

Hoijer, Harry. 1956. The chronology of the Athabascan languages. *International Journal of American Linguistics* 22: 219–32.

Hoover, Robert L. 1979. The mission at San Antonio de Padua. *Archaeology* 32(6): 56–58.

Hopkins, David M., ed. 1967. *The Bering Land Bridge.* Stanford, Calif.: Stanford Univ. Press.

———. 1979. Landscape and climate of Beringia during late Pleistocene and Holocene times. *In* Laughlin & Harper 1979, pp. 15–41.

Howard, Thomas F. K. 1980. Traces. *East Bay Express* 2(28): 1–4.

Hudson, Dee Travis. 1976. Marine archaeology along the southern California coast. *San Diego Museum Papers*, No. 9. San Diego.

Hudson, Travis, and Thomas Blackburn. 1978. The integration of myth and ritual in south-central California: The "Northern Complex." *Journal of California Anthropology* 5(2): 225–50.

Hudson, Travis, Georgia Lee, and Ken Hedges. 1979. Solstice observers and observatories in native California. *Journal of California and Great Basin Anthropology* 1(1): 39–63.

Hudson, Travis, Janice Timbrook, and Melissa Rempe. 1978. Tomol: Chumash watercraft as described in the ethnographic notes of John P. Harrington. *Ballena Press Anthropological Papers*, No. 9. Socorro, N.M.

Hudson, Travis, and Ernest Underhay. 1978. *Crystals in the Sky: An Intellectual Odyssey Involving Chumash Astronomy, Cosmology and Rock Art.* Socorro, N.M.: Ballena Press.

Hughes, Richard E. 1978. Aspects of prehistoric Wiyot exchange and social ranking. *Journal of California Anthropology* 5(1): 53–66.

Humphrey, Richard V. 1965. The La Purísima Mission cemetery. *Archaeological Survey Annual Report*, Vol. 7, pp. 179–92. Los Angeles: Univ. of California.

Hunt, Alice P. 1960. Archaeology of the Death Valley salt pan, California. *University of Utah Anthropology Papers*, Vol. 47. Salt Lake City.

Hunt, Charles B. 1975. *Death Valley: Geology, Ecology, Archaeology.* Berkeley: Univ. of California Press.

Hutchinson, William H. 1969. *California: Two Centuries of Man, Land and Growth in the Golden State.* Palo Alto: American West.

Ingles, Lloyd. 1965. *Mammals of the Pacific States.* Stanford, Calif.: Stanford Univ. Press.

Irving, W. N., and C. R. Harington. 1973. Upper Pleistocene radiocarbon-dated artifacts from the northern Yukon. *Science* 179: 335–40.

Irwin, Charles N. 1978. A material representation of a sacred tradition. *Journal of California Anthropology* 5(1): 90–95.

Jennings, Jesse D. 1974. *Prehistory of North America.* 2nd ed. New York: McGraw-Hill.

———, ed. 1978. *Ancient Native Americans.* San Francisco: Freeman.

Jennings, Jesse D., and Edward Norbeck, eds. 1964. *Prehistoric Man in the New World.* Chicago: Univ. of Chicago Press.

Jepson, Willis L. 1963. *A Manual of the Flowering Plants of California*. Berkeley: Univ. of California Press.

Jewell, Donald P. 1964. Archaeology of the Oroville Dam Spillway. *Archaeological Report*, No. 10(1), pp. 1–39. California Department of Parks and Recreation, Sacramento.

Johnson, Frederick, and John P. Miller. 1958. Review of *Pleistocene Man in San Diego* by George F. Carter. *American Antiquity* 24(2): 206–10.

Johnson, Jerald J. 1967. The archaeology of the Camanche Reservoir locality, California. *Sacramento Anthropological Society Papers*, No. 6. Sacramento.

———. 1970. Archaeological investigations at the Applegate Site (4-Ama-56). *Center for Archaeological Research at Davis Publications*, No. 2, pp. 65–144. Davis: Univ. of California.

———. 1973. Archaeological investigations in northeastern California (1939–1972). Unpublished doctoral dissertation, Department of Anthropology, University of California, Davis (also available from University Microfilms, Inc., Ann Arbor, Mich.).

———. 1978. Yana. *In* Heizer 1978a, pp. 361–69.

Johnson, Keith L. 1966. Site LAn-2: A late manifestation of the Topanga Complex in southern California prehistory. *University of California Anthropological Records*, Vol. 23, pp. 1–36. Berkeley.

———. 1976. Test excavations at the Old Tower Site (CA-Sha-192), Whiskeytown Recreation Area, Shasta County, California. Unpublished ms. on file, National Park Service, Tucson, Ariz.

Johnson, Keith L., and L. Skjelstad. 1974. The salvage archaeology of 4-Sha-177, Whiskeytown National Recreation Area, Shasta County, California. Unpublished ms. on file, National Park Service, Tucson, Ariz.

Johnson, LeRoy. 1968. Obsidian hydration rate for the Klamath Basin of California and Oregon. *Science* 165: 1354–56.

Johnston, Bernice E. 1962. *California's Gabrielino Indians. Frederick Webb Hodge Anniversary Publication Fund*, Vol. 8. Highland Park, Calif.: Southwest Museum.

Jordan, Lois B. 1973. *Mexican Americans: Resources to Build Cultural Understanding*. Littleton, Colo.: Libraries Unlimited.

Judge, James. 1977. *PaleoIndian Settlement in the Central Rio Grande Valley*. 2nd printing. Albuquerque: Univ. of New Mexico Press.

King, Chester D. 1962. Excavations at Parker Mesa (LAn-215). *Archaeological Survey Annual Report for 1961–1962*, pp. 91–155. Los Angeles: Univ. of California.

———. 1967. The Sweetwater Mesa Site (LAn-267) and its place in southern California prehistory. *Archaeological Survey Annual Report*, Vol. 9, pp. 25–76. Los Angeles: Univ. of California.

———. 1974. The explanation of differences and similarities among beads used in prehistoric and early historic California. *In* Bean & King 1974, pp. 75–92.

———. 1976. Chumash inter-village economic exchange. *In* Bean & Blackburn 1976, pp. 289–318.

———. 1978. Protohistoric and historic archaeology. *In* Heizer 1978a, pp. 58–68.

———. 1980. Social change at Tecolate Canyon: A comparison of mortuary contexts. Unpublished ms. presented at the 1980 annual meeting of the Society for California Archaeology, April 3–5, Redding.

King, Chester D., Thomas Blackburn, and Ernest Chandonet. 1968. The archaeological investigation of three sites on the Century Ranch, western Los Angeles County, California. *Archaeological Survey Annual Report*, Vol. 10, pp. 12–107. Los Angeles: Univ. of California.

King, Linda B. 1969. The Medea Creek Cemetery: An investigation of social organization from mortuary practices. *Archaeological Survey Annual Report*, Vol. 11, pp. 23–68. Los Angeles: Univ. of California.

King, Thomas F. 1971. The dead at Tiburon. *Northwest California Archaeological Society Occasional Papers*, No. 2, pp. 1–74. Daly City, Calif.

———. 1974. The evolution of status ascription around San Francisco Bay. *In* Bean & King 1974, pp. 35–54.

King, Thomas F., P. P. Hickman, and G. Berg. 1977. *Anthropological and Historic Preservation: Caring for the Nation's Clutter*. New York: Academic Press.

Kirk, Ruth, and Richard D. Daugherty. 1978. *Exploring Washington Archaeology*. Seattle: Univ. of Washington Press.

Koloseike, Alan, and M. Peterson. 1963. Macro-column shell analysis. Appendix III *in* Crabtree, Warren & True 1963, pp. 439–61.

Kowta, Makoto. 1969. The Sayles Complex: A later Milling-Stone assemblage from Cajon Pass and the ecological implications of its scraper planes. *University of California Publications in Anthropology*, Vol. 6. Berkeley.

Krantz, Grover. 1977. The populating of western North America. *Occasional Papers in Method and Theory in California Archaeology*, Vol. 1. San Francisco: Society for California Archaeology.

Krieger, Alex. 1964. Early man in the new world. *In* Jennings & Norbeck 1964, pp. 23–81.

Kroeber, Alfred L. 1925. Handbook of the Indians of California. *Bureau of American Ethnology Bulletins*, No. 78. Washington, D.C.: Smithsonian Institution.

———. 1939. Cultural and natural areas of native North America. *University of California Publications in American Archaeology and Ethnology*, Vol. 38, pp. 1–242. Berkeley.

———. 1962. The nature of land-holding groups in aboriginal California. *University of California Archaeological Survey Reports*, No. 56, pp. 19–58. Berkeley.

———. 1976. *Yurok Myths*. Berkeley: Univ. of California Press.

Kroeber, Alfred L., and Samuel A. Barrett. 1960. Fishing among the Indians of northwestern California. *University of California Anthropological Records*, Vol. 21, pp. 1–210. Berkeley.

Kroeber, Alfred L., and Edward W. Gifford. 1949. World renewal: A cult system of native northwest California. *University of California Anthropological Records*, Vol. 13(1): 1–156. Berkeley.

Kroeber, Theodora. 1959. *Ishi in Two Worlds*. Berkeley: Univ. of California Press.

Lampl, Michelle, and Baruch S. Blumberg. 1979. Blood polymorphisms and the origin of New World populations. *In* Laughlin & Harper 1979, pp. 107–23.

Landberg, Leif C. W. 1965. The Chumash Indians of southern California. *Southwest Museum Papers*, No. 19. Highland Park, Calif.

Langenwalter, Paul E., II. 1980. The archaeology of nineteenth-century Chinese subsistence at the Lower China Store, Madera County, California. *In* Schuyler 1980, pp. 257–80.

Lanning, Edward P. 1963. Archaeology of the Rose Spring Site, Iny-372. *University of California Publications in American Archaeology and Ethnology*, Vol. 49, pp. 237–336. Berkeley.

Lapp, Randolph M. 1977. *Blacks in Gold Rush California*. New Haven: Yale Univ. Press.

Laughlin, William S., and Albert B. Harper, eds. 1979. *The First Americans: Origins, Affinities and Adaptations*. Stuttgart and New York: Gustav Fischer.

Laughlin, William S., and Susan I. Wolf. 1979. The first Americans: Origins, affinities and adaptations. *In* Laughlin & Harper 1979, pp. 1–11.

Lavender, David. 1972. *California: Land of New Beginnings*. New York: Harper and Row.

Leakey, L. S. B., R. D. Simpson, and Thomas Clements. 1970. Man in America: The Calico Mountains excavations. *1970 Britannica Yearbook of Science and the Future*, pp. 64–79. Chicago: Encyclopedia Britannica.

Leakey, L. S. B., R. D. Simpson, Thomas Clements, Rainer Berger, and John Witthoff. 1972. *Pleistocene Man at Calico*. Bloomington, Calif.: San Bernardino County Museum Association.

Lee, Georgia, and Stephen Horne. 1978. The Painted Rock Site (SBa-502 and SBa-526): Sapaksi, the House of the Sun. *Journal of California Anthropology* 5(2): 216–24.

Leonard, N. Nelson, III. 1966. Ven-70 and its place in the Late Period of the western Santa Monica Mountains. *Archaeological Survey Annual Report*, Vol. 8, pp. 215–41. Los Angeles: Univ. of California.

———. 1971. Natural and social environments of the Santa Monica Mountains (6000 B.C. to A.D. 1800). *Archaeological Survey Annual Report*, Vol. 13, pp. 93–135. Los Angeles: Univ. of California.

Leonhardy, Frank C. 1961. The cultural position of the Iron Gate Site. Unpublished master's thesis, Department of Anthropology, University of Oregon, Eugene.

———. 1967. The archaeology of a late prehistoric village in northwestern California. *Museum of Natural History Bulletins*, No. 4. Eugene: Univ. of Oregon.

Levi, Jerome M. 1978. Wii'ipay: The Living Rocks—ethnographic notes on crystal magic among some California Yumans. *Journal of California Anthropology* 5(1): 42–52.

Lewis, Henry T., ed. 1973. Patterns of Indian burning in California. *Ballena Press Anthropological Papers*, No. 1. Socorro, N.M.

Libby, Willard F. 1955. *Radiocarbon Dating*. 2nd ed. Chicago: Univ. of Chicago Press.

Lillard, Jeremiah B., Robert F. Heizer, and Frank Fenenga. 1939. An introduction to the archaeology of central California. *Sacramento Junior College, Department of Anthropology Bulletins*, No. 2. Sacramento.

Loud, L. L. 1918. Ethnography and archaeology of the Wiyot territory. *University of California Publications in American Archaeology and Ethnology*, Vol. 14(3), pp. 221–436. Berkeley.

———. 1924. The Stege Mounds at Richmond, California. *University of California Publications in American Archaeology and Ethnology*, Vol. 17, pp. 355–72. Berkeley.

Lowie, Robert. 1937. *The History of Ethnological Theory*. Berkeley: Univ. of California Press.

MacNeish, Richard S. 1971. Early man in the Andes. *Scientific American* 224(4): 74–85.

———. 1976. Early man in the new world. *American Scientist* 64: 316–27.

Madsen, David B. 1978. Recent data bearing on the question of a hiatus in the eastern Great Basin. *American Antiquity* 43(4): 508–9.

Madsen, D. B., and M. S. Berry. 1975. A reassessment of northeastern Great Basin prehistory. *American Antiquity* 40(3): 391–405.

Mannion, Curtis. 1969. A report of three archaeological sites with historical components. *In* Thomas F. King, ed., The archaeology of the Buchanan Reservoir Region, Madera County, California, *San Francisco State University Anthropology Museum Occasional Papers*, No. 5, pp. 219–64. San Francisco.

Martin, Paul S., and Jeremy Sabloff. 1975. *A History of North American Archaeology*. Cambridge: Harvard Univ. Press.

Martin, Paul S., and Henry E. Wright, eds. 1967. *Pleistocene Extinctions: The Search for a Cause*. New Haven: Yale Univ. Press.

McCorkle, Thomas. 1978. Intergroup conflict. *In* Heizer 1978a, pp. 694–700.

McGimsey, Charles R., III. 1972. *Public Archaeology*. New York: Seminar Press.

McHargue, Georgess, and Michael Roberts. 1977. *A Field Guide to Conservation Archaeology in North America*. Philadelphia: Lippincott.

McKusick, Marshall B. 1961. Excavations at Goleta, Part 1: Methodology. *Archaeological Survey Annual Report for 1960–1961*, pp. 339–48. Los Angeles: Univ. of California.

McKusick, Marshall B., and R. S. Watson. 1959. Grinding implements from Vaquero Reservoir, San Luis Obispo and Santa Barbara Counties. *Archaeological Survey Annual Report for 1958–1959*, pp. 13–16. Los Angeles: Univ. of California.

Meighan, Clement W. 1950. Excavations in sixteenth-century shellmounds at Drake's Bay, California. *University of California Archaeological Survey Reports*, No. 9, pp. 27–32. Berkeley.

———. 1954. A late complex in southern California prehistory. *Southwestern Journal of Anthropology* 10: 215–27.

———. 1955. Archaeology of the North Coast Ranges, California. *University of California Archaeological Survey Reports*, No. 30, pp. 1–39. Berkeley.

———. 1959a. California cultures and the concept of an Archaic stage. *American Antiquity* 24(3): 289–305.

———. 1959b. The Little Harbor Site, Catalina Island: An example of ecological interpretation in archaeology. *American Antiquity* 24(4): 383–405.

———. 1965. Pacific Coast archaeology. *In* Henry E. Wright and David G. Frey, eds., *The Quaternary of the United States: A review volume for the VII Congress of the International Association for Quaternary Research*, pp. 709–22. Princeton, N.J.: Princeton Univ. Press.

———. 1978. California. *In* Taylor & Meighan 1978, pp. 223–40. New York: Academic Press.

Meighan, Clement W., and Hal Eberhart. 1953. Archaeological resources of San Nicolas Island, California. *American Antiquity* 19(2): 109–25.

Meighan, Clement W., and C. Vance Haynes, Jr. 1970. The Borax Lake Site revisited. *Science* 167: 1213–21.

Meighan, Clement W., and Robert F. Heizer. 1952. Archaeological exploration of sixteenth-century Indian mounds at Drake's Bay. *California Historical Society Quarterly* 31: 98–108.

Meighan, Clement W., and Francis Riddell. 1972. The Maru Cult of the Pomo Indians: A California Ghost Dance survival. *Southwest Museum Papers*, No. 23. Highland Park, Calif.

Merriam, C. Hart. 1955. *Studies of California Indians*. Berkeley: Univ. of California Press.

Mills, John E. 1950. Recent developments in the study of northwest California archaeology. *University of California Archaeological Survey Reports*, No. 7, pp. 13–24. Berkeley.

Minshall, Herbert L. 1976. *The Broken Stones*. La Jolla, Calif.: Copley Books.

Montgomery, Jean. 1968. *The Wrath of the Coyote*. New York: Morrow.

Mooney, Harold A. 1973. Plant communities and vegetation. *In* R. M. Lloyd and R. S. Mitchell, *A Flora of the White Mountains of California and Nevada*, pp. 7–17. Berkeley: Univ. of California Press.

Moratto, Michael J. 1970. Archaeology of the Buchanan Reservoir region, Madera County, California. *Treganza Museum of Anthropology Occasional Papers*, Vol. 7. San Francisco: California State Univ.

————. 1971. A study of prehistory in the Tuolumne River Valley, California. *Treganza Museum of Anthropology Occasional Papers*, Vol. 9. San Francisco: California State Univ.

————. 1973a. A survey of cultural resources in and near Redwood National Park, California. Unpublished ms. on file, Redwood National Park, Crescent City, Calif.

————. 1973b. The status of California archaeology. *Society for California Archaeology Special Reports*, No. 3. San Francisco.

Moratto, Michael J., Thomas F. King, and Wallace B. Woolfenden. 1978. Archaeology and California's climate. *Journal of California Anthropology* 5(2): 147–61.

Moriarty, James R., III. 1971. Mission San Diego de Alcalá. *In* Paul J. F. Schumacher, ed., Pacific West report, *Newsletter of the Society for Historical Archaeology* 4(3): 21–22. Ottawa.

————. 1973. With his boots on. *Masterkey* 47(2): 55–61.

Moriarty, James R., III, George Shumway, and Claude N. Warren. 1959. Scripps Estates Site I (SDi-525): A preliminary report on an early site on the San Diego coast. *Archaeological Survey Annual Report for 1958–1959*, pp. 187–216. Los Angeles: Univ. of California.

Moriarty, James R., III and William R. Weyland. 1971. Excavations at San Diego Mission. *Masterkey* 45(4): 124–37.

Munz, Philip A. 1970. *A California Flora*. Berkeley: Univ. of California Press.

Murray, Keith A. 1965. *The Modocs and Their War*. Norman: Univ. of Oklahoma Press.

Nelson, Nels C. 1909. Shellmounds of the San Francisco Bay region. *University of California Publications in American Archaeology and Ethnology*, Vol. 7(4), pp. 309–56. Berkeley.

————. 1910. The Ellis Landing shellmound. *University of California Publications in American Archaeology and Ethnology*, Vol. 7(5), pp. 357–426. Berkeley.

Ng, Pearl. 1972. *Writings on the Chinese in California*. San Francisco: R and E Research Associates.

O'Connell, James F. 1975. The prehistory of Surprise Valley. *Ballena Press Anthropological Papers*, No. 4, Socorro, N.M.

Odum, Eugene. 1971. *Fundamentals of Ecology*. 3rd ed. Philadelphia: Saunders.

Olsen, William H. 1961. Archaeological investigations at Sutter's Fort State Monument. *California State Division of Beaches and Parks Archaeological Report*, No. 1. Sacramento: Department of Parks and Recreation.

Olsen, William H., and Louis A. Payen. 1968. Archaeology of the Little Panoche Reservoir, Fresno County, California. *California State Department of Parks and Recreation, Archaeological Resources Section, Report*, No. 11. Sacramento.

Olsen, William H., and Francis A. Riddell. 1962. Salvage of the Rio Oso site, Yuba County, California. *California State Department of Parks and Recreation, Archaeological Resources Section, Report*, No. 6. Sacramento.

———. 1963. The archaeology of the Western Pacific Railroad relocation: Oroville Project, Butte County, California. *California State Department of Parks and Recreation, Archaeological Resources Section, Report*, No. 7. Sacramento.

Olsen, William H., and Norman L. Wilson. 1964. The salvage archaeology of the Bear Creek Site (SJo-112), a terminal central California Early Horizon site. *Sacramento Anthropological Society Papers*, No. 1. Sacramento: California State Univ.

Olson, Ronald L. 1930. Chumash prehistory. *University of California Publications in American Archaeology and Ethnology*, Vol. 28(1), pp. 1–21. Berkeley.

Orr, Phil C. 1943. Archaeology of Mescalitan Island and customs of the Canaliño. *Santa Barbara Museum of Natural History Occasional Papers*, No. 5. Santa Barbara.

———. 1956. Radiocarbon dates from Santa Rosa Island, I. *Santa Barbara Museum of Natural History Anthropological Bulletins*, No. 2. Santa Barbara.

———. 1968. *Prehistory of Santa Rosa Island*. Santa Barbara: Santa Barbara Museum of Natural History.

Osbourne, Carolyn M., and Harry S. Riddell, Jr. 1978. A cache of deer snares from Owens Valley, California. *Journal of California Anthropology* 5(1): 101–9.

Owen, Roger C. 1964. Early Milling Stone Horizon (Oak Grove), Santa Barbara County, California: Radiocarbon dates. *American Antiquity* 30(2): 210–13.

Owen, Roger C., Freddie Curtis, and Donald S. Miller. 1964. The Glen Annie Canyon Site, SBa-142: An Early Horizon coastal site of Santa Barbara County. *Archaeological Survey Annual Report for 1963–1964*, Vol. 6, pp. 431–517. Los Angeles: Univ. of California.

Payen, Louis A. 1961. Excavations at Sutter's Fort, 1960. *California State Division of Beaches and Parks Archaeological Report*, No. 3. Sacramento: Department of Parks and Recreation.

Payen, Louis A., and David S. Boloyan. 1963. "Tco'se," an archaeological study of the bedrock mortar-petroglyph at Ama-14, near Volcano, California. *California State Division of Beaches and Parks Archaeological Report*, No. 8. Sacramento: Department of Parks and Recreation.

Payen, Louis A., Carol H. Rector, Eric W. Ritter, R. E. Taylor, and J. E. Erickson. 1978. Comments on the Pleistocene age assignment and associations of a human burial from the Yuha Desert, California. *American Antiquity* 43(3): 448–52.

Payen, Louis A., and R. E. Taylor. 1976. Man and Pleistocene fauna at Potter Creek Cave. *Journal of California Anthropology* 3(1): 51–58.

Peak, A. S. 1976. Buchanan Reservoir Salvage Project, Madera County, California: Archaeological excavation. Unpublished ms. on file, U.S. Army Corps of Engineers, Sacramento.

Pearson, Roger. 1974. *Introduction to Anthropology*. New York: Holt, Rinehart & Winston.

Peck, Stuart L. 1955. An archaeological report on the excavation of a prehistoric site at Zuma Creek, Los Angeles County, California. *Archaeological Survey Association of Southern California Papers*, No. 2. Los Angeles.

Pendergast, David W., and Clement W. Meighan. 1959. The Greasy Creek Site, Tulare County, California. *Archaeological Survey Annual Report for 1958–1959*, pp. 1–10. Los Angeles: Univ. of California.

Phillips, George H. 1975. *Chiefs and Challengers: Indian Resistance and Cooperation in Southern California*. Berkeley: Univ. of California Press.

Pilling, Arnold R. 1978. Yurok. *In* Heizer 1978a, pp. 137–54.

Pisias, Niklas. 1978. Paleoceanography of the Santa Barbara Basin during the last 8000 years. *Quaternary Research* 9: 366–84.

Powers, Stephen. 1976. *Tribes of California*. Facsimile of 1877 ed. Berkeley: Univ. of California Press.

Pritchard, William E., Dorothy M. Hill, Sonia R. Purcell, and Roy Purcell. 1966. The Porter Rock Shelter Site (But-S177), Butte County, California. *Archaeological Survey Annual Report*, Vol. 8, pp. 279–86. Los Angeles: Univ. of California.

Ragir, Sonia. 1972. The Early Horizon in central California prehistory. *University of California Archaeological Research Facility Contributions*, No. 15. Berkeley.

Rasson, Judith. 1966. Excavations at Ahwahnee, Yosemite National Park, California. *Archaeological Survey Annual Report*, Vol. 8, pp. 165–83. Los Angeles: Univ. of California.

Rathje, William J. 1979. Modern material culture studies: Myths and a manifesto. *In* Schiffer 1979, pp. 1–29.

Reeves, B. O. K. 1973. The nature and age of the contact between the Laurentide and Cordilleran ice-sheets in the western interior of North America. *Arctic and Alpine Research* 5: 1–16.

Reinman, Fred M. 1964. Maritime adaptation on San Nicolas Island, California. *Archaeological Survey Annual Report*, Vol. 6, pp. 47–73. Los Angeles: Univ. of California.

Ricketts, Edward F., and Jack Calvin. 1968. *Between Pacific Tides*. 4th ed., revised by Joel W. Hedgpeth. Stanford, Calif.: Stanford Univ. Press.

Riddell, Francis A. 1951. The archaeology of site Ker-74. *University of California Archaeological Survey Reports*, No. 10, pp. 1–28. Berkeley.

———. 1955. Archaeological excavations on the Farallon Islands, California. *University of California Archaeological Survey Reports*, No. 32, pp. 1–18. Berkeley.

———. 1960. The archaeology of the Karlo Site (Las-7), California. *University of California Archaeological Survey Reports*, No. 53. Berkeley.

———. 1969. Pleistocene faunal remains associated with carbonaceous material. *American Antiquity* 34(2): 177–80.

Riddell, Francis A., and William H. Olsen. 1965. Archaeology of Mer-14, Merced County, California. Unpublished ms. on file, California State Department of Parks and Recreation, Sacramento.

———. 1969. An early man site in the San Joaquin Valley, California. *American Antiquity* 34(2): 121–30.

Riddell, Francis A., and William E. Pritchard. 1971. Archaeology of the Rainbow Point Site (4-Plu-S94), Bucks Lake, Plumas County, California. *University of Oregon Anthropological Papers*, Vol. 1, pp. 59–102. Eugene.

Ritter, Eric W. 1970. Northern Sierra foothill archaeology: Culture history and culture process. *Center for Archaeological Research at Davis Publications*, Vol. 2, pp. 171–84. Davis: Univ. of California.

Ritter, Eric W., Brian Hatoff, and Louis A. Payen. 1976. Chronology of the Farmington Complex. *American Antiquity* 41(3): 334–41.

Rocq, Margaret Miller, ed. 1970. *California Local History: A Bibliography and Union List of Library Holdings.* 2nd ed. Stanford, Calif.: Stanford Univ. Press.

——. 1976. *California Local History: A Bibliography and Union List of Library Holdings: Supplement to the Second Edition Covering Works Published 1961 Through 1970.* Stanford, Calif.: Stanford Univ. Press.

Rogers, David Banks. 1929. *Prehistoric Man of the Santa Barbara Coast.* Santa Barbara: Santa Barbara Museum of Natural History.

Rogers, Malcolm J. 1929. The stone art of the San Dieguito plateau. *American Anthropologist* 31(3), 454–67.

——. 1939. Early lithic industries of the lower basin of the Colorado River and adjacent desert area. *San Diego Museum Papers,* No. 3. San Diego.

——. 1945. An outline of Yuman prehistory. *Southwestern Journal of Anthropology* 1: 167–98.

——. 1968. *Ancient Hunters of the Far West.* San Diego: Copley Press.

Rogers, Spencer L. 1977. An early human fossil from the Yuha Desert of Southern California: Physical characteristics. *San Diego Museum Papers,* No. 12. San Diego.

Rozaire, Charles. 1960. The archaeology at Encino, California. *Archaeological Survey Annual Report for 1959–1960,* pp. 115–26. Los Angeles: Univ. of California.

Ruby, Jay W. 1961. Excavations at Zuma Mesa (LAn-40). *Archaeological Survey Annual Report for 1960–1961,* pp. 190–215. Los Angeles: Univ. of California.

——. 1966. Archaeological investigations of the Big Tujunga Site (LAn-167). *Archaeological Survey Annual Report,* Vol. 8, pp. 91–122. Los Angeles: Univ. of California.

Schenck, W. Egbert. 1926. The Emeryville shellmound: Final report. *University of California Publications in American Archaeology and Ethnology,* Vol. 18, pp. 91–122. Berkeley.

Schiffer, Michael J., ed. 1978. *Advances in Archaeological Method and Theory.* Vol. 1. New York: Academic Press.

——. 1979. *Advances in Archaeological Method and Theory.* Vol. 2. New York: Academic Press.

Schumacher, Paul J. F., ed. 1971. Pacific West report: California. *Newsletter of the Society for Historical Archaeology* 3(4): 16–18. Ottawa.

——, ed. 1972. Pacific West report: California. *Newsletter of the Society for Historical Archaeology* 5(1): 17–20. Ottawa.

Schuyler, Robert L. 1978. Indian–Euro-American interaction: Archaeological evidence from non-Indian sites. *In* Heizer 1978a, pp. 69–79.

——. 1979. *Historical Archaeology: A Guide to Substantive and Theoretical Contributions.* Farmingdale, N.Y.: Baywood.

——, ed. 1980. *Archaeological Perspectives on Ethnicity in America.* Farmingdale, N.Y.: Baywood.

Service, Elman R. 1975. *Origins of the State and Civilization: The Process of Cultural Evolution.* New York: Norton.

Sharp, Lawrence H. 1980. Speed, power, production and profit: Railroading in the Goosenest District, Klamath National Forest. Unpublished ms. on file, National Technical Information Service, Springfield, Va.

Shipek, Florence C. 1978. History of southern California mission Indians. *In* Heizer 1978a, pp. 610–18.

Shipley, William F. 1978. Native languages of California. *In* Heizer 1978a, pp. 80–90.

Shumway, George, Carl L. Hubbs, and James R. Moriarty III. 1961. Scripps Estate Site, San Diego, California: A La Jolla Site dated 5460 to 7370 years before the present. *Annals of the New York Academy of Sciences*, Vol. 93, pp. 37–132. Albany.

Simpson, Ruth DeEtte. 1961. Coyote Gulch: Archaeological investigations of an early lithic locality in the Mohave Desert of San Bernardino County. *Archaeological Survey Association of Southern California Papers*, No. 5. Bloomington, Calif.

Singer, Clay A., and Robert Gibson. 1970. LAn-243, Medea Creek Village: A functional lithic analysis. *Archaeological Survey Annual Report*, Vol. 12, pp. 184–203. Los Angeles: Univ. of California.

Sivertsen, Barbara J. 1980. A site activity model for kill and butchering activities at hunter-gatherer sites. *Journal of Field Archaeology* 7: 423–41.

Slaymaker, Charles. 1977. The material culture of Cotomko'tca: A Coast Miwok tribelet in Marin County, California. *Miwok Archaeological Preserve of Marin Papers*, No. 3. San Rafael, Calif.

Smith, C. E., and W. D. Weymouth. 1952. Archaeology of the Shasta Dam Area, California. *University of California Archaeological Survey Reports*, No. 18. Berkeley.

Smith, Gerald A., and Wilson Turner. 1975. *Indian Rock Art of Southern California*. Redlands, Calif.: San Bernardino County Museum Association.

Smith, Jack E. 1961. An archaeological survey of Vaquero Reservoir, Santa Maria, California. *Archaeological Survey Annual Report for 1960–1961*, pp. 161–74. Los Angeles: Univ. of California.

Smith, Jack E., and Jackie LaFave. 1961. Excavation of Site SLO-297, Vaquero Reservoir, San Luis Obispo County, California. *Archaeological Survey Annual Report for 1960–1961*, pp. 149–60. Los Angeles: Univ. of California.

Snow, Dean A. 1976. *The Archaeology of North America*. New York: Viking.

South, Stanley. 1977. *Method and Theory in Historical Archaeology*. New York: Academic Press.

———. 1979. Historic site content, structure, and function. *American Antiquity* 44(2): 213–37.

Stanford, Dennis. 1979. Bison kills for ice age hunters. *National Geographic* 155(1): 114–22.

Sterud, Eugene R. 1964. Report on salvage archaeological excavations at 4-Mno-382, the Mammoth Creek Site, Mono County, California. Unpublished ms. on file, California State Department of Parks and Recreation, Sacramento.

Steward, Julian H. 1933. Ethnography of the Owens Valley Paiute. *University of California Publications in American Archaeology and Ethnology*, Vol. 33(3), pp. 233–350. Berkeley.

———. 1938. Basin-Plateau aboriginal socio-political groups. *Bureau of American Ethnology Bulletins*, No. 120. Washington, D.C.: Smithsonian Institution.

Stewart, Omer C. 1978. Litigation and its effects. *In* Heizer 1978a, pp. 713–18.

Stickel, E. Gary. 1968. Status differentiation at the Rincon Site. *Archaeological Survey Annual Report*, Vol. 10, pp. 209–61. Los Angeles: Univ. of California.

Stickel, E. Gary, and Joseph L. Chartkoff. 1973. The nature of scientific laws and their relation to law-building in archaeology. *In* Colin Renfrew, ed., *The*

Explanation of Culture Change: Models in Prehistory, pp. 663–71. London: Duckworth.

Stickel, E. Gary, and Adrienne E. Cooper. 1969. The Chumash revolt of 1824: A case for an archaeological application of feedback theory. *Archaeological Survey Annual Report*, Vol. 11, pp. 5–21. Los Angeles: Univ. of California.

Susia, Margaret. 1962. The Soule Park Site (Ven-61). *Archaeological Survey Annual Report for 1961–1962*, pp. 157–234. Los Angeles: Univ. of California.

Taylor, R. E., ed. 1976. *Advances in Obsidian Glass Studies*. Park Ridge, N.J.: Noyes Press.

Taylor, R. E., and C. W. Meighan, eds. 1978. *Chronologies in New World Archaeology*. New York: Academic Press.

Taylor, Walter W. 1961. Archaeology and language in western North America. *American Antiquity* 25(1): 71–81.

Theodoratus, Dorothea, Joseph L. Chartkoff, and Kerry K. Chartkoff, eds. 1979. Cultural resources of the Gasquet–Orleans (G–O) Road, Six Rivers National Forest, California. Unpublished ms. on file, Six Rivers National Forest, Eureka, Calif.

Thomas, David B., and John Beaton. 1968. The Trancas Canyon Cemetery Site (4-LAn-197): An analysis of mortuary customs. *Archaeological Survey Annual Report*, Vol. 10, pp. 162–75. Los Angeles: Univ. of California.

Thomas, David H. 1978. Arrowheads and atlatl darts: How the stones got the shaft. *American Antiquity* 43(3): 461–72.

Thorensen, Timothy H. H. 1975. Paying the piper and calling the tune: The beginnings of academic anthropology in California. *Journal of the History of the Behavioral Sciences* 11(3): 257–75.

———. 1976. Kroeber and the Yurok, 1900–1908. *In* Kroeber 1976, pp. xix–xxviii. Berkeley: Univ. of California Press.

Treganza, Adan E. 1951. Old lime kilns near Olema. *In* Geologic Guidebook of the San Francisco Bay Counties, *State Division of Mines Bulletin* 154, pp. 65–72. San Francisco.

———. 1954. Fort Ross: A study in historical archaeology. *University of California Archaeological Survey Reports*, No. 23, pp. 1–26. Berkeley.

———. 1958a. Salvage archaeology in the Trinity Reservoir area, northern California. *University of California Archaeological Survey Reports*, No. 43, pp. 1–38. Berkeley.

———. 1958b. Archaeological excavations at the William B. Ide Adobe, Red Bluff, California. Unpublished ms. on file, California State Department of Parks and Recreation, Sacramento.

———. 1959. Salvage archaeology in the Trinity Reservoir area, northern California: Field season 1958. *University of California Archaeological Survey Reports*, No. 46, pp. 1–32. Berkeley.

———. 1968. Archaeological investigations at the William B. Ide Adobe, Red Bluff, California. *Robert E. Schenck Archives of California Archaeology*, No. 32. Society for California Archaeology, Treganza Museum of Anthropology, San Franisco State Univ.

Treganza, Adan E., and A. Bierman. 1958. The Topanga culture, final report on excavations, 1948. *University of California Anthropological Records*, Vol. 20(1), pp. 45–86. Berkeley.

Treganza, Adan E., and M. H. Heickson. 1960. Salvage archaeology in the Whiskeytown Reservoir area and the Wintu pumping plant, Shasta

County, California. *San Francisco State College Occasional Papers in Anthropology*, Vol. 1. San Francisco: California State Univ.

Treganza, Adan E., M. H. Heickson, and Wallace B. Woolfenden. 1969. The archaeology of the Black Butte Reservoir region, Glenn and Tehama counties, California. *San Francisco State College Occasional Papers in Anthropology*, Vol. 2. San Francisco: California State Univ.

Treganza, Adan E., and C. G. Malamud. 1950. The Topanga culture, first season's excavations at the Tank Site, 1947. *University of California Anthropological Records*, Vol. 12(4), pp. 129–70. Berkeley.

True, D. L. 1966. Archaeological differentiation of Shoshonean and Yuman speaking groups in southern California. Unpublished doctoral dissertation, Department of Anthropology, Univ. of California, Los Angeles.

———. 1968. Investigations of a late prehistoric complex in Cuyamaca Rancho State Park, San Diego County, California. *Archaeological Survey Monographs*, No. 1. Los Angeles: Univ. of California.

True, D. L., C. W. Meighan, and Harvey Crew. 1974. Archaeological investigations at Molpa, San Diego County, California. *University of California Publications in Anthropology*, Vol. 11. Berkeley.

Uhle, Max. 1907. The Emeryville shellmound. *University of California Publications in American Archaeology and Ethnology*, Vol. 7(1), pp. 1–106. Berkeley.

Wallace, William J. 1955. A suggested chronology for southern California coastal archaeology. *Southwestern Journal of Anthropology* 11(2): 214–30.

———. 1962a. Prehistoric cultural development in the southern California deserts. *American Antiquity* 28(2): 172–80.

———. 1962b. Archaeological explorations in the southern section of Anza-Borrego Desert State Park, California. *California State Division of Beaches and Parks Archaeological Reports*, No. 5. Sacramento: California State Department of Parks and Recreation.

———. 1962c. Archaeological investigations in the Arroyo Grande Creek Watershed, San Luis Obispo County, California. *Archaeological Survey Annual Report for 1961–1962*, pp. 23–91. Los Angeles: Univ. of California.

———. 1977. A half century of Death Valley archaeology. *Journal of California Anthropology* 4(2): 249–58.

———. 1978. Post-Pleistocene archaeology, 9000 to 2000 B.C. *In* Heizer 1978a, pp. 25–36.

Wallace, William J., and D. W. Lathrap. 1975. West Berkeley (CA-Ala-307): A culturally stratified shellmound on the east shore of San Francisco Bay. *University of California Archaeological Research Facility Contributions*, No. 29. Berkeley.

Wallace, William J., Edith S. Taylor, Roger J. Desautels, H. Robert Hammond, Herberto Gonzalez, James Bogart, and John Peter Redwine. 1956. The Little Sycamore shellmound. *Contributions to California Archaeology*, No. 2. Los Angeles: Archaeological Research Associates.

Warren, Claude N. 1967. The San Dieguito Complex: A review and hypothesis. *American Antiquity* 32(2): 168–85.

———. 1968. Cultural tradition and ecological adaptation on the southern California coast. *In* Cynthia Irwin-Williams, ed., Archaic prehistory in the western United States, *Eastern New Mexico University Contributions in Anthropology*, Vol. 3(1), pp. 1–14. Portales, N.M.

———. 1973. California. *In* Fitting 1973, pp. 213–50.

Warren, Claude N., and Marshall B. McKusick. 1959. Burial complex from the southern San Joaquin Valley, Tulare County, California. *Archaeological Survey Annual Report for 1958–1959*, pp. 17–26. Los Angeles: Univ. of California.

Warren, Claude N., and H. T. Ore. 1978. Approach and process of dating Lake Mohave artifacts. *Journal of California Anthropology* 5(2): 179–87.

Warren, Claude N., and Max G. Pavesic. 1963. Shell midden analysis of Site SDi-603 and ecological implications for cultural development of Bataquitos Lagoon, San Diego County, California. *Archaeological Survey Annual Report for 1962–1963*, Vol. 5, pp. 411–38. Los Angeles: Univ. of California.

Warren, Claude N., and D. L. True. 1961. The San Dieguito complex and its place in California prehistory. *Archaeological Survey Annual Report for 1960–1961*, pp. 246–337. Los Angeles: Univ. of California.

Warren, Claude N., D. L. True, and Ardith A. Eudey. 1961. Early gathering complexes of western San Diego County: Results and interpretations of an archaeological survey. *Archaeological Survey Annual Report for 1960–1961*, pp. 1–105. Los Angeles: Univ. of California.

Watson, Patty Jo, Stephen LeBlanc, and Charles Redman. 1978. *Explanation in Archaeology: An Explicitly Scientific Approach*. New York: Columbia Univ. Press.

Weaver, Muriel. 1972. *The Aztecs, the Maya and Their Predecessors*. New York: Seminar Press.

Wilke, Philip J. 1978. Cairn burials of the California deserts. *American Antiquity* 43(3): 444–47.

Willey, Gordon R. 1966. *Introduction to American Archaeology: Vol. 1, North and Middle America*. Englewood Cliffs, N.J.: Prentice-Hall.

Willey, Gordon R., and Philip Phillips. 1957. *Method and Theory in American Archaeology*. Chicago: Univ. of Chicago Press.

Willey, Gordon R., and Jeremy Sabloff. 1974. *A History of American Archaeology*. San Francisco: Freeman.

Williams, Stephen. 1971. *The Chinese in the California Mines, 1848–1860*. San Francisco: R and E Research Associates.

Wilmsen, Edwin, and Frank H. H. Roberts. 1978. Lindenmeier 1934–1974: Concluding report on investigations. *Smithsonian Contributions to Anthropology*, Vol. 24. Washington, D.C.: Smithsonian Institution.

Wire, Marcia V. V. 1961. Alamo Creek Site, San Luis Obispo County, California. *Archaeological Survey Annual Report for 1960–1961*, pp. 107–48. Los Angeles: Univ. of California.

Wormington, H. Marie. 1957. Ancient Man in North America. 4th ed. *Denver Museum of Natural History Popular Series*, No. 4. Denver.

————. 1971. Comments on early man in North America. *In* Richard J. Shutler, Jr., ed., Papers from a Symposium on Early Man in North America, New Developments 1960–1970, *Arctic Anthropology*, Vol. 8(2), pp. 83–91. Madison, Wisc.

Wright, Robert. 1971. Map showing locations of samples dated by radiocarbon methods in the San Francisco Bay region. *United States Geological Survey Miscellaneous Field Studies Map* MF-317. Menlo Park, Calif.

Yocum, Charles, and Ray Dasmann. 1965. *Pacific Coast Wildlife Region*. 2nd ed. Happy Camp, Calif.: Naturegraph.

INDEX

INDEX

Abalone: beads of, 118–20, 170–77 *passim*, 264; pendants of, 118–19, 175; as ornaments, 171, 184, 191, 363; fishhooks of, 185; as containers, 364

Abrading: in tool manufacture, 132

Abrading stone, 175, 366

Academic programs in California archaeology, 378–79

Acapulco, 253

Acorns: as prehistoric food, 40, 133, 147, 155, 166, 168f, 172f, 181, 187, 193, 228, 333; leaching of, 116–20; storage of, 156, 222

Adams, Richard, 358

Adaptation: focal, 41f, 134, 148, 183, 289, 324, 326, 328f; diffuse, 41, 74–77, 134, 148, 249, 301, 324, 328, 329; Pacific changes in, 147–49, 248–49

Adoption, 240

Adze, 195–98

Aerophysics Site, 161

Africans, 18

Agave, 91

Agriculture: Historical development of, 285, 287. *See also* Farming

Agua Hedionda Lagoon, 126

Ahwahnee village site, 182f, 389–90. *See also* Yosemite Valley

Alabaster, 120, 135, 214

Alameda County: Site 307, 129, 161, 180–81; Site 328, 161, 182f, 386

Alamo, 182f

Alaska: Russian colonization of, 257

Alaska lion: extinction of, 66–67

Albacore, 154

Albino deer, 199

Aleut Indians: as Russian allies, 309

Algonkian languages, 200f, 333

Alta California: colonization of, 257, 259, 272f

Altithermal climatic episode, 101, 105

Amargosa Tradition, 162, 178–82

Amateur-archaeology movement in California, 357–59, 373–76

Amboy, 287

"American Historical" school of anthropology, 351

American River, 168, 193

Amino acid racemization, 33–35

Amphibolite, 135

Anadromous fish, 94, 172, 230; salmon, 40, 93f, 117, 147, 151–52, 169, 187, 193, 228

Anathermal climatic episode, 101

Anchovy, 154

Andamanese hunter-gatherers, 63

Andesite, 132, 213